EQUALIZING JUSTICE

Millions of individuals worldwide struggle to understand and assert their legal rights without legal representation. *Equalizing Justice* examines how AI and other technologies can address this access-to-justice crisis by providing unrepresented litigants with knowledge and skills traditionally available only through lawyers. This volume takes a needs-first approach, identifying tasks that unrepresented litigants must complete and mapping specific technologies to each task, such as generative AI, computational logic, and document automation. The book highlights real-world applications, demonstrating proven impact, and presents case studies and interviews to explore both the potential positive outcomes and the challenges of AI for access to justice. *Equalizing Justice* argues that AI technologies offer unprecedented opportunities to create more equitable justice systems serving everyone, not just those who can afford representation, and that legal AI assistants should be treated as a public good accessible to all.

L. Karl Branting (1952–2024) was the Chief Scientist of Machine Learning for Computational Law at the MITRE Corporation (2007–2024). Karl served as the President of the International Association for Artificial Intelligence and Law (2004–2005), was a United States Supreme Court Fellow (2001–2002), and published more than 100 peer-reviewed research articles and books on artificial intelligence. Karl unexpectedly passed away while writing this book. The book was completed by Mia Bonardi, with contributions from Sarah McLeod (Chapters 2 and 9), Megan Ma (Chapter 2), Charlotte S. Alexander (Chapter 3), Elizabeth C. Tippett (Chapter 3), Hannes Westermann (Chapters 4, 8, and 12), Marco Giacalone (Chapters 4, 11, and 12), Rebecca Fordon (Chapter 5), Aniket Kesari (Chapter 6), Chinmayi Sharma (Chapter 6), Morgan A. Gray (Chapter 7), Jaromir Savelka (Chapters 7 and 16), Kiernan Moran (Chapter 13), Sateesh Nori (Chapter 14), Neel Guha (Chapter 15), Izak C. Rosenfeld (Chapters 15 and 17), Shraeya Iyer (Chapter 16), and Daniel W. Linna Jr. (Chapter 16).

Mia Bonardi is a research attorney at the Supreme Court of Guam. Mia was a member of Suffolk LIT Lab's Document Assembly Line Project and has published several articles at the intersection of human rights and technology.

Equalizing Justice

HARNESSING AI FOR LITIGANTS WITHOUT LAWYERS

L. KARL BRANTING

with MIA BONARDI

CAMBRIDGE
UNIVERSITY PRESS

CAMBRIDGE
UNIVERSITY PRESS

Shaftesbury Road, Cambridge CB2 8EA, United Kingdom

One Liberty Plaza, 20th Floor, New York, NY 10006, USA

477 Williamstown Road, Port Melbourne, VIC 3207, Australia

314–321, 3rd Floor, Plot 3, Splendor Forum, Jasola District Centre, New Delhi – 110025, India

Cambridge University Press is part of Cambridge University Press & Assessment, a department of the University of Cambridge.

We share the University's mission to contribute to society through the pursuit of education, learning and research at the highest international levels of excellence.

www.cambridge.org
Information on this title: www.cambridge.org/9781009779432
DOI: 10.1017/9781009779487

When citing this work, please include a reference to the DOI 10.1017/9781009779487

First published 2026

Cover image: filo / DigitalVision Vectors / Getty.

A catalogue record for this publication is available from the British Library

A Cataloging-in-Publication data record for this book is available from the Library of Congress

ISBN 978-1-009-77943-2 Hardback
ISBN 978-1-009-77946-3 Paperback

For Karl

Society cannot exist without law and order,
and cannot advance except through vigorous innovators.

Bertrand Russell

Contents

Figures

Tables

In Memoriam

Dr. L. Karl Branting
Chief Scientist of Machine Learning for Computational Law
The MITRE Corporation
November 16, 1952 – July 18, 2024

Dr. L. Karl Branting unexpectedly passed away on July 18, 2024, at the age of seventy-one. His loss is deeply felt, both personally by those who knew him and by the broader legal, artificial intelligence (AI), and access-to-justice communities.

Dr. Branting was the Chief Scientist of Machine Learning for Computational Law at the MITRE Corporation (2007–2024). He received a Ph.D. in computer science from the University of Texas at Austin (1991), a JD from Georgetown University (1980), and a BA magna cum laude in philosophy from the University of Colorado (1975). Dr. Branting served as the President of the International Association for Artificial Intelligence and Law (2004–2005) and as a US Supreme Court Fellow (2001–2002). He published more than 100 peer-reviewed research articles and books on AI and, in 2023, chaired an international workshop on AI for access to justice.

In addition to his innumerable professional accolades and achievements, Dr. Branting was an extraordinary human being. He was one of those rare individuals whose brilliance was matched by his kindness. Dr. Branting was known for his curiosity, intelligence, humility, and gregarious nature, which made him an incredible colleague and a beloved collaborator. These personal qualities significantly contributed to his ability to build strong, interdisciplinary teams that worked synergistically toward common goals.

As an academic, Dr. Branting mentored numerous students and researchers, instilling in them a rigorous approach to AI and Law. His teaching and research have inspired new generations of scholars to explore and expand upon his work, ensuring ongoing innovation and refinement of AI applications in the access-to-justice space.

Dr. Branting's extensive career in AI and Law significantly advanced applications for access to justice. His research in case-based reasoning, decision-support systems, and narrative-driven case elicitation provided profound insights into how AI can effectively assist unrepresented litigants. Starting in the early 1980s, he pioneered applications for legal AI in the access-to-justice space. His contributions consistently pushed the boundaries of what is achievable at the intersection of AI and Law, highlighting new possibilities for technology in the legal domain.

Dr. Branting's dedication to human rights and access to justice is reflected in each of his projects, showing a profound understanding of AI's potential to democratize access to legal resources. His recent and unexpected passing marks a significant loss to the field and cause, but his groundbreaking work will continue to inspire advancements in AI for access to justice for many years to come.*

–

Karl was a humble mentor and a creative collaborator. I will miss all the fun projects we might have worked on together.

Elizabeth C. Tippett, Professor, University of Oregon School of Law

Karl was a mentor and friend, and someone I deeply admired. He had a tireless passion for helping others and an infectious positivity and drive for increasing access to justice that energized and excited everyone he collaborated with. His creativity, encouragement, goofy sense of humor, generosity, humility, and profound insights helped expand what was possible and made hard work fun. He was truly an extraordinary person.

Sarah McLeod, Lead AI & NLP Engineer, The MITRE Corporation

My AI and Law course would not be complete without addressing two of Karl Branting's lasting contributions. Karl's GREBE was not only the first program to computationally represent judges' explanations of their decisions, but Karl evaluated it in a wholly new way with a human "judge" comparing legal analyses produced by law students and by GREBE while blinded to their source. His SCALE project applied machine learning to predict case outcomes and identify issues and factors in case texts, both of which would be useful for explaining predictions. The field and I will always miss Karl.

Kevin D. Ashley, Professor of Law and Intelligent Systems,
University of Pittsburgh

Karl's warmth, intellect, and curiosity were so powerful that they made an enormous impression even through a computer screen. Karl's memory will inspire me to continue exploring new ideas and always keep justice and equity at the center of my work, as he did throughout his truly remarkable career.

Charlotte S. Alexander, Professor of Law and Ethics,
Georgia Institute of Technology

* This in memoriam originally appeared in Mia Bonardi & L. Karl Branting, *Certifying Legal AI Assistants for Unrepresented Litigants: A Global Survey of Access to Civil Justice, Unauthorized Practice of Law, and AI*, 26 Colum. Sci. & Tech. L. Rev. 34, 105–06 (2025).

Karl was one of the brightest lights in the legal technology world. Our shared interests included document automation, access to justice, and music. His writings and talks were always exceptionally insightful and elegant. I was privileged to enjoy his friendship, and will long relish the occasions we had for collaboration.

Marc Lauritsen, President, Capstone Practice Systems

Karl was a dear friend and visionary who inspired my research focused on AI and Access to Justice. I was always amazed by his intelligence, kindness, and generosity. Our talks meant the world to me, and he is very missed. I am thankful for Karl's inspiration!

Amy J. Schmitz, Law Professor, The Ohio State University
Moritz College of Law

Karl was a pioneer at the intersection of artificial intelligence and law. He belonged to the first generation that recognized the potential of the computer to reshape and enhance our most fundamental social institutions. The research path that he and his fellow trailblazers charted decades ago is now bearing fruit. This book is a testament to Karl's vision and his dedication to using technology in service of justice.

Michael A. Livermore, Professor of Law,
University of Virginia

Karl's intelligence, curiosity, and kindness greatly inspired me, as did his can-do attitude and willingness to explore new approaches to improving the legal system through AI. I miss Karl greatly and am confident that his impact on the field will continue through his extensive research, this book, and the many people he inspired and mentored.

Hannes Westermann, Assistant Professor, Faculty of Law,
Maastricht University

Contributors

Charlotte S. Alexander, Georgia Institute of Technology

Rebecca Fordon, The Ohio State University Moritz Law Library

Marco Giacalone, Vrije Universiteit Brussel

Morgan A. Gray, University of St. Thomas School of Law

Neel Guha, Stanford University

Shraeya Iyer, Northwestern University

Aniket Kesari, Fordham Law School

Daniel W. Linna Jr., Northwestern Schools of Law & Engineering

Megan Ma, Stanford Law School

Sarah McLeod, The MITRE Corporation

Kiernan Moran, Quest for Justice

Sateesh Nori, New York University School of Law

Izak C. Rosenfeld, The MITRE Corporation

Jaromir Savelka, Carnegie Mellon University

Chinmayi Sharma, Fordham Law School

Elizabeth C. Tippett, University of Oregon School of Law

Hannes Westermann, Maastricht University

ADVISORS

Kevin D. Ashley, University of Pittsburgh

Marc Lauritsen, Capstone Practice Systems

Michael A. Livermore, University of Virginia School of Law

L. Thorne McCarty, Rutgers University

Amy J. Schmitz, The Ohio State University Moritz College of Law

VOLUNTEERS

Michelle Bernstein, Document Assembly Line Project

Julian A. Burlando-Salazar, WilmerHale

Marina S. Dolgova, Columbia Science and Technology Law Review

Simiao (Dante) Zhu, Columbia Science and Technology Law Review

Foreword

In a world where healthy food, clean water, decent shelter, and medical care are scarce for many, legal assistance can seem a luxury. Few societies provide significant help with legal issues to folks who cannot pay for it. Philanthropic and profit-making organizations have sought to address the shortage, but they have mostly come up short. The sad result is that the vast majority of legal problems and opportunities go without meaningful assistance, even when livelihoods, family integrity, and personal freedoms are at stake.

This is not due to a lack of resources. There are over 1,000 billionaires in the US alone,[1] and it is one of the worst performers in terms of access to justice.[2] Consumers reportedly spend more on Halloween costumes for their pets each year than total spending on legal services for the poor.[3] The global picture is not much better.[4]

To call this a "crisis" or an "emergency" distracts from the fact that this has always been a reality. Many of us who enlisted in the war on legal poverty half a century ago recognize that little has fundamentally changed, despite the best efforts of countless champions of innovation. Applicable technology has consistently advanced, but the underlying circumstances stubbornly persist.

Can the astonishing recent developments in artificial intelligence be leveraged to finally usher in transformative progress? Many hopeful signs, and daunting challenges, can be found in the ensuing pages. Few other topics offer such a combination of fascinating ideas and promising social goods.

1 Inti Pacheco et al., *What We Know about America's Billionaires: 1,135 and Counting*, Wall St. J. (Sep. 2, 2025), https://tinyurl.com/2s3554jv.

2 World Just. Project, Rule of Law Index 174 (2024) (ranking the US 31/47 in civil justice by income).

3 *Compare* Nat'l Retail Fed'n, *Halloween Spending to Reach Record $12.2 Billion as Participation Exceeds Pre-pandemic Levels* (Sep. 20, 2024), https://perma.cc/Q8X4-UQGE (reporting yearly pet costume spending at $700 million in 2021, 2022, and 2023) *with* Legal Servs. Corp., *LSC Appropriations*, https://perma.cc/A743-5NC9 (explaining the Legal Services Corporation received $560 million from Congress for 2023 and 2024).

4 *See generally* World Just. Project, *supra* note 2.

We deeply miss Karl's humble and loving brilliance, which shines in these pages through the words of those he inspired. And we owe a debt of gratitude to Mia for cat-herding such a brilliant group of experts to a phenomenal work of collaboration.

Settle back for education and encouragement!

Marc Lauritsen
President, Capstone Practice Systems

Preface

This book was born from a profound vision and an unexpected tragedy. Dr. L. Karl Branting, a pioneer at the intersection of AI and Law, had embarked on what he believed would be his most important work: a comprehensive guide to how AI and other technologies could bridge the justice gap for the millions of people who navigate the legal system unrepresented. When Karl passed away unexpectedly in July 2024, he had completed only a quarter of this ambitious project, leaving behind not just unfinished chapters but also unfulfilled conversations and unrealized ideas. Yet his vision endured, as did a community of scholars and practitioners who shared his unwavering commitment to equitable justice for all.

Karl's vision for this book was characteristically ambitious yet deeply practical. He sought to create something that had never existed before: a clear, accessible explanation of how the capabilities of AI could address the needs of unrepresented litigants. This was meant to be a roadmap for real change.

Karl understood that, when thoughtfully applied, AI could begin to address the crisis in access to justice by helping legal professionals serve more people, while enabling unrepresented people to understand their legal situations, find appropriate resources, and navigate otherwise insurmountable procedures. The technologies explored in this book, including computational logic, document automation, and generative AI, represent practical steps toward a more equitable legal system.

The tools highlighted in this book come alive through the journeys of their creators. Through interviews with the leaders behind innovations such as British Columbia's Civil Resolution Tribunal, AI-powered tools such as Upsolve's bankruptcy filing tool and JusticeBot, and platforms such as Hello Divorce, you will learn about the challenges, setbacks, and breakthroughs of each project. These are stories of determination and of teams "building a plane while flying it," driven by the belief that technology could help level the playing field for unrepresented litigants.

Those who knew Karl understood that his greatest strength lay not just in his technical brilliance, but in his ability to see possibilities where others saw obstacles. He possessed that rare combination of rigorous analytical thinking and genuine empathy that made him both a respected researcher and a beloved collaborator and mentor. His empathy extended naturally to nurturing emerging talent, as Karl believed deeply in elevating new voices. True to his spirit of mentorship, this book features contributions from early-career professionals and emerging scholars, the next generation of innovators who will carry forward his work.

As you engage with these chapters, I invite you to join a conversation that Karl would have loved to continue. Each technological innovation discussed here represents a foundation upon which further innovation can build. Karl's intellectual curiosity was infectious, and his approach to research was both methodical and imaginative. He would have encouraged readers to question assumptions, to see connections across disciplines, and to always ask: How can we do better? How can we reach more people? How can we make justice more accessible? And how will we know when we are succeeding?

The completion of this book was guided by the knowledge that it would never be the extraordinary book that Karl would have written himself. His unique combination of technical expertise, legal understanding, and human compassion created insights that cannot be fully replicated. The collective effort in these pages creates something Karl would have celebrated, his vision brought to life by those he inspired and refined by the community he helped build.

This book stands as both a practical guide and a call to action. It demonstrates what is possible when AI is deployed thoughtfully in the service of human dignity and justice. But more than that, it represents a continuing conversation that Karl began and that must be carried forward by all who believe that access to justice is not a luxury, but a fundamental human right.

This book is dedicated to Karl's memory, to his family, and to the individuals around the world who continue to seek justice in systems that remain frustratingly difficult to navigate. May the ideas contained in these pages contribute to the more equitable world that Karl envisioned and worked tirelessly to create.

Mia Bonardi

Acknowledgments

Completing this work would have been impossible without an extraordinary community of supporters who believed in Karl's mission and helped bring his vision to life. I thank Karl for offering me the opportunity to learn from him, though there would never have been enough time to absorb all the knowledge and wisdom he had to share.

While I cannot know precisely who Karl would have acknowledged, I am certain he would have been immensely grateful for everyone who contributed to making this book possible. I also want to thank everyone who helped Karl develop and refine his vision for this work.

My deepest gratitude goes to Karl's family, particularly his wife, Susan Branting, who not only supported the completion of this project but also meticulously edited every chapter.

The seventeen contributors delivered exceptional work under challenging circumstances. Each embraced the responsibility of advancing both the technical rigor and humanitarian goals that drove Karl's original conception of this project.

My sincere gratitude goes to the five esteemed advisors who generously shared their time and expertise to strengthen this work.

Special thanks go to Kiernan Moran, who began as a volunteer and ultimately emerged as a valued contributor to this work. I again thank Susan Branting for funding Kiernan's work.

I am grateful to Julian A. Burlando-Salazar for reviewing early drafts and for detailed editing. Thanks to Michelle Bernstein, who reviewed early drafts, designed some of the figures included in this book, and provided precise technical editing. Recognition goes to Marina S. Dolgova and Simiao (Dante) Zhu, both members of the Columbia Science and Technology Law Review, who generously volunteered to ensure all citations met Bluebook standards.

Appreciation goes to the innovators behind the Nevada Self-Help Chatbot, Pro Bono Net, Rentervention, Courtroom5, and the many other groundbreaking initiatives profiled in this book. Their willingness to share not only their successes but also their challenges and setbacks provides readers with concrete, actionable insights.

My gratitude extends to the MITRE Corporation for facilitating a smooth transition of Karl's materials during an incredibly difficult period. Dr. Ransom K. Winder deserves particular recognition for helping us recover significant portions of Karl's work and research during those early, uncertain days.

This book exists within an ecosystem of access to justice advocates, AI and Law researchers, and dedicated practitioners. It builds on the foundational contributions of countless individuals whose work made the innovations discussed in these pages possible.

Every person acknowledged here contributed to a mission rooted in the belief that justice should not be determined by one's ability to afford legal representation. In completing this work, I have tried to honor both Karl's collaborative spirit and our shared commitment to making legal systems more accessible, equitable, and just for all.

Author's Note

In honor of Karl, 100% of the royalties from this book will be donated to a nonprofit organization using artificial intelligence to expand access to justice.

Introduction

L. Karl Branting

Each day, millions of individuals around the world experience frustration, bewilderment, and failure when trying to understand or assert their legal rights. Without the assistance of an attorney, survivors struggle to obtain simple but necessary protection orders; tenants face horrific housing conditions or often illegal self-help evictions; consumers are victimized by assembly-line civil suits; and the retired, injured, or disabled struggle to obtain the benefits to which they are entitled.

Equality under the law is a fundamental principle of justice,[1] but it is increasingly elusive for most low-income and even moderate-income individuals throughout the world. Few individuals have the legal training and knowledge needed to effectively represent themselves in court, even in simple civil cases, or to navigate any but the most straightforward government benefits processes. Adequate legal representation imposes financial burdens that few individuals can afford. The growth in the number of individuals who lack the resources for adequate legal representation has been characterized as an "access-to-justice crisis."[2]

Ironically, the access to justice crisis has coincided with dramatic improvements in artificial intelligence ("AI") capabilities applicable to law. While the development of techniques for automating legal problem solving has been an area of active research for decades, their practical applications have primarily targeted attorneys and law firms, since they have had the greatest financial resources and incentives to adopt new legal technologies. However, for many years, a little-known community of judges, academics, and legal-aid attorneys has been exploring technologies to assist unrepresented litigants. The rapid advancement of AI techniques appropriate for law, particularly language processing, machine learning, and generative AI, has created an opportunity to extend this pioneering work to dramatically equalize access to justice.

[1] *See, e.g.*, G.A. Res. 217 (III) A, U.N. Doc. A/810, at art. 7, Universal Declaration of Human Rights (Dec. 10, 1948); U.S. Const. amend. XIV, § 1.

[2] *See, e.g.*, Nora Freeman Engstrom & David Freeman Engstrom, *The Making of the A2J Crisis*, 75 Stan. L. Rev. Online 146 (2024) (discussing origins and implications of the access-to-justice crisis).

The focus of this book is on technologies to help unrepresented litigants access an alternative source for the knowledge and skills that attorneys typically offer. *Unrepresented litigants* are individuals who, by circumstance or choice, represent themselves in legal proceedings without the assistance of a lawyer. Their unrepresented status may be due to various factors, including the inability to afford legal representation, lack of access to legal services, or the desire to handle their cases independently. Unrepresented litigants navigate the complexities of the legal system, which is built for lawyers and legal professionals, on their own, undertaking tasks such as filing documents, preparing legal arguments, and presenting their cases in courts. An unrepresented litigant is also referred to as a "self-represented litigant" (e.g., US, Canada, Australia), "litigant in person" (e.g., India, Singapore, UK), and "pro se litigant" (e.g., US).[3]

AI systems that aim to improve the ability of users to achieve their goals are called *decision support systems* or *intelligent assistants*, and when the goals are law-related, such systems are termed *legal AI assistants*. AI-driven tools can mitigate the problems unrepresented people face by streamlining legal processes and improving the efficiency of legal services.

Equalizing Justice is a resource for those who want to develop, use, or understand legal AI assistants as tools for improving access to justice. We focus on technologies that automate tasks faced by unrepresented litigants navigating the legal system. Our approach encompasses not only generative AI and machine learning but also more traditional computational logic systems. From document automation and computational logic to interactive technologies like dialogue systems and case elicitation tools, we examine a spectrum of tools that can meaningfully assist unrepresented litigants. By considering both advanced AI applications and more conventional computational approaches, we analyze how these technologies can collectively reduce barriers to justice by simplifying complex legal processes, improving information accessibility, and enhancing the overall experience for those without legal representation.

This book does not address applications of AI or other computer technology that function as autonomous decision processes, such as systems for calculating the probability of recidivism for the purpose of recommending sentences,[4] employment and tenant screening systems,[5] or systems for automatically calculating benefits.[6] Autonomous systems that impact individual rights and enforce penalties raise a

[3] Mia Bonardi & L. Karl Branting, *Certifying Legal AI Assistants for Unrepresented Litigants: A Global Survey of Access to Civil Justice, Unauthorized Practice of Law, and AI*, 26 Colum. Sci. & Tech. L. Rev. 34, 41 (2025).

[4] For a discussion of the COMPAS recidivism system, *see* Julia Dressel & Hany Farid, *The Accuracy, Fairness, and Limits of Predicting Recidivism*, 4 Sci. Adv. 1 (Jan. 2018) (corrected Mar. 30, 2018).

[5] *See* Statement of Interest of the United States at 4, Louis v. SafeRent Sols., No. 1:22-cv-10800 (D. Mass. Jan. 9, 2023), https://perma.cc/N4EZ-ZGU2.

[6] Virginia Eubanks, Automating Inequality: How High-Tech Tools Profile, Police, and Punish the Poor (2018).

range of procedural due process issues, including how such systems "do not provide any opportunity for meaningful cross-examination, knowledge of opposing evidence, or the true reasoning behind a decision."[7] Examination of issues regarding *autonomous systems* is an important topic, but it falls outside the scope of this book, which focuses on legal AI assistants to inform and empower the decisions of unrepresented litigants.

We argue that acceptance and adoption of legal AI technology in response to this access to justice crisis are imperative for two reasons. The first is simple fairness. A legal system that the average person cannot understand or use effectively fails to satisfy the fundamental principle of equality under the law. AI techniques that enable unrepresented individuals to understand or navigate the system governing their legal rights would help reduce the disparity in access to justice, thereby helping to level the playing field for all litigants, regardless of their resources.

A second reason is that a lack of access to justice gives rise to needless social costs. AI systems that handle common legal tasks can eliminate redundant effort across the legal system, where countless individuals separately struggle to understand identical procedures and requirements. A single investment in a system to automate the rules and procedures for common legal situations could relieve this redundancy. From this perspective, legal AI assistants for unrepresented litigants can be viewed as public goods, similar to roads, schools, and courthouses, whose costs and benefits are shared by all citizens. While there has long been a consensus on the value of publicly funded courts and judges, rather than passing the cost to litigants, the idea of treating software to improve access to justice as a similarly valued public good is relatively new.

Part I, *Addressing the Crisis in Access to Justice with Legal AI*, opens with Chapter 1, where we examine the magnitude and costs of the *global access to justice crisis*. Chapter 2 analyzes *the language gap* and explores the potential of generative AI to bridge it. Chapter 3 investigates the *needs of unrepresented litigants* and the tasks they must accomplish to assert their rights and defenses, laying the groundwork for future chapters to explain how AI and other technologies can assist them.

Part II, *Automating Legal Tasks with AI and Other Technologies*, demonstrates how certain legal AI and other technologies can automate the tasks unrepresented litigants need to assert their rights and engage with the legal system. Chapter 4 *introduces generative AI*, highlighting the recent technology that offers unparalleled capabilities for bridging the language gap, while also presenting many nuances and pitfalls. Chapter 5 traces the *history of legal AI and its evolution*. Chapter 6, on

7 Chris Chambers Goodman, *AI, Can You Hear Me? Promoting Procedural Due Process in Government Use of Artificial Intelligence Technologies*, 28 Rich. J.L. & Tech. 700, 711 (2022) (arguing that "algorithmic decision-making and the use of machine learning technologies violate most – if not all – of [Judge Friendly's] elements of a fair hearing" from his article, *Some Kind of Hearing*); *see also* Henry J. Friendly, *Some Kind of Hearing*, 123 U. Pa. L. Rev. 1267, 1279–95 (1975).

computational logic, explores techniques for modeling the rule-governed nature of law. Chapter 7, on *machine learning*, demonstrates capabilities for predicting case decisions and generalizing over cases. Chapter 8, on *document automation*, covers the widely adopted legal technology. Chapter 9, on *interactive legal technologies*, discusses chatbots, case elicitation, and legal design.

Part III, *Promising Applications*, highlights how legal AI and other technologies can address the needs of civil litigants, as discussed in Chapter 3. Chapter 10 emphasizes the importance of integrating these technologies to solve the full spectrum of litigants' needs. Chapter 11 explores *online dispute resolution ("ODR")*, a promising technological approach for equalizing the bias in favor of large-scale institutional plaintiffs. Chapter 12 reviews some uses of large language models ("LLMs") for the specific goal of increasing access to justice.

Part IV, *Today's Access to Justice Systems*, profiles tools offered both for free and at a cost. Chapter 13 profiles tools that are hosted directly by courts and tribunals, law schools, legal aid organizations, nonprofits, and companies. It also acknowledges that a business model for lawyers to provide low-cost consumer-facing tools and legal services to those in need is a critical part of the solution, highlighting several of the companies that do so already.

Part V, *Barriers and Risks*, acknowledges that while AI systems have great potential to benefit unrepresented litigants, there are also important barriers and risks to consider. Chapter 14 tackles prohibitions against the *unauthorized practice of law ("UPL")*, one of the most significant institutional barriers to adopting legal AI assistants. Chapter 15, on *AI assurance*, underscores the importance of reliability, privacy and accountability in legal AI technology.

Part VI, *Recommendations*, offers both technological and institutional recommendations for developers, legal aid organizations, nonprofits, courts, and other institutions looking to leverage AI or other technologies to assist unrepresented litigants. Chapter 16 outlines technological recommendations, specifically *technical methods for evaluating AI applications for legal tasks*. Chapter 17 addresses *institutional recommendations* and emphasizes that technological innovations alone will not be sufficient to solve the access to justice crisis. A variety of institutional reforms are needed, including simplifying legal procedures, increasing funding for legal services, and reducing restrictions on UPL, which all restrict the availability and affordability of legal services for unrepresented litigants.

PART I

Addressing the Crisis in Access to Justice with Legal AI

1

The Global Access to Justice Crisis

L. Karl Branting

1.1 INTRODUCTION

Justice is denied when individuals cannot navigate the legal system on their own or afford necessary legal assistance and when the system fails to deliver timely decisions. "Access to justice" refers to the ability of individuals to effectively and fairly use legal institutions and processes to seek and obtain remedies for their legal problems. It encompasses aspects such as affordability, availability of legal services, understanding of rights, and fairness in legal proceedings.

Lack of legal assistance is particularly acute for people experiencing poverty, with considerable consequences for both individuals and society. Unrepresented litigants are at a substantial disadvantage in legal proceedings compared with parties represented by an attorney: "Without representation, people lose custody of their children. They are evicted from their homes. Their assets or wages are seized. They are deported. Their lives are disrupted with significant financial and emotional impact."[1]

In *Rules for a Flat World*, Gillian Hadfield observed that "[h]alf the planet lives outside of any formal legal framework. The other half operates inside frameworks that have stagnated in the twentieth century – well designed for the nation-based mass-manufacturing economy but badly out of step with the digitized, global environment we now inhabit."[2]

This chapter discusses the multifaceted nature of the global access to justice crisis, highlighting countries with pervasive justice gaps and the severe consequences those gaps impose on people's lives. At the heart of this investigation are two

[1] Ralph Baxter, *Dereliction of Duty: State-Bar Inaction in Response to America's Access-to-Justice Crisis*, 132 Yale L.J.F. 228, 231 (2022); *see also* Martin Frankel, Carroll Seron & Gregg Van Ryzin, *The Impact of Legal Counsel on Outcomes for Poor Tenants in New York City's Housing Court: Results of a Randomized Experiment*, 35 Law & Soc'y Rev. 419, 419–34 (2001) (examining the effect of legal representation on outcomes for indigent tenants).

[2] Gillian K. Hadfield, Rules for A Flat World: Why Humans Invented Law and How to Reinvent It for a Complex Global Economy 3 (2016).

compelling reasons artificial intelligence ("AI") has emerged to mitigate this crisis: fairness and social costs. Four factors exacerbating the global access to justice crisis are: (1) growing societal complexity, (2) overprofessionalization, (3) bias toward institutional plaintiffs, and (4) the language gap. This chapter explores how increasing societal complexities create additional challenges for individuals seeking justice and examines how the legal profession's stringent requirements and gatekeeping practices limit access to legal services. Through this exploration, we aim to lay the groundwork for understanding both the scope of the crisis and the potential for technological tools to help bridge the access to justice gap.

1.2 MAGNITUDE OF THE CRISIS

The magnitude of the unmet global need for legal assistance is difficult to exaggerate. According to the World Justice Project, approximately 1.4 billion people have unmet civil or administrative justice needs, despite living in societies with functioning justice systems.[3] The report suggests that this estimate is likely conservative and elaborates: "Obstacles to addressing legal needs may include poor legal capability and knowledge, insufficient help or assistance, or resolution processes that are slow, expensive, or biased."[4] A 2019 analysis of twenty-nine Open Government Partnership countries found that only 41% of respondents with legal problems reported being able to get the help that they needed.[5] A closer look at individual countries confirms the magnitude of the global access to justice crisis.[6]

Argentina. In 2019, Argentina's Ministry of Justice and Human Rights of the Nation conducted an "Access to Justice and Conditions of Social Inequality" survey, which found that 70% of individuals who had a potential legal problem sought help or went to an institution to try to solve the problem, but after seeking help or advice, 62% of these people reported they were dissatisfied with the help.[7]

3 World Just. Project, Measuring the Justice Gap: A People-Centered Assessment of Unmet Justice Needs around the World 13 (2019), https://perma.cc/CM7W-TK3M [hereinafter World Just. Project, Measuring the Justice Gap]. This figure does not include the estimated 253 million individuals who live in "extreme conditions of injustice," such as being stateless, victims of modern slavery, or living in "fragile states with high levels of insecurity." *Id.*; *see also* Comm'n on Legal Empowerment of the Poor, Making the Law Work for Everyone (2008), https://perma.cc/VZ34-LFTD (discussing strategies to extend legal protections to impoverished communities).

4 World Just. Project, Measuring the Justice Gap, *supra* note 3.

5 *Justice Policy Series, Part 1: Access to Justice*, Open Gov't P'ship (Sep. 20, 2019), https://perma.cc/N5NJ-AV3B.

6 *See* Mia Bonardi & L. Karl Branting, *Certifying Legal AI Assistants for Unrepresented Litigants: A Global Survey of Access to Civil Justice, Unauthorized Practice of Law, and AI*, 26 Colum. Sci. & Tech. L. Rev. 34, 52–84 (2025).

7 Ministerio de Justicia y Derechos Humanos de la Nación [Ministry of Justice and Human Rights of the Nation], Acceso a la Justicia y condiciones de desigualdad social [Access to Justice and conditions of social inequality] 9 (2019) (machine translation by Google) (on file with Mia Bonardi).

Australia. In 2021, the Public Understanding of Law Survey ("PULS") interviewed over 6,000 respondents across Victoria and found that where legal needs existed, 78% went unmet.[8] PULS also found that most respondents received legal advice and met their needs via "non-legal" rather than traditional legal services. For those who did not seek advice, 30% cited reasons such as not knowing where to find help or feeling that seeking help would be futile.

Brazil. In a 2017 survey of about 1,000 people in Brazil's three largest cities, the World Justice Project found that of the 69% who experienced a civil legal problem in the past two years, 50% knew where to get advice and information, but only 13% were able to access help and of that, only 55% fully resolved their problem.[9] On average, it took respondents about six months to fix the problem.

Canada. According to the Law Society of Ontario, "over any three-year period, nearly half of all Canadian adults will experience at least one legal problem that they consider serious and difficult to resolve. However, Canadians do not seek professional assistance for more than 80% of their legal issues."[10]

China. A national legal needs survey has not been conducted for China.[11] However, according to the US Congressional-Executive Commission on China, "there is roughly one lawyer for every ten thousand individuals in China as compared to a ratio of one to 550 in the United States."[12]

Germany. A 2018 World Justice Project survey of about 1,000 people in Germany found that of the 68% of people who experienced a civil legal problem in the past two years, only 33% could access help, and only 43% said their problem was resolved.[13] On average, it took people about eleven months to solve their problem, and 43% experienced hardship because of their problem, whether it was health, economics, interpersonal, or substance abuse related.

India. The country with the greatest unmet need for legal services may be India, which has a backlog of more than 11 million civil cases, nearly a quarter of which are at least five years old.[14] Factors contributing to this backlog

[8] Nigel J. Balmer et al., The Public Understanding of Law Survey: Everyday Problems and Legal Need 10, 16 (Victoria Law Found, 2023), https://perma.cc/F3JE-3D43.

[9] World Just. Project, Global Insights on Access to Justice 25 (2019), https://perma.cc/98NY-KGDB [hereinafter World Just. Project, Global Insights] (summarizing survey results for Brazil).

[10] Law Soc'y of Ontario, *Access to Innovation: About A2I*, https://tinyurl.com/muc28xv5.

[11] Hongyao Wu, *People's Republic of China: National Report*, Glob. Access to Just. Project, https://globalaccesstojustice.com/global-overview-china/ (last visited May 28, 2025).

[12] Jayshree Bajoria, *Access to Justice in China*, Council on Foreign Rels. (Mar. 17, 2008, 3:00 PM EST), https://perma.cc/83MX-6GLS.

[13] World Just. Project, Global Insights, *supra* note 9, at 43 (summarizing survey results for Germany).

[14] Sameer Yasir, *"A Lifelong Nightmare": Seeking Justice in India's Overwhelmed Courts*, N.Y. Times (Jan. 13, 2024), www.nytimes.com/2024/01/13/world/asia/india-judicial-backlog.html.

include one of the world's lowest ratios of judges to population, at 21 per million people, and inefficient legal procedures.[15] India has an estimated 269.8 million people living below the poverty line,[16] and just five legal aid lawyers per 100,000 people,[17] so a vast number of individuals must face legal issues unrepresented.

New Zealand. A 2017 World Justice Project survey of about 1,000 people in New Zealand found that of the 63% of people who experienced a civil legal problem in the past two years, 72% knew where to get advice and information, but only 32% could access help, and only 44% said their problem was resolved.[18] On average, it took people about eight months to solve their problem, and 46% experienced hardship because of their problem, whether it was health, economic, interpersonal, or substance abuse related.

Nigeria. In 2022, the Hague Institute for Innovation of Law ("HiiL") surveyed 6,573 randomly selected adults across Nigeria and found that around 81% of Nigerians faced at least one legal issue in the past year, with many experiencing multiple legal issues.[19] Of these, 55% were resolved, and 82% of resolutions were considered fair or very fair. Common legal issues included neighbor disputes, domestic abuse, land disputes, crime, and housing problems.

Singapore. A 2019 World Justice Project survey of about 1,000 people in Singapore found that of the 50% of people who experienced a civil legal problem in the past two years, 67% knew where to get advice and information, and only 40% said their problem was resolved.[20] On average, it took people about nine months to solve their problem, and 45% experienced hardship because of their problem, whether it was health, economic, interpersonal issues, or substance abuse related.

South Africa. In 2022, Statistics South Africa published a survey of more than 30,000 residents regarding civil or justiciable (noncriminal) disputes which found that of the 21% of the population over the age of sixteen who had

[15] *Id*. Another estimate of the ratio of judges to population in India is nineteen judges for every 1 million people. John Clammer & Matthew Byrne, *The Village Says "No": Why Online ADR Is Not (Yet) Working in Rural India*, 3 LAW, TECH. & HUMS. 133, 134 (2021).

[16] Harsh Shrinet, *Relevance of Pro Bono Services in India's Battle for Justice and Equality*, 2 JUS CORPUS L.J. 1102, 1103 (2022).

[17] IndiaSpend & Suryanshi Pandey, Why Is the Quality of India's Free Legal Aid So Poor?, INDIA DEV. REV. (Jan. 20, 2023), https://perma.cc/2PP3-SN8B.

[18] WORLD JUST. PROJECT, GLOBAL INSIGHTS, *supra* note 9, at 77 (summarizing survey results for New Zealand).

[19] THE HAGUE INSTITUTE FOR INNOVATION OF LAW (HIIL), JUSTICE NEEDS AND SATISFACTION IN NIGERIA (2023), https://perma.cc/2KRV-ZFSU.

[20] WORLD JUST. PROJECT, GLOBAL INSIGHTS, *supra* note 9, at 94 (summarizing survey results for Singapore).

experienced one or more legal issues in the previous two years, most were due to "poor service from government and business."[21]

United Kingdom. Lack of legal representation is a rapidly growing problem in the UK due to a sharp decrease in annual spending on legal aid.[22] The UK Law Society found that 84.9% of welfare recipients in England and Wales do not have access to a legal aid provider, leaving them unable to challenge or appeal benefits decisions.[23] In only 18% of family law cases, both parties were represented, and neither was legally represented in 40%.[24] A 2019 online survey by the Law Society about the legal aid needs of nearly 30,000 people found that of the six in ten adults (64%) who experienced a legal issue in the last four years, 45% got nonprofessional help or no help.[25]

United States. In 2022, the Legal Services Corporation found that 92% of low-income Americans did not receive adequate or any legal assistance for their civil legal problems.[26] The same survey found that 74% of low-income households experienced one or more civil legal problems in the previous year, and the most common types of problems were consumer issues, health care, housing, and income maintenance. In 2015, at least one party was unrepresented by counsel in over 76% of all state court civil cases.[27] A survey conducted in 2019 on "Justice Needs and Satisfaction in the United States of America" found that more people used the Internet (31%) than lawyers (29%) as a resource for their legal issues.[28]

The data presented underscore the staggering magnitude of the global access to justice crisis. Across diverse nations, from developed economies such as Germany and the US to emerging markets such as India and Nigeria, the challenges in

21 Dep't: Stat. South Africa, Governance, Public Safety and Justice Survey GPSJS 2021/22, at v (2022), www.statssa.gov.za/publications/P0340/P03402022.pdf.

22 Gabrielle Garton Grimwood, Litigants in Person: The Rise of the Self-Represented Litigant in Civil and Family Cases, House of Commons Libr., at 13 (Jan. 14, 2016), https://tinyurl.com/5cuamx2e; Justice, *The State We're In: Addressing Threats & Challenges to the Rule of Law*, at 55 (Sep. 2023), https://perma.cc/8UHD-4X69.

23 *Welfare Benefits – Legal Aid Deserts*, The Law Soc'y (Feb. 21, 2024), https://perma.cc/8X9Y-S5T4.

24 Justice, *supra* note 22, at 56. The percentages in the text refer to the last quarter of 2022.

25 *Legal Needs of Individuals in England and Wales Report*, The Law Soc'y (Jan. 27, 2020), https://perma.cc/FZ8G-WM38.

26 Legal Servs. Corp., The Justice Gap Report: The Unmet Civil Legal Needs of Low-Income Americans 8 (2022), https://perma.cc/5BXH-ANNZ.

27 Paula Hannaford-Agor, Scott Graves & Shelley Spacek Miller, *The Landscape of Civil Litigation in State Courts*, Nat'l Ctr. For State Cts., at iv (2015), https://perma.cc/C28T-BU4A.

28 Inst. for the Advancement of the Am. Legal Sys. & The Hague Inst. for Innovation of Law, Justice Needs and Satisfaction in the United States of America, at 11 (2021), https://perma.cc/7CR2-EMFZ.

accessing legal assistance are pervasive and profound. The disparities in legal support, whether due to insufficient legal infrastructure, socioeconomic barriers, or systemic inefficiencies, highlight a universal shortfall in meeting civil and administrative justice needs.

The consistent theme is that a significant portion of the population faces legal issues without adequate resolution, often experiencing prolonged and unresolved disputes that profoundly impact their lives. These findings reveal the extensive gap in the delivery of legal services and underscore the urgent need for innovative tools to bridge this gap. Legal AI assistants tailored for unrepresented litigants are emerging as crucial tools in addressing this global crisis, providing a pathway to more equitable and efficient access to justice.

1.3 MOTIVATING FACTORS FOR IMPROVEMENT

These statistics underscore the critical need for enhanced access to legal assistance and highlight opportunities for ethical and pragmatic improvements. There are two primary motivations for developing AI systems to address the justice crisis: (1) fairness and (2) social costs.

1.3.1 *Fairness*

A legal system that the average person cannot understand or use effectively fails to satisfy the fundamental principle of equality under the law. The social contract underpinning representative democracies rests on a conception of fairness in which like cases are decided alike: *The Universal Declaration of Human Rights* states that "All are equal before the law and are entitled without any discrimination to equal protection of the law" (Article 7) and "Everyone is entitled to a fair and public hearing by an independent and impartial tribunal, in the determination of his rights and obligations" (Article 10).[29] Additionally, the principle of access to justice is enshrined in the *Charter of Fundamental Rights of the European Union*,[30] and the Equal Protection Clause of the Fourteenth Amendment to the US Constitution.[31] AI techniques that enable unrepresented individuals to understand or navigate the system that governs their legal rights would help reduce the disparity in access to justice, leveling the playing field for all litigants, regardless of resources.

[29] G.A. Res. 217 (III) A, Universal Declaration of Human Rights, arts. 7, 10 (Dec. 10, 1948).
[30] Charter of Fundamental Rights of the European Union art. 47, Oct. 26, 2012, 2012 O.J. (C 326).
[31] U.S. Const. amend. XIV, § 1.

1.3.2 *Social Costs*

Poorly functioning courts and the inability of unrepresented individuals to navigate the system that governs their legal rights impose significant social costs.[32] Economic growth rates are higher in economies with robust property rights and contract enforcement.[33] One particularly clear example is that foreign investment rates are higher in countries where courts effectively protect investors from having their assets seized by local residents or the government.[34]

AI systems that handle common legal tasks can alleviate the wasteful, duplicative effort by numerous individuals struggling with the same problems. A single investment in a system to automate the rules and procedures for common legal situations could relieve this redundancy, reducing the aggregate social costs of the civil legal system. From this perspective, AI systems for unrepresented litigants can be viewed as public goods, like roads, schools, and courthouses, whose costs and benefits are shared by all. While there has long been a consensus on the social value of publicly funding courts and judges, proposals to treat software as a similarly valued social good to improve access to justice are much newer.

More broadly, all functioning communities require predictable and well-known rules for resolving disputes and allocating resources. The importance of these rules is illustrated by the fact that such rules develop even in the absence of any external authority to enunciate and enforce them. For example, in medieval Europe, before the development of the modern state, "kings, nobles, guilds, church leaders, and town officials [competed] to supply the legal infrastructure to support the explosion of trade."[35] Those whose rules did a better job of supporting trade tended to grow wealthier and more powerful.

As an additional example, rules for resolving disputes over claims developed organically among miners during the California Gold Rush. There was no external authority to publicize or enforce these rules, but they were common knowledge among the miners, and miners enforced them in an informal collective fashion, for example, by respecting or defending lawful claims under the mining communities' rules and procedures.[36] Contemporary communities that exist outside the formal

[32] *See, e.g.*, Panayotis Kapopoulos & Anastasios Rizos, *Judicial Efficiency and Economic Growth: Evidence Based on European Union Data*, 71 Scottish J. Pol. Econ. 101, 101–31 (2024); *see generally* World Just. Project, Global Insights, *supra* note 9.

[33] Stephan Haggard & Lydia Tiede, *The Rule of Law and Economic Growth: Where Are We?*, 39 World Dev. 673, 673–85 (2011); *see also* Ernesto Dal Bó & Frederico Finan, At the Intersection: A Review of Institutions in Economic Development 40–50 (Econ. Dev. Inst. Working Paper Series WP16/11.01, 2016), https://perma.cc/T9TC-WSPV (protecting property rights encourages economic growth).

[34] Rafael La Porta, Florencio Lopez-de-Silanes & Andrei Shleifer, *Law and Finance after a Decade of Research*, *in* 2 Handbook of the Economics of Finance 425 (George M. Constantinides, Milton Harris & Rene M. Stulz eds., 2013).

[35] Hadfield, *supra* note 2, at 95.

[36] *Id.* at 26.

economy and legal system, such as homeless children in the slums of Lusaka, also develop rules that are observed and enforced by community members.[37] In all these cases, shared knowledge of rules is beneficial because it promotes confidence in fairness, reduces the potential for friction and conflict, and reduces the likelihood that disagreements will spiral into tit-for-tat retaliation.

1.4 CONTRIBUTING FACTORS TO THE CRISIS

Given the importance of efficient and comprehensible systems of legal rules, why are there so many societies in which most people cannot achieve an efficient, comprehensible, and fair resolution of their legal issues? Every society develops rules to resolve conflicts and allocate resources. As economies become more complex and interdependent, the rules and procedures necessary to resolve disputes correspondingly grow in complexity, and legal expertise becomes more professionalized, increasing the costs associated with each case. While increased specialization and professionalization benefit attorneys and may, in some ways, benefit large corporations and the wealthy, most individuals facing a legal problem lack the resources either to acquire the necessary specialized knowledge to represent themselves adequately or to hire an attorney educated in that specialized knowledge to represent them.

Thus, there are at least four critical factors that exacerbate the global access to justice crisis: (1) growing societal complexity, (2) overprofessionalization of the legal community, (3) a bias in favor of institutional plaintiffs, and (4) the language gap.

1.4.1 *Growing Societal Complexity*

As industrialized societies have become more economically and socially complex, so too have their governing rules and procedures. Complex rules and procedures complicate not only the justice systems of the complex societies in which they are developed but can also burden the justice systems in societies where they were not developed. For example, rules and procedures developed by colonizing nations are often left behind in less-industrialized former colonies, where they can lead, for instance, to "rococo complexity of the steps required to create and operate a legitimate business or transfer property rights."[38]

While economic and social complexity may account for the legal complexity of many areas, such as business, tax, and administrative law, it is at best a partial explanation of the intractability of the legal issues most common among unrepresented

[37] Chris Lockhart & Daniel Mulilo Chama, Walking the Bowl: A True Story of Murder and Survival among the Street Children of Lusaka (2022).

[38] Hadfield, *supra* note 2, at 329.

litigants, such as family law, landlord–tenant disputes, and problems involving credit, loans, or debt,[39] since these disputes usually involve a relatively stable set of predictable issues.

1.4.2 *Overprofessionalization of the Legal Community*

As the legal profession has grown more professionalized, both incentives and opportunities have grown for authorities to regulate the practice of law by, for instance, placing restrictions on who can provide legal advice and developing ever more complex legal procedures and doctrines that can be understood and navigated only by trained and credentialed professionals. Unauthorized practice of law ("UPL") rules that restrict the practice of law to licensed attorneys limit the availability of legal assistance for low-income individuals and contribute to the access to justice crisis.[40] See Chapter 14 for more on UPL.

1.4.3 *Bias toward Institutional Plaintiffs*

Economies of scale favor institutional plaintiffs over unrepresented defendants in civil courts, creating a strong financial incentive for corporate plaintiffs to sue individual defendants. In the US, this disparity is particularly evident in the rise of "assembly-line plaintiffs," which are typically financial services companies and debt collectors that file high volumes of low-value cases.[41] A study of data from trial courts of general jurisdiction across eighteen states revealed that the ten most frequent plaintiffs typically accounted for between 20% and 33% of all cases filed in 2019.[42] For example, just ten plaintiffs filed over 41% of all cases in twenty-one state court jurisdictions in New Jersey.[43] Similarly, just ten plaintiffs were responsible for more than 25% of all filings in twenty state-court jurisdictions in California.[44] These cases are nevertheless profitable because the majority of defendants default rather than dispute the claim, and because filing large volumes of almost identical cases lowers the cost of each case.[45]

Assembly-line cases illustrate that individuals without the resources to hire an attorney can be a source of profit for plaintiffs if they minimize the likelihood that

39 Legal Servs. Corp., *supra* note 26, at 8.

40 *See* Michele Cotton, *Experiment, Interrupted: Unauthorized Practice of Law versus Access to Justice*, 5 DePaul J. Soc. Just. 179, 181–83 (2012); S. Thomas, *Rethinking Unauthorized Practice of Law in Light of the Access to Justice Crisis*, 23 Prof. Lawyer 17–23 (2015).

41 Daniel Wilf-Townsend, *Assembly-Line Plaintiffs*, 135 Harv. L. Rev. 1704, 1708–10, 1732 (2022).

42 *Id.* at 1708, 1726–33.

43 *Id.* at 1708.

44 *Id.*

45 Peter A. Holland, *Junk Justice: A Statistical Analysis of 4,400 Lawsuits Filed by Debt Buyers*, 26 Loy. Consumer L. Rev. 179, 208 (2014).

A TAXONOMY OF LITIGATION BY STRATEGIC CONFIGURATION OF PARTIES

		Initiator, Claimant	
		One-Shotter	Repeat Player
Defendant	One-Shotter	Parent v. Parent (Custody) Spouse v. Spouse (Divorce) Family v. Family Member (Insanity Commitment) Family v. Family (Inheritance) Neighbor v. Neighbor Partner v. Partner OS vs OS I	Prosecutor v. Accused Finance Co. v. Debtor Landlord v. Tenant I.R.S. v. Taxpayer Condemnor v. Property Owner RP vs OS II
	Repeat Player	Welfare Client v. Agency Auto Dealer v. Manufacturer Injury Victim v. Insurance Company Tenant v. Landlord Bankrupt Consumer v. Creditors Defamed v. Publisher OS vs RP III	Union v. Company Movie Distributor v. Censorship Board Developer v. Suburban Municipality Purchaser v. Supplier Regulatory Agency v. Firms of Regulated Industry RP vs RP IV

FIGURE 1.1 A taxonomy of litigation by strategic configuration of parties. Republished with permission from Marc Galanter, the Law & Society Review, and Cambridge University Press.[46]

the claims will be contested. As shown in Figure 1.1, in *Why the "Haves" Come Out Ahead*, Marc Galanter depicts these assembly line plaintiffs as "repeat players" or "RPs" and others who typically only interact with the legal system once as "one-shotters" or "OSs."[47]

Galanter's taxonomy illustrates the strategic dynamics that make "RP vs. OS" cases systematically advantageous to RP plaintiffs and disadvantageous to OS defendants. Galanter argues, "Since they expect to litigate again, RPs can select to adjudicate (or appeal) those cases which they regard as most likely to produce favorable rules … [and t]hus, we would expect the body of 'precedent' cases – that is, cases capable of influencing the outcome of future cases – to be relatively skewed toward those favorable to RPs."[48] Unlike "OS vs. OS" cases, which involve disputes between individuals with similar resource constraints and legal inexperience, "RP vs. OS" cases create systematic imbalances. Repeat players can develop specialized expertise, pursue long-term strategic objectives, and select which cases to litigate based on their precedent-setting potential. Meanwhile, individual defendants typically encounter the legal system only once and lack

[46] Marc Galanter, *Why the "Haves" Come Out Ahead: Speculations on the Limits of Legal Change*, 9 Law & Soc'y Rev. 95, 107 (Figure 1) (1974).

[47] *Id.* at 97, 98–99.

[48] *Id.* at 101–02.

both the resources to mount vigorous defenses and the strategic incentives to consider broader legal implications.

The examples in Figure 1.1 for RP vs. OS cases, specifically Finance Co. v. Debtor, mirror exactly the types of high-volume, low-value cases that dominate civil dockets and contribute to the access-to-justice crisis.[49] These cases are profitable precisely because individual defendants usually default or settle quickly, allowing institutional plaintiffs to obtain favorable outcomes without facing the kinds of sustained legal challenges that might produce more balanced precedents.

1.4.4 *The Language Gap*

The language gap is a more fundamental obstacle to the ability of unrepresented litigants to understand their legal rights and defenses. It separates ordinary, everyday language from the language of legal rules. The language gap is not a product of legal professionalism, although legal professionalism exacerbates it. Rather, it is an unavoidable consequence of the fact that a rule that satisfies a fundamental principle of justice – that like cases be treated alike – must be expressed in language that is more general than the individual cases it covers. Chapter 2 is dedicated to the language gap because generative AI appears to provide several key capabilities needed to bridge it.

–

Individual litigants face what amounts to a perfect storm of disadvantages: they encounter complex rules they cannot understand, need professional services they cannot afford, face institutional opponents with systematic advantages, and must navigate a system using language and procedures designed for and by legal professionals.

As shown in Table 1.1, the "haves" enjoy cumulative advantages across parties, legal services, institutional facilities, and rules – "advantages which interlock, reinforcing and shielding one another."[50] Meanwhile, individual litigants face compounding disadvantages in each category, creating a structurally unequal contest from the outset. Meaningful reform requires confronting these deeply embedded structural inequalities rather than working around them. Although the AI applications highlighted in this book represent powerful tools for leveling these unequal playing fields, they remain technological patches on structural problems that ultimately require institutional reforms to be fundamentally resolved.

49 Wilf-Townsend, *supra* note 41, at 1708–10, 1732.

50 Galanter, *supra* note 46, at 124.

TABLE 1.1 *Why the "haves" tend to come out ahead*[51]

Element	Advantages	Enjoyed by
Parties	– ability to structure transaction – specialized expertise, economies of scale – long-term strategy – ability to play for rules – bargaining credibility – ability to invest in penetration	– repeat players (large, professional)*
Legal services	– skill, specialization, continuity	– organized, professional,* wealthy
Institutional facilities	– passivity – cost and delay barriers – favorable priorities	– wealthy, experienced, organized – holders, possessors – beneficiaries of existing rules – organized, attentive
Rules	– favorable rules – due process barriers	– older, culturally dominant – holders, possessors

* in the simple sense of "doing it for a living."
Source: Marc Galanter, the Law & Society Review, and Cambridge University Press.

1.5 CONCLUSION

The global access to justice crisis is a pervasive and multifaceted problem affecting millions of people worldwide. Individuals struggle to navigate complex legal systems, often facing significant barriers in resolving their legal issues.

Growing societal complexity has resulted in sophisticated yet opaque and inaccessible legal systems. Overprofessionalization has created restrictive gatekeeping mechanisms that limit legal assistance to credentialed professionals while pricing out those most in need of help. Institutional plaintiffs exploit systematic advantages as "repeat players," using economies of scale, specialized expertise, and strategic case selection to overwhelm individual defendants who encounter the legal system only once. And the language gap separates everyday communication and legal discourse.

As Galanter's framework demonstrates, these factors create cumulative advantages for the "haves" across the legal system while generating compounding disadvantages for individual litigants. The result is not just unequal access but systematically unequal outcomes that undermine the foundational principle that all are equal before the law.

51 *Id.* at 125 (Figure 3).

The motivations for addressing this crisis are twofold: fairness and social costs. Fairness demands that all individuals have equal access to justice, regardless of their economic status or legal expertise. The social costs of inadequate access to justice are substantial, impacting economic growth and overall social stability.

The AI technologies explored throughout this book offer powerful tools for addressing these structural inequalities. These applications can help bridge the language gap, provide guidance through complex procedures, and level the playing fields that favor institutional actors. Such technological interventions represent crucial progress toward expanding access to justice for millions who currently face legal systems that are formally open but practically closed to them.

Yet we must maintain clarity about both the promise and limitations of technological bridge building. While AI applications can meaningfully expand access to justice today, they remain bridges across structural divides rather than solutions to the underlying problems that create those divides. The ultimate goal is not to build better technological workarounds but to reform legal institutions themselves – creating courts designed for the people they serve, procedures accessible to everyone, and systems that prioritize justice delivery over professional gatekeeping.

Until such institutional transformation occurs, however, the responsible development and deployment of AI technologies offers a promising path forward. By leveraging these tools while working toward deeper structural reforms, we can begin to fulfill the promise that justice should be accessible to all, regardless of one's ability to afford a lawyer.

2

The Language Gap

L. Karl Branting, Sarah McLeod, and Megan Ma[*]

2.1 INTRODUCTION

Chapter 1 discussed four factors that exacerbate the global access to justice crisis: (1) growing societal complexity, (2) overprofessionalization, (3) bias toward institutional plaintiffs, and (4) the language gap. This chapter focuses on the fourth factor, the language gap. Generative AI appears to provide several key capabilities that may help bridge this gap. This section distinguishes three aspects of the language gap: (1) open texture, (2) legalese, and (3) the abstraction of legal predicates. Chapters 4, 9, and 12 further explore the potential of generative AI to address the language gap.

2.2 WHAT IS THE LANGUAGE GAP?

The language gap is a fundamental obstacle for unrepresented litigants trying to understand their legal rights and defenses. It separates ordinary, everyday language from the language of legal rules. The language gap is not solely a product of legal professionalism, although professionalism often exacerbates it. Instead, the gap is an unavoidable consequence of the fact that a rule satisfying a fundamental principle of justice – that like cases be treated alike – must be expressed in more general language than the individual cases it covers.

For example, consider how to create a rule that holds careless drivers responsible for harm caused by their carelessness. Such a rule must be expressed in more general language than the descriptions of any individual form of carelessness. It would be futile to try to enumerate every possible form of careless driving because the list would be endless, for example, reaching into the back seat while making a turn, drag racing on residential streets, and driving while impaired by a prescription drug. It is impossible to anticipate every example of carelessness, as new forms of

* This chapter is published with the permission of the MITRE Corporation. We thank Michael Livermore for his review of multiple drafts of this chapter.

careless behavior emerge over time, such as texting while driving or overreliance on self-driving mode.

Regardless of whether legal rules arise organically in response to the needs of a particular community, are enacted by regulation or statute, or evolve from court decisions under common law, they almost invariably contain abstract language that subsumes multiple situations. To continue with the previous careless-driving example, in most common law jurisdictions a defendant is liable to a plaintiff if the defendant "owed a duty of care" to the plaintiff (e.g., had a responsibility not to harm pedestrians in a crosswalk), "breached that duty" (e.g., did not look when driving through the intersection), and the plaintiff suffered "harm" that was "proximately caused by the breach of that duty" (e.g., was hit and injured by the defendant's car).[1] The abstract concepts of "duty of care," "breach," "harm," and "proximate cause" were developed by common law judges to cover the multiplicity of situations in which one person's carelessness can injure another, but their very abstractness often makes it challenging to determine whether they apply to new situations.[2]

The legal rules governing most cases involving unrepresented litigants are at the simpler end of the complexity spectrum; nevertheless, they contain abstract terms that are difficult for non-legal professionals to understand or apply. For example, in a typical US state, a survivor of domestic abuse can obtain a protection order against a person if the survivor can show that there is an intimate or domestic relationship with the person and that the person has committed or threatened abuse.[3] A typical statute lists types of relationships that satisfy "the intimate or domestic relationship" requirement, such as having a child with the person or having a sexual relationship with the person in the prior year, as well as types of abuse, such as child abuse or actions that result in fear of imminent serious bodily harm.[4] The terms on these lists are neutral and general, consistent with their function of covering a variety of typical possibilities. However, most people who are not legal professionals would struggle to understand what kind or frequency of intimate activities constitutes a "sexual relationship" or whether, for example, the statement "You'll be sorry" is sufficient to create a "fear of imminent serious bodily harm." In some states, these concepts are not defined by statute, but developed by judges through the common law, making some definitions more elusive.[5]

This example shows that solving a legal problem requires translating the facts of a situation into the abstract legal terms used in rules and statutes. Those terms are usually unfamiliar to people without legal training and unrepresented litigants often struggle to understand how their concrete experiences fit within the law.

1 57A AM. JUR. 2d *Negligence* § 68 n.6 (2025); 65 C.J.S. *Negligence* § 19 n.3 (2025).

2 65 C.J.S. *Negligence* § 1 (2025).

3 25 AM. JUR. 2d *Domestic Abuse and Violence* § 8 (2025); *see also* Lisa V. Martin, *The Importance of Civil Pathways to Protection Orders*, 113 GEO. L.J. 121, 131 (2024).

4 25 AM. JUR. 2d *Domestic Abuse and Violence* §§ 8–10 (2025).

5 *Id.* § 10.

Despite their challenges, the legal system expects unrepresented litigants to bridge this language gap on their own.

2.3 EXACERBATING THE LANGUAGE GAP

The complex dynamics behind the language gap can be analyzed in terms of three distinct elements: (1) open texture, (2) legalese, and (3) the abstraction of legal predicates. More concretely, the above examples suggest that the language gap goes beyond mere translation from legalese to ordinary language and back to legalese. Rather, multiple interacting factors increase the difficulty of accessing legal knowledge. Across these three elements, legal and linguistic features collaboratively muddy how people interpret legal rules.

To start, natural language is inherently fluid. In linguistics, this fluidity is described in terms of ambiguity and vagueness. Importantly, ambiguity and vagueness are distinguishable concepts, and both take multiple forms. The definition of *ambiguity* depends on the type of analysis. In syntax (rules for language structure), ambiguity refers to the *structure of the sentence* that enables more than one interpretation.[6] In semantics (the study of meaning in language), ambiguity refers to the *meaning in words* that have "more than one distinct meaning."[7] In pragmatics (how context affects meaning), ambiguity refers to *possible differences in context* that enable more than one interpretation.[8] Vagueness, on the other hand, appears predominantly in semantics and pragmatics. Unlike ambiguity, in both semantics and pragmatics, *vagueness* is defined by *indeterminacy*. A word is vague if it has a meaning "that does not distinguish between two or more different kinds of things."[9]

While they often appear in tandem, ambiguity and vagueness are not the same semantic property. That is, vagueness stems from uncertainty about a term's boundaries rather than from having multiple distinct meanings. Semantic ambiguity exists when a word has more than one meaning, but context makes the intended meaning clear. Consider, for example, "That idea is so novel!" versus "My latest novel will include three main characters." While the word "novel" has multiple meanings, each sentence clearly signals which meaning is intended. On the other hand, semantic vagueness reveals itself in the use of the word. For example, "The driver was going too fast." We understand what "too fast" means, but it is unclear exactly what speed is "too fast."

Similarly, vagueness in pragmatics is characterized by the strategic use of language. Consider, for example, the word "interesting," which is often used when a person does not want to take an explicit position on how they feel about a given

[6] Paul Elbourne, Meaning: A Slim Guide to Semantics 11 (2011).
[7] *Id.* at 59.
[8] *Id.* at 11.
[9] *Id.* at 34.

situation. By keeping the description vague, the person can avoid making any commitments at that moment.

Both ambiguity and vagueness found in natural language extend into the legal domain. Legal rules may be characterized by logical structures that, in theory, should provide clear paths to resolution, given a defined problem.[10] Alternatively, legal reasoning may follow a casuistic method, where circumstances and precedents associated with specific cases are used to reason about a law, or analogical reasoning, in which similarities between cases are used to answer legal questions. Yet in practice, neither form of reasoning presents itself neatly, and the open texture of natural language only exacerbates this.

What happens when we situate natural language in legal contexts? Consider a simple example: What is a sandwich? This precise issue was raised in the Worcester County Superior Court in Massachusetts when it considered whether a burrito was a sandwich in *White City Shopping Center, LP v. PR Restaurants, LLC*.[11] In 2006, White City Shopping Center ("White City") sought a declaratory judgment that it was not in violation of its commercial lease signed with PR Restaurants ("Panera"), a franchisee of Panera Bread Restaurants in New England. Chair 5 Restaurants, the operator of Qdoba Restaurants, wanted to open an outlet in White City to sell burritos. However, the commercial lease between White City and Panera contained an exclusivity clause preventing White City from entering into agreements with restaurants that would directly compete with Panera's sandwich sales. The lease agreement did not define "sandwich."

So, is a burrito a sandwich? Panera argued that any food product with bread and a filling is a sandwich. According to the Superior Court, it is not. From a semantic perspective, what set of objects does the word *sandwich* denote? Traits are crucial in classifying an object. *Componential semantics* regards the "set of primitive features that an object either must have or must not have in order to count as an instance of that term."[12] A simple example is the word *child*.[13] The deconstruction would look as follows:

+human
–adult

This denotation represents that a child is a human, not an adult. Using this methodology, Panera argued that a sandwich may be broken down into the following:

+bread
+filling

[10] Michael Genesereth, *Computational Law: The Cop in the Backseat*, CodeX – The Stan. Ctr. for Leg. Informatics 1–3 (2015), https://perma.cc/3TTV-CPV4.

[11] White City Shopping Ctr., LP v. PR Rests., LLC, No. 2006196313, 2006 WL 3292641 (Mass. Super. Ct. Oct. 31, 2006).

[12] Betty Birner, Language and Meaning 52 (2017).

[13] *Id.* at 14.

But this denotation is problematic as a further assessment requires understanding the primitive features of bread. Returning to the construction of a burrito, would a tortilla be considered bread? Panera argued that a tortilla qualifies as bread.[14] The Superior Court ruled that this argument was misplaced because the ordinary meaning of a word applies when interpreting unambiguous contractual terms. The court explained that Panera did not provide evidence that the term "sandwiches" was intended to include burritos.

But is the primitive feature of bread simply +flour? This question highlights the lack of clarity involved in componential semantics and the vicious circle involved in breaking down seemingly basic words. To resolve this conundrum, linguists often turn to prototypes – the archetypal example of a particular word – as a reference point. The more similar the object is to the prototype, the "more properly" the word applies to it.[15]

Linguists often discuss the parallel between prototype theory and the notion of fuzzy logic: the idea is that meaning is captured on a spectrum and is a matter of degree.[16] The understanding of a word depends on a process of continual refinement and a statistical calculation of likelihood. The inability to provide determinate parameters on the definition of "sandwich" suggests that, in law, ambiguity can quickly become vagueness, when contextualized by other compounding factors, such as business considerations.

We might also consider H. L. A. Hart's infamous "No Vehicles in the Park" hypothetical: A legal rule forbids you from taking a vehicle into the public park.[17] Plainly, this forbids an automobile. But what about bicycles, roller skates, and toy cars? What about airplanes? Are these "vehicles" for the purpose of this rule or not? For decades, this thought experiment has been used by law professors and their students to discuss and debate different interpretive strategies. Applying prototype theory, which suggests that individuals categorize objects based on their similarity to a "prototype" or ideal example, we can conceptualize archetypal vehicles (e.g., an automobile). We might even use componential semantics to parse what qualifies as a vehicle. Yet unlike the burrito, the complexity of this hypothetical stems not from the meaning of a vehicle, but how its meaning is affected by its existence in the park. In other words, even if there is consensus that something is indeed a vehicle, the operative question is whether it may enter the park. An ambulance or a fire truck would be considered archetypal vehicles but may be allowed in the park in case of an emergency.

But what happens if a drone is hovering above the park? More questions arise. Is the air above the park part of the park? Who is flying the drone? Was it flown

[14] *See* White City Shopping, 2006 WL 3292641, at *3 n.4.
[15] BIRNER, *supra* note 12, at 53.
[16] *Id.* at 54.
[17] H. L. A. Hart, *Positivism and the Separation of Law and Morals*, 71 HARV. L. REV. 593, 607 (1958).

by a child who was testing out a new video camera capable of capturing footage at 5,000 feet? Or was it flown by the employee of a large company (potentially located many miles away), delivering a shipment of goods to an area adjacent to the park? Answers to these questions require not only defining the meaning of "vehicle" but, more importantly, how the context modifies the meaning and logic of this legal rule.

While some may argue that a drone is a vehicle when a corporation flies it, or that a burrito should be considered a sandwich, the legal definitions of "sandwich" and "drone" change the quality of their ordinary meanings. In Section 2.4, we revisit seminal arguments of law and language scholars, specifically analyzing the relationship between the peculiarities of legal language and their role in accessing legal knowledge.

2.4 WRESTLING IN THE LANGUAGE GAP

In the preface of David Mellinkoff's pioneering text, *The Language of the Law*, he highlights a quote by legal historians on the significance of language: language is "no mere instrument which we can control at will; it controls us."[18] In other words, legal language drives behavior.

Mellinkoff states that this "customary language" used by lawyers and legal scholars includes a distinctive vocabulary, "certain mannerisms of compositions,"[19] and legalistic jargon, as well as words imported from other languages, such as Latin and French. He argues that the combination of these factors has led to the divergence between the language of the law and ordinary language. More specifically, he outlines nine characteristics that have made legal language a "specialized tongue."[20]

Among these characteristics, the majority draw attention to vocabulary. For Mellinkoff, the words of the language are problematic; a recurrent theme is that these terms of art are a significant source of confusion. Consider the first characteristic he discusses: the frequent use of common words with uncommon meanings. He highlights that words a lawyer understands are "incomprehensible" to those outside the community, as specific words often have an associated legal meaning.[21] Coupled with the continued use of arcane Latin words and phrases, understanding legal language requires regular visits to a specialized reference text: *Black's Law Dictionary*. For example, in the US, a Latin term still used by courts and lawyers for unrepresented litigants is "pro se," which means "for self" or "in one's own behalf." Importantly, Mellinkoff points to an existing conversion process between legal and ordinary language. Despite the language of the law being housed within the exact

18 David Mellinkoff, The Language of the Law vii (1963) (citing 1 Pollock and Maitland, The History of English Law 87 (2d ed. 1898); Oliver Wendell Holmes, The Common Law 382 (1881); 2 Bacon, Works 192–93 (Montagu ed. 1825)).

19 Mellinkoff, *supra* note 18, at 3.

20 *Id.* at 11.

21 *Id.* at 12.

linguistic vehicle (i.e., natural language) as common speech, the differences in the lexicon are sufficiently vast that translation is required.

However, Mellinkoff's discussion around the seemingly esoteric vocabulary of the law serves the purpose of an incisive commentary. He notes that the historical reasons for their existence are often justified as reasons for their current use. The bridge between vocabulary and arguments for their continued practice centers around the discussion of precision. Mellinkoff stresses the law's emphasis on, and perhaps obsession with, precision. He characterizes the law as requiring "extraordinary precision" yet being full of "weasel words."[22] Precision is a deliberate choice whereby flexibility is deployed intentionally. In effect, Mellinkoff delineates the boundaries between clarity and precision in the interpretive space.

He describes the legal language as a "viscous sea of verbiage," leading to a "muddiness" in understanding.[23] For Mellinkoff, "if there is any meaning, it is hard to find."[24] Interestingly, he defines clarity based on several structural peculiarities: (1) long sentences;[25] (2) awkward sentences;[26] and (3) "tortured metaphors."[27] These three factors contribute to the language's inability to communicate effectively. Clarity is associated with the capacity to communicate, whereas precision is a matter of choosing the appropriate vocabulary. As a result, clarity is directly correlative with meaning-making. Precision is merely a stylistic choice or an aesthetic decision.

So why, then, is Mellinkoff concerned with precision? He argues that precision is often referenced as a virtue and a response to any criticism of the language. The characteristic of being precise is fundamental to its existence. Moreover, precision (as in the word choice to convey an idea exactly as intended) fosters accuracy (an unambiguous outcome); the language of the law is exact. Consequently, even if the language is obscure, it is necessarily so.[28] Mellinkoff alludes to the irony of the legal language, that form precedes substance. Precision is intimately linked with certainty and the ancestry of its use. For these reasons, precision reigns over clarity. Other defects of the language are a small sacrifice in exchange for precision.

While Mellinkoff interprets clarity as a substantive trait, he concedes that the argument for precision often traverses into the territory of clarity. Those familiar with the language consider that precision enables clarity because the vocabulary is

22 *Id.* at 21 (citing H. Cairns, *Language of Jurisprudence*, *in* LANGUAGE: AN ENQUIRY INTO ITS MEANING AND FUNCTION 232, 258 (Anshen ed. 1957); STUART CHASE, THE TYRANNY OF WORDS 324 (1938)).

23 *Id.* at 24 (citing STUART CHASE, THE TYRANNY OF WORDS 327 (1938)).

24 *Id.* at 25.

25 *Id.* at 26 (suggesting that an average of 176 words in a sentence is not anything out of the ordinary).

26 *Id.* (suggesting that even shorter sentences with innumerable dependent clauses make sentences unclear).

27 *Id.* (pointing to imagery and artful use of literary devices as not providing any useful information).

28 *See id.* at 291 (considering the argument raised by Sir Ernest Gowers on legal language).

already understood.[29] This suggests that Mellinkoff is posing an argument not to the legal community but, more broadly, to the public by breaking down the barrier to legal literacy.

Perhaps again, with an ironic touch, he reflects on definite meaning and whether the language of the law has ever had any. He concludes that the "only reason for [the language's] existence" is what he labels as "flexibles."[30] Mellinkoff points to the classic example, the word "reasonable." There has never been a "real definition" of the term.[31] Yet legal text is riddled with this word. What Mellinkoff suggests is evident: the arguments for precision, often grounded in certainty, bury language's heavy dependence on flexible words. While "reasonable" is an obvious instance, he considers other words that are not observably vague. He references Old and Middle English words, such as "aforesaid," "heretofore," "forthwith," and "hereafter." The most infamous is "whereas," which he calls the "most persistently typical and most consistently vague word in the language of the law."[32] Mellinkoff notes that the word takes on innumerable meanings, often with immense polarity. "Whereas" became a term of art when English legal forms were hardened in the eighteenth century, borrowed from the "loose usage" in Middle English common speech.[33]

We may infer the inconvenient truth that ordinary language applied in legal contexts could never fully be understood by the ordinary person. This is because legal language is colored by existing mechanisms that gentrify common speech to legal form. Ordinary discourse placed in legal contexts refurbishes its common form into one that follows the rules of legalese. This transformation is so complete that even simple words become inaccessible. For example, when a contract "lacks consideration," ordinary readers might assume it is rude or thoughtless, missing the intended meaning that it is invalid because no value was exchanged. The legal system has effectively created a parallel language that looks like English but operates by entirely different rules.

Peter Tiersma argues that these stylistic features suggest that legal language follows its own linguistic rules.[34] That is, the distinct "characteristics" of legal language are, in fact, inherent to its formulation. Legal language is characterized by syntactic and semantic constraints, as well as a distinct grammar. The language of the law is its own separate language; it is, in fact, integral to the law's function. This raises fundamental questions about the relationship between language and legal concepts. If we expressed "due process" in completely different words, would it still be the same concept? Can legal concepts be expressed through symbols, numbers, or different

[29] *Id.* at 292.
[30] *Id.* at 301.
[31] *Id.* (citing Chief Justice Goddard's opinion in R. v. Summers, [1952] 1 All E.R. 1059–60 (Can.)).
[32] *Id.* at 321.
[33] *Id.* at 323.
[34] Peter M. Tiersma, Legal Language 49 (1999).

languages and retain their meaning? Are legal concepts inseparable from their particular verbal formulations?

Some scholars have argued that legal concepts can exist in different forms. Since the 1950s, Layman E. Allen has fervently argued for using symbolic logic to express legal concepts.[35] In short, he demonstrated that symbolic logic can help unpack complex sentence structures. Nevertheless, hesitations remained about the usefulness of symbolic logic for drafting documents.[36] These arguments largely centered on the limits of symbolic logic in resolving legal complexity: namely, that the limit is beyond a question of increasing precision, but simply that most ambiguity is unknowable.[37] In other words, the law has an open texture and is inherently incomplete.

Two possible conclusions may be drawn: (1) legal concepts can exist only in natural language, or (2) legal concepts could exist in alternative forms, provided those forms incorporate natural language's essential characteristics. The first conclusion suggests that natural language is the law's signature. The second conclusion is less absolutist and more nuanced. It suggests that, even accepting a deconstructionist view, there must necessarily be a mirroring and, at the very least, a mapping of the ways in which legal concepts have taken shape through writing. This suggests that for the law to communicate outside of legalese *and* natural language, any alternative language must behave as if it could already speak the language.

2.5 HOW AI CAN HELP

If we conclude that natural language is the only way to express legal concepts, then recent advancements in AI offer tools for making legalese more accessible to ordinary people. As will be discussed in greater detail in Chapter 4, the introduction of large language models ("LLMs") has effectively provided a universal translator across domain-specific languages to the average person. Leveraging AI breakthroughs that date as far back as the 1940s,[38] these models derive their capabilities from their ability to transform encoded knowledge in ways that are understandable outside the original context. Consider a directive (i.e., prompt) to OpenAI's ChatGPT requesting an explanation of the US Constitution for a fifth grader and – as a fun exercise to demonstrate the flexibility of these models – in the voice of a pirate.[39]

35 *See* Layman E. Allen, *Symbolic Logic: A Razor-Edged Tool for Drafting and Interpreting Legal Documents*, 66 Yale L.J. 833, 833 (1957); Layman E. Allen, *Some Uses of Symbolic Logic in Law Practice*, 3 Mod. Uses Logic L. 119, 119 (1962).

36 *See* Robert S. Summers, *A Note on Symbolic Logic and Law*, 13 J. Leg. Ed. 486, 490–91 (1961) (responding to Layman E. Allen arguments in *supra* note 35).

37 *Id.* at 492.

38 *What Is a Neural Network?*, IBM (Oct. 6, 2021), https://perma.cc/55JV-7LBB.

39 Megan Ma, ChatGPT-5, "Explain to me the US Constitution as a fifth grader" (Aug. 10, 2025) (see Extract 2.1); Megan Ma, ChatGPT-5, "Explain to me the US Constitution as a pirate" (Aug. 10, 2025) (see Extract 2.2).

EXTRACT 2.1 ChatGPT-5 explains the Constitution as a fifth grader.

explain to me the U.S. Constitution as a fifth grader

Sure! Here's a simple explanation of the **U.S. Constitution** like you're in 5th grade:

What is the U.S. Constitution?
The **U.S. Constitution** is the **most important rulebook** for how the United States government works. It's kind of like the instruction manual for running the country.

Why is it important?
It helps everyone know:

- **Who is in charge** of what
- **What powers** they have
- And **what rights** the people have

When was it written?
It was written in **1787**, a long time ago, by a group of smart people called the **Founding Fathers**.

What's in the Constitution?
Here are the main parts:

1. **Preamble**
This is like the introduction. It starts with:

> "We the People of the United States…"

It says the Constitution is made by the people, for the people.

EXTRACT 2.2 ChatGPT-5 explains the Constitution as a pirate.

explain to me the U.S. Constitution as a pirate

Aye aye, matey! 🏴‍☠️ Hoist the sails and gather 'round, for I be tellin' ye the tale of the **U.S. Constitution**, pirate-style!

🗺 What Be the U.S. Constitution?
Arrr! 'Tis the **mighty map o' laws** that shows how the landlubbers of the United States run their great ship o' government. It's the code they follow to keep their country sailin' smooth and not sinkin' into chaos!

📜 The Preamble – The Opening Scroll

The scroll begins with a mighty phrase:

> **"We the People…"**

That means the crew (the people!) be in charge o' the ship, not just the captain or the rich merchants.

The Three Mighty Masts (Branches o' Government)
Every good ship needs strong masts to hold the sails – and this Constitution ship has **three**:

1. **Congress (Legislative Branch)** – These scallywags make the laws! Ye got the House of Representatives and the Senate, argghh!
2. **The President (Executive Branch)** – The big captain o' the ship! Makes sure the laws be carried out.
3. **The Courts (Judicial Branch)** – These sea judges tell if laws follow the Constitution, or if someone be walkin' the plank!

The Bill o' Rights – The Treasure Chest o' Freedoms
Ahoy! The first 10 **amendments** be called **the Bill o' Rights**, and they be precious like gold!

LLMs are also capable of processing additional information, provided as context, and summarizing that additional context when formulating a response. However, at the time of writing, these summaries are not always as precise as legal language requires. Figure 2.1 displays a prompt provided to Anthropic's Claude Sonnet 4 requesting help for a hypothetical tenant who is questioning the legality of the location of an installed water heater in their rental home. A PDF copy of the Seattle Residential Code, specifically regarding "Boilers and Water Heaters," is provided for reference.[40] The prompt requests that the model reference specific sections of the Residential Code in its response. Extract 2.3 shows the model's response.

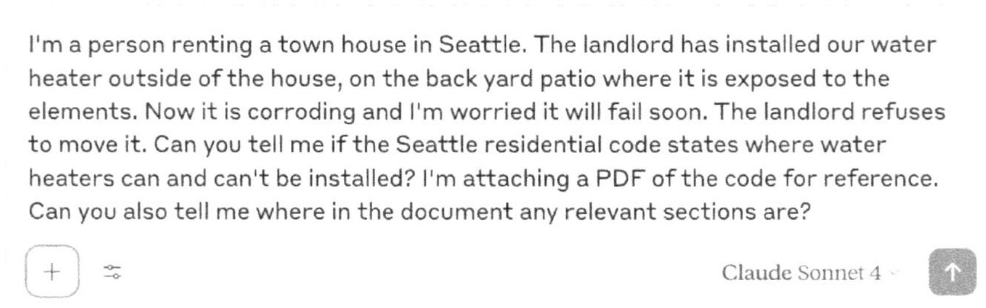

FIGURE 2.1 A prompt accompanied by a PDF sent to Claude Sonnet 4 requesting help with a landlord–tenant dispute.[41]

[40] *See* Seattle, Wash., Residential Code ch. 20 §§ M2001–06 (2021).
[41] Sarah McLeod, Anthropic's Claude Sonnet 4, "I'm a person renting a town house in Seattle ..." (Aug. 10, 2025).

EXTRACT 2.3 The response from Claude Sonnet 4 requesting help with a landlord dispute.

Looking at the Seattle Residential Code Chapter 20 you provided, I can see the relevant requirements for water heater installation locations.
The key sections are:

Section M2005.2 – Prohibited locations (page 20–2):

- "Fuel-fired water heaters shall not be installed in a room used as a storage closet"
- "Water heaters located in a bedroom or bathroom shall be installed in a sealed enclosure so that combustion air will not be taken from the living space"

Section M2005.1 – General (page 20–2):

- States that "Water heaters shall be installed in accordance with Chapter 5 of the State Plumbing Code, the manufacturer's instructions and the requirements of this code"
- Also mentions that "Water heaters installed in an attic shall comply with the requirements of Section M1305.1.2"

However, I notice that this chapter doesn't specifically address outdoor installation requirements or prohibitions for water heaters exposed to weather elements. The code references that water heaters must be installed according to:

1. Chapter 5 of the State Plumbing Code
2. Manufacturer's instructions
3. The requirements of this code

Since the document you provided only contains Chapter 20 and doesn't include Chapter 5 of the State Plumbing Code or other relevant sections that might address outdoor installations, weatherproofing, or corrosion protection requirements, I'd recommend:

1. Checking the manufacturer's installation instructions for your specific water heater model – these typically specify indoor installation or require weather protection for outdoor units
2. Looking at Chapter 5 of the Washington State Plumbing Code for additional location requirements
3. Checking if there are specific provisions elsewhere in the Seattle code about protecting equipment from weather damage

The fact that your water heater is corroding due to weather exposure suggests it may not be installed according to manufacturer's instructions, which would be a code violation under Section M2005.1.

Claude Sonnet 4

What is particularly fascinating about the ability of these models to provide such seemingly sensible responses is precisely their inability to understand language in any human-like sense. LLMs leverage a type of neural network architecture known as transformers.[42] Transformers allow LLMs to generate each word conditioned on all the data in their context window, which can include an entire conversation, a few sentences, or just a few words. Given exposure to vast quantities of text and having "seen" words in numerous contexts, LLMs engage in a complex array of pattern matching and next word prediction. Therefore, meaning and interpretation do not hold the same value to these machines as they do for humans. Because there is no internal "signified" attached to the "signifier,"[43] these systems prioritize highly accurate imitation and endless recombination of patterns rather than understanding.

These qualities of LLMs, in effect, align with such conclusions on how an alternative vehicle (i.e., technology) might be capable of communicating the law. This, in turn, enables a scalable translation mechanism that detaches linguistic form from meaning and treats legal language as a statistical game of word association. The challenges of ambiguity, vagueness, jargon, and the open texture of legal language, which prevent unrepresented litigants from understanding which legal remedies are available for their situation, can in principle be mitigated, and interpreting legalese as a layperson becomes more feasible.

However, these qualities also have weaknesses that create challenges, especially when applying them within legal contexts. LLMs can interpret natural language and seem to provide detailed and helpful output; however, the quality of a response is often a concern. These models are prone to hallucinations and can provide responses that are irrelevant at best and inaccurate at worst (see Section 12.7.1 and Section 16.2.3). There is also strong evidence that these models are still incapable of learning a unified theory or principled "world model" (i.e., an internal representation that can be used to explain the answers they produce) required for consistent interpretation and application.[44] Similarly, Romero argues that LLMs are still only capable of making observations and predicting outcomes based on those observations; they cannot learn a unified theory of how a system works and use it to explain the underlying cause of new or seemingly unrelated phenomena.[45]

[42] Ashish Vaswani et al., *Attention Is All You Need*, ARXIV 1, 2 (Aug. 2, 2023), https://perma.cc/7M2Q-72HA.

[43] FERDINAND DE SAUSSURE, COURSE IN GENERAL LINGUISTICS 10 (Bloomsbury Revelations ed. 2013).

[44] Keyon Vafa et al., *What Has a Foundation Model Found? Using Inductive Bias to Probe for World Models*, ARXIV 1, 1–2 (July 10, 2025), https://perma.cc/XWP8-RTKB.

[45] *See* Alberto Romero, *Harvard and MIT Study: AI Models Are Not Ready to Make Scientific Discoveries*, ALGORITHMIC BRIDGE (July 15, 2025), https://perma.cc/3EZJ-ENFY (providing an approachable discussion on inductive bias, the dichotomy between prediction and explanation, and its importance in the experiments described in the paper).

There is also the practical matter that an AI providing legal advice may run afoul of unauthorized practice of law ("UPL") restrictions, which vary across jurisdictions. Chapters 4, 9, and 12 address generative AI in more detail, and Chapter 14 focuses on UPL.

The above examples highlight the practical ways in which unrepresented litigants are interacting with this new technology, particularly in circumstances where self-help tools are not available in their jurisdiction. There is also an increasing number of tools and resources available to the legal community, providing both a means for building LLM-based legal self-help tools and for assessing the performance of LLMs in legal tasks. Chapter 8 outlines how AI can be used to assist with legal document automation. LLM-based legal chatbots are discussed in Chapter 9. Chapter 12 explores current research and the potential ways LLMs can be used to increase access to justice. Chapter 12 also introduces the LegalBench project, which is an ongoing collaborative effort to build a benchmark consisting of different legal reasoning tasks.

2.6 CONCLUSION

The language gap is a fundamental challenge for unrepresented litigants and addressing it has the potential to improve access to justice in significant ways. But improvement will require more than translation from legalese to ordinary language and back. The characteristics of language that give it its expressive power and make it an ideal medium for expressing legal concepts, including the use of vagueness and ambiguity, also exacerbate the problem. Several characteristics of legalese also contribute to the language gap, including a distinct vocabulary, the tension between clarity and precision, the structural peculiarities of legal language, and the challenge of achieving definite meaning.

The fundamental challenge posed by the gap between ordinary discourse and the abstract language of legal rules in access to justice is further compounded by other factors: growing legal complexity, increased costs and decreased availability of legal expertise, and economic incentives for lawsuits against unrepresented defendants.

Recent advancements in AI have the potential to help close this gap. This chapter presented a few simple examples of how AI can be used to assist unrepresented litigants in civil cases. The remainder of this book explores additional ways that AI technology, in particular generative AI, can address these challenges to improve access to justice: guiding litigants through the mazes of rules that arise in complex legal systems; providing alternative decision forums that assist unrepresented litigants in understanding and responding to claims against them; and bridging the language gap.

3

The Needs of Civil Litigants

*L. Karl Branting, Charlotte S. Alexander, and Elizabeth C. Tippett**

3.1 INTRODUCTION

If we accept the reality that unrepresented litigants will remain a part of the legal system – either because they cannot find a lawyer, cannot afford a lawyer, or do not want a lawyer – it is worth considering whether technology could help.

Understanding the tasks associated with each stage of litigation is a necessary first step. A task-based approach lets us think about how technology could help litigants without lawyers at a granular level. Technological tools may be specific to plaintiffs or defendants, may be useful only at particular stages but not others, or may be offered by the court system or by third parties.

This chapter identifies the tasks associated with each stage of litigation, laying a foundation for later chapters to explore the role that technology could play in closing the global access to justice gap.[1] We offer the task-based framework as a jumping-off point for later chapters' work on taxonomizing, mapping, and assessing the welter of legal AI and other technological innovations. The framework helps match technologies to the specific needs of unrepresented civil litigants at various stages of their journeys.

We use the term "litigants" and "litigation" broadly to refer to any dispute that is filed, or threatened to be filed, in court. However, the following framework incorporates the practical reality that a vanishingly small proportion of civil litigation ends in a bench or jury trial. Instead, most such disputes are resolved through some form of settlement, whether through negotiation or mediation.[2]

* We thank Michael Livermore for his review of multiple drafts of this chapter.

[1] Of course, litigation is not the only stage at which lawyers work, nor the only context in which individuals might need legal assistance. Lawyers perform a variety of other tasks for clients, such as dealmaking, compliance advice, risk assessment, due diligence, and contract drafting. The implications of AI for bridging the access to justice gap for legal needs other than litigation are addressed in Chapter 11, *Online Dispute Resolution*.

[2] *See infra* Chapter 11, *Online Dispute Resolution*. The task-based model does not incorporate arbitration, a process that typically serves as an alternative to litigation. Many consumers are compelled to arbitrate their claims as a result of binding arbitration provisions in service contracts, such as cell phone agreements. *See, e.g.*, AT&T Mobility LLC v. Concepcion, 563 U.S. 333, 336 (2011).

3.2 LITIGATION TASKS AND STAGES

We consider litigation tasks chronologically, starting before the initiation of proceedings and continuing through the resolution of the claims. An unrepresented litigant might complete each task without help, but doing so without legal expertise is often very difficult and fraught with peril. Figure 3.1 shows nine tasks organized into five litigation stages. The following discussion identifies cross-cutting themes and begins to sketch opportunities for technological intervention.

Figure 3.1 presents a task-based model of civil litigation. Each task appears as a row, arranged from top to bottom. Both plaintiffs and defendants must complete tasks on this list, and tasks may recur at different stages of the litigation.

The top row of Figure 3.1 shows the stages of litigation in chronological order from left to right: Recognition, Evaluation, Initiation, Litigation, and Resolution. Each stage's column contains the tasks litigants must complete during that stage.

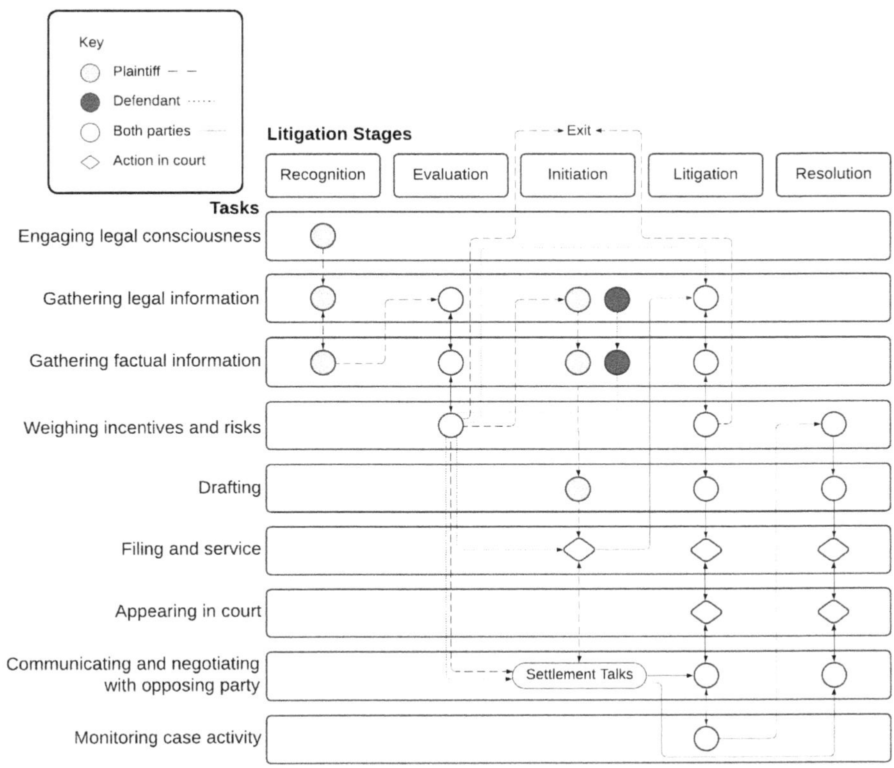

FIGURE 3.1 Task-based model of civil litigation.

The model is limited to the trial level of a case and therefore does not include tasks associated with appeals.[3]

Tasks are depicted as shapes. Circles represent tasks performed independently of the court, and diamonds represent tasks that involve the court. White circles indicate tasks that both the plaintiff and defendant must complete, gray circles represent only the tasks that the plaintiff must complete, and black circles are reserved for tasks that the defendant must complete.

Figure 3.1 also includes arrows that show how tasks flow from one stage to the next, including junctures at which parties may seek to resolve a case through settlement before the claim is fully adjudicated. Although not formally a stage of litigation, the model also includes "Exit" points, shown at the top of Figure 3.1, where a plaintiff may unilaterally abandon litigation rather than continue to an adjudicated or negotiated resolution. (The model assumes that defendants who unilaterally abandon litigation will face a default judgment, which appears in the Resolution stage.)

Next, we describe the five stages of litigation and the tasks associated with each stage.

3.2.1 *Recognition*

The first stage, Recognition, is exclusively the province of plaintiffs. This stage occurs pre-litigation, when the plaintiff first becomes aware of a legal issue and begins to gather information about the relevant legal and factual context. The engaging legal consciousness task occurs here, as the plaintiff adopts a perception of their problem that is influenced and bounded by the law. As socio-legal scholar Susan Silbey describes it, legal consciousness is the practice of drawing on the law to provide meaning for the activities of daily life: "[T]he study of legal consciousness traces the ways in which law is experienced and interpreted by specific individuals as they engage, avoid, or resist the law and legal meanings."[4] Drawing on another foundational framework from William L. F. Felstiner, Richard L. Abel, and Austin Sarat, legal consciousness involves "naming," or "saying to oneself that a particular experience has been injurious," and "blaming," or the "transformation from perceived injurious experience to grievance."[5] The third item in the

[3] When a case is appealed, no further fact-gathering occurs. Instead, an appellate court is limited to the record developed at the trial stage. A model attempting to illustrate the tasks associated with appeals would be similar to the one described, but with the "engaging legal consciousness" and "gathering factual information" tasks removed. The "recognition" stage of litigation would also be absent, as parties would already be aware of the claim.

[4] *See, e.g.*, Lynette J. Chua & David Engel, *Legal Consciousness Reconsidered*, 15 ANN. REV. L. & SOC. SCI. 335, 336–41 (2019) (defining and summarizing literature on legal consciousness).

[5] William L. F. Felstiner, Richard L. Abel & Austin Sarat, *The Emergence and Transformation of Disputes: Naming, Blaming, Claiming*, 15 LAW & SOC'Y REV. 631, 635 (1981); *see also* LEGAL SERVS. CORP., THE JUSTICE GAP REPORT: THE UNMET CIVIL LEGAL NEEDS OF LOW-INCOME AMERICANS 8, 45 (2022), https://perma.cc/5BXH-ANNZ ("People are more likely to seek

triplet described by Felstiner et al., "claiming," appears later in our diagram at the Initiation stage.

Once a plaintiff has conceptualized a problem as a grievance for which the law may provide a remedy, they gather legal and factual information. These tasks require research about substantive legal rights and protections, as well as the preliminary marshaling of evidence: obtaining witness statements or promises of support, gathering documents, researching the defendant, and writing a chronology or narrative.

3.2.2 *Evaluation (Plaintiff's Version)*

In the second stage, Evaluation, the plaintiff continues to gather legal and factual information, but now with an eye toward assessing the strength of their claim: what they might likely recover, what recovery would require, how long it would take, who would need to be involved, what forms or templates are available, and how much it would cost. At this stage, the plaintiff also weighs their own incentives and appetite for risk. The information the defendant gathers during the Initiation stage, after the lawsuit is filed and they have been served, informs their Evaluation-stage tasks, as discussed in Section 3.2.4.

Here, the term "facts" refers to the relevant events that precipitated the claim. This is the who, what, when, where, and sometimes the why of events, when the motives of the actors are legally relevant. The terms "legal information" or "law" refer to the substantive legal rules that give rise to a cause of action, such as a statute or common law claims, as well as the procedural rules that govern litigation, such as the Federal Rules of Civil Procedure or state equivalents.[6]

The facts and the law are distinct but related in that the law dictates which facts matter. Consider, for example, a simple statutory claim for an employee's unpaid wages upon termination, based on the following statute: "When an employer discharges an employee … all wages earned and unpaid at the time of the discharge or termination become due and payable not later than the end of the first business day after the discharge or termination."[7] Relevant facts under this statute, and likely case law interpreting it, may include: (1) the employee's rate of pay, as promised by the employer in a contract, policy, practice, or oral agreement; (2) the date of the

legal help for problems that are more obviously 'legal' like those involving legal documents and court proceedings.").

6 In this model, we treat the law as fixed, although the law is constantly evolving as a result of new case law and legislation. There is also a difference between the law on the books and the law as practiced, based on local customs and norms. The model also does not consider the effect of judicial ideology or preferences in legal outcomes. These dynamic factors may be difficult to address via technological solutions, as there may be little training data for an AI tool that captures unwritten local customs and norms or judicial ideology. All of these factors might manifest themselves in litigation patterns shown on docket sheets or in judicial opinions, which could serve as an imperfect proxy for and signal of the underlying, unrecorded custom, norm, or ideology.

7 Or. Rev. Stat. § 652.140 (2023).

termination; (3) any policies or contractual provisions placing conditions precedent on when a wage is "earned"; and (4) the amount (if any) the employee was actually paid upon termination.

However, even a relatively straightforward statute such as this may implicate additional complexities that are difficult for unrepresented plaintiffs to navigate. For example, there may be a legal question about what qualifies as a "wage" and whether it includes bonuses, certain forms of incentive pay, or vacation pay. Alternatively, the employer might argue that the worker was actually an independent contractor and not an employee, giving rise to a threshold dispute about the individual's employment status. That dispute implicates additional legal standards regarding the definition of "employee" for the purposes of wage and hour law,[8] as well as a plethora of error facts relevant to employee status, such as the amount of control exercised by the employer, the duration of the relationship, the skill required, and other factors. To be genuinely helpful to unrepresented litigants, technology designed to assist plaintiffs in Evaluation-stage tasks would need to incorporate these complexities and convey them in an actionable way.

We view the tasks at the Evaluation stage through the lens of rational choice theory, which predicts that litigants will file suit – or keep litigating once in court – when the expected value of litigation exceeds its expected costs.[9] Represented litigants can rely on their lawyers' experience to perform this weighing process and advise on a course of action. Lawyers and paralegals commonly conduct an initial evaluation at the intake stage, combining legal research with some assessment of the facts to determine whether the elements of the claim are met in light of legal precedent. Unrepresented litigants, if they undertake this task at all, are left to their own devices: attempting to gather the correct legal and factual information about precedent, process, and remedies; assessing the strengths and weaknesses of their case; and considering potential outcomes before deciding whether to proceed.

As Figure 3.1 illustrates, after weighing incentives and risks, plaintiffs may decide to "exit" and abandon the march toward litigation, or they may engage informally with the defendant in settlement talks. Alternatively, they may proceed to file a lawsuit.

3.2.3 *Initiation*

The third stage, Initiation, marks the point at which formal legal action begins. This stage is also exclusively the plaintiff's domain, involving ongoing gathering of factual

[8] Or. Bureau of Lab. & Indus., Employee or Independent Contractor, https://perma.cc/LYV6-PGQ8.

[9] George L. Priest & Benjamin Klein, *The Selection of Disputes for Litigation*, 13 J. Legal Stud. 1, 4 (1984) ("[T]he determinants of settlement and litigation are solely economic, including the expected costs to parties of favorable or adverse decisions, the information that parties possess about the likelihood of success at trial, and the direct costs of litigation and settlement").

and legal information to clarify filing requirements, understand procedures, and continue to amass evidence. The plaintiff must also draft a complaint or complete a court-provided form, pay a filing fee or seek to proceed *in forma pauperis* (as an indigent person who does not have to pay fees), file the complaint with the court (in hard copy or electronically, depending on the court), obtain a summons, and execute proper service of process or obtain a waiver from the defendant or defendants. This filing and service step is represented in Figure 3.1 by a diamond, indicating the first formal, court-involved step in the litigation process. This is typically the first point at which the defendant is formally notified of the litigation, which triggers the defendant's own pathway through the Evaluation stage described next in Section 3.2.4.

3.2.4 *Evaluation (Defendant's Version)*

The defendant begins gathering legal and factual information at the Initiation stage, after the plaintiff has filed the complaint. This sequence is illustrated by the black circles under the Initiation stage in Figure 3.1. Although both the plaintiff and defendant are subject to the same substantive legal rules, the defendant may be focused on different aspects of the law than the plaintiff, such as potential defenses and damages. The defendant may likewise focus on different aspects of the procedural rules, such as a motion to dismiss or a motion for summary judgment.

Likewise, although both the plaintiff and defendant share a common set of facts, the defendant may have access to facts that are unavailable to the plaintiff until discovery, such as the defendant's own internal correspondence and business records, and employee witnesses. Corporate defendants may engage in extensive prediscovery fact-finding to inform their litigation strategy and settlement stance, as well as to fulfill their duties to preserve evidence. Many of these facts would ultimately be disclosed to plaintiffs represented by attorneys, who have the expertise to request relevant documents through discovery and to depose witnesses. Unrepresented parties, however, are not well-positioned to make use of these discovery tools. Consequently, they can be at a severe informational disadvantage.[10]

As illustrated in Figure 3.1, defendants use the legal and factual information gathered at the Initiation stage to inform their internal assessment of the case and strategy ("weighing incentives and risks"), followed by settlement talks, further litigation, or exit.

In this context, "exit" refers to a default judgment resulting from the defendant's failure to further engage in litigation, such as failing to file a responsive pleading or appear in court. Default judgments are a serious risk for unrepresented defendants

[10] For a more in-depth discussion of the structural disadvantages that unrepresented parties face in litigation, *see* Section 1.4.3; Marc Galanter, *Why the "Haves" Come Out Ahead: Speculations on the Limits of Legal Change*, 9 LAW & SOC'Y REV. 95, 114–19 (1974) (conceptualizing lawyers and their clients as benefiting from their repeat player status in the legal system).

such as individuals defending debt-collection claims in small claims court. These individuals often do not have access to counsel, may lack any information on the applicable legal rules or procedures, and may not even be aware that their failure to respond will result in a default judgment. In fact, many collection agencies use small claims court as a mass clearinghouse to obtain default judgments on "consumer debt which others have already deemed uncollectible."[11] Peter Holland observes that "robo-signing and fraud are rampant in this industry, and … the debt buyers who pursue these claims often lack proof necessary to show that they own the debt, and often lack proof even that a debt was ever owed in the first place."[12] These actors bet on the fact that unrepresented litigants rarely appear at their court hearing, enabling them to launder bad debt into debt that can be enforced as a court judgment.[13]

3.2.5 *Litigation and Resolution*

We address the fourth and fifth stages, Litigation and Resolution, together because all tasks except one, monitoring case activity, occur in both stages. (Monitoring case activity is no longer required once a case is resolved.)

Unlike prior stages, Litigation includes the active involvement of the court, as shown in Figure 3.1 as "Appearing in court." Judicial involvement can sometimes be beneficial for unrepresented litigants, especially when judges provide guidance on the court's procedures. Litigants, likewise, are often eager for court involvement when it aligns with their vision of what it means to have a "day in court." However, the Litigation stage also reveals the vast gap between what an unrepresented litigant can achieve on their own and the skill and expertise required to prevail in litigation and make informed decisions.[14]

Litigation can involve several tasks similar to those in earlier stages of the proceeding, specifically gathering legal and factual information and weighing options; however, the process of doing so tends to be highly formalized. For example, while plaintiffs might have marshaled witnesses and gathered documents on their own earlier in the proceedings, they may be compelled to do so in the context of responding to discovery requests. Likewise, plaintiffs will almost certainly be unable to gather documents or testimony from the other side through informal means. Instead, that

11 Peter A. Holland, *The One Hundred Billion Dollar Problem in Small Claims Court: Robo-Signing and Lack of Proof in Debt Buyer Cases*, 6 J. Bus. & Tech. L. 259, 259 (2011).

12 *Id.*

13 *Id.*

14 *See, e.g.*, Victor D. Quintanilla, Rachel A. Allen & Edward R. Hirt, *The Signaling Effect of Pro se Status*, 42 Law & Soc. Inquiry 1091, 1091 (2017) (demonstrating pro se status' adverse influence on stereotypes of claimants and settlement awards received); *see also* Emily S. Taylor Poppe & Jeffrey J. Rachlinski, *Do Lawyers Matter? The Effect of Legal Representation in Civil Disputes*, 43 Pepp. L. Rev. 881, 885 (2016) (showing professional legal representation is associated with better outcomes for litigants across a wide range of substantive areas of law).

information must be obtained through document requests, interrogatories, depositions, and subpoenas, and may be enforced by a motion to compel.

Similarly, in cases outside of small claims court, parties cannot present their factual and legal arguments in an unstructured live hearing before the court. Most briefing occurs pretrial, where the parties are expected to present or oppose claims through motions, as illustrated in Figure 3.1 under "Filing and service." Most such motions are initiated by defendants seeking a dispositive decision on a pretrial motion, such as a motion to dismiss or a motion for summary judgment.[15] Unrepresented litigants must also ensure that their filings comply with pleading requirements and that they file and serve documents within applicable deadlines.

Communicating and negotiating with the opposing party are also important parts of the litigation process, even outside the settlement context. Under the Federal Rules of Civil Procedure, the parties are expected to meet and confer early in the litigation and to generate a joint discovery plan,[16] as well as to negotiate to resolve any discovery disputes.[17] The parties must also coordinate deposition dates and other logistics regarding discovery. Additionally, parties may negotiate deadline extensions or waivers of service.

Litigation also requires regular communication with, and appearances before, the court. Parties are expected to participate in various proceedings, such as pretrial conferences, settlement conferences, hearings on motions, and trial.

Resolution represents the final stage of the case, when the parties settle and dismiss the case voluntarily before litigation ends or when the case ends because of a court ruling or jury verdict. The most common form of resolution in civil litigation is settlement, whether through direct negotiation, mediation, or a court-supervised settlement conference.[18] Otherwise, cases are resolved through motions, such as motions to dismiss, for summary judgment, or for default judgment, or through a bench or jury trial. Trials are the least common form of resolution, representing less than 4% of civil cases.[19]

Throughout the litigation process, parties should continue to evaluate their case and assess whether a settlement would resolve their case in a satisfactory yet realistic manner. For example, if discovery reveals that a case is substantially stronger or weaker than originally assumed, those facts should inform the parties' evaluation of the case. Likewise, if a judge signals at a hearing that they are strongly inclined to

[15] FED. R. CIV. P. 12, 56.
[16] FED. R. CIV. P. 26(f).
[17] FED. R. CIV. P. 37(a).
[18] Measurements of settlement rates can vary by case type and involve considerable uncertainty because court dockets do not always indicate why a case terminates. However, a 2001–2002 study of federal cases suggests that a strong majority of civil cases (with the exception of constitutional cases) are resolved through settlement. Theodore Eisenberg & Charlotte Lanvers, *What Is the Settlement Rate and Why Should We Care?*, 6 J. EMPIRICAL LEGAL STUD. 111, 133 (2009).
[19] *Id.* at 128.

grant or deny a motion, that signal influences how the parties view the overall prospects and settlement value of the case.

An informed settlement is often preferable to a court-imposed outcome because it avoids the transaction costs (e.g., time, energy, fees) of further litigation and reduces uncertainty about how a court might rule. Here, too, however, unrepresented litigants are at a distinct disadvantage because they lack the expertise to predict how a court is likely to resolve their case. Legal expertise is likewise helpful for understanding the implications of a court-imposed outcome, whether it be the significance of an adverse court ruling, the available opportunities for appeal, or the challenges in collecting on a favorable court judgment.

Parties may attempt settlement negotiations multiple times during litigation but fail to reach an agreement, and then return to litigation. For example, parties might attempt mediation or settlement while a summary judgment motion is pending but fail to reach an agreement because they have vastly different predictions about the outcome of the motion. If the court grants summary judgment, the case is dismissed and thus is "resolved" by the court. If the court denies summary judgment and allows the case to proceed, it may subsequently be "resolved" by a bench or jury trial. Alternatively, the parties may return to the bargaining table and resolve the case through a negotiated settlement before trial.

3.3 OBSERVATIONS AND THEMES

Figure 3.1 reveals four themes, along with a limitation of the task-based taxonomy. First, some tasks repeat and recur throughout litigation, particularly the gathering of legal and factual information and the weighing of that information to decide how to proceed. Artificial intelligence might be a good match for a particular task at multiple points during litigation, though the specific application of a given task might demand different technological capabilities. For example, technology that furnishes legal information at the pre-filing stage might capably gather details through a structured interview and return a set of options to a litigant regarding the claims they might file. However, to assist the same litigant in legal analysis at a later stage in the litigation, the technology would need to incorporate new facts and legal developments in the case and then deliver information in a format that would be useful for that stage of litigation, such as a motion, a discovery request, or a settlement proposal. The density of arrows flowing to and from the Evaluation stage illustrates the central role that evaluation plays throughout litigation, as parties weigh the current merits of their claims in light of new information. Lawyers engage in these updated assessments constantly, while unrepresented litigants may struggle to recognize the significance of new factual, legal, and procedural developments.

Second, any of these tasks could theoretically be performed without legal counsel but can be difficult to carry out competently without assistance. Drafting, filing, and serving legal pleadings is particularly difficult for unrepresented litigants. Other tasks, like gathering facts, appear to be nonlegal in nature but are actually closely intertwined with legal judgments. As previously discussed, knowing which facts to collect is almost impossible without knowing which types of facts are most closely related to the legal elements and defenses of a claim. Similarly, an unrepresented litigant might be a capable negotiator in other contexts but may be poorly positioned to evaluate a proposal from the other party without legal advice.

AI could add value by furnishing at least some of the expertise that would be furnished by a lawyer by, for example, identifying relevant deadlines, providing updates on case status, or automating document drafting.[20] Although such simple forms of assistance are not equivalent to legal counsel, they could nevertheless help bridge some of the vast gaps between represented and unrepresented litigants. Evolving technology could also come close to assisting with more complex legal tasks. For example, our research suggests that machine learning technology could combine with a corpus of legal briefs to identify relevant cases to cite in opposition to a motion for summary judgment.[21] Although such technology could fail to detect new and emerging cases, it could approximate the task of legal research for unrepresented litigants otherwise ill-equipped to identify relevant case law.

Third, Figure 3.1 reveals that both the plaintiff and the defendant ultimately perform similar or identical tasks. This is illustrated by the predominance of white circles and diamonds in the chart, which represent tasks that both the plaintiff and the defendant perform. In addition, both the plaintiff and the defendant engage in gathering factual and legal information, although the defendant performs these tasks later than the plaintiff. In particular, the preliminary research and claim evaluation that the plaintiff performs before filing are performed by the defendant after filing. The mirrored nature of legal tasks suggests that technology developed to assist either the plaintiff or the defendant could be usefully adapted to serve the other side. For example, sophisticated proprietary generative AI technology developed to assist corporate defendants in litigation could be adapted to assist unrepresented plaintiffs if that technology were made available to developers working on access to justice tools.[22] In other words, one major access to justice challenge arises not from the technology's suitability for the needs of unrepresented litigants but rather from the privatized and cost-prohibitive nature of the technology.[23]

[20] *See supra* Introduction.

[21] *See* Elizabeth Tippett, Charlotte Alexander, Karl Branting, Paul Morawski, Carlos Balhana, Craig Pfeifer & Sam Bayer, *Does Lawyering Matter? Predicting Judicial Decisions from Legal Briefs, and What That Means for Access to Justice*, 100 TEXAS L. REV. 1157, 1190 (2022).

[22] As Mia Bonardi and L. Karl Branting observed, existing generative AI tools have primarily been designed for use by lawyers, who are better positioned to craft prompts for the models and interpret the outputs. The bigger challenge is how this technology can be made useful for unrepresented litigants. *See* Mia Bonardi & L. Karl Branting, *Certifying Legal AI Assistants for Unrepresented Litigants: A Global Survey of Access to Civil Justice, Unauthorized Practice of Law, and AI*, 26 COLUM. SCI. & TECH. L. REV. 34, 98–99 (2025).

[23] Galanter, *supra* note 10, at 98 (noting the advantages of repeat players in the legal system).

Fourth, the chart reveals a practical barrier to using technological substitutes for attorney representation: many litigation tasks require some level of in-person or interpersonal interaction with the court or opposing counsel. These include in-person or remote court appearances, as well as communications and negotiations with the other side. Although current generative AI technology could support such interactions, implementation of such technology faces both the legal barrier of unauthorized practice of law rules[24] and a likely hostile reaction from opposing counsel and the court to automated interactions. Lawyers also perform other "human" functions that are not listed in the chart but may be equally important to clients, such as managing expectations, acknowledging client concerns and frustrations, and empathizing with loss and disappointment. Leveling the playing field for unrepresented plaintiffs relying on technological assistance may require other interventions, such as making attorneys available for limited in-person appearances or providing additional court resources or personnel to unrepresented plaintiffs.[25]

Lastly, we note a limitation in the task-based taxonomy illustrated in Figure 3.1. While most tasks fall within the broad categories described previously, each category comprises both generalizable tasks and highly individualized or idiosyncratic tasks. Generalizable tasks, such as gathering general information about the legal system, accessing forms, and completing forms, are typically the most readily automated and have already been automated with some degree of success.[26] Idiosyncratic tasks specific to the facts and legal issues in a case, such as articulating the legal relevance of a particular fact in a motion or arguing why one line of legal authority is more applicable than another to this particular case, are more challenging to automate.[27]

Although a particular technology might be well-suited to a generalizable task in one of the task categories, that technology might be poorly suited to address idiosyncratic tasks within that same category. Providing robust assistance to an unrepresented litigant to complete a litigation-related task that includes both generalizable and idiosyncratic components may require combining multiple technologies or supplementing technological measures with human support.

3.4 CONCLUSION

This chapter has developed a task-based model of civil litigation to explore how technology might take on some tasks, in whole or in part, to aid unrepresented litigants. This approach highlights some key characteristics and potential limitations of automated legal assistance: tools likely need to be able to integrate new

[24] *See infra* Chapter 14: The UPL Barrier; *see also* Bonardi & Branting, *supra* note 22.

[25] *See, e.g.*, Sarah Martinson, *How Courts Can Use Generative AI to Help Pro Se Litigants*, Law360 (May 3, 2024, 7:03 PM), https://perma.cc/8EK3-H59S (describing court-based innovations such as chatbots and form-completion software to aid pro se litigants).

[26] *See infra* Chapter 8: Document Automation.

[27] *See infra* Chapter 5: The Origins of Legal AI.

factual and legal developments dynamically as litigation progresses; tools might serve both defendants and plaintiffs; and tools might be unsatisfactory where litigants are expected to engage in direct, synchronous communication with the court or opposing counsel.

Subsequent chapters engage more deeply with the promise and limitations of technological approaches for unrepresented litigants. Chapter 4 introduces generative AI, Chapter 6 covers computational logic systems, Chapter 9 discusses dialogue systems such as chatbots, and Chapter 12 explores generative-AI-powered form completion and information extraction. Applications of these technologies could be relevant to every task at each stage of litigation: gathering information, translating legal rules into plain language, strategizing, presenting claims, and communicating with the court and opposing parties. Chapter 7 considers the potential of AI to predict case outcomes, which is especially relevant to the Evaluation stage. Chapter 8 explores tools developed for document automation, which are at least relevant to tasks during the Initiation and Litigation stages. Chapter 11 assesses online dispute resolution ("ODR"), which is at minimum relevant to tasks during the Evaluation, Litigation, and Resolution stages.

As we noted at the outset of this chapter, self-representation is common in civil litigation. Yet unrepresented litigants repeatedly fall through the cracks of the court system, suffering high loss rates regardless of the merits of their claims or defenses, if they even bring claims or defenses to court in the first place.[28] As Dr. Branting wrote in the Introduction, there is hope that "AI-driven tools can mitigate the problems unrepresented people face by streamlining legal processes and improving the efficiency of legal services," helping to close the justice gap and equalize access to justice in the US and around the world.

[28] *See* Holland, *supra* note 11.

PART II

Automating Legal Tasks with AI and Other Technologies

4

Introduction to Generative AI

*Hannes Westermann and Marco Giacalone**

4.1 INTRODUCTION

The release of ChatGPT in the fall of 2022 heralded a new era of artificial intelligence. ChatGPT enables the public to interact with a sophisticated AI system using a natural chat interface. Using a novel approach to artificial intelligence, known as generative AI, ChatGPT offers immense capabilities across many different tasks, such as text drafting, computer programming, translation, and even creative tasks such as ideation and poetry. What is more, it is incredibly easy to use and can carry out these tasks after simply being asked by the user in natural language.

These models have led to an enormous surge in interest in artificial intelligence across industry, academia, and society. Furthermore, the development of such models has advanced at a rapid pace. Today, generative AI models can generate images[1] and videos,[2] interact in strikingly human-sounding voices,[3] and perform sophisticated reasoning tasks.[4] As this development is poised to continue, experts believe that generative AI models will significantly impact many areas of society.[5]

The new capabilities of generative AI systems, and their ability to perform many reasoning and drafting tasks without specific training, make them very interesting for use in the legal field. A growing body of researchers is exploring their capabilities in

* We thank Michael Livermore for his review of multiple drafts of this chapter.

1 *DALL·E 2*, OpenAI, https://openai.com/index/dall-e-2/ (last visited July 10, 2025).

2 *Sora*, OpenAI, https://openai.com/index/sora/ (last visited July 5, 2025).

3 *Voice Mode FAQ*, OpenAI, https://tinyurl.com/mptdp4m4 (last visited July 10, 2025).

4 *Learning to Reason with LLMs*, OpenAI, https://tinyurl.com/4fyzzdvz (last visited June 18, 2025); DeepSeek-AI et al., *DeepSeek-R1: Incentivizing Reasoning Capability in LLMs via Reinforcement Learning*, arXiv 1 (Jan. 22, 2025), https://perma.cc/5YD8-E6PG.

5 Erik Brynjolfsson, Danielle Li & Lindsey R. Raymond, *Generative AI at Work* 1 (Nat'l Bureau of Econ. Rsch., Working Paper No. 31161, 2023), https://perma.cc/ZJ5W-H85G.

performing legal reasoning and accomplishing legal tasks. For example, generative AI systems have been shown to answer many questions on bar exams[6] and perform statutory reasoning.[7] Likewise, commercial entities are starting to make use of generative AI to support their clients. For example, LexisNexis and Thomson Reuters Westlaw are exploring how generative AI can enhance their offerings.[8]

In light of these developments and the global crisis in access to justice discussed in Chapter 1, more and more research is exploring the use of generative AI to improve access to justice. We will explore many such use cases over the coming chapters. However, to obtain the greatest benefits from this technology and avoid inappropriate use cases that may have harmful outcomes, understanding the capabilities and limitations of generative AI is crucial. Thus, in this chapter, we situate the development of generative AI in light of previous AI approaches and briefly discuss the opportunities and challenges of such models. This exploration will inform several aspects of the analysis in the succeeding chapters. Chapter 12 directly explores the uses of generative AI for access to justice, but many of the other chapters (such as Chapter 8, *Document Automation*; Chapter 11, *Online Dispute Resolution*; and Chapter 9, *Interactive Legal Technologies*) also feature elements and discussions of generative AI. Therefore, we aim for this brief introduction to the technology to serve as a foundation for further discussion of generative AI.

4.2 NATURAL LANGUAGE PROCESSING

To understand what makes generative AI and large language models special, it is important to understand what came before in the field of working with natural language. The legal field is largely based on textual documents, such as contracts, laws, case law, and doctrine. Thus, most projects that aim to use AI to tackle access to justice also focus on the processing of text, for example, by interacting with laypeople via text, providing legal information, or helping to fill out forms.

In computer science, the field of processing text is known as natural language processing ("NLP"). It includes tasks such as machine translation, spoken dialogue systems, machine reading, social media mining, and sentiment analysis.[9] Many of

6 Daniel Martin Katz et al., *GPT-4 Passes the Bar Exam*, 382 PHIL. TRANSACTIONS ROYAL SOC'Y A 1, 1 (2023).

7 Andrew Blair-Stanek, Nils Holzenberger & Benjamin Van Durme, *Can GPT-3 Perform Statutory Reasoning?*, ARXIV 1 (May 10, 2023), https://perma.cc/9WE3-R977.

8 *LexisNexis Launches Lexis+ AI, a Generative AI Solution with Hallucination-Free Linked Legal Citations*, LEXISNEXIS (Oct. 25, 2023), https://perma.cc/W2HG-2SX3; *CoCounsel – Generative AI assistant for professionals*, THOMSON REUTERS, https://perma.cc/8297-4G7P; THOMSON REUTERS, *AI-Powered Legal Research: Where Legal Research Meets Generative AI*, (Nov. 15, 2023), https://perma.cc/57ZQ-AVKY.

9 Julia Hirschberg & Christopher D. Manning, *Advances in Natural Language Processing*, 349 SCIENCE 261, 261 (2015).

these tasks could be applied to the legal domain: for example, to understand a user request, analyze legal documents (e.g., court decisions), and communicate legal information to legal professionals or people seeking legal advice.[10]

However, language is variable, ambiguous, and context-dependent,[11] making it difficult for computers to handle. In the field of artificial intelligence, various approaches have been explored.

4.3 ARTIFICIAL INTELLIGENCE

Artificial intelligence can be defined as the field that "aims to build intelligent entities."[12] AI has long been a focus of research. In fact, the term *artificial intelligence* was coined in 1956, at a conference at Dartmouth.[13] Initially, much of the development focused on so-called *symbolic AI* approaches, which rely on the encoding of and reasoning with symbols representing reality.[14] For NLP, this could consist of aiming to explicitly capture the rules and vocabulary of human language.[15] This approach thus relies on the explicit encoding into a computer system of the rules that govern a problem, which has the advantage of being easy to explain, as the specific rules that were used to reach a decision can be examined.[16] However, such systems can be expensive to implement[17] and struggle with certain kinds of problems, for example, those relying on intuition.[18]

Another powerful approach to AI lies in *machine learning*. Here, instead of explicitly providing rules and symbols to a computer system, algorithms are used to "train a model" of the patterns underlying a task, based on a set of training samples given to the system. This model can then be used to carry out the same task on new, previously unseen examples.[19] For example, after being trained on images of cats and dogs, such a model could look at a new image and determine whether it contains a cat or a dog. Various algorithms exist for machine learning.[20] Deep learning is a

10 João Dias et al., *State of the Art in Artificial Intelligence Applied to the Legal Domain*, ARXIV 1 (Mar. 10, 2022), https://perma.cc/XQE2-BSCD.

11 Hirschberg & Manning, *supra* note 9, at 261; STUART J. RUSSELL & PETER NORVIG, ARTIFICIAL INTELLIGENCE: A MODERN APPROACH 823–24 (4th ed. 2021).

12 RUSSELL & NORVIG, *supra* note 11, at 1.

13 Bruce G. Buchanan, *A (Very) Brief History of Artificial Intelligence*, 26 AI MAG. 53, 57 (2005).

14 H. R. EKBIA, ARTIFICIAL DREAMS: THE QUEST FOR NON-BIOLOGICAL INTELLIGENCE 24 (2008).

15 Hirschberg & Manning, *supra* note 9, at 261.

16 Bruce G. Buchanan & Reid G. Smith, *Fundamentals of Expert Systems*, 3 ANN. REV. COMPUT. SCI. 1, 23, 26 (1988).

17 *Id.* at 19.

18 Terence Horgan & John Tienson, *Representations Without Rules*, 17 PHIL. TOPICS 147, 151 (1989).

19 Pedro Domingos, *A Few Useful Things to Know about Machine Learning*, 55 COMMC'NS ACM 78 (2012).

20 *Id.*

machine learning architecture relying on "neural networks," bearing a superficial resemblance to the human brain.[21] It has emerged as a powerful method of handling unstructured data such as images, text, and spoken voice.[22] Despite these advances, there are limitations on what these models can accomplish. For example, they often require large training datasets of task-specific data.[23] Creating such datasets can be an expensive and complex endeavor.

4.4 GENERATIVE AI

Generative AI is a subset of artificial intelligence focused on generating media.[24] Often, these models can be directed by simple textual instructions to, for example, generate images, sounds, videos, or text. Of particular importance for us are so-called large language models ("LLMs"), which focus on understanding and generating text and have led to a huge revolution in NLP.[25]

LLMs are machine learning systems, based on sophisticated deep learning models.[26] These models have been trained on enormous corpora of textual documents to predict the next word in a sequence, based on a sequence of words. For example, the model could be given the sequence "to be or not to …" and be asked what a likely next word would be. After being trained on billions of textual documents, such models start to form a general "understanding" of the patterns underlying human language.[27] Now, after being given a sequence of, for example, the words "the word for bread in French is," the model might respond with "pain." Likewise, after being asked to complete the sequence "The best thing to do if your employer refuses to pay you is …," the model may generate a plausible answer based on the millions of documents it has seen, which likely include legal documents.

Next, models such as ChatGPT are trained on human feedback to become better at human interactions.[28] This training process alters how a model responds, making it easier to guide using so-called prompts, which contain queries or instructions

[21] RUSSELL & NORVIG, *supra* note 11, at 750.

[22] Yann LeCun, Yoshua Bengio & Geoffrey Hinton, *Deep Learning*, 521 NATURE 436 (2015).

[23] Domingos, *supra* note 19, at 84–85; Nithya Sambasivan et al., *"Everyone Wants to Do the Model Work, Not the Data Work": Data Cascades in High-Stakes AI*, PROC. CHI CONF. ON HUM. FACTORS IN COMPUT. SYS. 1 (2021).

[24] Brynjolfsson, Li & Raymond, *supra* note 5.

[25] Bonan Min et al., *Recent Advances in Natural Language Processing via Large Pre-Trained Language Models: A Survey*, 56 ACM COMPUT. SURV. 1 (2024).

[26] Ashish Vaswani et al., *Attention Is All You Need*, ARXIV 1 (June 12, 2017), https://perma.cc/C9DM-GNUC.

[27] Tom Brown et al., *Language Models Are Few-Shot Learners*, 33 ADVANCES IN NEURAL INFO. PROCESSING SYS. 1 (2020), https://perma.cc/9GNG-9LDX.

[28] Long Ouyang et al., *Training Language Models to Follow Instructions with Human Feedback*, ARXIV 1 (Mar. 4, 2022), https://perma.cc/6PMP-APBV.

from the user. With the general level of language understanding and knowledge acquired during training, the models can perform a variety of tasks on request, including poetry, coding, translation, general advice, and drafting various types of documents. However, knowing how to interact with the model in the most specific way can still be a challenge.[29] This has led to the field of "prompt engineering," which focuses on optimizing prompts in the best way.[30]

There are a variety of LLMs available on the market today, and development continues at a rapid pace. The most famous example is likely ChatGPT, which was released to the public in 2022 and quickly gathered over 100 million users.[31] Since then, several updated versions have been released, improving the general performance of the model and adding functionality such as the ability to understand images as well as text.[32] Other models include the Claude series by Anthropic[33] and Gemini by Google.[34] Most recently, models with advanced reasoning capabilities have been the focus of a great deal of research. They include OpenAI o1[35] and o3,[36] as well as DeepSeek-R1.[37] These models can make a plan for how to solve a certain task before executing it, which can improve their performance on tasks requiring sophisticated reasoning, such as math and coding.[38] Such models are likewise able to power so-called agentic AI, which can autonomously decide how to tackle complex, long-term tasks with little human oversight.[39]

Most of the aforementioned models are commercial and are therefore accessed via a chat interface or an application programming interface ("API"), which enables the integration of these models into other software systems. However, there are also open models that can be downloaded to the user's computer and run locally,

29 Simon Willison, *Think of Language Models like ChatGPT as a "Calculator for Words,"* Simon Willison's Weblog (Apr. 2, 2023), https://perma.cc/5UW6-WY35.

30 *Prompt Engineering*, OpenAI, https://perma.cc/5YY2-DH2F.

31 Krystal Hu, *ChatGPT Sets Record for Fastest-Growing User Base – Analyst Note*, Reuters (Feb. 2, 2023), https://perma.cc/VW45-876G.

32 OpenAI, *GPT-4 Technical Report*, arXiv 1 (Mar. 15, 2023), https://perma.cc/A24F-RYD9; *Hello GPT-4o*, OpenAI, https://perma.cc/M2UP-25LX.

33 *The Claude 3 Model Family: Opus, Sonnet, Haiku*, Anthropic (2024), https://perma.cc/95QL-QMV5.

34 *Introducing Gemini: Our Largest and Most Capable AI Model*, Google (Dec. 6, 2023), https://perma.cc/ZS2K-X3KC; *Introducing Gemini 2.0: Our New AI Model for the Agentic Era*, Google (Dec. 11, 2024), https://perma.cc/43JU-MBRS.

35 *OpenAI o1 System Card*, OpenAI (Dec. 5, 2024), https://perma.cc/5PH7-7PFM.

36 *OpenAI o3-mini System Card*, OpenAI (Jan. 31, 2025), https://perma.cc/2RQG-63P7.

37 DeepSeek-AI et al., *supra* note 4.

38 OpenAI, *supra* note 36.

39 Deepak Bhaskar Acharya, Karthigeyan Kuppan & B. Divya, *Agentic AI: Autonomous Intelligence for Complex Goals – A Comprehensive Survey*, 13 IEEE Access 18912 (2025).

provided the user has sufficient computational power. Notable open LLMs include the Llama family by Meta,[40] and the DeepSeek-R1 model.[41]

4.5 OPPORTUNITIES AND CHALLENGES

Now that we have gained an overview of generative AI as a technology, we can explore some opportunities and challenges inherent in using such models, with a focus on the legal domain.

4.5.1 *Opportunities*

One of the biggest opportunities presented by large language models lies in their ability to perform very sophisticated reasoning in text. They have led to a huge increase in the capabilities of NLP, revolutionizing the field.[42] Recent models, such as Llama and DeepSeek, have hundreds of billions of parameters and are trained on trillions of tokens of text.[43] Interestingly, the more parameters a model has, and the more high-quality data a model is trained on, the "smarter" it seems to become.[44] Today, LLM results are increasingly competitive with human performance on tasks such as predicting the outcomes of studies[45] and checking facts.[46] On many standardized exams, such as sections of the SAT and some AP exams, GPT-4 would place in the 80th or 90th percentile of test takers.[47]

Another big advantage of generative AI is that such models are flexible. Unlike most machine learning models, which can carry out a specific task, LLMs have learned an "understanding" of language and the world through being trained on enormous corpora of text.[48] They are thus "foundation models" that can be used for a wide variety of tasks, based on adjustments to the prompt.[49] This flexibility is important for applying machine learning in the legal field, which was previously

[40] Hugo Touvron et al., *LLaMA: Open and Efficient Foundation Language Models*, ARXIV 1 (Feb. 27, 2023), https://perma.cc/Z2CH-XVWQ.

[41] DeepSeek-AI et al., *supra* note 4.

[42] Arkaitz Zubiaga, *Natural Language Processing in the Era of Large Language Models*, 6 FRONT. A.I. (2024).

[43] Aaron Grattafiori et al., *The Llama 3 Herd of Models*, ARXIV 1 (Nov. 23, 2024), https://perma.cc/55W6-GM5X; DeepSeek-AI et al., *supra* note 4.

[44] Jordan Hoffmann et al., *Training Compute-Optimal Large Language Models*, ARXIV 1 (Mar. 29, 2022), https://perma.cc/7D7X-K7W8.

[45] Xiaoliang Luo et al., *Large Language Models Surpass Human Experts in Predicting Neuroscience Results*, 9 NAT. HUM. BEHAV. 305 (2024).

[46] Jerry Wei et al., *Long-Form Factuality in Large Language Models*, ARXIV 1 (Nov. 7, 2024), https://perma.cc/9LDT-6PZQ.

[47] OpenAI, *supra* note 32.

[48] Brown et al., *supra* note 27.

[49] Rishi Bommasani et al., *On the Opportunities and Risks of Foundation Models*, ARXIV 1 (July 12, 2022), https://perma.cc/YJV6-P4TZ.

constrained by the limited availability of specific, annotated documents.[50] The speed with which LLMs can be adapted to new tasks and their output tweaked by altering the prompt is unparalleled.

4.5.2 *Challenges*

Of course, LLMs are not magical. There are still a number of limitations to consider in their deployment. A significant limitation is their tendency to "hallucinate" answers to questions.[51] This means that they invent information that sounds correct. Studies have shown that such issues arise when asking questions about legal information in specific domains,[52] or when asking the model to explain the content of court cases.[53]

This issue is especially significant when coupled with the human tendency to overestimate and anthropomorphize AI systems. This is known as the ELIZA effect, after an early AI system that acted as a psychologist and elicited long conversations, despite clearly being governed by very simple rules.[54] This effect may lead users to trust and rely on information provided by an AI system, even if they know that it is an AI.[55] Thus, confidently incorrect responses provided by AI systems could lead users to make bad decisions. For more on hallucinations, see Sections 12.7.1 and 16.2.3.

LLMs also raise further concerns because they can exhibit bias. Depending on how they are trained, such models may absorb biases spread across the textual training data and exhibit such bias in their answers.[56] Biased responses can have significant implications in legal contexts where fairness and accuracy are paramount.[57] For more on bias in the context of reliability, see Section 15.2.1.

50 Masha Medvedeva, Martijn Wieling & Michel Vols, *Rethinking the Field of Automatic Prediction of Court Decisions*, 31 A.I. & L. 195 (2023); Zhe Zheng et al., *Pretrained Domain-Specific Language Model for Natural Language Processing Tasks in the AEC Domain*, 142 Comput. in Indus. 103733 (2022).

51 Ziwei Ji et al., *Survey of Hallucination in Natural Language Generation*, 55 ACM Comput. Surv. 248:1 (2023).

52 Jinzhe Tan, Hannes Westermann & Karim Benyekhlef, *ChatGPT as an Artificial Lawyer?*, ICAIL Workshop A.I. for Access to Just. (2023), https://perma.cc/ZW7V-E66A.

53 Jakub Drapal, Hannes Westermann & Jaromir Savelka, *Using Large Language Models to Support Thematic Analysis in Empirical Legal Studies*, 379 Legal Knowledge and Information Sys. 197 (Giovanni Sileno, Jerry Spanakis & Gijs van Dijck eds., 2023).

54 Ekbia, *supra* note 14, at 8.

55 *Id.*

56 Emily M. Bender et al., *On the Dangers of Stochastic Parrots: Can Language Models Be Too Big?* 🦜, Proc. ACM Conf. Fairness, Accountability & Transparency 610 (2021), https://perma.cc/SKW5-ULCR.

57 Ninareh Mehrabi et al., *A Survey on Bias and Fairness in Machine Learning*, 54 ACM Comput. Surv. 1 (2022); Alexandra Chouldechova & Aaron Roth, *A Snapshot of the Frontiers of Fairness in Machine Learning*, 63 Commc'ns ACM 82 (2020); Neel Guha et al., *Legalbench: A Collaboratively*

Finally, there are operational risks to LLMs. For example, when using hosted versions of LLMs (such as ChatGPT and Gemini), the data submitted to prompt the model may be used to train future versions of these models, which could have implications for privacy and confidentiality.[58] Furthermore, there can be significant costs (both environmental[59] and monetary) associated with running LLMs at scale.

4.6 CONCLUSION

Generative AI and LLMs represent a significant technological leap forward, with particular relevance to legal applications. Their ability to understand context, process natural language, and generate human-like responses presents important opportunities to address access to justice challenges. At the same time, understanding the limitations of these models is crucial in ensuring that they are deployed safely and in ways that effectively address the complex issue of access to justice.

Built Benchmark for Measuring Legal Reasoning in Large Language Models, 36 ADVANCES IN NEURAL INFO. PROCESSING SYS. 2 (2024), https://perma.cc/JRJ8-2T63.

58 Mindy Nunez Duffourc, Sara Gerke & Konrad Kollnig, *Privacy of Personal Data in the Generative AI Data Lifecycle*, 13 NYU J. INTELL. PROP. & ENT. L. 219, 245–46 (2023).

59 Bender et al., *supra* note 56.

5

The Origins of Legal AI

*Rebecca Fordon and L. Karl Branting**

5.1 INTRODUCTION

The creation of an artificial person has been a dream of humankind for millennia, from Talos, the giant bronze automaton that guarded Crete in Greek legend, to the Golem of ancient Jewish tradition. Science fiction writers have imagined robotic assistants (e.g., R2-D2 and C-3PO in the *Star Wars* saga), antagonists (e.g., HAL 9000 in *2001: A Space Odyssey* and M3GAN in *M3GAN*), and romantic partners (e.g., Samantha in *Her* and Ava in *Ex Machina*), but robotic lawyers seem to be absent from even the most dystopian of these fictional worlds.[1]

Science fiction robots typically possess traits that are essential for effective lawyers, including *general intelligence*, the full range of human reasoning abilities, and *personhood*, encompassing self-awareness, self-worth, goals, experiences, and emotions. An AI system with general intelligence and personhood would presumably have no difficulty dispensing advice about even the most complex legal problems after suitable training, such as reading every legal treatise, statute, and court decision. Sadly, no AI system has either general intelligence or personhood, notwithstanding the astonishing capabilities of large language models ("LLMs"), as discussed in Chapters 4, 9, and 12. Indeed, there is no convincing theory of what process could lead to an artificial system with these characteristics.

Instead, most useful AI applications have resulted from emulating individual human problem-solving capabilities through specific *algorithms*, that is, through precisely defined procedures that are amenable to automation. In general, AI technologies have been painstakingly developed to solve specific categories of problems. The main categories of AI capabilities and typical applications of those capabilities include:

* We thank Kevin D. Ashley for his review of multiple drafts of this chapter.

1 This is not to say that attorneys do not appear in dystopian science fiction. An episode of the *FarScape* series is set on a planet, Litigara, 90% of whose disputatious population consists of attorneys. *See Dream a Little Dream (FarScape Season 2, Episode 8)*, FARSCAPE FANDOM, https://perma.cc/79S2-7KVU.

Reasoning – Logical inference, analogical reasoning
Understanding – Computational linguistics, computer vision
Planning – Action sequencing, design
Acting – Goal-directed dialogue, robotics
Learning – Outcome prediction

For example, *logical inference*, the kind of reasoning used in solving geometry problems or logic puzzles (listed as an application of "Reasoning"), was among the first technologies to be described as "artificial intelligence" or "AI." These early AI systems, which date back to the 1950s, included proving mathematical theorems[2] and playing checkers.[3]

We define legal AI as the application of AI technologies to legal tasks and processes. Legal AI systems employ reasoning capabilities to analyze legal arguments and precedents, understanding capabilities to process legal texts and documents, planning capabilities to develop legal strategies, interaction capabilities to engage with legal professionals and litigants, and learning capabilities to identify patterns in legal outcomes. These systems range from tools that automate routine document review and legal research to sophisticated applications that can analyze case outcomes and generate legal documents. This potential is particularly relevant for unrepresented litigants, as AI can play a pivotal role in addressing the justice gap by making legal processes more understandable, predictable, and navigable.

The AI community was initially optimistic that tasks that were easier for people – such as conversation, recognizing images, and manipulating physical objects – would soon be within reach, given that tasks as challenging for people as mathematics and board games could be mastered by AI systems. However, it soon became clear that the opposite was true: Tasks closer to the ordinary human social and physical world were much harder to automate than abstract logical activities that lack the subtleties and complexities of human experience.[4] AI applications that are now taken for granted, including automated speech recognition, highway route planning, grammar checking, and autonomous vehicle control, did not develop out of the general logic-based techniques of the 1950s, but were the products of decades of research focused on the unique characteristics of each of these tasks.

A similar story unfolded in the subfield of AI and Law research. In the 1950s, some scholars argued that legal rules, norms, and arguments could be accurately modeled using mathematical logic.[5] The development of general-purpose techniques for automated inference based on logical rules[6] provided a method for implementing

[2] Allen Newell & Herbert A. Simon, *The Logic Theory Machine – A Complex Information Processing System*, 2 IRE Trans. Info. Theory 61, 61–79 (1956).

[3] Arthur L. Samuel, *Some Studies in Machine Learning Using the Game of Checkers*, 3 IBM J. Rsch. & Dev. 210, 210–29 (1959).

[4] Melanie Mitchell, Artificial Intelligence: A Guide for Thinking Humans 103–04 (2019).

[5] Layman E. Allen, *Symbolic Logic: A Razor-Edged Tool for Drafting and Interpreting Legal Documents*, 66 Yale L.J. 833 (1957).

[6] John C. Shaw & Herbert A. Simon, *Report on a General Problem-Solving Program*, 1 Proc. Int'l Conf. on Info. Processing 256 (1959).

this approach in the form of logic-based legal reasoning systems.[7] It seemed to many that an age of legal AI had dawned and that "legal expert systems" could fully automate legal expertise.[8] Yet despite adoption in specialized applications, such as automated insurance claim settlement advisors,[9] logic-based models failed to live up to the optimism of their advocates.[10]

This chapter explores the reasons behind the failed millenarian dream of providing legal advice as cleanly and decisively as theorem-proving or chess. It traces the development of legal AI across three waves: (1) the "First Wave" of knowledge-based and logic-driven systems, which culminated in the 1980s and 1990s, (2) the "Second Wave" of data-centric predictive models in the 2000s and 2010s, and (3) the "Third Wave" from the 2010s to the present. The latest wave represents a sophisticated synthesis, combining the data-driven approaches of the Second Wave with the knowledge representation and reasoning capabilities of the First Wave, while adding robust natural language processing ("NLP") for improved human–AI interaction. This hybrid approach is showing exciting progress in marrying the ability of modern legal AI systems to both analyze patterns in legal data and engage in meaningful legal discourse, grounded in formal legal knowledge and reasoning. Even as the Third Wave continues to evolve, some experts are already envisioning a Fourth Wave of legal AI that would focus on deeper human–machine collaboration rather than new model architectures.

As with AI in general, progress in AI and Law has been achieved by working from the bottom up, starting with the needs of litigants, lawyers, and courts and developing technologies to satisfy those needs, rather than from the top down by attempting to address all problems using a single AI method, such as computational logic (as discussed in Chapter 6). An exploration of these technologies for unrepresented litigants must therefore start with an analysis of their needs, as outlined in Chapter 3.

5.2 FIRST WAVE OF LEGAL AI (1980S–1990S): LOGIC-BASED SYSTEMS

The First Wave of legal AI, spanning the 1980s through the 1990s, was characterized by an ambitious vision: to capture legal reasoning through formal logic and rules-based computational systems.[11] This period's optimism stemmed from an apparent natural fit between legal reasoning and early AI approaches. Legal analysis, with its

[7] *See* L. Thorne McCarty, *Reflections on TAXMAN: An Experiment in Artificial Intelligence and Legal Reasoning*, 90 HARV. L. REV. 837 (1977); Marek J. Sergot et al., *The British Nationality Act as a Logic Program*, 29 COMMC'NS ACM 370, 370–86 (1977).

[8] Richard E. Susskind, *Expert Systems in Law: A Jurisprudential Approach to Artificial Intelligence and Legal Reasoning*, 49 MOD. L. REV. 168 (1986).

[9] D. A. Waterman & Mark Peterson, *Rule-Based Models of Legal Expertise*, *in* COMPUTING POWER AND LEGAL REASONING 627 (Charles Walter ed. 1985).

[10] *See, e.g.*, Anja Oskamp & Marc Lauritsen, *AI in Law Practice? So Far, Not Much*, 10 A.I. & L. 227 (2002).

[11] Bruce G. Buchanan & Thomas E. Headrick, *Some Speculation about Artificial Intelligence and Legal Reasoning*, 23 STAN. L. REV. 40 (1970).

emphasis on structured reasoning and formal logic, seemed ideally suited for the rule-based expert systems that dominated AI research at the time.[12]

This perceived alignment manifested in several ways. First, legal reasoning has historically relied on structured forms, such as syllogistic reasoning and precedent-based logic, which appear compatible with computational approaches. As Rissland observed, "rule-based techniques are but one component in a full model of legal argument, [but] they can be satisfyingly powerful from the perspective of building useful applications."[13] Second, much of the law, particularly in civil law systems, is based on codified statutes that aim for clarity and predictability. Such qualities made it seem amenable to rule-based AI systems.

Early attempts to formalize legal reasoning (which were not focused on unrepresented litigants) led researchers to develop and apply several specialized forms of logic to capture different aspects of legal analysis. As shown in Table 5.1, the most prominent were *deontic logic*, which introduces formal operators to model normative concepts like rights, obligations, and permissions (e.g., "it is obligatory that" or "it is permitted that"); *defeasible logic*, which accommodates the defeasibility of legal rules by allowing conclusions to be withdrawn when exceptions or stronger rules apply; and *temporal logic*, which incorporates time-based operators such as "before," "after," and "until" to represent rules that depend on specific temporal sequences.[14] Deontic logic excels at structuring duties and entitlements within a legal framework. Defeasible logic captures the inherently non-monotonic nature of legal reasoning, where rules can be overridden. Temporal logic enables precise modeling of legal rules that hinge on timing. Each faces challenges in formal representation, especially when dealing with nested conditions, conflicting rules, or ambiguous temporal language. Notable practical examples included Waterman and Peterson's Legal Decision-making System ("LDS") at the RAND Corporation, which assessed the worth of product liability cases for settlement purposes, and McCarty's TAXMAN project, which modeled aspects of corporate tax law.[15] Branting's Protection Order Advisor, developed in collaboration with the Idaho Supreme Court, was one of the first such systems designed for unrepresented litigants.[16] These systems demonstrated that rule-based approaches could handle certain well-defined legal tasks, particularly in areas with clear statutory frameworks.

Deontic logic, aimed at modeling normative concepts central to law, provided formal operators for obligations ("it is obligatory that"), permissions ("it is permitted that"), and prohibitions ("it is forbidden that"). For example, Waterman and Peterson's LDS employed deontic logic through a sophisticated system of chained if–then rules that

[12] Edwina L. Rissland, *Artificial Intelligence and Law: Stepping Stones to a Model of Legal Reasoning*, 99 Yale L.J. 1957, 1958 (1990).

[13] *Id.* at 1978.

[14] *Id.* at 1975.

[15] *See* McCarty, *supra* note 7; D. A. Waterman & Mark A. Peterson, Models of Legal Decision Making (1981), https://perma.cc/F84Y-P9NP.

[16] L. Karl Branting, *An Advisory System for Pro Se Protection Order Applicants*, 14 Int'l Rev. L. Computs. & Tech. 357, 361 (2000).

TABLE 5.1 *Forms of logic applied to legal reasoning.*

Logic type	Definition	Primary purpose in law	Key operators/features	Example use	Challenges
Deontic logic	A formal system for expressing normative concepts like obligations and rights.	Formalizing duties, permissions, and prohibitions.	"It is obligatory that (O)," "It is permitted that (P)," "It is forbidden that (F)."	LDS used it to evaluate legal obligations and permissions through nested if–then rules in product liability.	Complex interplay of norms; modeling interactions between multiple obligations and exceptions.
Defeasible logic	A non-monotonic logic allowing conclusions to be withdrawn in light of new information.	Handling rules with exceptions and rule conflicts.	Rule prioritization, exception handling, rebuttal rules.	Representing how a general liability rule may be overridden by a specific statutory defense.	Determining rule strength and systematizing when one rule should override another.
Temporal logic	A logic for reasoning about propositions qualified in terms of time.	Modeling rules that depend on sequence, duration, or timing.	Temporal operators: "Before," "After," "Until," "Since."	Used in modeling time-bound legal conditions, such as residency duration in the British Nationality Act.	Legislative time clauses often have ambiguous or implicit assumptions that resist clean formalization.

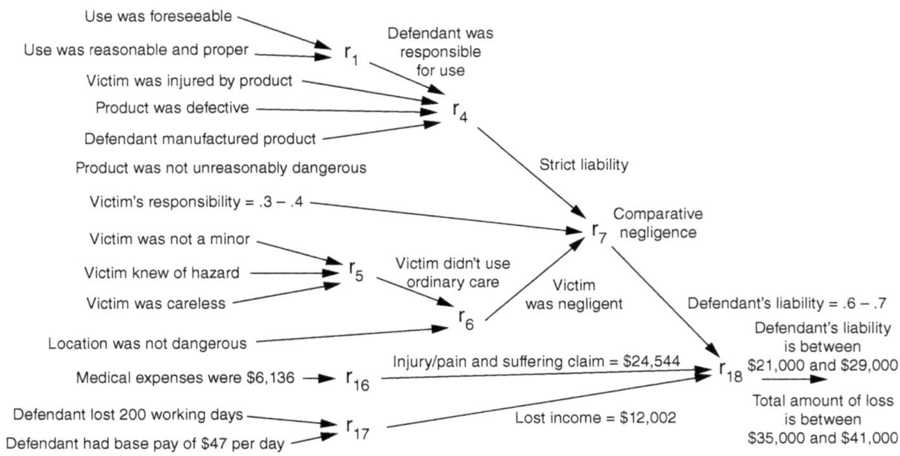

FIGURE 5.1 Representation of computer output for a drain-cleaner case. Republished with permission from the RAND Corporation.[17]

evaluated legal obligations, permissions, and prohibitions in product liability cases.[18] For instance, Rule 4 in LDS (the strict liability definition) contained multiple nested conditions that had to be satisfied, including whether the plaintiff was injured by the product, whether the incidental-sale defense was inapplicable, whether the defendant was responsible for the product's use, and whether specific jurisdictional requirements were met.[19] As shown in Figure 5.1, these rules would trigger other rules in sequence. For example, Rule 1 (determining if the defendant was responsible for use) would feed into Rule 4 (strict liability), which would then connect to Rules 5 and 6 (evaluating user negligence), and ultimately flow into Rule 7 (comparative negligence) to determine final liability proportions and settlement ranges.[20] This chain of deontic reasoning allowed the system to systematically evaluate legal duties and permissions while accounting for complex interactions between different aspects of product liability law, such as how a user's negligence might modify a manufacturer's strict liability obligations.[21]

Defeasible logic was developed to handle a key characteristic of legal rules: they admit exceptions and can be overridden by other rules in certain circumstances. Unlike classical logic, where conclusions necessarily follow from premises, defeasible logic allows for tentative conclusions that can be defeated by stronger contrary evidence or rules.[22] This mapped well onto legal reasoning, where rules

[17] WATERMAN & PETERSON, *supra* note 15, at 20 (Figure 4).

[18] *Id.* at 13–14.

[19] *Id.* at 16.

[20] *Id.* at 18–21.

[21] *Id.* at 20–21.

[22] Donald H. Berman & Carole D. Hafner, *Obstacles to the Development of Logic-Based Models of Legal Reasoning*, *in* COMPUTER POWER AND LEGAL LANGUAGE: THE USE OF COMPUTATIONAL MODELS IN LINGUISTICS, ARTIFICIAL INTELLIGENCE, AND EXPERT SYSTEMS 183, 185–86 (1988).

often have implicit exceptions and conclusions that must be revised as new information emerges. However, encoding the relative strength of competing rules and determining when exceptions should apply proved difficult to systematize.

Temporal logic added operators to handle time-dependent rules and reasoning, which are crucial in areas like contract law, where timing and sequence matter. This allowed for the representation of concepts such as "before," "after," and "until" in formal rules. However, as Sergot and colleagues found in their work on the British Nationality Act, even seemingly straightforward temporal conditions in legislation often harbored ambiguities that made formal logical representation problematic.[23]

Early projects attempted to translate legal rules and reasoning into computational logic. McCarty's TAXMAN project, while primarily focused on semantic information processing, incorporated several types of logical reasoning to model corporate reorganization law. Beyond the basic predicate logic used for representing facts about corporations and stock ownership, TAXMAN employed aspects of temporal logic to track the sequence of corporate transactions and state changes over time.[24] The system maintained a timeline of corporate events and could reason about the ordering of transactions, which was crucial for applying concepts like the "step transaction" doctrine.[25] TAXMAN also exhibited characteristics of defeasible reasoning, particularly in its handling of partial pattern matches and multiple interpretations of reorganization types, such as when a transaction could potentially qualify as both a Type B and a Type C reorganization.[26] While not explicitly using deontic logic, TAXMAN did need to represent and reason about permissions and requirements in corporate tax law, such as the conditions under which reorganizations could qualify for tax-free treatment.[27] While TAXMAN could successfully analyze certain well-defined statutory requirements, it struggled to capture more nuanced judicial doctrines like "continuity of interest" and "business purpose" that required reasoning about underlying principles rather than just formal rules.[28] This highlighted a key challenge in legal AI: the need to bridge formal logical representations and the more flexible, principle-based reasoning characteristic of legal analysis.

Branting's Generator of Recursive Exemplar-Based Explanations ("GREBE") integrated rule-based and case-based approaches using what Branting termed an "impartial" control strategy for legal analysis, as shown in Figure 5.2.[29]

[23] Sergot et al., *supra* note 7, at 383.
[24] McCarty, *supra* note 15, at 865–67.
[25] *Id.* at 848–49.
[26] *Id.* at 844–45.
[27] *Id.* at 846–48.
[28] *Id.* at 892–93.
[29] L. Karl Branting, Reasoning with Rules and Precedents: A Computational Model of Legal Analysis 63, 145, 155 (2000); *see also* L. Karl Branting, Integrating Rules and Precedents for Classification and Explanation: Automating Legal Analysis (1991) (Ph.D. thesis, University of Texas at Austin) (on file with Mia Bonardi). Not coincidentally, the grebe (pronounced grēb) is a type of bird. For further commentary, *see* Kevin D. Ashley, Artificial Intelligence and Legal Analytics: New Tools for Law Practice in the Digital Age 93–97, 105 (2017).

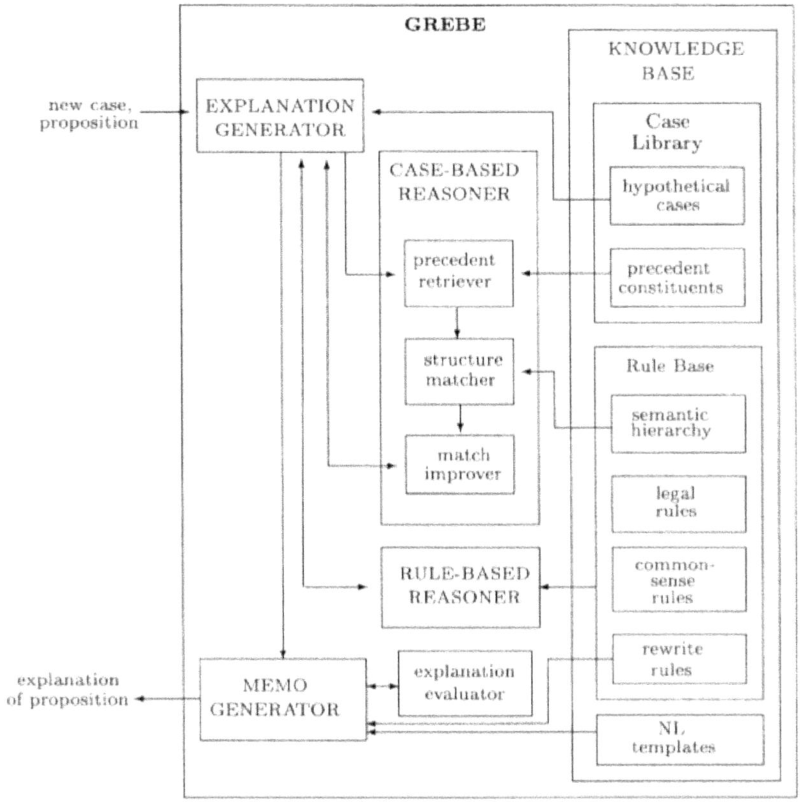

FIGURE 5.2 A schematic representation of GREBE's architecture. Republished with permission from Springer Nature.[30]

Branting categorized GREBE as *impartial*, distinguishing it from the purely case-based, rule-based, or hybrid approaches at the time:

> Systems that use both rules and cases can be further subdivided based on whether they use case elaboration or goal reformulation … but the best performance requires both.
>
> …
>
> [I]f both a rule and precedent are applicable to a goal, the choice is based on the strength of the resulting explanation, rather than on an arbitrary ordering scheme. A control strategy that permits rules and precedents to be used in this complementary fashion, imposing no arbitrary ordering restrictions, is impartial.[31]

[30] BRANTING, *supra* note 29, at 64.
[31] *Id.* at 145, 155.

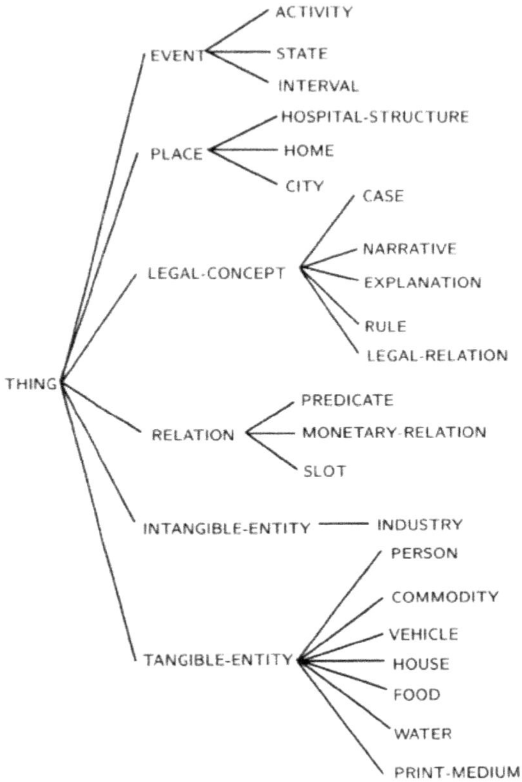

FIGURE 5.3 The top two levels of GREBE's object taxonomy. Republished with permission from Springer Nature.[32]

Implemented in Common Lisp for Texas workers' compensation law, GREBE employed defeasible logic in its case-based reasoning component, allowing general legal principles to be overridden by more specific rules or compelling factual distinctions when comparing new cases to precedents.[33] The system incorporated temporal logic to handle the sequencing of events crucial to workers' compensation claims.[34] Figure 5.3 displays the top two levels of GREBE's object taxonomy, which encompasses frames for events, tangible and intangible entities, places, legal concepts, and relations.

GREBE employed deontic logic through inference rules derived from judicial opinions, such as "the inference that if an activity constitutes a duty of employment, then each necessary step of that activity is a duty of employment as well."[35] A key

[32] *Id.* at 72.

[33] *Id.* at 67–70.

[34] *Id.* at 71–74.

[35] *Id.* at 65.

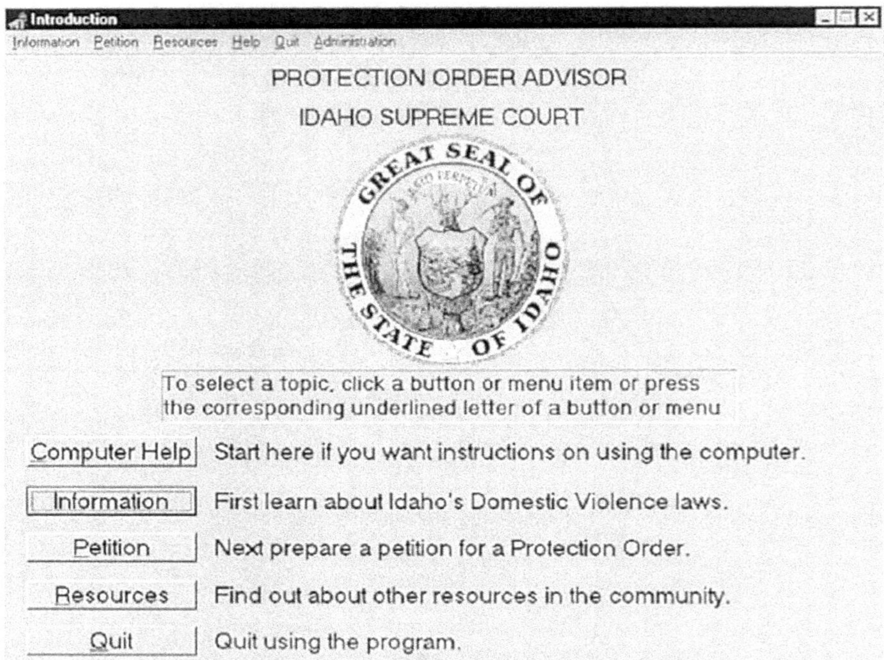

FIGURE 5.4 The POA's introduction screen (2000). Republished with permission from the Taylor & Francis Group and the Idaho Supreme Court.[36]

contribution was the computational model of *ratio decidendi*, which represented the authoritative content of precedents as justification structures consisting of reasoning steps that linked abstract legal predicates to other predicates and to specific case facts.[37]

Building on these early explorations of formal logic in legal AI, Branting's Protection Order Advisor ("POA"), designed for the Idaho Supreme Court in the late 1990s and no longer in use, demonstrated how even basic rule-based reasoning can provide meaningful assistance to unrepresented litigants in practice (Figure 5.4).[38]

Designed as a comprehensive four-module system, the POA first informed users about available types of legal relief through hypertext explanations, then used rule-based reasoning to determine whether they could make a prima facie showing for a protection order by systematically eliciting relevant facts from users (Figure 5.5).[39]

36 *Id.* at 363 (Figure 1).
37 *Id.* at 27–62.
38 Branting, *supra* note 16, at 359.
39 *Id.* at 360.

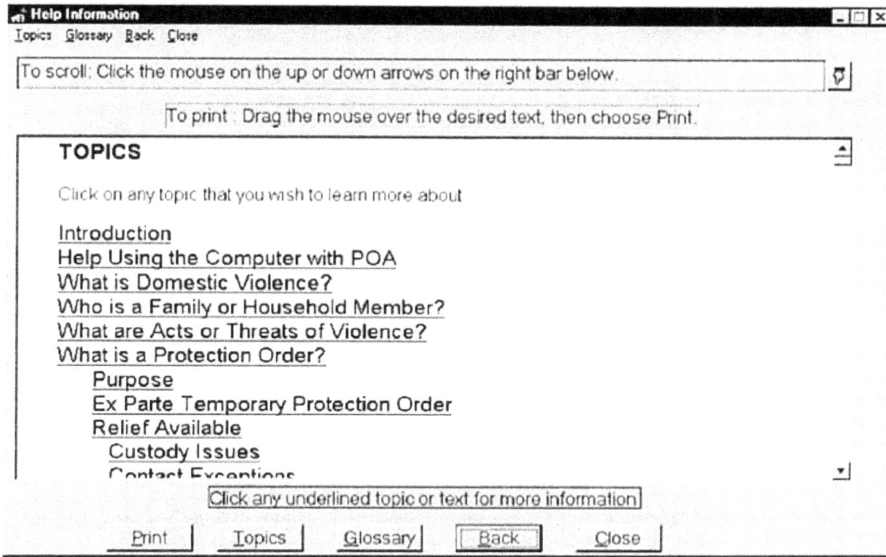

FIGURE 5.5 The POA's help file topics (2000). Republished with permission from the Taylor & Francis Group and the Idaho Supreme Court.[40]

Rather than employing the sophisticated deontic, defeasible, or temporal logic systems being developed in academic research, the POA used straightforward if-then rules to guide domestic abuse survivors through Idaho's protection order process, checking whether two key statutory requirements were met: (1) the existence of actual or threatened violence and (2) a qualifying domestic relationship between the parties (Figure 5.6).[41]

Once eligibility was established, the system informed users of procedural requirements and elicited the necessary information (Figure 5.7).

After gathering all required information, the system automatically generated the necessary legal documents, including both the petition for the protection order and the service information sheet needed by law enforcement (Figure 5.8).[42]

Using backward-chaining inference implemented in Prolog, the system worked backward from eligibility determinations to identify required facts, while employing simple inference rules to reduce user burden by automatically completing obvious data relationships and detecting logical inconsistencies in user responses.[43] This practical approach proved effective precisely because protection order eligibility,

40 *Id.* at 364 (Figure 2).
41 *Id.* at 365.
42 *Id.* at 365–66.
43 *Id.* at 366.

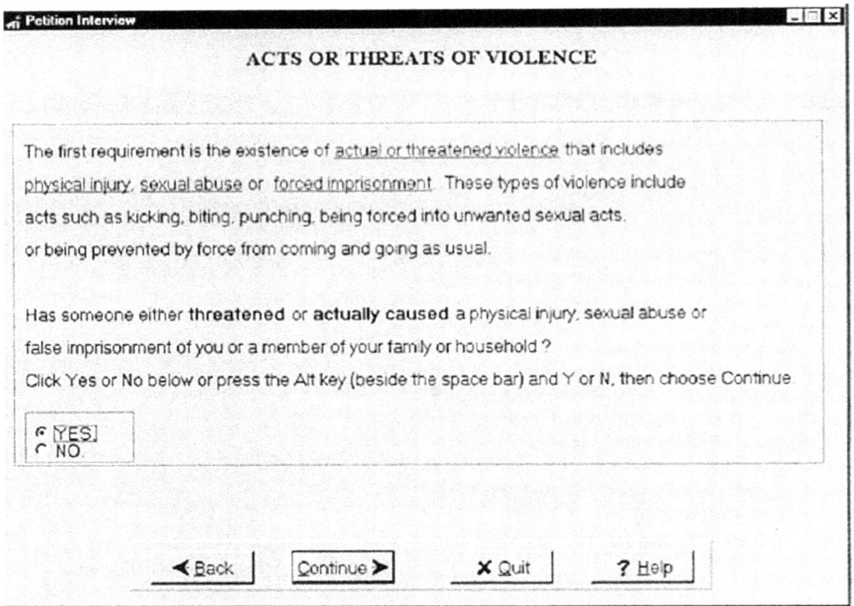

FIGURE 5.6 The POA asked whether the violence requirement for a protection order was satisfied (2000). Republished with permission from the Taylor & Francis Group and the Idaho Supreme Court.[44]

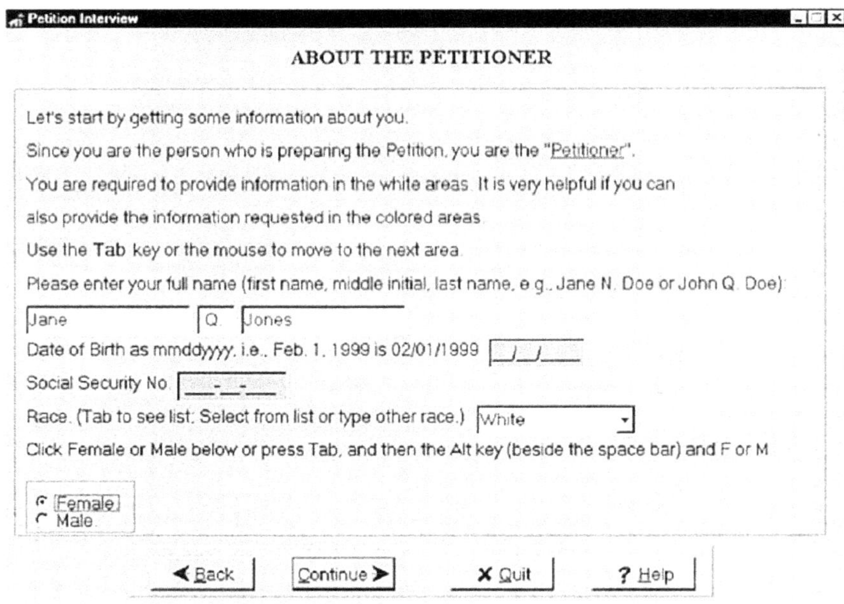

FIGURE 5.7 The POA elicited the required information (2000). Republished with permission from the Taylor & Francis Group and the Idaho Supreme Court.[45]

44 *Id.* (Figure 3).
45 *Id.* at 366 (Figure 4).

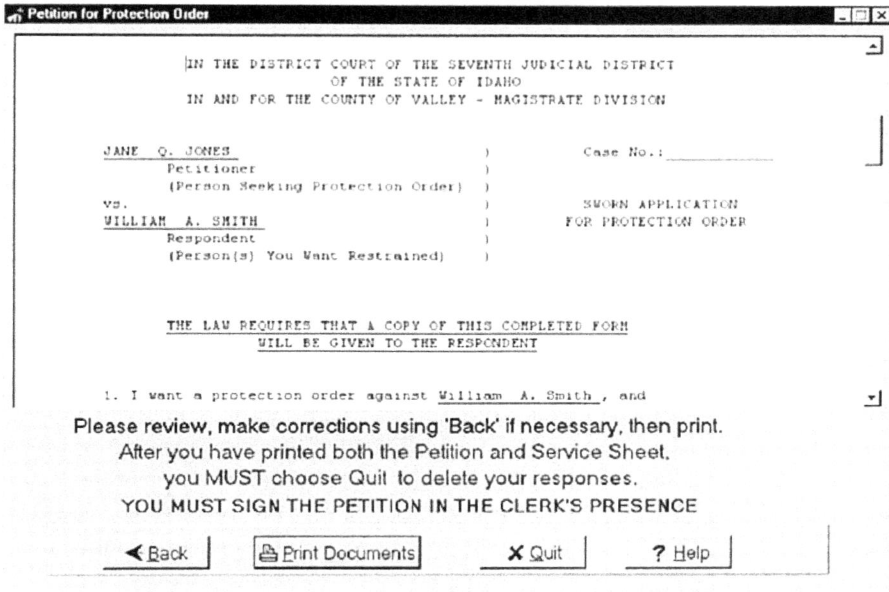

FIGURE 5.8 Sample petition for protection order drafted by the POA (2000). Republished with permission from the Taylor & Francis Group and the Idaho Supreme Court.[46]

unlike many areas of law, involves relatively clear-cut statutory criteria rather than complex legal concepts requiring nuanced interpretation.[47] The POA's success illustrated that while formal logic systems could capture the theoretical complexity of legal reasoning, unrepresented litigants often needed something different: reliable guidance through well-defined legal processes rather than sophisticated analysis of ambiguous legal concepts.[48] By focusing on accessibility and practical utility, the POA showed how AI could bridge formal legal requirements and access to justice. The POA provided a template for legal aid technology that prioritized helping real people navigate the legal system over advancing the frontiers of computational legal reasoning.[49]

As Oskamp and Lauritsen noted in a 2002 retrospective, despite initial enthusiasm, logic-based expert systems struggled to gain widespread adoption in commercial legal practice.[50] Several fundamental challenges emerged: (1) legal reasoning is inherently ambiguous and interpretive, making it difficult to translate into authoritative formal logic; (2) building such systems required rare dual expertise

[46] *Id.* at 367 (Figure 5).
[47] *Id.* at 359–60.
[48] *Id.* at 359.
[49] *Id.* at 368.
[50] Oskamp & Lauritsen, *supra* note 10, at 228.

and intense manual effort, limiting scalability beyond narrow, routine domains; and (3) legal practice involves complex, context-sensitive reasoning and advocacy that resist replication through rigid rule-based approaches. We examine each challenge below.

First, legal analysis proved far more complex than the simple application of rules to facts. Legal texts are often ambiguous, so multiple alternative logical representations are possible, which is to say that those performing the conversion can, and frequently do, disagree. Worse, none of the alternative logical representations is authoritative; that is, the original text expresses a valid rule if it is enacted or enunciated by an authoritative legal entity,[51] but representations of this text in logic are simply interpretations that may or may not be valid.[52] Finally, even in those aspects of legal assistance that seem amenable to being automated with logic, there are disagreements about the particular variety of logic that is most appropriate for legal applications. Specialized logics have been developed that formalize rights, prohibitions, and obligations (deontic logic), rules with exceptions (defeasible logic), and rules with specific time bounds (temporal logic),[53] but there is no consensus about which specialized logic features are necessary or sufficient to faithfully model human legal reasoning.[54]

Second, the development of these systems was labor-intensive and required rare expertise in both legal analysis and computational logic. This made them difficult to scale beyond narrow applications. Success stories tended to be in areas with routine situations and limited outcomes, such as tax preparation software like TurboTax, rather than more complex legal reasoning tasks.[55] Even these narrow applications required extensive manual coding.

Finally, navigating legal systems entails multiple tasks besides just applying rules to facts. Legal reasoning encompasses diverse modes, including "reasoning with cases, rules, statutes and principles" as well as understanding procedural rules, strategic planning, and crafting persuasive arguments.[56] Rule-based systems struggled

[51] H. L. A. HART, THE CONCEPT OF LAW (1961).

[52] An exception to this observation is "Rules as Code," rules that are enacted in the form of computational logic rather than text. The applications of Rules as Code have largely been confined to highly formal domains, like building codes. *See, e.g.*, Matthew Waddington, *Rules as Code*, 37 L. CONTEXT 170 (2020); Rónán Kennedy, *Rules as Code and the Rule of Law: Ensuring Effective Judicial Review of Administration by Software*, 16 LAW, INNOVATION & TECH. 170 (2024).

[53] Guido Governatori et al., *Logic and the Law: Philosophical Foundations, Deontics, and Defeasible Reasoning*, *in* HANDBOOK DEONTIC LOGIC AND NORMATIVE SYSTEMS 657 (2021).

[54] Rissland, *supra* note 12, at 1975.

[55] Oskamp & Lauritsen, *supra* note 10, at 230–31; *see* KARL N. LLEWELLYN, THE BRAMBLE BUSH 41–69 (1930); BENJAMIN N. CARDOZO, THE NATURE OF THE JUDICIAL PROCESS 13–33 (1921); *see also* EDWARD H. LEVI, AN INTRODUCTION TO LEGAL REASONING 1–27 (1949).

[56] Rissland, *supra* note 12, at 1961; *see also* L. KARL BRANTING, REASONING WITH RULES AND PRECEDENTS 6–7 (2000) (describing a framework for integrating rule-based reasoning and case-based reasoning as "complementary processes for classification and explanation in legal analysis").

to replicate core lawyering tasks like analogizing favorable cases, distinguishing contrary ones, anticipating counter-arguments, and creating artful hypotheticals.[57] The contextual, nuanced, and adversarial nature of legal analysis proved far more complex than the binary logic that characterized First Wave AI systems. Even in statutory domains requiring extensive rule application, legal interpretation demands a "special set of skills and knowledge" that incorporates procedural expertise, contextual understanding, and professional judgment.[58] The limitations of purely logic-based approaches led to important insights about the nature of legal reasoning itself. As Rissland observed, "[T]asks closer to the ordinary human social and physical world were much harder to automate than abstract logical activities that lack the subtleties and complexities of human experience."[59] This realization prompted a shift away from attempts to reduce all legal reasoning to formal logic, toward more nuanced approaches that could better handle the complexity and ambiguity inherent in legal analysis.

While logic-based expert systems struggled to gain widespread adoption in commercial legal practice, Oskamp and Lauritsen noted significant adoption in government contexts, including social welfare and taxation systems in Australia, the Netherlands, and the US.[60]

They also noted that legal-aid offices offered web-based expert systems, and courts offered advisory and form-generation services to self-represented litigants.[61]

This First Wave, while falling short of its grandest ambitions, laid the groundwork for future developments in legal AI. It demonstrated both the potential and the limitations of formal logical approaches to legal reasoning, while highlighting the need for more sophisticated methods that could better address the nuanced, context-dependent nature of legal analysis. These insights would prove invaluable as the field moved into its Second Wave, which would embrace more data-centric approaches to legal AI.

5.3 SECOND WAVE (2000S–2010S): DATA-CENTRIC PREDICTIVE MODELS

The transition from the logic-based systems of the 1970s to 1990s to data-centric models beginning in the 2000s marked a fundamental shift in legal AI. The data-centric paradigm emerged as a response to what Karl Branting identified as

[57] Rissland, *supra* note 12, at 1957–58.

[58] Oskamp & Lauritsen, *supra* note 10, at 232; *see* McCarty, *supra* note 15 at 837–38.

[59] Rissland, *supra* note 12, at 1959.

[60] Oskamp & Lauritsen, *supra* note 10, at 228–29.

[61] *Id.* at 229.

two persistent obstacles that had constrained logic-based legal systems: (1) the challenge of creating authoritative logical representations of legal texts and (2) the difficulty of bridging the gap between legal terminology and ordinary language.[62] Rather than attempting to solve the problems of logic-based models directly through better formalisms or knowledge engineering, the data-centric approach effectively "finessed" them by exploiting "knowledge latent in legal corpora."[63]

This foundational infrastructure for data-centric approaches had been developing since the 1950s. Beginning with the Health Law Center at the University of Pittsburgh in 1956 and continuing through the 1970s, when LEXIS and CLIRS became available to the legal profession, computerized legal information systems had been creating vast digital repositories of legal materials.[64] These early legal information retrieval systems, while not employing machine learning themselves, established both the technological infrastructure and professional culture that would prove essential for Second Wave developments. They demonstrated that lawyers would adopt computational tools for practical advantage and, crucially, created the large-scale digitized legal datasets that machine learning approaches would require. The shift to data-centric approaches involved a deliberate trade-off: What these approaches gained in scalability and adaptability, they sacrificed in explanatory transparency.[65]

5.3.1 *Machine Learning Enters Law*

Central to the Second Wave was the application of machine learning ("ML") – computational methods that learn patterns from data rather than relying on explicitly programmed rules.[66] This capability proved transformative for processing the massive volumes of legal text that had become available through digitization.

The power of ML lies in its ability to handle the scale and complexity that had overwhelmed earlier approaches. As detailed in Chapter 7, ML techniques ranging from decision trees to neural networks can process thousands of legal documents, identify predictive features, and generate insights about legal patterns that would be impossible for human analysis alone.[67]

[62] L. Karl Branting, *Data-Centric and Logic-Based Models for Automated Legal Problem Solving*, 25 A.I. & L. 5, 6–11 (2017).
[63] *Id.* at 6.
[64] For a comprehensive history of early legal information systems, *see* Colin Tapper, Lawyers and Machines: The Technology of Legal Practice (1963).
[65] Branting, *supra* note 62, at 5.
[66] For a detailed technical explanation of ML approaches, *see infra* Chapter 7: Machine Learning.
[67] *See infra* Section 7.4.1: Extracting Features from Legal Texts.

This disconnect between ML's pattern-finding power and its inability to explain its reasoning created a fundamental tension that would define much of the Second Wave. Legal practice demands not just accurate predictions but explanations that can support arguments and justify decisions. As Ashley noted, lawyers are "expected to justify their legal conclusions symbolically by citing some legal authorities in support," making unexplained numerical predictions of limited value in legal contexts.[68] The challenge of developing ML systems that could both predict and explain would become a driving force in legal AI research.

5.3.2 *Initial Resistance in the AI and Law Community*

Despite ML's dramatic success in other domains, the AI and Law community was initially slow to adopt corpus-based approaches. From the late 1990s to the early 2000s, while statistical methods had become fundamental in computational linguistics, the proportion of papers reporting corpus-based work at international conferences on AI and Law increased only slightly, from about 18% in 1997 to about 21% in 2003.[69]

This resistance stemmed from several factors unique to the legal domain. First, there was a fundamental cultural mismatch between legal training and statistical approaches. Attorneys' professional education emphasized generating and evaluating textual arguments rather than statistical prediction. As one analysis noted, predictive ability is "much less central to legal expertise than articulating the most cogent argument for a given outcome."[70] Legal professionals were trained to think in terms of precedent, interpretation, and persuasive reasoning rather than pattern recognition and statistical forecasting.

Second, technical barriers complicated the adoption of standard NLP methods in legal contexts. Legal texts posed unique challenges that existing parsing methods could not handle effectively. The syntactic complexity of legal language, with its deeply nested enumerations, conditional clauses, and statutory cross-references, made standard computational linguistics approaches inadequate.[71] Legal documents required specialized processing techniques that the broader NLP community had not developed.

Third, access to large-scale legal datasets remained severely limited. Unlike general NLP research, which has benefited from openly available corpora such

68 Kevin D. Ashley, *Reasoning with Cases and Hypotheticals in HYPO*, 34 INT'L J. MAN-MACHINE STUD. 753, 765 (1991).

69 Serena Villata et al., *Thirty Years of Artificial Intelligence and Law: The Third Decade*, 30 A.I. & L. 561, 569 (2022).

70 *Id.*

71 *Id.* at 569–70 (citing Leora Morgenstern, *Knowledge Representation for Legal Texts*, *in* LAW AND LOGIC 265–80 (2014)).

as Wikipedia and news articles, legal AI researchers have faced significant barriers in obtaining sufficient training data. In the US, access to legal decisions remained fragmented, with court records often locked behind paywalls or proprietary platforms.[72] This lack of accessible data delayed researchers' abilities to develop robust ML models and slowed the adoption of statistical approaches in the legal domain.

5.3.3 *Task-Based Complementarity*

A critical insight from this period was the recognition that different categories of legal tasks naturally aligned with different computational approaches. Data-centric approaches did not render logic-based systems obsolete; rather, they revealed that certain legal tasks benefited more from statistical pattern recognition than from formal deduction. Branting developed a taxonomy of legal tasks to illustrate this complementarity, showing that the choice between approaches should depend on the specific type of legal problem at issue.[73]

Tasks such as legal analysis and argument generation, which depend on the generation or analysis of highly rule-governed discourse, remained better suited to logic-based approaches. These tasks required the kind of explicit reasoning and justification that symbolic AI systems could provide. In contrast, tasks involving prediction, retrieval, trend analysis, and document classification saw dramatic improvements through data-centric methods. These applications could benefit from ML's ability to identify patterns across large datasets without requiring detailed representations of legal reasoning.

This task-oriented perspective offered a more nuanced view than simply declaring one approach superior to the other. Instead, it suggested that computational legal reasoning, like human legal reasoning, requires multiple complementary approaches tailored to specific types of legal problems. This theoretical framework helped explain both the successes and limitations of Second Wave systems, while also pointing toward the hybrid approaches that would eventually emerge.

5.3.4 *Second Wave Applications and Innovations*

The Second Wave eventually produced a range of practical applications that demonstrated the value of data-centric approaches for specific legal tasks. These applications generally targeted efficiency gains in document-intensive legal workflows rather than attempting to replicate human legal reasoning.

[72] *Id.* at 570.
[73] Branting, *supra* note 62, at 8–11.

Legal Research and Analytics transformed how lawyers approached case law research. Platforms like Lex Machina emerged to analyze litigation patterns, judicial behavior, and case outcomes using ML techniques applied to court filings and decisions.[74] These systems could identify trends invisible to traditional legal research, such as which attorneys were most successful before particular judges, how specific legal arguments performed across different jurisdictions, and the likelihood of success for ongoing legal matters. By analyzing historical case data, judicial behavior, and jurisdictional trends, these tools helped practitioners make informed decisions about settlement options and litigation strategies.[75] However, these predictive systems were often criticized for focusing on statistical generalizations rather than the relative strength of competing legal arguments.

Contract Analysis and Review represented one of the earliest successful applications of Second Wave AI. By the early 2010s, AI-powered tools like Kira Systems and RAVN were helping legal professionals extract and analyze key clauses from complex agreements.[76] These systems used NLP to identify obligations, risks, and inconsistencies across large volumes of contracts, dramatically reducing the time required for due diligence and compliance reviews.

Document Automation evolved beyond simple template filling to offer more sophisticated document generation capabilities (see Chapter 8). These tools could automatically generate standard legal documents, from wills to employment contracts, by using ML to understand contextual patterns in legal drafting. While not fully "intelligent," these systems marked a significant improvement over earlier approaches by offering more nuanced and context-aware document generation.[77]

e-Discovery and Technology Assisted Review ("TAR") represented perhaps the most successful and widely adopted Second Wave commercial application. In TAR, attorneys manually tagged representative sets of documents as relevant or irrelevant to discovery requests, and ML algorithms used these examples to classify remaining documents automatically.[78] TAR received approval for use in US federal courts in 2012 and in the UK in 2016, demonstrating institutional acceptance of ML approaches for appropriate legal tasks.[79]

74 For a description and history of Big Data-based legal analytics programs, including Lex Machina, *see* Zsolt Zodi, *Big-Data-Based Legal Analytics Programs. What Will Data-Driven Law Look Like?*, 10 Acta Univ. Sapientiae: Legal Stud. 287 (2021).

75 *See infra* Section 7.4.2: Predicting Case Outcomes.

76 Ilias Chalkidis & Dimitrios Kampas, *Deep Learning in Law: Early Adaptation and Legal Word Embeddings Trained on Large Corpora*, 27 A.I. & L. 171, 173–74 (2019).

77 *See generally* Richard Susskind, The Future of Law: Facing the Challenges of Information Technology 239–52 (1996). For a fuller discussion of document automation, *see infra* Chapter 8: Document Automation.

78 Maura R. Grossman & Gordon V. Cormack, *Technology-Assisted Review in E-Discovery Can Be More Effective and More Efficient than Exhaustive Manual Review*, 17 Rich. J.L. & Tech. 1 (2011).

79 Da Silva Moore v. Publicis Groupe, 287 F.R.D. 182 (S.D.N.Y. 2012); Pyrrho Investments Ltd v. MWB Property Ltd [2016] EWHC 256 (Ch).

Compliance and Risk Management tools emerged to help organizations navigate complex regulatory environments. These systems could track changes across vast bodies of regulations and identify compliance risks using ML approaches that could monitor evolving legal standards continuously. Financial institutions, healthcare providers, and multinational corporations began using AI systems to maintain compliance with frameworks such as the General Data Protection Regulation ("GDPR") and anti-money laundering laws.[80]

5.3.5 *Limitations and Challenges*

Despite their demonstrated potential to improve efficiency in specific legal tasks, Second Wave systems faced significant limitations that constrained their broader adoption. The most fundamental challenge was the "black box" problem. While complex algorithms could achieve impressive predictive accuracy, they often could not provide explanations for their decisions. This became particularly problematic in the legal domain, where transparency in decision-making is crucial for professional and ethical reasons.[81]

Data quality issues also posed significant challenges. The effectiveness of ML systems depended heavily on the quality and representativeness of their training data.[82] In many cases, the legal data used to train predictive models was incomplete, imbalanced, or reflected historical biases, leading to AI tools that were either ineffective or systematically biased. The lack of standardization in legal data further complicated training processes, which required consistent, structured inputs to function effectively.

Professional skepticism represented another major barrier to adoption. As noted by Branting in 2017, the predictive capabilities of AI systems were impressive; however, these models still lacked the ability to articulate legal arguments or justify legal decisions in the way a human lawyer might. The legal profession's emphasis on precedent, justification, and reasoned argument created natural resistance to "opaque" algorithmic decision-making that could not be explained or defended in traditional legal terms.[83]

Institutional resistance also played a significant role in limiting adoption. Many legal organizations, particularly traditional or conservative firms, were reluctant to

80 David Freeman Engstrom et al., Government by Algorithm: Artificial Intelligence in Federal Administrative Agencies (2020), https://perma.cc/P8D7-K2QQ.

81 *See infra* Section 7.3: Interpretable and Explainable Machine Learning.

82 Edwina L. Rissland, *Artificial Intelligence and Law: Stepping Stones to a Model of Legal Reasoning*, 99 Yale L.J. 1957 (1990); Marc Lauritsen, *Technology Report: Building Legal Practice Systems with Today's Commercial Authoring Tools*, 1 A.I. & L. 87 (1992). *See also infra* Section 7.4.2: Predicting Case Outcomes (discussing data quality challenges in legal prediction).

83 Branting, *supra* note 62; *see generally* Cathy O'Neil, Weapons of Math Destruction: How Big Data Increases Inequality and Threatens Democracy (2016).

adopt technologies that threatened to disrupt established workflows or replace tasks that lawyers had previously performed. Legal ethics and data privacy concerns further complicated integration efforts, as firms worried about inadvertently violating confidentiality agreements or misusing sensitive client information through large-scale data aggregation.[84]

Finally, a disconnect persisted between AI research capabilities and the demands of actual legal practice. While Second Wave systems demonstrated impressive performance on specific tasks, many remained limited in scope, addressing routine activities like document review rather than the complex reasoning and judgment that characterize much legal work. As some scholars noted, despite enthusiasm among academics and technologists, many AI tools still lacked the sophistication required to perform the nuanced interpretive work that lawyers routinely engage in.[85]

5.3.6 *Bridge to the Third Wave*

The Second Wave laid crucial foundations for the future evolution of AI and Law. The period's experiences highlighted both the potential of data-centric approaches and the persistent need for explainability in legal applications. This growing recognition that legal AI systems needed to combine the scalability of ML with the transparency of logical reasoning pointed toward the hybrid approaches that would characterize the Third Wave.

The development of increasingly sophisticated NLP capabilities, particularly the emergence of LLMs discussed in Chapter 4, began to offer new possibilities for addressing the explainability challenge that had previously limited Second Wave systems.[86] These advances suggested that future AI systems might provide both accurate predictions and legally meaningful explanations, combining the best elements of data-centric and logic-based approaches.

As Branting suggested, the future of legal AI likely rested with hybrid systems that could leverage ML's pattern recognition capabilities while incorporating the structured reasoning and justification that legal practice demands.[87] The Second Wave's emphasis on practical effectiveness and scalability, combined with growing awareness of the need for transparency and explainability, set the stage for more sophisticated approaches that would attempt to bridge the gap between computational power and legal reasoning.

The increasing availability of legal datasets, the maturation of ML techniques, and the growing commercial interest in legal technology, evidenced by the emergence

84 *See* Model Rules of Pro. Conduct r. 1.6 (confidentiality), r. 5.5 (unauthorized practice).

85 Oskamp & Lauritsen, *supra* note 10.

86 *See infra* Section 7.2.1: Machine Learning in Natural Language Processing.

87 Branting, *supra* note 62, at 11; L. Karl Branting, *Artificial Intelligence and the Law from a Research Perspective*, 14 SciTech Law. 32 (2018).

of hundreds of legal tech companies during this period, created an ecosystem ready for the next wave of innovation.[88] The challenge moving forward would be developing systems that could harness the demonstrated capabilities of data-centric approaches while addressing the explanatory requirements that remained essential for meaningful integration into legal practice.

5.4 THIRD WAVE (LATE 2010S–PRESENT)

Legal practice demands something unique from AI: not just accuracy, but accountability. When an AI system recommends a legal strategy, summarizes a contract, or predicts a case outcome, lawyers need to understand *why* and be able to explain that reasoning to clients, opposing counsel, and judges. Legal work requires transparency, adherence to established rules and precedents, and the ability to provide reasoned justifications – qualities that distinguish it from many other professional domains.

This recognition has led many scholars and technologists to advocate for "hybrid AI" approaches that combine the clarity and normative reliability of logic-based systems with the adaptability and processing power of ML.[89] In this vision, AI systems would mirror how lawyers actually work: applying formal rules and precedents while drawing insights from patterns in large volumes of cases and documents. The legal domain, which demands both principled reasoning and practical scalability, seems ideally suited for such integration.

Yet the reality of legal AI today tells a different story. While the aspiration for hybrid systems has inspired important research and some commercial tools, most widely deployed legal AI applications rely almost exclusively on LLMs and statistical approaches. These systems excel at generating fluent legal text and processing vast amounts of information quickly, but they operate through statistical associations rather than legal reasoning. They cannot explain their outputs in terms of applicable law, precedent, or established legal principles.

The notion of a "Third Wave" of legal AI, characterized by the integration of logic-based and data-centric methods, draws considerable inspiration from Karl Branting's work. For example, in his 2017 article, Branting articulated the limitations of both traditional logic-based systems and purely statistical models while proposing a hybrid framework that draws on the strengths of each. Logic-based systems, he explained, can mirror the rule-governed nature of legal discourse and offer explainability through deductive inference, but they are hampered by practical

[88] As of 2025, the Stanford CodeX Legal Tech Index listed over 3,000 companies providing AI-driven legal services. *See CodeX TechIndex*, STAN. L. SCH., https://perma.cc/FA5V-WLKH.

[89] *See, e.g.*, A. Sakshi et al., *Emerging Trends in Hybrid Information Systems Modeling in Artificial Intelligence, in* HYBRID INFORMATION SYSTEMS (Ramakant Bhardwaj et al. eds., 2024).

challenges in rule formalization and the evaluation of open-textured legal concepts in natural language. By contrast, data-centric systems offer scalability and adaptability through pattern recognition in large corpora yet tend to be opaque and poorly suited for tasks requiring argumentation, justification, or normative reasoning. Branting thus proposed a synthesis: a model that "exploits the complementarity" of symbolic and empirical techniques to enable automated legal reasoning that is both scalable and intelligible.[90]

Branting's hybrid model does not envision a single architecture or technology stack, but rather a conceptual framework for matching the right tools to the right legal tasks. For instance, statistical methods may be well-suited to predictive tasks such as estimating litigation outcomes or parsing document structure, whereas rule-based models may be more appropriate for tasks that demand fidelity to legal norms, such as generating justifications or applying codified law. This pluralist framework foreshadowed what this chapter proposes as the "Third Wave" of legal AI: systems that integrate formal legal knowledge with ML to emulate more closely the actual practice of legal reasoning.[91] In a 2018 follow-up piece, Branting emphasized that the future of AI and Law would depend on bridging the technical, institutional, and linguistic divides between legal formalism and computational scalability.[92]

However, the trajectory of legal AI development since Branting's prescient analysis reveals how challenging this bridge-building has proven to be. While some systems have attempted genuine integration of symbolic and statistical approaches, many others have pursued the path of least resistance: deploying LLMs that can process legal text fluently without grappling with the deeper challenges of legal reasoning, explainability, or normative grounding. The result thus far is a legal AI ecosystem that embraces hybrid ideals in theory while remaining fragmented and often opaque in practice, with significant implications for how AI can and should serve the legal system.

5.4.1 *Technological Foundations*

The Third Wave emerged from the convergence of several technological developments that began in the 2010s, well before the public breakthrough of systems like ChatGPT. Early advances in deep learning, particularly recurrent neural networks ("RNNs") and long short-term memory ("LSTM") networks, demonstrated superior performance in legal text processing tasks.[93] These neural architectures could better

[90] Branting, *supra* note 62, at 6–7.
[91] *Id.* at 24–25.
[92] Branting, *supra* note 87.
[93] *See, e.g.*, Ilias Chalkidis & Dimitrios Kampas, *Deep Learning in Law: Early Adaptation and Legal Word Embeddings Trained on Large Corpora*, 27 A.I. & L. 171, 178 (2018).

capture the sequential and contextual nature of legal language compared to earlier statistical methods.

A crucial innovation was the development of semantic vector spaces specifically adapted for legal concepts. Unlike general-purpose language models, these systems could represent legal relationships – such as the hierarchical structure of statutory law or the analogical connections between cases – in mathematically tractable forms.[94] Knowledge graphs emerged as another key technology, allowing AI systems to explicitly represent legal concepts, their relationships, and their evolution over time.

Finally, the transformer revolution of the late 2010s provided the architectural foundation for the most dramatic Third Wave advances. Transformer-based models like BERT and GPT demonstrated unprecedented capabilities in natural language understanding and generation.[95] Legal applications quickly followed, with domain-specific models like LamBERTa (a BERT-based model designed for Italian legal texts) showing how these general-purpose architectures could be adapted for legal language processing.[96]

These technological advances seemed to point toward a future where AI could combine the best of both worlds: the scalability and pattern recognition of ML with the transparency and rule-based reasoning that legal practice demands. Yet, as we will see, the path from technological capability to practical legal application has proven far more complex than these early advances suggested. The tools that could enable hybrid AI exist, but building systems that lawyers can trust and courts can accept remains an ongoing challenge.

5.4.2 A *Spectrum of Hybridization in Recent Research*

A review of recent publications in AI and Law reveals a spectrum of integration between symbolic and statistical methods. This suggests that while fully hybrid AI systems remain underdeveloped, there is increasing experimentation with hybrid architectures and layered approaches. Rather than a uniform adoption of "hybrid AI," the legal AI field is advancing through a diverse array of combinations that vary in degree, purpose, and conceptual alignment with the hybrid paradigm.

One of the clearest examples of intentional hybrid architecture is found in recent work on sentence boundary detection ("SBD") for legal texts. The study combines deep learning models, including domain-specific transformer architectures like

94 Serena Villata et al., *Advances in Legal Knowledge Representation*, 30 A.I. & L. 565, 573 (2022).

95 Jacob Devlin et al., *BERT: Pre-training of Deep Bidirectional Transformers for Language Understanding*, Proc. NAACL-HLT 4171, 4171 (2019).

96 Andrea Tagarelli & Andrea Simeri, *Unsupervised Law Article Mining Based on Deep Pre-Trained Language Representation Models with Application to the Italian Civil Code*, 29 A.I. & L. 1 (2022).

LegalBERT, with a statistical conditional random field ("CRF") model. By embedding the output of a convolutional neural network ("CNN")-based deep learning model into the CRF, the researchers created a pipeline that integrates statistical sequence modeling with contextual neural representations, resulting in a 4% F1-score improvement over the baseline. This is a concrete instantiation of hybrid AI, not just in design but in performance gains, demonstrating how symbolic or statistical models can be enriched by neural methods rather than replaced by them.[97]

A more implicit form of integration is observed in legal judgment summarization research, which combines structural and semantic features of legal texts using different models for distinct document sections. Here, the symbolic structure of legal judgments, such as the tripartite division into facts, rationale, and verdict, is leveraged to inform the use of semantic summarization models like Lawformer. While not symbolic reasoning in the traditional AI sense, this method introduces a modular architecture that assigns different NLP tools to sub-tasks based on document structure, approximating the logic-driven segmentation that a rule-based system might impose.[98]

Other studies reinforce the continued relevance of symbolic logic in areas where statistical learning still struggles. For example, recent research on modeling legal precedents introduces a factor-based approach that explicitly accommodates multiple interpretations of legal cases and seeks to reconcile inconsistent precedents using formal reasoning frameworks.[99] These efforts to extend legal logic models show that the symbolic side of AI is far from obsolete – especially in domains like precedent reasoning, where legal norms, not patterns in data, define correctness. Similar motivations underlie work exploring deontic logic in the context of inconsistent precedent bases, reinforcing the idea that explainable, rule-grounded reasoning remains vital in legal contexts.[100]

Even models that appear purely data-driven often involve human-in-the-loop or modular strategies that hint at emerging hybrid norms. A two-stage classification system for legal petitions in Brazil, for instance, combines transformer-based feature extraction with a downstream support vector machine ("SVM") classifier, incorporating human-curated annotations during training to localize relevant text segments. This setup not only reflects a technical layering of models but also reflects the hybrid ambition to ground statistical performance in domain-specific legal understanding.[101]

[97] Reshma Sheik et al., *Legal Sentence Boundary Detection Using Hybrid Deep Learning and Statistical Models*, 33 A.I. & L. 519 (2024).

[98] Jingpei Dan et al., *Enhancing Legal Judgment Summarization with Integrated Semantic and Structural Information*, 33 A.I. & L. 271 (2023).

[99] Adam Rigoni, *Toward Representing Interpretation in Factor-Based Models of Precedent*, 33 A.I. & L. 199 (2024).

[100] Ilaria Canavotto, *Reasoning with Inconsistent Precedents*, 33 A.I. & L. 137 (2023).

[101] Yuri D. R. Costa et al., *Automating Petition Classification in Brazil's Legal System: A Two-Step Deep Learning Approach*, 33 A.I. & L. 227 (2023).

Taken together, these articles suggest that "hybrid AI" in law is not a monolithic or fully realized methodology, but rather a direction of travel. While many current systems remain dominated by large-scale statistical models, a growing number of implementations leverage legal structure, logical formalism, or modular integration to bridge the divide between statistical power and symbolic clarity. This heterogeneity should temper overly optimistic claims about the state of hybrid AI, but it also shows that the field is actively grappling with the hybrid ideal in increasingly sophisticated ways.

5.4.3 *Hybrid AI in Applied Legal Technology*

While academic experiments continue to push the boundaries of hybrid models, several applied systems in commercial legal technology already exemplify key aspects of hybrid AI. These tools demonstrate how logic-based reasoning, structured legal knowledge, and statistical modeling can work together in real-world settings.

IBM Watson Discovery combines NLP capabilities with a legal knowledge graph. Legal professionals can pose complex queries, and Watson retrieves relevant documents using NLP, then filters and organizes results through a structured network of legal sources. The system's reliance on a knowledge graph enables traceability, allowing users to follow the AI's answer back to a cited statute or precedent.[102]

Westlaw Edge incorporates legal ontologies and citation networks into its AI-powered search functions, enabling re-ranking of results based on legal authority and topical relevance. This creates an AI that recognizes keyword similarity and prioritizes documents with higher jurisprudential weight.[103]

Hybrid e-discovery platforms combine predictive ML for clustering or prioritizing documents with symbolic tagging rules to identify privileged or confidential information. These tools support large-scale document review while retaining explainability.[104]

Academic neuro-symbolic systems for tasks like contract analysis and legal question answering illustrate cutting-edge implementations. In one model, an LLM extracts structured data from insurance policies, which is then fed into a formal logic program to determine claim eligibility. This hybrid architecture significantly outperformed either component alone.[105]

102 *IBM Watson Discovery*, IBM, https://perma.cc/A6S4-3DE7; *see also* Jaspreet Singh Dhani et al., *Similar Cases Recommendation Using Legal Knowledge Graphs*, IBM (2021), https://perma.cc/5DWQ-54MR.

103 *Westlaw Edge – AI-Powered Legal Research*, THOMSON REUTERS, https://perma.cc/4XSC-XRFB.

104 *See, e.g.*, *Tagging Along with AI: The Powerful Simplicity of Logikcull's "Suggested Tags,"* LOGIKCULL, https://perma.cc/KF4A-P4QP.

105 Manuj Kant et al., *Equitable Access to Justice: Logical LLMs Show Promise*, ARXIV 1 (Oct. 13, 2024), https://perma.cc/54Y6-UN6X.

These examples demonstrate that hybrid AI is becoming a reality. Yet they also reveal the limits of current implementations: the symbolic components often require heavy upfront investment and domain-specific tuning, making pure LLM models more attractive for general-purpose tasks. The legal tech industry is blending these paradigms, but full hybridization remains uneven across domains and vendors.

5.4.4 *Limitations and Challenges*

Despite its promise, hybrid AI in the legal domain faces several structural and technical challenges. First, building and maintaining the symbolic components of hybrid systems, such as expert rules, ontologies, or knowledge graphs, remains labor-intensive and requires ongoing domain expertise. While ML can scale efficiently with data, symbolic systems often require manual updates to reflect legal changes, jurisdictional nuances, or evolving standards of interpretation.

Second, integration itself can be non-trivial. Bridging symbolic and statistical systems requires careful architectural design to ensure that the outputs of one component are usable by the other. In many systems, this means mapping unstructured text to structured representations that symbolic components can understand. This task often depends on natural language understanding techniques that remain error-prone in complex legal language.

Third, while hybrid systems aim for explainability, this goal can be undermined if the statistical parts of the system dominate decision-making. For example, if a hybrid e-discovery tool relies heavily on clustering algorithms but only lightly incorporates legal tagging rules, the symbolic reasoning may not meaningfully constrain or justify the system's outputs. Thus, true explainability requires not just the presence of symbolic logic, but its genuine integration into the reasoning process.

Fourth, hybrid systems can raise challenges for reproducibility and validation. Because they often involve complex pipelines with multiple layers of inference and transformation, tracing the provenance of a given legal output can be difficult, especially when statistical elements include opaque neural networks. This is particularly problematic in high-stakes legal contexts where decisions must be justified, audited, and defended.

Finally, the uneven pace of development across the legal AI ecosystem means that hybrid models may be infeasible for smaller firms or public institutions lacking the resources to build or adopt such tools. As large tech providers push forward with proprietary hybrid solutions, questions of accessibility, standardization, and ethical deployment remain unresolved.

In sum, while hybrid AI represents a compelling vision for the future of legal technology, reconciling the strengths of formal reasoning with the scalability of data-driven methods, it also presents real barriers to widespread and equitable adoption.

Overcoming these challenges will require not only technical innovation but also institutional commitment to transparency, interpretability, and interdisciplinary collaboration.

5.4.5 *Primarily Generative Approaches*

While the vision of hybrid AI has inspired both research and commercial development, it is also important to acknowledge that many of the most widely used legal AI tools today are not hybrid in any meaningful sense. Instead, they rely almost exclusively on LLMs or statistical ML approaches, with little or no integration of formal legal knowledge or symbolic logic.

These systems, such as GPT-based legal chatbots, contract review platforms, and legal summarization tools, excel at parsing natural language and generating fluent, seemingly coherent legal text. Their appeal lies in their flexibility and speed: they can be trained on large corpora of legal documents and quickly deployed to handle tasks like answering legal questions, drafting contracts, or extracting clauses. However, their outputs are generated through statistical associations rather than logical inference, and they generally do not provide explanations grounded in legal reasoning or authoritative sources.

Despite their limitations, these non-hybrid tools have gained significant traction in the legal market, in part because they are easier to develop, require less domain-specific knowledge engineering, and can be adapted to a wide range of use cases with minimal customization. Their popularity highlights a pragmatic trade-off: while they may lack transparency and normative rigor, they often deliver usable results faster and at a lower cost than fully hybrid systems.

One of the most visible recent developments is the rise of AI "agents," which are systems that attempt to simulate legal reasoning through multi-step or multi-role workflows.[106] These tools chain together multiple AI operations, allowing users to query legal databases, generate document summaries, and apply legal rules through orchestrated interactions. A legal agent might research a client's question by first identifying relevant statutes, then finding related cases, and then drafting a summary that synthesizes the findings. While these agents are often marketed as enhancing explainability or supporting legal reasoning, in reality their operations depend almost entirely on the same statistical language models that power simpler AI tools.

Despite offering structured outputs, agent-based systems are vulnerable to the same opacity and unpredictability that characterize their constituent models.

[106] Emily Hamilton, *2025 Is the year of AI agents, OpenAI CPO Says*, Axios (Jan. 23, 2025), https://perma.cc/R6B8-7F3T; *see, e.g.*, Li Zhang & Kevin D. Ashley, *Mitigating Manipulation and Enhancing Persuasion: A Reflective Multi-Agent Approach for Legal Argument Generation*, arXiv 1 (June 3, 2025), https://perma.cc/NN37-6VFG.

Studies show that chain-of-thought prompting, while useful for generating stepwise answers, often produces reasoning that is more narrative than logically sound.[107] As a result, even well-performing agents may produce convincing but unfounded explanations – an effect known as rationalization rather than reasoning. In high-stakes legal contexts, this can be particularly dangerous, as it may lead users to over-trust outputs that appear deliberate but lack grounding in legal norms or verifiable precedent.

These challenges have particular significance for access to justice. Generative AI tools are becoming increasingly accessible to smaller firms, solo practitioners, and legal aid organizations that serve low-income clients. In principle, this democratization of AI capabilities could help address the justice gap by making sophisticated legal analysis more affordable and accessible. A rural lawyer could use AI to research complex federal regulations, while a legal aid attorney could use AI to quickly analyze hundreds of housing court cases for patterns of landlord violations.

However, the opacity of current generative AI systems means that the clients who most need reliable legal representation – those who cannot afford multiple attorneys or extensive appeals – may be most vulnerable to AI errors. A wealthy client whose AI-assisted lawyer makes a mistake might have resources to pursue other remedies, but a low-income tenant facing eviction might not. The promise of AI democratizing legal services could become a reality of two-tiered justice: sophisticated hybrid AI for those who can afford transparent, explainable systems, and opaque generative AI for everyone else.

The market has responded to these limitations with increasingly sophisticated commercial tools that attempt to bridge the gap between basic generative AI and the transparency lawyers need. Platforms like Harvey AI, adopted by major law firms, including Paul Weiss, represent a new category of legal-specific AI systems that combine LLMs with legal workflow management, firm-specific training, and enhanced security features.[108] These tools go beyond generic AI assistants by incorporating legal document templates, firm precedents, and practice-specific workflows. A partner using Harvey might receive not just a contract draft, but one that follows firm style guidelines, incorporates standard clauses from the firm's precedent library, and flags potential issues based on the firm's prior experience.

However, while these enhanced platforms represent a significant step forward in user experience and reliability, they remain fundamentally generative rather than hybrid systems. Harvey and similar tools are essentially sophisticated wrappers around statistical language models. They may be trained on legal-specific data and

[107] Yanda Chen et al., *Reasoning Models Don't Always Say What They Think*, ARXIV 1 (2025), https://perma.cc/9RC8-B6WZ.

[108] *Paul, Weiss Partners with Harvey on New AI Workflows Innovation*, HARVEY (June 11, 2025), https://perma.cc/XD5A-PMPV.

integrated with legal workflows, but they still generate outputs through pattern recognition rather than formal legal reasoning. They cannot explain why a particular contract clause is legally appropriate beyond statistical associations in their training data, nor can they engage in the kind of rule-based analysis that would constitute genuine legal reasoning. This represents an important middle ground: they are more sophisticated and legally oriented than generic AI tools, yet they still fall short of the hybrid ideal that would combine statistical power with symbolic legal knowledge.

Recent research has begun to explore more structured agent architectures that incorporate knowledge graphs, symbolic rule modules, or case-based reasoning.[109] These neuro-symbolic agents aim to tether LLM-generated reasoning to explicit legal standards, creating systems that not only simulate legal workflows but also enforce legal coherence. Yet these are early-stage efforts, and most commercially available agents still lack persistent memory, formal rule representation, or genuine analogical reasoning. Thus, while legal AI agents represent a major step forward in interface design and workflow automation, they are best understood as scaffolding rather than substitutes for true legal reasoning.

This trend underscores the tension at the heart of legal AI today between the normative aspirations of hybrid reasoning and the commercial incentives driving rapid deployment of LLM-based tools. As regulatory and professional standards evolve, the legal community will need to grapple with how, and whether, non-hybrid systems can be trusted in roles that affect legal rights, obligations, and outcomes.

5.4.6 *A Fourth Wave?*

Some researchers and technologists have begun to speculate about a possible "Fourth Wave" of legal AI – one defined less by new model architectures than by deeper integration between humans and machines. In this emerging vision, AI tools do not merely assist or automate discrete legal tasks; they become embedded collaborators in the legal workflow, supporting reasoning, dialogue, and judgment in more seamless and dynamic ways.

This trend is visible in the design of hybrid systems that foreground transparency and human control. Rather than replacing legal professionals, such systems aim to augment human decision-making by handling information overload, surfacing relevant authorities or clarifying rule applicability while preserving space for human interpretation and normative evaluation. The emphasis shifts from automation to alignment: tools are judged not only by their predictive accuracy but by how well they support legal reasoning and deliberation.

[109] Kant et al., *supra* note 105.

Whether this evolution marks a distinct "Fourth Wave" or a maturing Third Wave remains to be seen. What is clear is that the future of legal AI lies in systems that are not only powerful and scalable but also interpretable, participatory, and consistent with legal values.

5.5 CONCLUSION

Today's legal AI tools can draft contracts, review thousands of documents for litigation, and predict case outcomes with impressive accuracy – capabilities that would have seemed like science fiction in the 1980s. But getting here required confronting a fundamental challenge: law is simultaneously systematic and subjective, rule-based and interpretive, precedent-bound and constantly evolving. Three generations of developers have approached this paradox from different angles, first attempting to encode legal rules into logical systems, then mining patterns from vast legal databases, and now combining both approaches. Each generation learned from its predecessors' limitations, gradually abandoning dreams of fully automated legal reasoning in favor of tools that could handle specific, practical tasks. The result is a technology that excels at some aspects of legal work while struggling with others, revealing as much about the nature of law as it does about the limits of computation.

The First Wave's logic-based systems demonstrated both the appeal and the limitations of attempting to reduce legal reasoning to formal rules. While these systems succeeded in narrow, well-defined domains like protection order eligibility, they ultimately revealed that legal analysis involves far more than applying rules to facts. The ambiguity of legal language, the contextual nature of legal interpretation, and the adversarial character of legal practice all resisted capture in formal logic. Yet this wave established a crucial principle: legal AI systems must be able to explain and justify their conclusions in ways that align with legal reasoning.

The Second Wave's embrace of machine learning and data-centric approaches achieved remarkable gains in efficiency and scalability. Systems could now process vast legal corpora, identify patterns invisible to human analysis, and automate document-intensive workflows. However, the "black box" problem limited their adoption for tasks requiring transparency and accountability. This wave taught us that while statistical pattern recognition has immense value for certain legal tasks, the legal profession's demand for explanatory reasoning cannot be ignored.

The Third Wave represents an ongoing attempt to synthesize these lessons through hybrid approaches that combine the transparency of logic-based systems with the power of machine learning. The vision is compelling: AI systems that can both process legal information at scale and provide reasoned explanations grounded in legal principles. Yet the reality of current implementation reveals a more complex picture. While some systems genuinely integrate symbolic and statistical approaches, many of today's most widely deployed legal AI tools, including sophisticated platforms like Harvey AI, remain fundamentally generative rather than hybrid. They excel at producing fluent legal text but cannot engage in genuine legal reasoning or provide explanations rooted in formal legal knowledge.

This gap between aspiration and implementation has profound implications for access to justice. The democratizing potential of AI to make legal services more affordable and accessible remains real, but it comes with risks. If transparent, explainable hybrid systems remain expensive and complex while opaque generative tools proliferate in legal aid and small practice settings, we risk creating what Drew Simshaw calls "two-tiered systems" where the least trustworthy AI tools serve those who most need reliable legal representation.[110]

[110] Drew Simshaw, *Access to A.I. Justice: Avoiding an Inequitable Two-Tiered System of Legal Services*, 24 YALE J.L. & TECH. 150, 156 (2022).

6

Computational Logic

*L. Karl Branting, Aniket Kesari, and Chinmayi Sharma**

6.1 INTRODUCTION

While recent discourse around AI and Law has centered on data-driven applications such as large language models ("LLMs"), an earlier and still important subset of AI exists: computational logic in the law.[1] This technology has the potential to revolutionize how we engage with the legal system, including in ways that can dramatically improve access to justice.

While the law can sometimes feel ambiguous, relying on difficult-to-define concepts like "the reasonable person" or "intermediate scrutiny," many legal rules are clear and logical. These scenarios exhibit what we call "computational structures": legal processes that can be systematically broken down into clear decision points and if–then rules that a computer can process. For example, determining tax liability, zoning compliance, or eligibility for certain benefits or protections all have computational structures because they follow defined rules that lead to predictable outcomes based on specific inputs. Computational logic takes these clear, structured rules and translates them into precise instructions, or code, that a computer can execute.[2]

Think of it as encoding the law into a series of if–then statements: if a certain fact is true, then a specific legal outcome necessarily follows. A simple example in the context of housing and eviction law might be: If a tenant has lost income due to a pandemic and has provided proper documentation, then they may be protected from eviction for nonpayment of rent. By systematically walking tenants through these rules, computational logic could help individuals understand their rights and defenses against eviction, offering immediate assistance in critical situations.

* We thank Kevin D. Ashley for his review of multiple drafts of this chapter.

[1] Marek J. Sergot et al., *The British Nationality Act as a Logic Program*, 29 COMMC'NS ACM 370, 371 (1986).

[2] One key distinction that can be made is between data-centric and logic-based models. Whereas logic-based models use these structured rules directly, data-centric models attempt to use statistical inference to infer legal rules. *See* L. Karl Branting, *Data-Centric and Logic-Based Models for Automated Legal Problem Solving*, 25 A.I. & L. 5, 6–7 (2017).

What makes this technology particularly exciting is its potential to break down barriers to justice. At its core, the problem is twofold. First, the law is not self-executing; it requires interpretation and application. Legal rules are often written in complex language, full of technical jargon and cross-references, making them nearly impossible for a person without legal representation to fully understand, let alone use effectively to vindicate their rights.[3] The numbers are staggering: unrepresented litigants are far more likely to lose their cases compared to those with lawyers.[4]

Second, the cost of legal representation is exorbitantly high for many people. Hiring an attorney can easily run into thousands or even tens of thousands of dollars, even for relatively straightforward cases. This makes justice inaccessible to large portions of the population, particularly low-income individuals, who are often the ones most in need of legal protection. Unrepresented litigants are left to navigate a legal labyrinth without guidance, often leading to unfavorable outcomes simply because they do not know how to effectively present their cases.[5]

However, the law need not be so inaccessible. Many areas of law, such as tax, property, housing, and family law, lend themselves well to computational logic because they involve processes that follow clear, structured rules.[6] By encoding these rules into technology, we can create tools that help people understand and navigate the law without needing expensive legal assistance.

Imagine a tenant facing eviction who can enter their circumstances into an accessible online system. That system could walk them through their potential legal defenses, such as the right to a moratorium on evictions due to financial hardship, by asking simple, clear questions. When combined with other AI tools, the system could generate a legal argument based on the tenant's responses, guiding the tenant through the necessary steps to assert their rights.

By integrating computational logic into user-friendly software, we can empower individuals to engage directly with the legal system. This approach not only reduces costs but also opens a path for ordinary people to protect their rights effectively, especially in critical areas like housing, where the consequences of legal issues can be life changing.[7] In this way, computational logic offers a powerful tool to address one of the most persistent challenges in the legal field: access to justice.

3 *See* Sarah Lawsky, *Coding the Code: Catala and Computationally Accessible Tax Law*, 75 SMU L. Rev. 535, 538–40 (2022).

4 *See* Sande L. Buhai, *Access to Justice for Unrepresented Litigants: A Comparative Perspective*, 42 Loy. L.A. L. Rev. 979, 985 (2009).

5 *See id.* (showing unrepresented litigants had greater difficulty not only in understanding and applying the finer points of the substantive law but even in conceptualizing the key claims or defenses of their case).

6 *See, e.g.*, Symbium, *A Stanford-Led Team Is Enabling Instant Permits by Automating the Legal Analysis of Building Codes with 100% Accuracy*, Medium (Sep. 16, 2024), https://perma.cc/Q2GN-9N69.

7 *See* Philip Sales, *Algorithms, Artificial Intelligence, and the Law*, 105 Judicature 22, 24 (2021).

This chapter explores the role of computational logic in the legal system, with a particular emphasis on how it can level the playing field for individuals who might otherwise be left without legal assistance. It begins by introducing the concept of computational logic and explaining how it works in the context of AI. It then examines its applications across various legal domains, such as tax law, zoning regulations, and protection orders, showing how these rule-based systems can simplify complex legal tasks. Next, it delves into the ways computational logic improves access to justice by making legal processes more transparent and affordable. However, no technology is without its challenges, so the chapter also looks at the limitations of these systems, including their rigidity and potential biases. Finally, it considers how advances in AI, coupled with smart legal reforms, could make computational logic even more powerful in improving the accessibility and fairness of the legal system.

By the end of this chapter, it should be clear that computational logic is not just a relic of early AI; it is a powerful tool that has the potential to reshape the legal landscape and expand access to justice for all.

6.2 WHAT IS COMPUTATIONAL LOGIC?

At its core, computational logic is about transforming human rules, like legal statutes, into a format that can be processed and applied by a computer. Through interactions with the computer, these rules and their application are then made accessible to unrepresented litigants. The simplest form of computational logic involves encoding the law into a series of "if–then" statements: if a certain fact is true, then a specific legal outcome follows. This structure allows for decision-making based on straightforward, binary inputs, often involving "yes" or "no" answers. However, computational logic can handle more complex scenarios too, where the inputs may not be binary but fall within a predefined range of acceptable responses. These responses could be imagined as a dropdown menu, with all relevant answers carefully considered during the system's design.

The first key component of computational logic is the code itself: how the law is translated into computational instructions. The law is often more rigid in certain areas, where legal outcomes depend on a fixed set of conditions. For example, in eviction law, the system could be programmed to check whether a tenant's rights have been violated under local housing codes. A system might ask questions like, "Has the landlord provided adequate notice for eviction?" or "Did the tenant notify the landlord of necessary repairs?" These queries represent logical checkpoints: each response determines the next step in the process, similar to an attorney going through a checklist of facts needed to meet the legal threshold for a defense.

The second component is the interface: the means through which users interact with the system. For computational logic to be truly effective, it requires a user-friendly interface that makes the process of entering information as simple as possible for non-experts. The system then generates an output, such as a recommendation or a legal document, that reflects the user's legal position based on the facts they provided. For example, the system could produce a document advising a tenant that they may be able to argue that their landlord failed to maintain habitable conditions in their home, which could serve as a defense against eviction based on the tenant's responses to the system's questions.

To illustrate how computational logic might work in a real-world legal scenario, consider the case of a tenant facing eviction for nonpayment of rent. Many states allow tenants to raise a defense against eviction if the landlord has failed to make necessary repairs, such as fixing a broken heater during winter. The following sample interaction demonstrates how a computational logic system might guide a tenant through this process:

CLIENT: My landlord is evicting me.
SYSTEM: Why is your landlord evicting you?
CLIENT: I stopped paying the rent.
SYSTEM: Why did you stop paying the rent?
CLIENT: The heater in my place broke, and it's been really cold.
SYSTEM: Did you tell your landlord about the heater by certified mail?
CLIENT: No.
SYSTEM: Did you talk to your landlord about the heater?
CLIENT: Yes, they told me to deal with it.
SYSTEM: How long ago did you notify your landlord?
CLIENT: Over a month ago.
SYSTEM: Did your landlord do anything to fix the heater?
CLIENT: No.
SYSTEM: Then you may have satisfied the requirements for a defense against your eviction. The judge will decide.

Based on these responses, the system could provide a recommendation: "You might be able to stop the eviction. You appear to meet the requirements for the defense of the breach of the implied warranty of habitability. Tell the judge that your landlord failed to repair a safety-related defect after you notified them, which might help you stay in your home." It might also provide the tenant with a list of resources, such as phone numbers for legal aid or forms for filing an action in housing court.

6.2.1 *The Code*

Prolog is one of the earliest and most influential systems based on computational logic and shows some of the basic mechanics of these systems. The heart of any computational logic system is the inference engine, which processes the user's inputs and applies legal rules to generate conclusions. This process is driven by

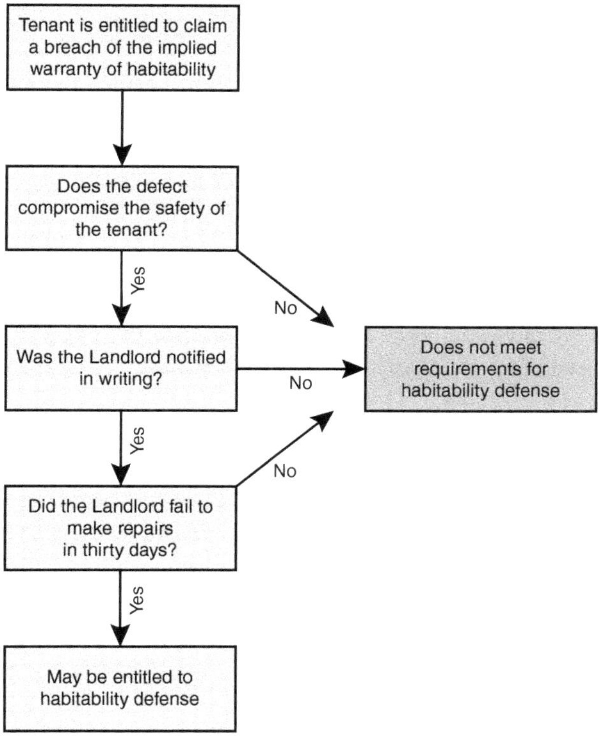

FIGURE 6.1 Decision tree working backward from the conclusion.

if–then statements that mirror legal rules. The design of a Prolog system begins by translating a legal rule, such as the conditions under which a tenant is entitled to a habitability defense, into a decision tree.[8]

The decision tree in Figure 6.1 is built by starting with the legal conclusion at the top, for example, "Tenant is entitled to claim a breach of the implied warranty of habitability," and working downward.

At a high level, we observe that there are several if–then conditions that govern the logical flow. In Prolog, each if–then statement corresponds to a specific point in the decision tree. The "if" parts of the statement ascertain the relevant facts: Did the tenant notify the landlord about the defect? Was the defect severe enough to affect the safety of the premises? Did the landlord fail to repair the defect within a reasonable time? And the "then" part concludes whether the tenant meets the legal standard. For example, the Prolog system might include rules such as: **If** the defect compromises the tenant's safety, **and** if the landlord was notified in writing, **and if**

[8] WILLIAM F CLOCKSIN & CHRISTOPHER S. MELLISH, PROGRAMMING IN PROLOG 3 (5th ed. 2003).

the repairs were not made within 30 days, **then** the tenant has a valid defense under the habitability law.

By breaking down the law into a series of questions, Prolog helps to create a logical framework in which the conditions for a legal rule are tested and met (or not), based on the user's inputs. In Prolog, the logic for a system guiding a tenant through an eviction case could look as follows. Lines that start with the percent sign ("%") are notes, not code.

```
% Base facts and rules for habitability defense
% Rule: If defect compromises safety, landlord
% was notified, and landlord failed to repair in 30 days
habitability_defense(Safety, Notified, Repair) :-
    Safety == yes,
    Notified == yes,
    Repair == no.
% Rule: Habitability defense fails if conditions not met
% Note: Prolog would typically cover this rule without
  having to define it but it is shown to illustrate the
  example
habitability_defense(Safety, Notified, Repair) :-
      (Safety == no; Notified == no; Repair == yes),
      fail.
% Helper predicates
compromises_safety(Defect, yes) :- Defect == yes.
compromises_safety(_, no).
notified_landlord(Notification, yes) :- Notification ==
yes.
notified_landlord(_, no).
failed_repair(Timeline, no) :- Timeline == no.
failed_repair(_, yes).
% Example queries:
% ?- habitability_defense(yes, yes, no).
% true.
% ?- habitability_defense(no, yes, no).
% false.
```

This sample code would produce a decision tree like Figure 6.2. This approach enables the system to follow a comprehensive decision tree that covers scenarios in which the habitability defense applies. In both Figures 6.1 and 6.2, each node on the tree is a question about a relevant fact, and each branch represents a possible answer, ultimately determining whether the tenant can proceed toward the legal conclusion.

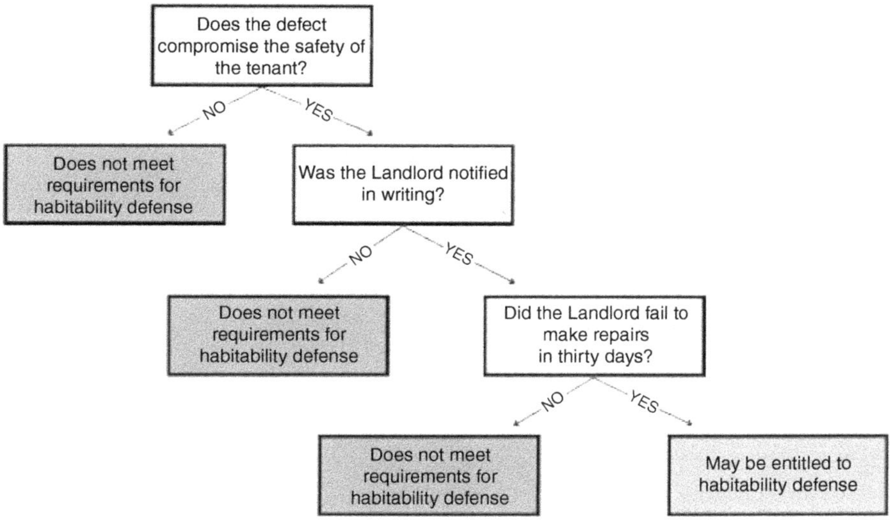

FIGURE 6.2 Logical progression of user questions leading to a legal conclusion.

Once legal rules have been converted from the original text into a computational logic representation, they can be used to reason about how the rules would apply to facts provided by a litigant. This reasoning can be performed by a Prolog interpreter, which is a computer program that can read Prolog rules and answer questions based on those rules. An unrepresented litigant can then access the system through an interface that works from the bottom up through the decision tree, as shown in Figure 6.1. From the user's perspective, the process works in reverse: the system begins by asking factual questions to gather relevant information. These questions start at the top of the decision tree and work downward toward the legal conclusion.

For example, a tenant facing eviction for nonpayment of rent might start by responding to a series of questions such as:

- Why did you stop paying rent?
- Did you notify your landlord about the defect?
- How long ago did you notify your landlord?
- Did your landlord attempt to repair the issue?

Each question corresponds to a point on the decision tree, and depending on the user's response, the system moves along a specific path. If the user's responses match the conditions in the decision tree, they continue moving upward, getting closer to the legal conclusion that they may be entitled to a habitability defense.

However, if the user's response does not satisfy one of the conditions, for example, if they did not notify the landlord about the defect, the system will determine that they cannot proceed further on that particular path. This means that the user is effectively "off" the decision tree, and the system may conclude that they do not meet the requirements for the habitability defense.

6.2.2 *Limitations*

While computational logic systems like Prolog can be powerful tools for guiding users through legal rules, they have significant limitations. Although one of the key strengths of computational logic is its ability to distill complex legal questions into a series of simple, manageable queries,[9] computational logic is less effective when legal issues require interpretation or involve a high degree of ambiguity.[10] Laws are not always clear-cut; they often hinge on subjective terms or require nuanced understanding, which can make it difficult for computational systems to function effectively. For example, terms like "reasonable," "substantial," or "good faith" often appear in legal statutes but are inherently ambiguous. In these instances, human interpretation is typically necessary to make sense of these legal standards, and computational logic struggles to account for this ambiguity. Put differently, questions such as "Was your workplace environment hostile or abusive?" admit a wide range of possible answers, and the follow-up questions needed to elicit sufficient detail are too numerous to be captured by a series of if–then statements. For an employee filing a harassment claim, this lack of flexibility could mean that the system misses critical nuances, like the context of behavior or the cumulative effect of multiple incidents, leaving them without the full legal support they need to pursue their claim.

One key limitation is that these systems are most effective when applied to legal problems with clear computational structures and are only as good as the rules they are programmed to follow.[11] A Prolog system relies on structured, predictable inputs: clear yes/no answers or choices from a predefined set of responses. This works well when the law is clear and applies to a narrow set of factual scenarios.

Prolog is just one of many computational logic languages, and a Prolog interpreter is just one type of "inference engine," that is, an algorithm for reasoning with computational logic. Another example is the advent of "no-code" applications.[12] No-code applications can improve the design of interfaces for computational logic systems. These platforms enable developers to create software using graphical interfaces instead of traditional programming code. By designing applications through flowcharts and decision trees, no-code applications simplify the creation of user-friendly, intuitive interfaces that reflect the underlying legal logic. These applications can

9 *See* Lawsky, *supra* note 3, at 555.

10 *See* Kevin D. Ashley, Artificial Intelligence and Legal Analytics: New Tools for Law Practice in the Digital Age 38 (2017).

11 Subarna D., *Prolog-Programming: Features and Disadvantages*, Eng'g Notes, https://perma.cc/VA6P-A8SS.

12 Cheyenne Kolosky, *What is No-Code?: Understanding No-Code Development*, Knack (Mar. 30, 2024), https://perma.cc/32SL-YDFX.

be easily customized and iterated based on user feedback, making them a valuable tool for building accessible and effective legal interfaces without requiring extensive coding expertise. As projects become more complex, no-code applications may not be the right tool when goals include flexibility and depth, among others.

However, real-life legal situations are often more complex than can be captured by even the most flexible or sophisticated decision tree. The range of possible responses to certain questions can be too vast or ambiguous to be captured by simple if–then statements. For instance, if a tenant's response is that they notified the landlord verbally rather than in writing, but there was an informal agreement about repairs, the Prolog system might fail to account for this nuance. As a result, the system could prematurely conclude that the tenant is not entitled to a habitability defense, even though, under certain circumstances, a human attorney might argue otherwise.

This inherent limitation of Prolog systems means that users could be misinformed about their legal rights if the system fails to consider specific factual details or nuances that fall outside the rigid structure of the decision tree. Therefore, it is crucial that any Prolog-based legal system include caveats and disclaimers. The system's outputs should clearly state that while the user may not meet the requirements under the rules as defined in the system, there could be other legal avenues or mitigating circumstances that the system is not equipped to consider.

For example, the system might conclude: "Based on the information provided, it appears you do not qualify for a habitability defense. However, there may be other factors or legal arguments that a lawyer could assess more thoroughly."

The inference process described earlier shares some similarities with the way an attorney might reason about whether a client is entitled to a particular defense. An attorney would typically consider the elements required for a habitability defense and would ask about facts to determine whether each of these elements would be satisfied under the client's story.

Figure 6.3 shows schematically a general model of a legal advisor based on computational logic. Legal text, such as the rules for obtaining a protection order, is manually translated by the system implementer into a logical representation that an inference engine can use to provide answers to queries posed by a user. This model is a kind of Platonic ideal in which the rules, once they have been represented as logic, need no interpretation to guide problem solving other than a completely generic inference engine like the Prolog interpreter.

6.2.3 *The Interface*

A computational logic legal system is only as effective as the interface through which users interact with it.[13] The interface serves as the crucial communication

[13] Oliver R. Goodenough & Preston J. Carlson, *Words or Code First? Is the Legacy Document or a Code Statement the Better Starting Point for Complexity-Reducing Legal Automation?*, 382 PHIL. TRANS. R. SOC'Y A 3 (2024).

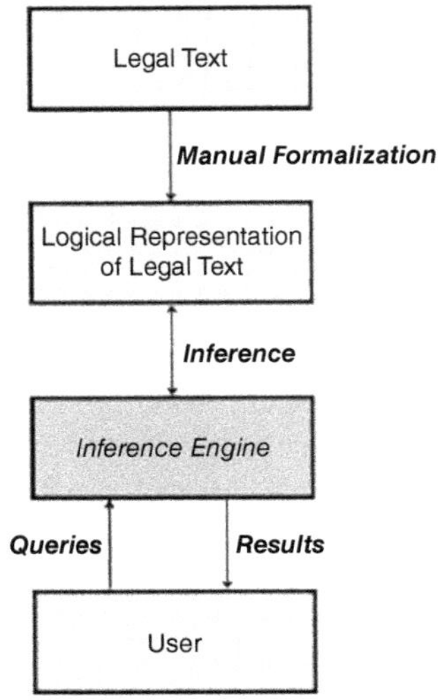

FIGURE 6.3 An architecture for a legal advisor based on computational logic. Republished with permission from the MITRE Corporation.

bridge between the person seeking legal help and the AI-powered system. Its design is vital in making the system accessible and intuitive, particularly for people without legal expertise. A well-designed interface has two primary functions:

1. Soliciting Information: It gathers the relevant information from the user in a format that the system needs to make accurate legal decisions.
2. Providing Explanations: It delivers clear and understandable explanations of the system's decisions, including both positive explanations (why a user qualifies for a legal remedy) and negative explanations (why they do not qualify).

If access to justice is limited because the law is difficult to comprehend or navigate, a computational logic system intended to solve this problem cannot itself be difficult to understand or use. The interface should not simply rely on computational logic but must also be designed with a focus on user experience, ensuring seamless communication between the user and the system. This is particularly important in sensitive legal situations, such as intimate partner violence or domestic abuse, where individuals often have urgent and critical legal needs but limited access to justice.

Consider the example of a person seeking a protection order in a domestic abuse case. For example, in many jurisdictions, a person ("Petitioner") can obtain a protection order against another person ("Respondent") if the Petitioner can show that there is an intimate or domestic relationship with the Respondent and that the Respondent has committed or threatened violence or abuse.[14] The requirement of an intimate or domestic relationship is satisfied by having had a child with Respondent or having had "a sexual relationship within one year," and the violence or abuse requirement is satisfied by child abuse or threats that create fear of imminent, serious bodily harm.[15]

As the following sample interaction demonstrates, a system that contained just these rules could answer simple questions and engage in a dialogue that could be helpful to someone with limited knowledge of the requirements for a protection order:

CLIENT: I want to keep my ex-boyfriend away from me.
SYSTEM: Has the person threatened you or put you in fear of imminent, serious bodily harm?
CLIENT: Yes.
SYSTEM: Have you had a child with the person?
CLIENT: No.
SYSTEM: Have you had a sexual relationship with the person within the last year?
CLIENT: Yes.
SYSTEM: Then you may have satisfied the requirements for a protection order. The judge will decide.

In Prolog, this logic could look as follows:

```
% Base facts and rules for determining eligibility
% for a protection order
% Rule: Eligible for protection order if there is a
% threat and either a child or recent sexual
% relationship exists
protection_order(Threat, Child, Relationship) :-
 Threat == yes,
 (Child == yes; (Relationship == yes)).
% Example queries:
?- protection_order(yes, no, yes).
true.
?- protection_order(yes, no, no).
false.
```

[14] 25 AM. JUR. 2d *Domestic Abuse and Violence* §§ 8–10 (2025); *see also* Lisa V. Martin, *The Importance of Civil Pathways to Protection Orders*, 113 GEO. L.J. 121, 131 (2024); *see, e.g.*, MD. CODE ANN., FAM. LAW §4-506 (LexisNexis 2022).

[15] *See supra* note 14; *see generally* L. Karl Branting, *Data-Centric and Logic-Based Models for Automated Legal Problem Solving*, 25 A.I. & L. 5 (2017) (elaborating on this vignette in detail).

In terms of the litigants' needs discussed in the previous section, this system elicits case facts, for example, "Has the person threatened you or put you in fear of imminent serious bodily harm?" until it has acquired sufficient facts to support a prima facie case for the relief that the client seeks or until it has no more rule conditions to ask about. If the facts do not support one rule, that is, "Have you had a child with the person?," the system tries another, that is, "Have you had a sexual relationship with the person within the last year?"

The interface plays a critical role here. It must ask these questions in a way that is sensitive, clear, and appropriate for someone in a vulnerable and possibly traumatic situation. It should avoid legal jargon and present the questions in simple, comprehensible terms, while also ensuring that the responses it gathers align with the legal requirements embedded in the system's computational logic.

Moreover, the interface should give users the right level of control. For instance, should the system allow free-form text answers, or should it rely on predefined options like checkboxes or dropdown menus? Free-form text may provide more nuanced responses but can complicate the system's ability to process the information, while dropdown menus can restrict user input but offer greater precision. A computational logic system, without the help of additional forms of AI, is less likely to be able to parse long text responses to determine whether they satisfy the conditions in the decision tree.[16]

Other design choices involve how to elicit relevant facts from the user. Should a user interface simply allow a user to type a free response narrative and then use some other system to extract the relevant facts? Or should a user click radio buttons for all facts that apply? Or perhaps the system should help the user work through the if–then logic themselves and provide facts one at a time? Or should the system allow users to select the relevant facts first by toggling among different scenarios and thereby locking them into one decision path? These choices all have important implications for the eventual computation because they can directly influence user behavior.

In situations where users are seeking a protection order, the system can avoid directly asking whether the user was in "fear of imminent harm," which is a legal standard, or even whether they "felt threatened," a subjective question that may be hard to answer, by instead guiding the user through a series of specific questions about abusive behaviors or circumstantial factors that legally qualify as putting someone in "fear of imminent harm." For instance, the system could ask whether the alleged abuser made repeated threats, displayed violent behavior in the past, has access to weapons, has mental health conditions, has control over the user's finances or other important documents, has damaged property, or has a history of substance abuse. However, it is important that the system make clear that this

16 Maryna Dorash, *Machine Learning vs. Rule-Based Systems in NLP*, Medium (Dec. 26, 2017), https://perma.cc/DY7J-XC5V.

list of behaviors is not exhaustive and that users are not required to select only one answer. The system should allow users to select as many behaviors as apply because, in many cases, a combination of factors such as ongoing threats, substance abuse, and a history of violence may meet the legal standard for "fear of imminent harm," even if no single factor would be sufficient on its own. This approach ensures that the system is flexible enough to capture the full context of the user's situation, while guiding them with clarity and empathy, especially during times of emotional distress.

Another critical role of the interface is in providing explanations for the system's decisions. Users need to understand not just what the system concludes but *why* it arrived at that conclusion. This is critical both to satisfy principles of due process and to reduce the risk of misunderstanding, miscommunication, or missing information – errors that, if left unaddressed, could affect a user's entitlement to legal privileges or protections. Explanations fall into two categories:

1. *Positive Explanations*: These explain why the system determined that the user meets the legal requirements. For instance, "You might qualify for a protection order because you had an intimate relationship with the person and showed they could harm you." Positive explanations should ideally map out which of the user's answers contributed to a positive finding.
2. *Negative Explanations*: These are especially important when the system determines that the user does *not* meet the legal standard. In such cases, the system should not only say, "You do not qualify for a protection order," but also explain why: "You do not qualify for a protection order because the law only gives protection for threats from the last six months."

These explanations should be sensitive to the user's situation. In domestic abuse cases, for example, an explanation that is too brief or overly technical could leave the user feeling confused or unsupported. Explanations that offer actionable next steps can provide clarity and comfort.[17] For example, suggesting the user seek legal advice and directing them to pro bono legal services available close by.

As mentioned earlier, it is also essential for the interface to include disclaimers that clarify the system's limitations. A computational logic system cannot account for every possible circumstance. For example, a system might determine that someone does not meet the requirements for a protection order based on the facts they input, but there could be other facts the system did not ask about that would change the outcome. The interface should communicate this clearly, perhaps stating something like, "Based on the information provided, you do not qualify for a protection order. However, there may be other factors or legal avenues that a lawyer

[17] Margaret Hagan, *Measuring What Matters: Developing Human-Centered Legal Q-and-A Quality Standards through Multi-Stakeholder Research* (Dec. 1, 2024), https://tinyurl.com/mv6b9pdy.

could help you explore." And the system could provide them with resources for local pro bono legal aid.

6.3 HOW IS COMPUTATIONAL LOGIC DIFFERENT FROM DATA-DRIVEN AI?

Many recent advances in AI and Law have been based on machine learning ("ML") approaches, a subset of artificial intelligence that enables systems to automatically learn from and improve with experience without being explicitly programmed. While these approaches share some similarities with computational logic, the key difference lies in their methodology. ML models, such as random forests, neural networks, and, more recently, LLMs, may also use if–then structures to make predictions or decisions.[18] However, the critical distinction is how these if–then rules are generated. In computational logic systems, the rules are designed by human experts who use their domain knowledge to build the system's logic in advance. In contrast, ML uses data-adaptive techniques (methods, algorithms, or systems that can automatically adjust their parameters or behavior based on the specific characteristics of the input data they are processing) to infer patterns and rules from large datasets.[19]

This difference in methodology has two significant implications for access to justice. First, ML requires vast amounts of data to function effectively. This can be problematic in areas of law where large datasets are unavailable or difficult to obtain, which limits the applicability of ML in certain legal contexts. Second, the rules produced by ML are not always intuitive to humans. While one of the strengths of ML is its ability to uncover hidden or non-obvious relationships in data, this can lead to decision-making processes that seem counterintuitive or opaque to users.[20] This lack of transparency and interpretability may hinder access to justice, as it becomes harder for individuals, especially those without formal legal training, to understand or challenge decisions made by ML models.

In contrast, computational logic systems are effective even with little or no data, and can be purposely designed to align with human reasoning and legal principles. Because these systems rely on the encoding of an expert's knowledge rather than on data, they can be designed to reflect the logical structure of the law itself. This makes computational logic particularly useful for certain types of legal applications where clarity, simplicity, and fidelity to the law are crucial for expanding access to justice. Users can follow the system's decision-making process step by step, making

[18] Karin Kelley, *What Is Machine Learning? A Comprehensive Guide for Beginners*, Caltech Blog (Feb. 12, 2024), https://perma.cc/6KW7-XSK5.

[19] *Id.*

[20] Saurabh Bagchi, *What Is a Black Box? A Computer Scientist Explains What It Means When the Inner Workings of AIs Are Hidden*, The Conversation (May 22, 2023), https://perma.cc/K86G-YTG2.

it easier to explain legal problems and options, especially to people with limited legal knowledge or education. These systems are inherently auditable, which gives users the ability to challenge errors or inconsistencies.

Computational logic systems offer a distinct advantage in their ability to be modified when laws change, allowing legal experts to update the underlying rules to reflect new standards.[21] For example, when states revise their eligibility criteria for public benefits to exclude prior marijuana convictions, a computational logic system's decision tree can be readily adjusted to reflect this change, removing what was previously a disqualifying factor from the sequence of if–then statements. Similarly, when jurisdictions modify their eviction procedures, such as by extending notice periods from 30 to 60 days, the computational rules can be updated with the new timeframe. This flexibility allows for the rapid implementation of legal changes, ensuring that individuals receive current and accurate guidance. ML models, on the other hand, require retraining with updated data whenever new legal precedents arise. This retraining process can be time-consuming and costly, and it may not always yield understandable changes in the model's behavior. For people seeking justice, the inability to easily adapt or modify a ML system in response to new information can create barriers to legal recourse.[22]

However, this adaptability is also a double-edged sword: while the systems can be modified, they must be actively maintained and updated to remain accurate. Without regular review and updates, these systems risk providing outdated advice that could harm rather than help individuals seeking legal assistance. This maintenance burden is particularly challenging in areas of law that change frequently or vary significantly by jurisdiction, requiring constant vigilance and resources to keep the systems current.

However, computational logic is not a one-size-fits-all tool. Some legal problems are better addressed with data-driven approaches. Tasks such as algorithmic auditing, fraud detection, and early intervention in legal processes can benefit from ML's ability to handle complex, high-volume data. Similarly, LLMs offer new ways of analyzing and interpreting legal texts at scale. The choice between ML and computational logic ultimately depends on the specific goals of the legal task at hand.

6.4 APPLICATIONS OF COMPUTATIONAL LOGIC IN LAW

There are already several examples of computational logic used in law, including for protection orders and housing rights, as discussed earlier. Some of these systems

[21] Hamish Fraser & Tom Barraclough, *Governing Digital Legal Systems: Insights on Artificial Intelligence and Rules as Code*, MIT COMPUTATIONAL L. REP. (Oct. 14, 2024), https://perma.cc/ZQQ6-AMC4.

[22] L. Karl Branting, *Data-Centric and Logic-Based Models for Automated Legal Problem Solving*, 25 A.I. & L. 5, 17–18 (2017).

are designed with consumer needs in mind, while others focus on modeling legal codes and statutes to aid lawyers, judges, and legal scholars. Still others are oriented toward question-answer systems that aim to expand access to justice by providing legal guidance directly to those who may not have access to traditional legal representation. These systems can play a critical role in simplifying legal complexities and making legal processes more transparent for the public.

Perhaps the most familiar example of computational logic that people encounter is computational versions of the US tax code. Several consumer products, such as TurboTax and H&R Block, use a form of computational logic to assist users in preparing their tax returns.[23] These systems translate the complicated tax code into a series of guided questions, allowing users to file their taxes accurately without needing to understand the intricate legal language of federal, state, and local tax codes. Another example is Catala, a specialized programming language designed to formalize the US tax code.[24]

The tax code is particularly well-suited to computational approaches because the majority of filers have relatively simple taxes. A handful of if–then statements can help users determine whether to take the standard deduction or explore other deductions. More broadly, the US tax code exhibits clear computational structures with well-defined rules and exceptions, which makes it an ideal candidate for computational systems. For example, all income may be taxable, but if the income came from an inheritance, it is not taxable unless the inheritance exceeds a certain limit (about $13 million at the time of writing), in which case the excess amount is taxable.

Similarly, computational logic can be highly effective in navigating complex regulatory frameworks like local zoning laws, which often feature clear if–then rules. For instance, a city may zone certain areas for single-family dwellings, but buildings older than 50 years may be "grandfathered in" and exempt from this restriction. One example of a computational logic zoning technology is Symbium, an application designed to help users visualize and understand whether specific permits are possible at their address.[25] For example, a homeowner might want to build an accessory dwelling unit ("ADU") but be unsure whether zoning laws require a parking space for the new structure. This type of question can be modeled computationally by checking the local regulations on parking spaces per residence, determining whether ADUs are permissible, and then verifying whether ADUs are subject to the same parking requirements or have different regulations.

Importantly, these systems not only assist consumers but also enhance transparency and consistency in the application of laws. By automating the application of

[23] Michael Genesereth, Prof., Stanford University, Presentation at the Stanford University CodeX FutureLaw Conference: *The Cop in the Backseat: Embedding Law in Everyday Life* (May 2015).

[24] Lawsky, *supra* note 3, at 537–38.

[25] SYMBIUM, https://perma.cc/V7Q2-CN7C.

legal rules, computational logic can reduce the risk of human error and help ensure that laws are interpreted consistently, helping both legal professionals and the public better understand their legal rights and obligations.

6.5 OPPORTUNITIES

Access to justice is often hindered by numerous barriers, including high legal fees, limited awareness of available legal services, language obstacles, and logistical difficulties in obtaining representation.[26] Computational logic addresses these challenges by simplifying legal processes and making them more accessible to the general public, especially to unrepresented litigants. By breaking down complex legal rules into clear, understandable steps, computational logic empowers individuals to navigate legal systems more efficiently, reduces the cost and reliance on professional legal representation, and helps make the justice system more inclusive and equitable.

6.5.1 *Reducing Legal Costs*

One of the most immediate ways computational logic improves access to justice is by reducing legal costs. As a baseline matter, getting any amount of legal advice involves paying attorneys hundreds of dollars; if individuals cannot afford an attorney, they may be unable to determine whether they are entitled to a defense against their eviction or a protection order.[27] An AI system leveraging computational logic could help inform them about their rights and the likelihood of success based on their specific circumstances before they decide to hire counsel.

But also, many legal processes, such as filling out forms, gathering necessary documentation, or determining eligibility for legal remedies, can be automated using logic-based AI systems. These systems guide individuals through legal procedures step by step, providing support that lawyers traditionally offer. For example, Suffolk University Law School's Document Assembly Line Project, profiled in Section 13.6, leverages Docassemble, which uses computational logic to assist people in preparing necessary legal documents.[28] By answering a series of if–then questions, users can ensure they have all the required paperwork for their case, eliminating the need to hire a lawyer

[26] Natalie Anne Knowlton et al., *Paths to Justice: Identifying Barriers to Equity in the Justice System*, INST. FOR THE ADVANCEMENT OF THE AM. LEGAL SYS. 1 (Feb. 22, 2022), https://perma.cc/TEP5-KUN4.

[27] LEGAL SERVS. CORP., THE JUSTICE GAP REPORT: THE UNMET CIVIL LEGAL NEEDS OF LOW-INCOME AMERICANS 9 (2017), https://perma.cc/T4M8-US9P.

[28] Suffolk University Law School, *Introduction to the Document Assembly Line*, SUFFOLK LIT LAB, https://perma.cc/5NCH-NFAU.

for routine tasks. While document preparation and assembly can be complicated, it is fundamentally a structured problem that lends itself to codified rules. By guiding people through the structure, they can access the court, administrative agencies, and other legal institutions capable of providing relief in common situations.

6.5.2 *Increasing Efficiency and Speed*

Computational logic also increases efficiency by automating time-consuming legal tasks, allowing individuals to get answers to their legal questions much faster.[29] Unrepresented litigants who might otherwise spend weeks or months trying to understand complex legal language can use computational logic systems to get immediate guidance. This efficiency not only benefits individuals but also reduces strain on legal systems, allowing them to handle cases more swiftly and to allocate resources to more complex issues that require human oversight. For instance, a system that helps tenants understand whether their landlord has unlawfully withheld a security deposit can deliver a clear answer within minutes by walking the user through the relevant legal criteria.

6.5.3 *Clarity of Rules and Transparency in Decision-Making*

Another significant advantage of computational logic is that it promotes clarity and transparency. Legal rules, especially when applied in a court or administrative setting, can often feel opaque to the general public.[30] Computational logic breaks down these rules into understandable, logical steps, helping users comprehend the decisions made about their cases. Proof trees generated by computational logic systems can visually map out the reasoning behind a decision, showing how specific facts relate to legal rules. For example, a system designed to assess whether someone qualifies for a protection order can link facts like the nature of the relationship and the presence of a threat to legal standards, making the reasoning behind the decision clear and easy to follow. This transparency builds trust in the system and helps users better understand their rights and responsibilities.

Clarity can also help reduce overhead for the legal system as a whole. The more efficiently people can get answers to their legal questions and navigate legal services themselves, the less they need to rely on lawyers and courts to do the same work. Of course, computational logic cannot supplant the legal work of human beings entirely but can instead act as a supplement for everyday problems that have computational structures.

[29] Chay Brooks, Cristian Gherhes & Tim Vorley, *Artificial Intelligence in the Legal Sector: Pressures and Challenges of Transformation*, 13 Cambridge J. Regions, Econ. & Soc'y 135, 137 (2020).

[30] *See* Stephanos Bibas, *Transparency and Participation in Criminal Procedure*, 81 N.Y.U. L. Rev. 911 (2006).

6.5.4 *Ability to Experiment with Legal Theories*

A benefit of computational logic is that it allows users to test or experiment with legal theories before formally presenting them in court. For example, a user could input different factual scenarios into the system to see whether their claim might be successful. This feature enables individuals to explore various legal strategies without the cost or risk of hiring a lawyer prematurely. A tenant could, for example, input the details of a situation involving a landlord dispute, changing facts to see what legal remedies might be available if the circumstances were different. This kind of experimentation empowers users to better prepare their cases or determine whether it is worth pursuing legal action at all.

6.5.5 *Consistent Application of the Law*

Computational logic also allows for consistency in the application of the law. Human decision-makers, such as judges, can be influenced by unconscious biases, emotions, or external factors. A computational logic system, however, applies legal rules consistently, ensuring that similar cases have similar outcomes. Consistency is especially important for marginalized groups who may face bias or unequal treatment in traditional legal settings. By removing some of the variability in decision-making, computational logic promotes fairness and can help reduce discriminatory outcomes in the justice system.

6.5.6 *Language and Disability Inclusiveness*

Computational logic systems can also be more inclusive of different languages and disabilities. Access to translation and accessibility resources in the judicial system has been a longstanding problem.[31] Many computational logic systems can be designed to operate in multiple languages, making legal guidance available to people who speak languages other than English. Additionally, these systems can be adapted for users with disabilities, ensuring that legal processes are accessible to individuals who may have difficulty reading or hearing. For example, a system could provide text-to-speech functionality for individuals with visual impairments or could incorporate sign language interpretation for users who are deaf.

6.5.7 *Collecting Data for Systemic Improvement*

Computational logic systems can also collect and analyze data on how users interact with the system, offering valuable insights into trends in the law. For instance, these systems can track common issues faced by tenants in eviction cases or patterns

[31] *See* Laura K. Abel, *Language Access in the Federal Courts*, 61 Drake L. Rev. 593 (2013).

in family law disputes, which could inform legal reform or policy changes. By gathering information on how and why people seek legal remedies, these systems can help researchers and policymakers better understand the challenges faced by certain populations and craft more targeted resources.

6.6 CHALLENGES

While computational logic systems offer significant potential for improving access to justice, they also face important constraints and challenges that must be carefully considered. These limitations range from technical hurdles in implementing rule-based systems to broader concerns about the appropriate role of automation in legal decision-making. Understanding these challenges is crucial not only for developing more effective computational logic tools but also for ensuring they are deployed responsibly and ethically in legal contexts. This section examines several key limitations that currently affect the implementation and effectiveness of computational logic in expanding access to justice.

6.6.1 *Amorphous Legal Concepts*

Computational logic legal systems can lack nuance. They are built around a rigid structure of if–then statements that capture specific legal rules and exceptions. While this structure works well in highly procedural areas of law, such as tax law or zoning codes, it struggles with the nuances of human communication and non-standard facts that often arise in legal cases. For instance, legal concepts such as "reasonableness" in tort law or "*mens rea*" (the intent to commit a crime) in criminal law are inherently subjective and depend on a variety of factors that cannot be neatly codified into a computational system. The sheer number of relevant variables makes it difficult, if not impossible, to predefine every possible scenario in a decision-tree format.

6.6.2 *Accuracy and Misleading Information*

Even in areas where computational logic works relatively well, it is never perfectly accurate. There are always outlier facts or anomalous situations that might still be legally relevant but are difficult to predict or account for in a system that relies on predefined logic. For example, a system assessing eligibility for a protection order might miss an unusual but critical fact that a human lawyer would catch, such as lesser-known sociocultural behavioral norms in a minority community that affect the degree to which an individual is put in imminent fear of harm. Even with systems equipped with disclaimers, users may over-rely on the apparent objectivity of the computer's output, potentially to their detriment. This "veneer of objectivity" can mislead users into believing that the system's conclusions are final or absolute, when in fact the system may have overlooked critical nuances.[32]

6.6.3 *Rigidity*

One of the major advantages of computational logic systems is their ability to apply the law consistently, ensuring that similar cases receive similar outcomes. However, the flip side of consistency is a lack of adaptability. Additionally, legal processes often require human discretion and empathy. Judges may consider personal narratives, life circumstances, or the broader context of a case to reach a just outcome, even when the formal legal requirements are not fully met. Computational logic lacks the flexibility to adapt to these human factors, leading to the rigid application of legal rules that may not serve the interests of fairness or justice.

6.6.4 *Perpetuating Unjust Laws*

Relatedly, computational logic systems will universally apply the law, regardless of whether the law itself is fair or just. This can lead to the widespread enforcement of laws that may perpetuate injustice. For example, if a system is designed to automate evictions based on nonpayment of rent, it may not consider the broader social context, such as a global pandemic or local housing crisis, that might lead a human judge to halt the eviction in the interest of equity. This issue becomes particularly problematic in areas of law where systemic bias may be baked into the rules, such as sentencing guidelines or immigration law.[33] More access to biased laws does not create more justice; it can simply spread injustice more widely and consistently.

6.6.5 *Need for Constant Updates*

A key challenge for computational logic systems is keeping them up to date with the latest legal standards. Whether through legislative amendments, new judicial rulings, or evolving administrative guidelines, laws change frequently, and a system that is not kept up to date can quickly become inaccurate or irrelevant. Maintaining the accuracy of such systems requires substantial resources and ongoing attention, which poses a practical limitation on their widespread adoption.

[32] Artue Klingbeil et al., *Trust and Reliance on AI – An Experimental Study on the Extent and Costs of Overreliance on AI*, 160 COMPUT. HUM. BEHAV. 1, 1 (2024).

[33] *See* Max M. Schanzenbach & Emerson H. Tiller, *Reviewing the Sentencing Guidelines: Judicial Politics, Empirical Evidence and Reform*, 75 U. CHI. L. REV. 715, 722 (2008); Fatma E. Marouf, *Implicit Bias and Immigration Courts*, 45 NEW ENG. L. REV. 417, 422–23 (2011).

6.6.6 *Lack of Counterfactual Reasoning*

One of the most significant limitations of computational logic is its inability to offer counterfactual reasoning.[34] In many legal cases, individuals need to understand not only why they do not qualify for a legal remedy but also what circumstances would need to change for them to qualify. Human lawyers are skilled at providing this kind of feedback, explaining to a client, for example, "If your relationship with the person had ended more recently, you might qualify for a protection order." Computational logic systems struggle to produce such alternative legal outcomes, leaving users without a clear path forward or guidance on how to adjust their situation to better meet legal standards.

6.6.7 *Unauthorized Practice of Law Restrictions*

Finally, there are concerns about whether the use of AI for legal services constitutes the unauthorized practice of law ("UPL"). The American Bar Association ("ABA") and state bar associations regulate the legal profession to ensure that only qualified individuals provide legal advice.[35] Some computational logic systems, particularly those marketed to the general public, have raised red flags in certain jurisdictions because they were found to have crossed the line into providing legal advice without oversight from licensed attorneys.[36] As these technologies evolve, there will need to be clear guidelines around how computational logic systems can be used in ways that comply with UPL regulations and uphold professional legal standards. For more on UPL, see Chapter 14.

6.7 FUTURE DIRECTIONS

While computational logic already plays an important role in improving access to justice, its potential lies in both expanding its capabilities and integrating it with forms of advanced AI. By addressing current limitations and incorporating new techniques, computational logic can become a more powerful tool for navigating complex legal systems and improving outcomes for individuals seeking justice.

34 Judea Pearl, *Causal Inference: Proceedings of Workshop on Causality: Objectives and Assessment at NIPS 2008*, 6 PROCEEDINGS MACH. LEARNING RSCH. 39, 39 (2010).

35 *See* MODEL RULES OF PRO. CONDUCT r. 5.5 (AM. BAR ASS'N 2024).

36 *See, e.g.*, Janson v. LegalZoom.com, Inc., 802 F. Supp. 2d 1053, 1062–65 (W.D. Mo. 2011) (finding that LegalZoom's preparation of legal documents constituted the practice of law within the meaning of Missouri's practice of law statute). *But see* Medlock v. LegalZoom.com, Inc., No. 2012-208067, 2013 S.C. LEXIS 362, at *13 (S.C. Oct. 18, 2013) (finding that LegalZoom's services "do not constitute the practice of law").

6.7.1 *Enhancing Legal Guidance with Case-Based Reasoning*

One promising avenue for the future of computational logic in law is the development of case-based reasoning. Unlike traditional computational logic, which operates solely on predefined if–then rules, case-based reasoning allows AI systems to compare the facts of a current case to past cases with known outcomes.[37] This approach could provide users with more nuanced guidance, particularly in cases where a strict application of legal rules may not immediately lead to success.[38] Specifically, this would mitigate traditional computational logic's inability to provide comprehensive explanations for negative decisions.

For instance, in an eviction case, a tenant might be denied protection under a computational logic system because they did not provide written notice to their landlord about needed repairs. However, with case-based reasoning, the system could compare this scenario to previous cases where verbal notice was accepted due to the landlord's history of neglect. The system could then offer feedback, suggesting that while the tenant may not qualify based on the strict letter of the law, they could explore arguments used in similar cases to strengthen their position. This approach mirrors the way human attorneys draw on case law and precedent to craft legal arguments and could provide unrepresented litigants with more comprehensive guidance when navigating the legal system.

Similarly, in domestic abuse cases where protection orders are sought, case-based reasoning could help users understand why their application was denied and what changes might make them eligible. For example, the system might explain, "Your protection order was denied because your last intimate contact with the respondent was more than six months ago. However, in similar cases where other forms of abuse were documented, the court has granted protection orders despite the time lapse." By comparing a user's case to similar successful ones, case-based reasoning can help litigants adjust their strategies or pursue alternative legal remedies.

Case-based reasoning would be a layer on top of the computational logic decision tree. The output of the system would be an application of the rule, as informed by the if–then conditions, but the output would be contextualized by providing comparisons to past cases with similar facts.[39]

6.7.2 *Combining Logic-Based AI and Machine Learning*

Technologically, incorporating case-based reasoning into computational logic, which traditionally relies on if–then decisions, would require moving beyond the

[37] Katie Atkinson et al., *Explanation in AI and Law: Past, Present, and Future*, 289 A.I. 1, 7 (2020).

[38] L. Karl Branting, Reasoning with Rules and Precedents, A Computational Model of Legal Analysis (1999).

[39] *See* L. Karl Branting, *Stratified Case-Based Reasoning in Non-Refinable Abstraction Hierarchies*, Ass'n Advancement A.I. Tech. Rep. 29 (1997); *see also* L. Karl Branting, *Stratified Case-Based Reasoning: Reusing Hierarchical Problem Solving Episodes*, 1 Int'l Joint Conf. A.I. Org. 384 (1995).

fixed structure of decision trees. The future of computational logic in law therefore lies in its integration with other AI techniques, particularly ML and natural language processing ("NLP") (a branch of AI that enables computers to understand, interpret, and generate human language). While computational logic excels at handling clear, structured rules, its effectiveness is limited when dealing with ambiguous or subjective legal standards. ML, by contrast, demonstrates strength in identifying patterns within large datasets and can accommodate more flexible, data-driven decision-making. By combining the transparency of computational logic with the adaptability of ML, legal systems could strike a balance between interpretable decision-making and nuanced reasoning.[40]

Consider the case of domestic abuse protection orders. A hybrid system could use logic-based AI to process rule-driven aspects, such as verifying relationship status and documenting the history of threats, while simultaneously employing ML to analyze broader patterns in domestic abuse cases. This ML component could identify less obvious risk factors or behavioral patterns that courts have historically considered when granting protection orders. The result would be more comprehensive and nuanced recommendations that maintain explainability while incorporating insights from both structured rules and historical case patterns.

This hybrid approach could also enhance accessibility for diverse user groups. By incorporating NLP capabilities, these systems could offer real-time translations and more intuitive interfaces for non-English speakers or individuals with disabilities. ML models could be trained to account for varying user experiences and communication styles, while the underlying computational logic would ensure consistent application of legal rules.

The integration of these technologies offers a path to more equitable justice. Rather than having case-based reasoning serve merely as a supplementary layer atop computational logic, a truly hybrid model would weigh insights from both processes to deliver more informed, tailored, and explainable legal guidance. This approach maintains the crucial transparency of rule-based systems while adding the flexibility needed to address complex legal situations that do not fit neatly within predefined categories.

6.8 CONCLUSION

Computational logic represents a powerful tool for expanding access to justice by making legal processes more transparent, accessible, and efficient. By translating complex legal rules into clear, actionable steps, it empowers unrepresented litigants to navigate the legal system with greater confidence. However, as this chapter

[40] *See* L. Karl Branting, *Data-Centric and Logic-Based Models for Automated Legal Problem Solving*, 25 A.I. & L. 5, 19 (2017).

has explored, there are still challenges to address, such as the rigidity of rule-based systems, the difficulty of handling ambiguous legal standards, and the need for constant updates to reflect changing laws.

Looking forward, the integration of computational logic with other AI techniques, such as ML and case-based reasoning, offers exciting potential for even more tailored and effective legal tools. Hybrid approaches that combine the clarity of logic-based AI with the adaptability of ML can provide more nuanced, data-informed guidance. As the legal landscape evolves, computational logic will continue to play a crucial role in making justice more accessible, equitable, and efficient for all.

7

Machine Learning

*L. Karl Branting, Morgan A. Gray, and Jaromir Savelka**

7.1 INTRODUCTION

A hallmark of intelligence is the ability to respond appropriately to new situations, an ability that usually depends on learning from prior experiences. It is therefore unsurprising that techniques enabling computers to learn from prior experiences have been an important topic in AI since its inception. This chapter introduces several key concepts of machine learning ("ML") with a focus on its applications in the legal domain, particularly in addressing the access to justice gap.

ML refers to several data-based computational methods that rely on data to detect patterns. Unlike symbolic AI systems, where rules must be explicitly coded, ML systems identify patterns in data and develop models that can make predictions or decisions without being explicitly programmed for the specific task. Both ML and symbolic AI have been important in AI and Law, with respective strengths and weaknesses in domains where rules are complex, outcomes depend on numerous factors, and vast amounts of textual data must be processed.

The legal domain presents unique challenges and opportunities for ML applications. Legal reasoning requires not just prediction but explanation: decisions must be justified with reference to established principles, precedents, and statutory frameworks. This requirement for interpretability shapes how ML can be effectively deployed in legal contexts. Legal jargon is specialized and nuanced, requiring ML systems to learn complex terminology and reasoning patterns.

This chapter will explore the evolution of ML in AI generally before examining its specific applications in law. We will begin with the historical context of ML in AI, tracing its development from early experiments to today's state-of-the-art language models capable of understanding and generating nuanced legal text. We will then examine various ML approaches relevant to legal applications, including supervised learning techniques that learn from labeled examples, self-learning methods that

* We thank Michael Livermore for his review of this chapter.

identify patterns without explicit guidance, neural networks that model complex relationships, and embeddings that capture the meaning of legal language.

The chapter will also address feature extraction in legal contexts, explaining how different types of information – from metadata about cases to lexical patterns in legal documents to derived features that capture legally meaningful concepts – can support prediction in legal contexts. We will give particular attention to interpretability and explainability, exploring how ML systems can provide not only predictions but also explanations that are crucial to legal reasoning.

Throughout the chapter, we will consider both the potential of ML technologies and the unique constraints of legal reasoning that shape their implementation. The goal is not simply to predict legal outcomes but to develop systems that can meaningfully support legal reasoning, enhance access to justice, and transform how legal services are delivered.

7.2 THE HISTORY OF MACHINE LEARNING IN AI

In view of learning's key role in intelligence, ML was one of the earliest areas of study in the emerging field of AI. Among the earliest learning systems was the checkers-playing program developed by Arthur Samuel in the 1950s, which improved its performance by a form of *reinforcement learning*[1] in which the current best-performing version of the program was pitted against a series of variants. When a variant won, it was promoted to be the new best-performing version; otherwise, the old version was retained. This process was repeated until the system stopped improving.[2] This approach to learning, in conjunction with vastly more computing power and a variety of clever algorithmic innovations, led almost 60 years later to AlphaZero, a program that went in mere hours from knowing nothing but game rules to being among the world's strongest players in multiple games, including chess, go, and shogi.[3]

Another important area in ML is *neural networks*, an approach to computer intelligence inspired by human neural anatomy. In 1943, neurophysiologist Warren McCulloch and logician Walter Pitts published a paper on the computing capability of a single computing unit resembling an individual human neuron.[4] A biological neuron, that is, a nerve cell in an animal's nervous system, receives excitatory and inhibitory signals from other neurons and emits signals based in part on the

[1] Ashish Kumar Shakya, Gopinatha Pillai & Sohom Chakrabarty, *Reinforcement Learning Algorithms: A Brief Survey*, 231 EXPERT SYS. APPLICATIONS 1, 2 (2023).

[2] Arthur L. Samuel, *Some Studies in Machine Learning Using the Game of Checkers*, 3 IBM J. 211, 211 (1959).

[3] David Silver et al., *Mastering Chess and Shogi by Self-Play with a General Reinforcement Learning Algorithm*, ARXIV 1, 1 (Dec. 5, 2017), https://perma.cc/RK23-QWWJ.

[4] Warren S. McCulloch & Walter Pitts, *A Logical Calculus of the Ideas Immanent in Nervous Activity*, 5 BULL. MATH. BIOPHYSICS 115, 115 (1943).

combination of the input signals.[5] The McCulloch-Pitts model, a predecessor to Rosenblatt's *perceptron*,[6] is a simplification of a biological neuron in which the output of the neuron depends only on the values of the inputs and a simple calculation – essentially just testing whether the sum exceeds a given threshold – performed on these inputs.[7]

A mathematical analysis showed that perceptrons could learn to identify patterns of inputs.[8] Suppose that each input is a numerical representation of a feature of an animal (say, the first feature was 0 if the entity had feathers and 1 if it had hair, and the second feature was 0 if it had two legs and 1 if it had 4 legs) and the output is 0 or 1 depending on the actual category of the animal (say, 0 means bird and 1 means mammal). A simple learning procedure would enable a perceptron to learn to distinguish a bird from a mammal based on examples of each. For each example in which the perceptron made a wrong prediction, the weights associated with the prediction would be adjusted to make that prediction less likely (e.g., the weight associated with the number of legs might be adjusted downward, and the weight associated with feathers vs. hair adjusted upward). There was great excitement at this development of what seemed to be a general-purpose mechanism for learning and perception.

The excitement and US government funding over perceptrons came dramatically off the rails in 1971 after Minsky and Papert demonstrated that perceptrons could learn only the simplest concepts.[9] This triggered what has been known as the first "AI Winter," a period when AI research funding was very scarce despite the development of numerous novel ML algorithms that did not have perceptrons' limitations.[10]

Development of these new ML algorithms was dominated by a *supervised learning* approach in which each algorithm is trained on a set of examples. Each example consisted of a set of features (observations, as in the example above, or disease symptoms) and a category label (e.g., the type of animal or disease). In this paradigm, the examples are divided into a training set and a smaller testing set; the accuracy of a model created from the training set can be measured by its performance on the testing set. By averaging over repeated splits between training and testing sets, one can

5 *Id.*

6 Frank Rosenblatt, *The Perceptron – A Perceiving and Recognizing Automaton (Project Para)*, *in* 85 CORNELL AERONAUTICAL LABORATORY REPORT, No. 85-460-1 (1957).

7 McCulloch & Pitts, *supra* note 4, at 120.

8 *Id.*

9 MARVIN MINSKY & SEYMOUR A. PAPERT, PERCEPTRONS: AN INTRODUCTION TO COMPUTATIONAL GEOMETRY, EXPANDED EDITION 193 (MIT PRESS ed. 1988) (1969) (Perceptrons can learn what are termed "linearly separable" concepts, i.e., those that have an orderly decision boundary between one category and another (e.g., mammal vs. bird). Even the simplest concept of the form either A or B but not both is beyond the capacity of a perceptron to learn).

10 STUART J. RUSSELL, PETER NORVIG & ERNEST DAVIS, ARTIFICIAL INTELLIGENCE: A MODERN APPROACH 24 (Pearson 3d ed. 2010).

get an improved estimate of the accuracy of the learning method. Influential learning methods developed and improved under the supervised learning paradigm during this period include decision-tree induction,[11] Bayes nets,[12] and nearest-neighbor classifiers.[13]

Two important developments in the 1980s significantly advanced the field of ML. The first was the establishment of a collection of standard databases at the University of California, Irvine, that enabled researchers around the world to directly compare the performance of algorithms on supervised learning tasks.[14] A second development was a new algorithm for training neural networks consisting of multiple layers of neurons. Such networks do not have the limitations of single-neuron perceptrons but can, in principle, learn arbitrarily complex concepts.[15]

Despite these advances in ML, the focus of AI in the 1980s and early 1990s was primarily on manually constructed "expert systems"[16] and "knowledge bases"[17] that were intended to emulate human levels of understanding and performance. Expert systems, which were typically based on the computational logic approach described in Chapter 6, could achieve levels of performance comparable to human experts in narrow domains. However, the requirement of manual engineering made such systems very expensive to build, validate, and update or to scale up to cover a broad area of expertise. Exaggerated claims about the potential of expert systems and connectionism, an approach to AI based on neural networks, led to a second AI Winter from the late 1980s through the early 1990s.[18] Although ML had little visibility during the rise of expert systems and the ensuing AI Winter, several ML applications of some legal relevance inconspicuously came into wide use. Credit card companies began using decision-tree induction and other learning algorithms to detect potentially fraudulent transactions and customers by training on known instances and non-instances of fraud.[19]

In the 2000s, dramatic improvements in the ability to store, process, and analyze large datasets created enormous hype for *Big Data*, *data science*, and *data mining*. "Big Data" referred to the new capabilities of handling very large datasets, "data

11 J. Ross Quinlan, *Induction of Decision Trees*, 1 MACH. LEARNING 81, 81 (1986).

12 Judea Pearl, *Bayesian Networks: A Model of Self-Activated Memory for Evidential Reasoning*, 7 PROC. ANN. CONF. COGNITIVE SCI. SOC'Y 329 (Technical Report CSD-850021 R-43, 1985).

13 David W. Aha, Dennis Kibler & Marc K. Albert, *Instance-Based Learning Algorithms*, 6 MACH. LEARNING 37 (1991).

14 *See* UCI MACH. LEARNING REPOSITORY, https://perma.cc/Q8Q5-W9RG.

15 David E. Rumelhart, Geoffrey E. Hinton & James L. McClelland, *A General Framework for Parallel Distributed Processing, in* PARALLEL DISTRIBUTED PROCESSING: EXPLORATIONS IN THE MICROSTRUCTURE OF COGNITION: FOUNDATIONS 35, 74–76 (1986).

16 PETER JACKSON, AN INTRODUCTION TO EXPERT SYSTEMS (2d ed. 1990).

17 DOUGLAS B. LENAT & R.V. GUHA, BUILDING LARGE KNOWLEDGE-BASED SYSTEMS: REPRESENTATION & INFERENCE IN THE CYC PROJECT (1989).

18 James Hendler, *Avoiding Another AI Winter*, 23 IEEE INTELLIGENT SYS. 2, 2–3 (2008).

19 Tom M. Mitchell, *Does Machine Learning Really Work?*, 18 AI MAG. 11, 11 (1997).

science" to techniques capable of analyzing such datasets,[20] and "data mining" to the process of extracting useful information from large datasets, often using simple statistical tools and the types of supervised learning methods that had lost prominence during the Second AI Winter.[21] See Chapter 5 for a discussion of the three waves of legal AI.

Although this may not always be true in law,[22] a remarkable theoretical observation from this period is that the size of a dataset used to train an algorithm can be more important than the quality of the algorithm itself.[23] This realization created a strong incentive to develop datasets at the scale of all the transactions of large businesses,[24] telephony,[25] and the entire World Wide Web.[26]

Concurrent with the dramatic expansion of dataset sizes, a new approach to training neural networks was developed that permits efficient training of networks with many layers and with individual processing units capable of remembering prior states.[27] The performance of this approach, referred to as *deep learning*, quickly exceeded the performance of alternative learning methods in image recognition, autonomous vehicle control, and many other domains.[28]

7.2.1 *Machine Learning in Natural Language Processing*

Because law is a largely text-driven domain, the research community has focused on natural language processing ("NLP"). When deep learning techniques, originally

[20] *See* Andrea De Mauro, Marco Greco & Michele Grimaldi, *A Formal Definition of Big Data Based on Its Essential Features*, 65 LIBRARY REV. 122, 122 (2016).

[21] *See* Xindong Wu et al., *Top 10 Algorithms in Data Mining*, 14 KNOWLEDGE & INFO. SYS. 1, 33 (2008).

[22] *See* Lucia Zheng et al., *When Does Pretraining Help? Assessing Self-Supervised Learning for Law and the CaseHOLD Dataset of 53,000+ Legal Holdings*, 18 PROC. INT'L CONF. ON A.I. & L. 159, 167 (2021) (discussing the marginal effect of domain pretraining for legal NLP).

[23] Alon Halevy, Peter Norvig & Fernando Pereira, *The Unreasonable Effectiveness of Data*, 24 IEEE INTELLIGENT SYS. 8, 12 (2009).

[24] *See, e.g.*, Yen-Liang Chen, Jen-Ming Chen & Ching-Wen Tung, *A Data Mining Approach for Retail Knowledge Discovery with Consideration of the Effect of Shelf-Space Adjacency on Sales*, 42 DECISION SUPPORT SYS. 1503, 1503 (2006) (developing data mining schemes to discover relationship between relative spatial distance of displayed products and items' unit sales in retail stores).

[25] *See, e.g.*, Nathan Eagle & Alex (Sandy) Pentland, *Reality Mining: Sensing Complex Social Systems*, 10 J. PERS. & UBIQUITOUS COMPUTING 255, 255 (2006) (collecting data from 100 mobile phones to measure information access and use in different contexts and recognize social patterns).

[26] *See, e.g.*, Adam Kilgarriff & Gregory Grefenstette, *Introduction to the Special Issue on the Web as Corpus*, 29 COMPUTATIONAL LINGUISTICS 333, 333 (2003) (discussing scientists and technologists' increasingly turning to the Web as a source of language data).

[27] YOSHUA BENGIO, Ian Goodfellow & Aaron Courville, DEEP LEARNING 18 (2015).

[28] *See, e.g.*, Jia Deng et al., *Imagenet: A Large-Scale Hierarchical Image Database*, PROC. IEEE CONF. COMPUT. VISION & PATTERN RECOGNITION 1 (2009) (discussing the effectiveness of deep learning in image recognition); Mariusz Bojarski, *End to End Learning for Self-Driving Cars*, ARXIV 1, 1 (Apr. 25, 2016), https://perma.cc/65ZD-MAHD (training convolutional neural network for autonomous driving).

developed for image recognition, were adapted for NLP, several new capabilities of great importance to AI and Law emerged. The key training method was a form of weakly supervised learning via a self-attention mechanism and a large corpus of natural language texts. In this method, the neural network is trained using a procedure called masking to predict a word removed from a text passage.[29] As in the perceptron example described above,[30] if the prediction is wrong, weights contributing to that prediction throughout the network are slightly altered to make the prediction less likely, and if the prediction is correct, the weights throughout the network are slightly altered in the opposite direction. The training process can be implemented in different ways. In the BERT implementation, 15% of the tokens[31] are randomly selected for masking at each training step. In this implementation, words are randomly removed, and the model is trained to predict the word based on the surrounding context.[32] This process is typically repeated over a number of training steps, called epochs. The Big Data revolution meant that this training process could be applied to giant datasets, including snapshots of the entire World Wide Web.[33] The deep-network architecture that is most widely used is termed a *transformer language model* (i.e., transformer). Where the parameters of the model are large, such as 405 billion,[34] we refer to it as a *large language model ("LLM")*. The most common method modeling approach for LLMs is autoregressive,[35] which focuses on predicting the next most likely word in a sequence.[36]

One remarkable capability is the ability to quantify the similarity between pairs of words. The *distributional hypothesis*, sometimes summarized as "[y]ou shall know a word by the company it keeps,"[37] is that the meaning of a word is determined by its relationships to other words. This idea is key, as the context-reliant training of transformers and LLMs reflects the distributional hypothesis. Another useful implementation is to rely on distributional representations in the form of *semantic vector*

[29] One well known example of this procedure is the BERT Language Model. *See generally* Jacob Devlin et al., *BERT: Pre-training of Deep Bidirectional Transformers for Language Understanding*, ARXIV 1, 1 (May 24, 2019), https://perma.cc/M8PJ-SHDW (introducing the new language representation model, BERT, and its effectiveness in natural language processing tasks).

[30] Rosenblatt, *supra* note 6.

[31] A token is a word or part of a word. DANIEL JURAFSKY & JAMES H. MARTIN, SPEECH AND LANGUAGE PROCESSING: AN INTRODUCTION TO NATURAL LANGUAGE PROCESSING, COMPUTATIONAL LINGUISTICS, AND SPEECH RECOGNITION WITH LANGUAGE MODELS 15 (3rd ed. 2025).

[32] Devlin et al., *supra* note 29, at 4.

[33] *See* OpenAI et al., *GPT-4 Technical Report*, ARXIV 1, 25 (Mar. 4, 2024), https://perma.cc/WX6B-2LRY.

[34] Aaron Grattafiori et al., *The Llama 3 Herd of Models*, ARXIV 1, 1 (Nov. 23, 2024), https://perma.cc/NPT5-RQ3M.

[35] Autoregressive generation relies on "a language model to incrementally generate words by repeatedly sampling the next word conditioned on our previous choices." JURAFSKY & MARTIN, *supra* note 31, at 167.

[36] *Id.*

[37] John Rupert Firth, *A Synopsis of Linguistic Theory*, *in* STUDIES IN LINGUISTIC ANALYSIS 1, 11 (1957).

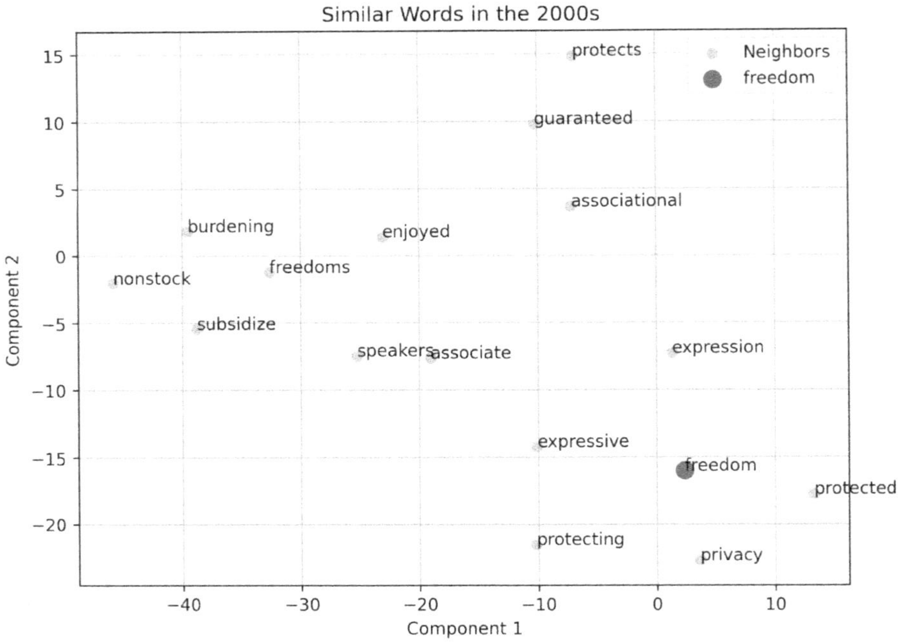

FIGURE 7.1 The word "freedom" and similar words based on US Supreme Court opinions from 2000 to 2009. Caselaw Access Project (2025). Retrieved December 10, 2025.

embeddings.[38] By measuring the similarity of words in embedding space, we can understand their similarity. Words that occur in similar contexts typically have similar meanings. As shown in Figure 7.1, using US Supreme Court opinions from 2000 to 2009, we can examine the word "freedom" and its similar neighbors using word embeddings created with Word2Vec.[39]

In one example, a remarkable illustration of the expressiveness of this approach is that the vector-space representation of "king," minus the representation of "man," plus the representation of "woman" is almost exactly the representation of "queen."[40]

Embeddings can scale from individual words into embeddings for sentences, paragraphs, and larger texts. The distance between two meanings in this representation can be measured using a simple mathematical calculation (vector cosine).[41] In sum,

[38] Tomas Mikolov et al., *Efficient Estimation of Word Representations in Vector Space*, ARXIV 1, 1 (Jan. 16, 2013), https://perma.cc/8EYD-5RSZ.

[39] *Id.* at 11; *Word2Vec*, GOOGLE, https://perma.cc/S4HE-HXRF.

[40] JURAFSKY & MARTIN, *supra* note 31, at 125; *see also* Elliott Ash & Daniel L. Chen, *Case Vectors: Spatial Representations of the Law Using Document Embeddings*, *in* LAW AS DATA: COMPUTATION, TEXT & THE FUTURE OF LEGAL ANALYTICS 313 (Michael A. Livermore & Daniel N. Rockmore eds., 2019).

[41] JURAFSKY & MARTIN, *supra* note 31, at 110.

semantic vector spaces are a transformative technique for automating the analysis of meaning.

7.2.2 Applications of Natural Language Processing

One important capability of language models is significantly improved performance in *document classification*, a supervised learning task of assigning a document to a category based on its text. Traditional document classification tasks included identifying a document's genre, author, or topic. As will be discussed below, document classification is an important legal AI task. The significance of transformers for document classification is that converting documents into a semantic-vector representation makes it much easier to classify them based on meaning. Classifiers based on transformers, such as BERT, consistently outperform earlier approaches and are currently the dominant approach to document classification.[42] This capability is particularly important in the context of technology assisted review ("TAR") in the e-discovery context.[43]

A recent and highly important property of language models, particularly LLMs, is the ability to generate sequences of fluent, idiomatic text, which is especially relevant to NLP. LLMs' pre-training learns a model capable of generating *autoregressively*, meaning word by word, conditioned on the input prompt.[44] For example, "Pat's attorney pointed to the" is much more likely to be followed by "signature line" than by "oil tanker." This next-word prediction can be repeated based on the sequence so far to produce a sentence that is highly probable in the context of the previous words. Using a large context window, LLMs can use context words much earlier in the text to estimate the probability of the next words generated by the model.[45] So, if the previous words were "After hours of fruitless attempts at reaching a compromise, Pat's attorney pointed to the," the most probable next word might be "door," whereas if the previous words were only "After 45 minutes of waiting for a decision, Pat's attorney pointed to the," the most probable next word might be "clock."[46]

Relatedly, *modern dialogue systems*, now commonly known as generative AI, combine the capacity of LLMs to generate sequences of highly probable text with further fine-tuning of these models on conversational data using supervised learning. The purpose of fine-tuning is to adhere to the conventions of human

[42] Santiago González-Carvajal & Eduardo C. Garrido-Merchán, *Comparing BERT Against Traditional Machine Learning Text Classification*, ARXIV 1, 3 (Jan. 12, 2021), https://perma.cc/AN6T-ND57.

[43] Eugene Yang et al., *Goldilocks: Just-Right Tuning of BERT for Technology-Assisted Review*, *in* ADVANCES IN INFORMATION RETRIEVAL 502, 503 (Jaap Kamps et al. eds., 2022).

[44] JURAFSKY & MARTIN, *supra* note 31, at 178.

[45] Grattafiori et al., *supra* note 34, at 14.

[46] *Id.*

discourse, including tracking topics across multiple conversational turns, providing relevant responses, maintaining consistency, emulating a persona, avoiding contradictions, and observing conversational etiquette. As discussed in more detail in Chapter 12, these transformers and LLMs have made a significant impact on AI and Law.

7.3 INTERPRETABLE AND EXPLAINABLE MACHINE LEARNING

ML models make predictions based on inputs. However, in many applications, a prediction standing alone is of limited value unless accompanied by an explanation. This may be especially true in certain domains, such as law. The key reason is that the purpose of a prediction may often be to guide future actions, and the explanation can indicate what actions should be taken in light of the prediction. For example, if the US Securities and Exchange Commission uses an ML model to identify a suspicious trader for investigation, an explanation of the reasons this trader was flagged could help guide the investigation in the most informative direction.[47] An explanation of a prediction of a coronary event might suggest health interventions to make the event less likely. Similarly, the explanation for a loan denial by a financial institution could help a customer take corrective action to improve their credit rating and could help the institution avoid charges of bias or discrimination. Another example is that the explanation for a prediction that a motion for summary judgment would fail, given a particular jurisdiction, brief, and judge, might suggest changes to a brief or venue.[48] In law, it may often not be the prediction of an outcome that has utility, but an argument or explanation in favor of a specific legal conclusion. According to Ashley, when discussing the inclusion of a numerical weight to a factor, "[s]uch numbers are meaningless for judges and attorneys as a means of evaluating a problem, not least because they are expected to justify their legal conclusions symbolically by citing some legal authorities in support."[49] In some cases, ML models may be of utility in law to the degree they are interpretable.

Some ML models are easier to reason about than others. For example, one approach to ML builds ("induces") a decision tree that correctly predicts as many as possible of the training examples.[50] Decision trees, specifically, are useful because

47 For a discussion of this and other examples involving federal agencies, *see* DAVID FREEMAN ENGSTROM ET AL., GOVERNMENT BY ALGORITHM: ARTIFICIAL INTELLIGENCE IN FEDERAL ADMINISTRATIVE AGENCIES (Feb. 19, 2020), https://perma.cc/AV2Q-H2VK.

48 L. Karl Branting et al., *Predictive Features of Persuasive Legal Texts*, PROC. AUTOMATED SEMANTIC ANALYSIS INFO. L. TEXT 1 (2020) [hereinafter Branting et al., *Legal Texts*].

49 Kevin D. Ashley, *Reasoning with Cases and Hypotheticals in HYPO*, 34 INT'L J. MAN-MACH. STUD. 753, 758 (1991).

50 *See* Quinlan, *supra* note 11.

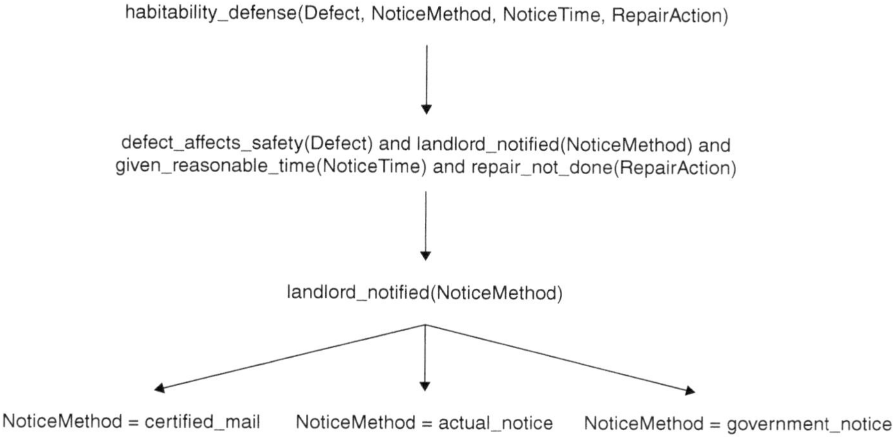

FIGURE 7.2 A "proof tree," also called a "goal tree," showing the justification for the conclusion that the tenant meets the requirements to show their landlord provided them with unsafe or unlivable housing conditions.

they conform to "'hierarchical and dichotomous structure' often employed in judicial decisions to answer questions and they are easily interpretable."[51]

Suppose, for example, that the decision tree shown in Figure 7.2 predicts that John has a defense from eviction based on the implied warranty of habitability. One way to explain this prediction is to look at the case facts along the path from the root of the tree to the leaf node that contains the prediction: There was a dangerous defect in the rental unit, John notified the landlord of the defect, and the repair was not provided. In Maryland, for example, there is a rebuttable presumption that a landlord's failure to make repairs within 30 days of receiving notice is unreasonable.[52] Fully understanding this explanation might require some knowledge of law, but there is no mystery about how the system comes to its conclusion: at each decision point, a given fact directs the path toward a leaf node representing one way to prove the conclusion.

In contrast, deep learning systems are notoriously opaque. Such systems have a large number of neural layers, units, and connections, each contributing in some way to the prediction, but it is very difficult to understand exactly how. The US government research agency Defense Advanced Research Projects Agency ("DARPA") funded a multiyear study of explainable deep learning, but no overall

[51] Morgan Gray et al., *Empirical Legal Analysis Simplified: Reducing Complexity through Automatic Identification and Evaluation of Legally Relevant Factors*, 382 PHI. TRANS. R. SOC. A 1, 3 (2023) (quoting Jonathan Kastellec, *The Statistical Analysis of Judicial Decisions and Legal Rules with Classification Trees*, 7 J. EMPIR. LEG. STUD. 202, 210 (2010)) [hereinafter Gray et al., *Empirical*].

[52] MD. CODE ANN. REAL PROP. § 8-211(h).

general solution was identified.[53] One approach is to have a separate ML model find the best rationalization for a prediction made by a neural system.[54] On the face of it, providing a post-hoc justification, such as a Shapley-based value or other post-hoc-explainability technique,[55] for a conclusion reached by other means seems particularly inappropriate in law, where explaining the facts and law that require a particular conclusion is vital.[56] Yet as we shall see, precisely this approach has been used in a deployed AI legal advisor.

In summary, ML techniques date back to the beginnings of AI. Training paradigms include supervised learning (from manually labeled examples), unsupervised learning (the model learns patterns from the data), and self-attention (e.g., learning the importance of words based on their context in text). Although current neural network systems outperform earlier learning algorithms, they lack explanatory capability.

7.4 MACHINE LEARNING IN LAW OVERVIEW

One way ML could assist individual litigants would be if models could be trained on prior cases *en masse* and then applied to the facts of each individual litigant's case to predict the likely outcome. Intuitively, the prior decisions of any court are a naturally occurring training set for supervised learning, so an algorithm trained on such a collection could be expected to be a powerful tool for understanding how a new case would be decided. However, many complications lurk in this appealing scenario.

The first complication is the requirement of identifying a set of features to represent existing (training) and novel (litigant's) cases. Features that can be determined only by individually reading and analyzing each case are not practical for real applications because of the huge volume of new cases[57] (e.g., 353,170 filings in US district courts in 2023[58] and roughly 64.6 million cases in US state courts in 2022).[59]

53 David Gunning & David W. Aha, *DARPA's Explainable Artificial Intelligence (XAI) Program*, 40 AI MAG. 44, 57 (2019).

54 One of the best-known of these approaches is LIME (Local Interpretable Model Agnostic Explanations). *See* Andreas Holzinger et al., *Explainable AI Methods – A Brief Overview*, *in* XXAI – BEYOND EXPLAINABLE AI 13, 15–17 (2020).

55 Scott M. Lundberg & Su-In Lee, *A Unified Approach to Interpreting Model Predictions*, 31 PROC. INT'L CONF. NEURAL INFO. PROCESSING SYS. 4768, 4768 (2017).

56 Masha Medvedeva & Pauline Mcbride, *Legal Judgment Prediction: If You Are Going to Do It, Do It Right*, PROC. NAT. L. LANGUAGE PROCESSING WORKSHOP 73, 80–81 (2023).

57 Some scholars estimate that for a single issue there are roughly 40,000 cases on point that would need to be analyzed. *See* Morgan Gray et al., *Toward Automatically Identifying Legally Relevant Factors*, *in* 362 LEGAL KNOWLEDGE AND INFORMATION SYSTEMS 53, 54 (Enrico Francesconi, Georg Borges & Christoph Sorge eds., 2022) [hereinafter Gray et al., *Factors*].

58 U.S. CTS., *Federal Judicial Caseload Statistics 2023*, https://perma.cc/S4SY-UAT3.

59 NAT'L CTR. FOR STATE CTS., *Court Statistics Project* (Mar. 6, 2024), https://tinyurl.com/4vrry5mp.

To predict the outcome of a novel case using this model, the facts of the litigant's case must be represented in the same way as the past cases. This poses a number of challenges that must be overcome. For example, how should the precedent be represented as training data?

One promising approach is to use factors with a longstanding history in AI and Law. Factors are "stereotypical patterns of fact that tend to strengthen or weaken a[n] argument in favor of a legal claim."[60] Factors have long been employed in computational models of legal reasoning as a way to represent facts for legal argument.[61] Factors have recently been used as training data in ML models to predict the outcome or a court's conclusion as to whether a police officer has reasonable suspicion.[62] Regardless of how legal information is represented in training data, humans typically must manually annotate the data. Recent scholarship, however, has made progress in automatically identifying important features from legal text.[63]

Even if an effective representation of legal knowledge in a case were identified, simply informing a litigant that their case is likely to be successful or unsuccessful may be of limited use. This prediction is more valuable when delivered in a decision-support framework that helps the litigant understand their legal situation and suggests ways to improve their likelihood of prevailing or to mitigate the consequences of a likely failure.

When an international community of researchers in AI and Law began to coalesce in the 1980s, the primary interest was in logical and cognitive models of legal reasoning.[64] There were two main reasons for the comparative lack of interest in statistical ML approaches. First, there were very few publicly available datasets for training ML systems for legal tasks. Case collections were held by a handful of large vendors of legal information retrieval services (e.g., Westlaw and LexisNexis) who were generally unwilling to license their collections for research purposes. In any event, there was little interest in ML techniques that operated directly on legal text. Second, researchers of the day were particularly focused on computational modeling of two activities: providing advice to clients (legal expert systems) and engaging in argumentation (computational models of legal reasoning). AI systems for providing advice to clients, which were broadly termed *legal expert systems*,

[60] Kevin D. Ashley, Artificial Intelligence and Legal Analytics: New Tools for Law Practice in the Digital Age 73 (2017).

[61] Ashley, *supra* note 49, at 757; Vincent Aleven, *Using Background Knowledge in Case-Based Legal Reasoning: A Computational Model and an Intelligent Learning Environment*, 150 A. I. 183, 186 (2003); Alison Chorley & Trevor Bench-Capon, *Using Heuristic Search to Automate the Construction of Case Law Theories*, 13 A.I. & L. 9, 9–10 (2005).

[62] Gray et al., *Empirical*, *supra* note 51, at 1.

[63] *See, e.g.*, Morgan A. Gray et al., *Can GPT Alleviate the Burden of Annotation?*, *in* 379 Legal Knowledge and Information Systems 157 (Giovanni Sileno, Jerry Spanakis & Gijs van Dijck eds., 2023) (discussing utilization of GPT models in text annotation).

[64] Trevor Bench-Capon, *Thirty Years of Artificial Intelligence and Law: Editor's Introduction*. 30 A.I. & L. 475, 476 (2022).

largely adhered to the computational logic paradigm described in Chapter 6. Legal expert systems were generally intended to demonstrate how, as a matter of law, legal conclusions follow from a given set of facts. The only form of uncertainty in this framework arises from *the language gap* described in Chapter 2, in that terms occurring in legal rules are often *open-textured*, for example, abstract, context-dependent, vague, or ambiguous.[65] As discussed, attorneys may dispute whether, for example, a driver was exercising "reasonable care" at the time of an accident, but bridging the gap computationally can be difficult. Nevertheless, systems such as Bruce McClaren's SIROCCO made progress by reasoning in situations involving open-textured legal rules, designed to cover a broad range of conduct.[66] The second popular research area was the simulation of litigators' disputation via *argumentation models*.[67] This line of research is at the intersection of jurisprudential theory and formal logic.[68]

All the while, a practical application arose in *TAR*, also termed *predictive coding* or *e-discovery*, in which supervised ML was used to determine the relevance or responsiveness of a document to a discovery request.[69] In TAR, attorneys manually tagged a representative set of documents as relevant or irrelevant. Each document was converted into a set of features consisting of the occurrence or frequency of predefined keywords in each document. While these keywords were selected manually, the detection of the keywords was straightforward to automate. The documents, together with the relevant/irrelevant tags, were used as a training set for an ML algorithm. The resulting model was then used to classify the remaining documents as relevant or irrelevant, obviating the burden on attorneys of examining every document for relevance.[70] TAR has been approved for use in US federal courts since 2012[71] and in the UK since 2016.[72] While TAR improves the lives of attorneys in large cases involving extensive discovery, it has little relevance for unrepresented litigants, whose cases seldom involve discovery.

The development of the Supreme Court Database ("SCDB") in the US provided an opportunity to test the predictability of Supreme Court decisions. The SCDB

65 Anne von der Lieth Gardner, An Artificial Intelligence Approach to Legal Reasoning 3–4 (1987).
66 Bruce M. McLaren, *Extensionally Defining Principles and Cases in Ethics: An AI Model*, 150 A.I. 145, 145 (2003).
67 Henry Prakken & Giovanni Sartor, *A Dialectical Model of Assessing Conflicting Arguments in Legal Reasoning*, 4 A.I. & L. 331, 331 (1996).
68 Phan Minh Dung, *On the Acceptability of Arguments and Its Fundamental Role in Nonmonotonic Reasoning, Logic Programming and N-Person Games*, 77 A.I. 321, 321 (1995).
69 The Sedona Conference, *The Sedona Conference Best Practices Commentary on the Use of Search and Information Retrieval Methods in E-Discovery*, 8 Sedona Conf. J. 189, 199 (2007).
70 Maura R. Grossman & Gordon V. Cormack, *Technology-Assisted Review in E-Discovery Can Be More Effective and More Efficient than Exhaustive Manual Review*, 17 Rich. J.L. & Tech. 1, 3–4 (2011).
71 Da Silva Moore v. Publicis Groupe, 287 F.R.D. 182, 193 (S.D.N.Y. 2012).
72 Pyrrho Invs. Ltd. v. MWB Prop. Ltd., [2016] EWHC 256 (Ch).

contains cases spanning over 200 years. Furthermore, the cases have been assigned values by expert scholars for as many as 240 variables, including "chronological variables, case background variables, justice-specific variables, and outcome variables."[73] Given these elaborately and expertly curated features, supervised learning methods such as decision tree induction were demonstrated to be predictable to a reassuring degree.[74]

7.4.1 *Extracting Features from Legal Texts*

If predictive models are to be used, training data must be identified. For example, SCALE, a system that predicts a case outcome with explanations, used relevant sentences representing facts, contentions, findings, and decisions.[75] There are four general approaches to automatically extracting predictive features from legal texts. The first is to represent a document using *metadata*, information about the document that is external to its content. For a court filing, this might include the court where the document is filed, the judge handling the case, the type of filing (e.g., complaint, answer, motion for summary judgment), the attorney submitting the document, the party represented by the attorney, and any other information likely to be recorded when the document is filed. Case metadata has been shown to be surprisingly predictive of judges' decisions in federal civil litigation. An early system demonstrated 64% accuracy in predicting the outcomes of intellectual property claims after training on ten years of prior cases.[76] Interestingly, but perhaps not surprisingly, the most predictive features were found to be the identity of the judge, the plaintiff's law firm, the defendant's identity, and the district where the claim was filed.[77]

A second approach goes beyond the metadata by extracting a set of simple *lexical features* that can be directly observed from the text. Simple lexical features are well known from the *Information Retrieval ("IR")* community, which developed the techniques used by the large legal search engines like Westlaw and Lexis/Nexis. The simplest feature could be a count of the number of times a term (word, number, symbol, etc.) occurs in a document. Such a *term frequency vector* represents the number of times every term occurs in a document, typically with the most common

[73] Daniel Martin Katz, Michael J. Bommarito II & Josh Blackman, *A General Approach for Predicting the Behavior of the Supreme Court of the United States*, 12 PLoS ONE 4 (Apr. 12, 2017).

[74] *Id.*; Theodore Ruger et al., *The Supreme Court Forecasting Project: Legal and Political Science Approaches to Predicting Supreme Court Decision Making*, 104 Colum. L. Rev. 1150, 1194 (2004); Aaron Russell Kaufman, Peter Kraft & Maya Sen, *Improving Supreme Court Forecasting Using Boosted Decision Trees*, 27 Pol. Analysis 381, 386 (2019).

[75] L. Karl Branting et al., *Scalable and Explainable Legal Prediction*, 29 A.I. & L. 213, 221–22 (2021) [hereinafter Branting et al., *Scalable*].

[76] Mihai Surdeanu et al., *Risk Analysis for Intellectual Property Litigation*, 13 Proc. Int'l Conf. on A.I. & L. 116, 116 (2011).

[77] *Id.*

words (such as articles) eliminated. On the face of it, this document representation seems grotesquely unintuitive: what can a list of word counts really tell you? Surprisingly, a key discovery by the IR community is that documents on similar topics – and therefore relevant to the same queries – often have a very high vector cosine, and those on unrelated topics have a low vector cosine.[78] While there has been an abundance of refinements to the vector space model for information retrieval, it continues to play a central role in the most widely used IR systems.[79]

A slightly more expressive lexical feature could be an n-gram, a sequence of n successive terms (e.g., the first 3-gram of the Gettysburg Address is ["four," "score," "and"], and the next 3-gram is ["score," "and," "seven"]). Legal documents can be automatically converted into frequency vectors of n-grams that can be used as features for outcome prediction. Note that a 1-gram representation is identical to a term frequency vector. Once again, it may seem remarkable that such shallow features have any predictive value, but a series of different research projects showed that, under some circumstances, an n-gram representation can be surprisingly predictive. N-grams have been used to study the evolution of legal language.[80]

A third approach to automatically extracting predictive features from legal texts is to develop a separate ML model that converts the text into a set of *derived features* and uses these derived features, rather than the original lexical features, for prediction. The motivations for using derived features include both improved explanatory capability and possibly improved accuracy.[81]

Recently, LLMs have been applied to extract features from legal texts. Typically, a transformer-based model goes through a process called fine-tuning. This process involves using annotated data that represent a legal feature. For example, Gray et al. used a fine-tuned RoBERTa model to identify legally relevant factors in court opinions.[82] Mumford et al. used a BERT model to perform factor ascription.[83] The process of fine-tuning may be costly due to the need for expert-annotated data. However, state-of-the-art LLMs have been put to the same kinds of feature

[78] The cosine similarity between two term frequency vectors is a standard approximate measure of similarity between the texts represented as vectors. The vector cosine similarity between identical documents is 1.0, whereas a pair of documents that share no terms have a vector cosine of 0.0.

[79] David Dubin, *The Most Influential Paper Gerard Salton Never Wrote*, 52 LIBR. TRENDS 748, 748 (2004).

[80] Daniel Martin Katz et al., *Legal N-Grams? A Simple Approach to Track the "Evolution" of Legal Language*, *in* 235 LEGAL KNOWLEDGE AND INFORMATION SYSTEMS 167, 167 (Katie M. Atkinson ed., 2011).

[81] Kevin D. Ashley & Stefanie Brüninghaus, *Automatically Classifying Case Texts and Predicting Outcomes*, 17 A.I. & L. 125, 149 (2009); *see also* Mohammed Falakmasir & Kevin D. Ashley, *Utilizing Vector Space Models for Identifying Legal Factors from Text*, *in* 302 LEGAL KNOWLEDGE AND INFORMATION SYSTEMS 183, 185 (Adam Wyner & Giovanni Casini eds., 2017).

[82] Gray et al., *Empirical, supra* note 51, at 55.

[83] Jack Mumford, Katie Atkinson & Trevor Bench-Capon, *Reasoning with Legal Cases: A Hybrid ADF-ML Approach*, *in* 362 LEGAL KNOWLEDGE AND INFORMATION SYSTEMS 93 (Enrico Francesconi, Georg Borges & Christoph Sorge eds., 2022).

extraction tasks without the need for fine-tuning.[84] The prospect of automatically extracting legally relevant features from legal text could open a number of opportunities to represent cases.

7.4.2 *Predicting Case Outcomes*

Since 2016, a series of research projects have demonstrated that ML models trained on large collections of published decisions are capable of predicting the outcome of a case based only on the statement of facts in that opinion.[85] A 2020 study on decisions by the European Court of Human Rights ("ECtHR") achieved an accuracy of 75% in predicting whether the Court found a violation of the European Convention on Human Rights ("ECHR"). In roughly 88% of cases, the ECtHR found a violation, meaning that 88% accuracy could be obtained just by always predicting a violation. The experimenters, therefore, used a subset of cases that was equally balanced between violations and non-violations (a random guess would be 50% accurate).[86] However, 65% accuracy was obtained using only the judges' surnames. This suggests that the 75% accuracy might have been based on other features that are unrelated to the merits of the case.[87]

Another example of this phenomenon, involving surprisingly high accuracy based on factors that may be unrelated to the merits of the case, was observed in a project focused on predicting decisions by the World Intellectual Property Organization ("WIPO") on domain name disputes.[88] WIPO cases include sections setting forth the procedural history, the factual background, the parties' contentions, discussion and findings, and the decision. A model trained to predict case decisions based on an n-gram representation of the text in the procedural history, the factual background, and contentions sections achieved a roughly 95% F-measure. However, the most informative features[89] included the 4-grams "respondent did not submit" and "not submit any response" and the 2-gram "default on," phrases that seem to indicate that

[84] Gray et al., *Factors*, *supra* note 57, at 157; Jaromir Savelka et al., *Can GPT-4 Support Analysis of Textual Data in Tasks Requiring Highly Specialized Domain Expertise?*, ARXIV 1, 10 (June 24, 2023), https://perma.cc/78EH-XV3Y; Dor Bernsohn et al., *LegalLens: Leveraging LLMs for Legal Violation Identification in Unstructured Text*, ARXIV 1, 8 (Feb. 6, 2024), https://perma.cc/88L4-SRTD.

[85] *See, e.g.*, Nikolaos Aletras et al., *Predicting Judicial Decisions of the European Court of Human Rights: A Natural Language Processing Perspective*, 2 PEERJ COMPUT. SCI. 1, 1 (2016) (using NLP and ML to predict the outcome of cases tried by the European Court of Human Rights based solely on textual content).

[86] Masha Medvedeva, Michel Vols & Martijn Wieling, *Using Machine Learning to Predict Decisions of the European Court of Human Rights*, 28 A.I. & L. 237, 247, 256 (2020).

[87] *Id.*

[88] L. Karl Branting, *Automating Judicial Document Analysis*, PROC. 2ND WORKSHOP ON AUTOMATED SEMANTIC ANALYSIS INFO. LEGAL TEXT 1 (2017).

[89] Feature weights were estimated using *information gain*. *See* Daphne Koller and Mehran Sahami, Toward Optimal Feature Selection, 13 PROCS INT'L CONF. MACH. LEARNING 284 (1996).

the respondent failed to respond to the complaint or suffered a default. These are procedural rather than substantive features; no n-grams that obviously involve intellectual property concepts were found to be informative. Moreover, approximately 90% of WIPO cases are decided in favor of the complainant. A model that says "the complainant always wins" would achieve 90% accuracy. In sum, the performance of models trained on lexical features in predicting ECtHR and WIPO decisions is less impressive than it seems at first glance. Moreover, these models have very little explanatory capacity beyond identifying n-grams that were important to the model and those that were not.

The statement of facts of a legal decision is generally written by the same judges who decide the case, so it is hardly surprising that the facts anticipate the decision.[90] To be useful, a model must make predictions based only on the information available to a litigant prior to the decision, and what information is in fact "available" to litigants at this stage is nuanced. One way to explore this is to see whether complainants' own words are predictive. Branting et al. described an effort to apply the techniques that worked well in ECtHR and WIPO prediction to attorney misconduct complaints submitted to the bar association of a large US state.[91] The complainant's information included a free-text description of the events justifying the complaint and the relationship between the complainant and the respondent-attorney. The task was to predict whether the case would be forwarded for a full investigation or, instead, whether the case should be closed before an investigation because it failed to state a "colorable" (i.e., prima facie) claim.

Disappointingly, prediction based on the lexical features of the complainant's statements was only slightly better than chance. Slightly better, but still poor, performance was obtained by adding metadata, such as information from the bar association's attorney database regarding prior complaints against the attorney. Better still, but still mediocre, results were obtained using as features the "allegation codes" intake staff had assigned to each case before the decision was made whether to send the case forward for investigation. Adding lexical features to the allegation codes did not improve performance.[92] These experiments suggest that learning methods that work well on judges' highly standardized statements of fact perform poorly on text from indignant, untrained laypeople.

There is, of course, an intermediate point between statements of facts by judges who know the outcome and unrepresented litigants who do not know how to frame or describe their situation in legally relevant terms, namely, texts written by attorneys. In a novel application of ML, researchers compared the predictiveness of a

[90] L. Karl Branting et al., *Judges Are from Mars, Pro Se Litigants Are from Venus: Predicting Decisions from Lay Text*, *in* 334 Legal Knowledge and Information Systems 215, 218 (Serena Villata, Jakub Harašta & Petr Kremen eds., 2020).

[91] *Id.* at 216.

[92] *Id.* at 217.

variety of features of legal writing to try to identify which features should receive the most emphasis in training attorneys.[93] Using a corpus of 864 federal employment cases involving summary judgment motions, the study explored the accuracy of models to predict whether motions for summary judgment would be granted or denied based on the text of the briefs submitted by the moving and opposing parties. A model trained on an n-gram feature representation of the text of the briefs was only weakly predictive of whether the motion would be granted. Factors related to lawyering skills appeared to make much more of a difference (probably because they were easier to detect using simple lexical techniques). These included citing briefs similar to those cited by other winning briefs, filing more and longer briefs, emphasizing strong points through positive intensifiers, and addressing weak points through hedging.[94] In a study involving 7,904 motions to strike in Connecticut state courts, combining a semantic embedding[95] representation of the document texts with case metadata produced the highest accuracy in predicting whether the motion would be granted, roughly 63%.[96] However, the resulting models were opaque in the sense of not being capable of explaining their predictions.

An early exploration of derived features for legal prediction used an ML model to identify "factors" relevant to trade secret disputes that had been manually developed by expert attorneys (e.g., whether the plaintiff took security measures, whether the product was unique, etc.) and then used these factors to predict the outcome of the cases or to perform case-based argumentation.[97] A second system was an extension of the WIPO prediction work described above, in which an ML model was trained to predict the features representing findings in the justifications of published opinions, for example, the respondent's domain name was "confusingly similar" to a trademark belonging to the complainant, or the respondent has "no rights or legitimate interest" in the domain name.[98] In an evaluation involving 16,024 WIPO cases, an F-measure of 92.2% was achieved using n-grams alone. To facilitate explainability, an alternative approach was tested in which the findings features were predicted first, and then the outcome was predicted based on those features. Predictive performance on the ultimate decisions was lowered to 79.5%, but the predictions were much more understandable because they included the findings that justified them.[99]

93 Branting et al., *Legal Texts*, *supra* note 48.

94 Elizabeth C. Tippett, Charlotte Alexander, Karl Branting, Paul Morawski, Carlos Balhana, Craig Pfeifer & Sam Bayer, *Does Lawyering Matter? Predicting Judicial Decisions from Legal Briefs, and What That Means for Access to Justice*, 100 Texas L. Rev. 1157, 1185–86 (2022).

95 *See supra* Section 7.2.1 for an explanation of embeddings.

96 Devin J. McConnell et al., *Case-Level Prediction of Motion Outcomes in Civil Litigation*, 18 Proc. Int'l Conf. on A.I. & L. 99, 103 (2021).

97 Ashley & Brüninghaus, *supra* note 81.

98 Branting et al., *Scalable*, *supra* note 75, at 233; Lisa Ferro et al., *Scalable Methods for Annotating Legal-Decision Corpora*, Proc. Nat. Legal Language Processing Workshop 12, 14 (2019).

99 Branting et al., *Scalable*, *supra* note 75, at 228.

Recent work has tried to incorporate precedents into outcome predictions to provide some basic explanatory capability, for example, by identifying precedents that have similar facts and that support the outcome; by identifying terms, sentences, or paragraphs that are particularly important to the decision;[100] or by incorporating a mix of highly interpretable and less interpretable models.[101] For the most part, outcome prediction models are "black boxes" whose predictions cannot be explained in any comprehensible way. Although some work is underway in ML explainability, and the power of LLMs shows promise in relieving longstanding bottlenecks, much remains to be done in legal decision prediction with ML.

7.5 CONCLUSION

This chapter traced the evolution of ML in the legal domain, from early developments to today's complex language models. ML techniques offer promising capabilities for legal applications while also presenting unique challenges inherent to legal reasoning and justice system requirements.

The history of ML reveals cycles of breakthroughs and limitations. Current neural network approaches, particularly transformers and LLMs, have demonstrated unprecedented capabilities in processing legal text, capturing meaningful relationships between legal concepts in ways previously not possible.

However, significant challenges persist, including representing legal cases effectively as training data, extracting legally relevant features, and providing explanations rather than just predictions. The requirement for interpretability remains perhaps the most persistent challenge. While some ML approaches like decision trees offer inherent interpretability, more powerful neural approaches often function as "black boxes," limiting their utility where explanation is essential. Recent advances in using transformer-based models to automatically identify legal factors show promise in addressing feature extraction challenges.

Despite these obstacles, ML has considerable potential to enhance access to justice by automating routine legal work, predicting outcomes to inform decision-making, and potentially reducing costs associated with legal services. Looking forward, improvements in explainable AI, automated feature extraction, and integration with decision-support frameworks will enhance ML's utility in legal contexts.

[100] *See, e.g.*, Josef Valvoda & Ryan Cotterell, *Towards Explainability in Legal Outcome Prediction Models*, ARXIV 1, 4–5 (Mar. 25, 2024) (discussing a novel approach to legal NLP through developing a taxonomy of legal precedents), https://perma.cc/K3LG-96RH.

[101] *See, e.g.*, Morgan A. Gray et al., *Automatic Identification and Empirical Analysis of Legally Relevant Factors*, 19 PROC. INT'L CONF. A.I. & L. 101, 101 (2023) (addressing how to automatically identify certain factors in the text of legal decisions and analyze their roles in court decisions to predict drug interdiction auto stop cases).

8

Document Automation

*L. Karl Branting, Mia Bonardi, and Hannes Westermann**

8.1 INTRODUCTION

In courtrooms around the globe, individuals attempting to navigate the legal system without an attorney face a daunting maze of procedures, forms, and technical language. While access to legal representation remains a critical challenge worldwide, document automation has emerged as a powerful tool that can significantly reduce barriers to justice for unrepresented litigants.

Document automation serves as a stepping stone toward justice, often enabling unrepresented litigants to progress surprisingly far, even in complex legal proceedings without professional legal assistance. The technology acts as a virtual guide, transforming complex legal forms into accessible, interview-style interactions that help unrepresented individuals present their cases effectively to the court. By breaking down complex legal documents into simple, understandable questions, document automation systems can make intimidating court processes more accessible to those without legal training.

The significance of document automation technology lies in its ability to address multiple barriers simultaneously. Complex legal terminology becomes more accessible through plain-language interfaces, often made available in multiple languages to serve diverse populations. Traditionally scattered across various court websites or available only in person, some required forms have become accessible through centralized document automation platforms. Document automation can particularly benefit rural communities and those with limited mobility, as digital access eliminates the need for repeated courthouse visits simply to obtain the correct form. The often complex and confusing logic of forms is broken down into small, manageable steps that ask for one piece of information at a time, and then automatically place it in the correct spot in the form, resulting in fewer errors.

Getting in front of a judge represents a critical milestone in many legal matters, and document automation technology has proven effective in helping litigants

* We thank Marc Lauritsen for his review of multiple drafts of this chapter.

reach this pivotal stage. When documents are properly prepared and filed, courts can process cases more efficiently, and litigants are more likely to have their matters heard. The technology helps ensure that paperwork meets court requirements the first time, reducing the frustration and delays caused by rejected filings. This is especially important in cases involving time-sensitive matters, such as housing disputes or protection orders, where procedural delays can have serious consequences.

Through the strategic implementation of document automation, courts and legal aid organizations are streamlining legal processes and reducing longstanding barriers to justice. Document automation serves as a practical demonstration of how innovation can democratize access to legal remedies, particularly for vulnerable populations who might otherwise be unable to assert their rights effectively. As we examine the role of document automation in expanding access to justice, we will explore the technical foundations and theories of document automation, as well as the evolution of document automation systems. We also examine how document automation systems have evolved from simple form-filling tools to sophisticated platforms that can guide users through complex legal procedures.

8.2 THE IMPORTANCE AND CHALLENGES OF DOCUMENTS IN THE LEGAL FIELD

Legal documents play a crucial role in many important tasks in the legal system. For example, to initiate a claim in court, individuals must identify, fill out, and submit a form or court submission containing information regarding the cause of action and the factual basis. The other party responds, again by completing a legal document, and the court then assesses the case. Beyond the court system, individuals are free to enter into contracts, for example, for the sale of specific goods, which typically require legal documents with specific requirements and legal consequences. In other words, legal documents are the foundation of many legal procedures and actions and are thus a core part of many legal tasks.

Lawyers are trained to decide which document is relevant for a particular legal situation, identify the correct form or document type, draft or complete the document, and understand the legal consequences of such a document. Laypeople, on the other hand, may struggle with many of these steps.

First, interacting with a form or document requires the litigant to understand the underlying need for the document. Laypeople may lack awareness that a particular situation gives rise to legal rights or consequences,[1] and thus fail to take any action, such as deciding to complete a certain form or document. Legal consciousness is discussed further in Section 3.2.1.

[1] Ab Currie, *The Legal Problems of Everyday Life*, *in* 12 SOCIOLOGY OF CRIME, LAW AND DEVIANCE 1, 56 (Rebecca L Sandefur ed., 2009).

Second, completing a form or drafting a legal document requires identifying the correct legal document type. Steenhuis, Willey, and Colarusso note that "[w]ithin a single jurisdiction, court systems may provide litigants with up to 1,500 standardized forms that address different legal rights."[2] Relevant forms may be spread across various websites, making them difficult to locate. Knowing which form to use may require a legal assessment, which again may be difficult for laypeople. Not knowing which form to use was one of the most common issues identified by Macfarlane as part of the National Self-Represented Litigants Project.[3] When drafting a more open-ended legal document, such as a contract, these issues may be exacerbated. For example, there may be no form or template for the person to complete, requiring them to start from scratch.

Third, completing or drafting a document is a significant challenge. Forms can impose a number of formal requirements, such as specific formatting, complex logical reasoning (e.g., certain sections only needing to be completed in specific situations), and even complex calculations. While people have knowledge of some information that a form may require (such as name or address), other fields may require litigants to locate pieces of information across various other documents, such as a driver's license number or the length of a lease.[4] Locating the correct information can itself be a challenge. Errors in meeting these formal requirements may result in stressful adjournments or even dismissal.[5]

Furthermore, beyond the formal requirements, there are also substantive requirements for completing forms. The more difficult fields require a narrative that explains why a particular criterion is satisfied, from the litigant's perspective.[6] For example, when filing a claim against a landlord, a litigant will need to explain which obligation the landlord breached. Drafting this section requires selecting legally relevant facts and organizing them into a coherent, legally sound, and complete narrative. Failing to properly establish the substantive requirements of a case in the initial filing, may lead to the case being dismissed.

Form completion can present a significant challenge for laypeople, as illustrated by an experiment by Branting et al. They sought to predict the outcome of cases involving attorney misconduct complaints based on complaint forms filed by laypeople. Such predictions can be made quite accurately when they are based on, for example,

[2] Quinten Steenhuis, Bryce Willey & David Colarusso, *Beyond Readability with RateMyPDF: A Combined Rule-Based and Machine Learning Approach to Improving Court Forms*, 19 Proc. Int'l Conf. A.I. & L. 287 (2023).

[3] Julie Macfarlane, The National Self-Represented Litigants Project: Identifying and Meeting the Needs of Self-Represented Litigants: Final Report 8–9 (2013), https://perma.cc/V4TF-76L8.

[4] Caroline Jarett & Gerry Gaffney, Forms that Work: Designing Web Forms for Usability (2008); Steenhuis, Willey & Colarusso, *supra* note 2.

[5] Macfarlane, *supra* note 3.

[6] Steenhuis, Willey & Colarusso, *supra* note 2.

the fact sections from court cases, but fail completely when using only material compiled by laypeople. As the authors state, "The root problem is that pro se litigants seldom know what facts they need to establish or how to articulate and organize the facts in a manner that makes their claims amenable to evaluation."[7] Salyzyn et al. reached a similar conclusion, noting that the requirement to provide information such as the desired outcome often requires the person completing the form to possess legal knowledge, which can prevent laypeople from engaging with the legal system.[8]

Overall, incorrectly completed forms and documents can lead to significant delays and even cause litigants to fail to enforce their rights. Next, we explore how a form can be integrated into a document automation platform and how this type of system can support laypeople in overcoming the issues described above.

8.3 DEFINING DOCUMENT AUTOMATION

Document automation systems fundamentally transform how unrepresented litigants navigate the legal system's documentary requirements. These systems rely on pre-drafted templates, including intake forms, court forms, motions, letters, and more, which are then customized based on user responses to interview questions or automatically populated with information without requiring the user to enter it manually (Figure 8.1). Common document automation platforms in the access to justice space include Gavel, A2J Author, HotDocs, LawHelp Interactive, and Docassemble. These platforms address many of the essential tasks that civil litigants must complete, as identified in Chapter 3, serving both to simplify complex legal processes and to guide users through necessary documentation requirements.

The process of document automation transforms static templates into dynamic, personalized documents through a systematic approach that accommodates various document formats and platform capabilities.

8.3.1 *Setting Up the Template*

Document automation begins with template preparation, though the specific approach varies depending on the document format. For DOCX documents, the process starts with placing fields throughout the template. These fields, typically denoted by curly braces `{ }` or square brackets `[ ]`, serve as placeholders that the automation software will later populate with user-specific information. For instance, a standard letter might include fields like `{recipient_name}` or `{recipient_address}`, each representing a piece of information that will be customized

7 Karl Branting et al., *Judges Are from Mars, Pro Se Litigants Are from Venus: Predicting Decisions from Lay Text*, *in* 334 LEGAL KNOWLEDGE AND INFORMATION SYSTEMS 215 (Serena Villata, Jakub Harašta & Petr Kremen eds., 2020).

8 Amy Salyzyn et al., *Literacy Requirements of Court Documents: An Underexplored Barrier to Access to Justice*, 33 WINDSOR YEARBOOK OF ACCESS TO JUSTICE 263 (2016).

FIGURE 8.1 Document automation system workflow illustrating how templates are converted into user-specific legal documents through guided interviews.

for each use. Consistent naming of fields and variables supports long-term maintenance, and clear documentation of those fields and variables saves valuable time during troubleshooting and updates. In Figure 8.2, square brackets are used to represent the variable fields in the sample lease agreement.

PDF templates require a different approach because of their unique structure. Using specialized PDF-editing software such as Adobe Acrobat, developers must draw fields onto the document where variable content should appear. These fields function similarly to their DOCX counterparts but offer additional formatting and validation capabilities specific to the PDF format. The placement of these fields requires careful consideration of the document's layout and final appearance.

8.3.2 *Deploying the Template*

After preparing the template, the next phase involves deploying it within the chosen document automation platform. This stage requires careful attention to detail because it establishes the foundation for all future document generation. The

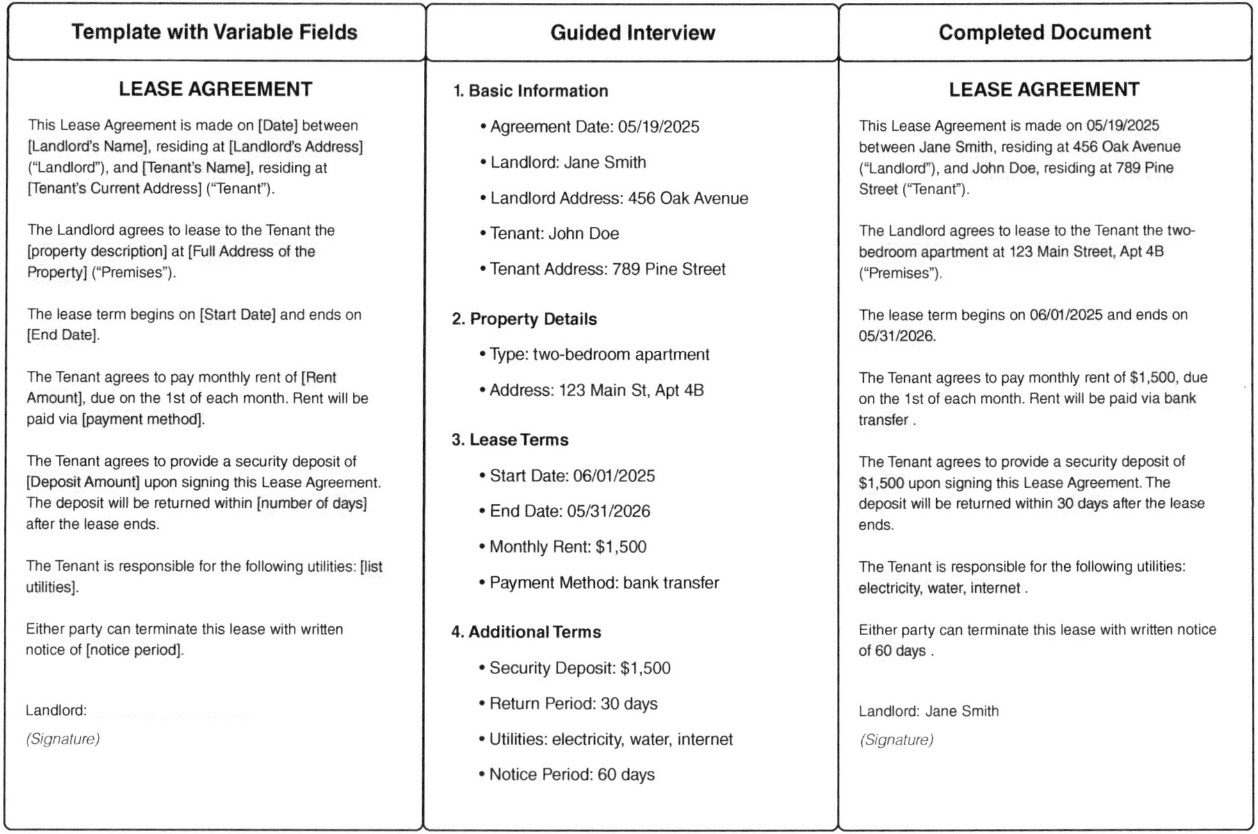

FIGURE 8.2 Sample automation of a lease agreement showing the process of populating variable fields from a template (left) with information entered by the user in a guided interview (center) to produce the final document (right).

developer must first upload the template to the platform, and ensure that all fields are correctly recognized and preserved.

The questions that the users see are a critical component of template deployment. These questions must be crafted thoughtfully to gather all necessary information while providing an intuitive experience for users. The complexity of this process varies significantly between platforms. Some platforms offer simple drag-and-drop interfaces that enable rapid development without coding knowledge, while others provide sophisticated programming options for creating more complex, dynamic interactions.

8.3.3 *Interacting with the User*

When developing forms for unrepresented litigants, it is standard practice to design questions in plain language at a 6th–8th grade reading level. Once the questions are written, the variables and labels in the DOCX or PDF are aligned with the user's responses. In other words, when users enter their information or respond to a question, those responses are linked to variables and the corresponding fields in the template. In Figure 8.2, the guided interview is represented in the center column, matching the lease agreement's variable fields to the users' answers to the interview questions.

8.3.4 *Generating Documents*

When users complete an interview, their responses are inserted into the template, producing a personalized and completed document. In Figure 8.2, this final step is represented in the rightmost column, with the lease agreement completed using the user's responses to the guided interview.

The overview of the document automation process in Figure 8.1 and the practical lease agreement generation in Figure 8.2 demonstrate how users can complete sometimes complex legal forms through plain language, guided interviews.

8.4 DOCUMENT AUTOMATION COMPARED WITH TRADITIONAL METHODS

Document automation represents a significant advancement over traditional manual form completion and document drafting methods. In traditional form completion, unrepresented litigants must repeatedly enter identical information across multiple documents, increasing both the time required and the likelihood of transcription errors. Manual drafting also leads to formatting inconsistencies, as users attempt to replicate legal document standards without technological support. These traditional methods do not offer validation of entered information, leaving errors to be discovered only upon court filing or review. Furthermore, litigants may struggle

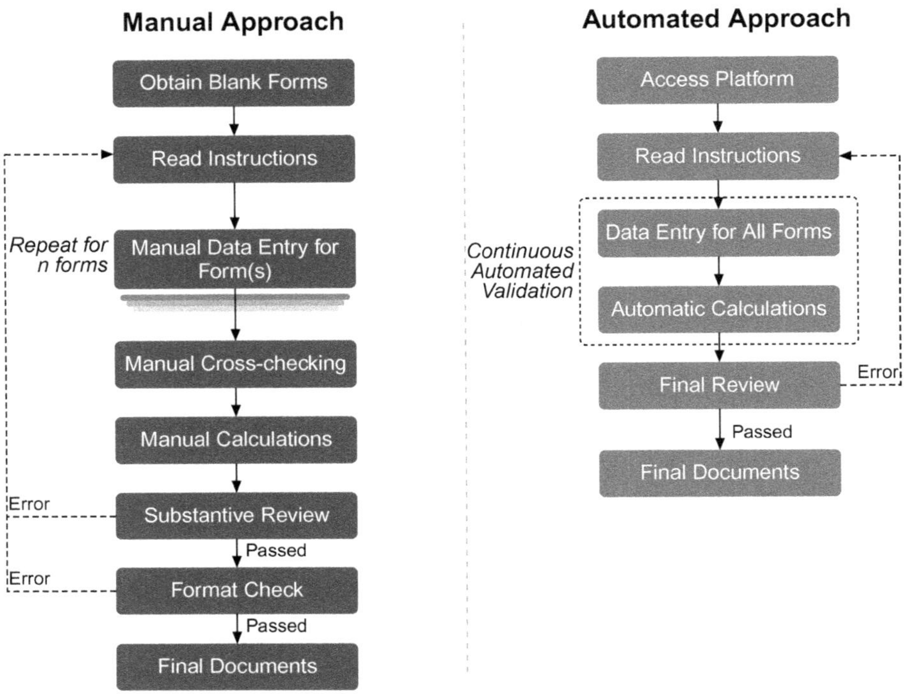

FIGURE 8.3 Manual document preparation process (left) compared to streamlined automated workflow (right), showing the elimination of repetitive steps and error cycles.

to determine which information is legally relevant to include, reducing their likelihood of success in court.[9]

The efficiency gains from automation are substantial. A single data entry point populates all related documents, eliminating redundancies and ensuring consistency across documents. Built-in validation catches errors immediately rather than after submission, while automated calculations eliminate mathematical errors that are common in financial disclosures and other calculations. Automation maintains consistent formatting and legal language across all generated documents, ensuring compliance with court standards. Simplified guidance can help litigants determine which information to include.

The evolution from traditional manual document preparation to automated systems represents a fundamental shift in legal-document processing methodology. As illustrated in Figure 8.3, the manual approach requires multiple steps, with multiple potential points of failure and inefficiency. This process requires separate data entry for each form, thereby creating redundant work when a litigant must fill out multiple forms. Error correction through manual document preparation requires substantial backtracking.

[9] Branting et al., *supra* note 7, at 218.

By contrast, the automated approach is streamlined. Rather than treating each form as a separate entity requiring individual attention, the automated system employs a unified data-collection methodology through a guided interview process. This single point of data entry, coupled with real-time validation, represents a paradigm shift in document preparation. Error handling and validation play crucial roles in maintaining document quality. Implementing validation rules helps prevent common issues such as missing information or incorrectly formatted data. Plain language instructions and support resources further enhance the user experience, reducing confusion and minimizing errors during document creation process. The system's ability to generate multiple documents from a single dataset not only increases efficiency but also ensures consistency across all documents.

Several crucial advantages of the automated approach are clear. Eliminating redundant data entry and manual cross-checking steps directly addresses common barriers that unrepresented litigants face. Integrating automated validation before document generation, rather than after manual completion, represents a proactive approach.

This transformation in document-processing methodology represents a significant advancement for access to justice initiatives, particularly for unrepresented litigants who may lack familiarity with filing requirements. The automated system's ability to guide users through a structured data collection process while ensuring consistency and compliance with legal standards demonstrates the technology's potential to bridge crucial gaps in delivering legal services.

8.4.1 *Beyond Basic Fillable Forms*

While fillable PDF forms, such as those created with Adobe Acrobat, represent an improvement over paper forms, they offer limited functionality compared to comprehensive document automation systems. Fillable forms typically present static fields for data entry without logic-driven guidance or error detection: they cannot adapt questions based on prior responses or skip irrelevant sections, forcing users to navigate unnecessary complexity.

Document automation platforms, by contrast, employ logic to create dynamic interviews tailored to each user's circumstances. These systems can:

- modify questions based on previous responses,
- calculate values automatically,
- populate multiple related documents from a single interview,
- store information for future use,
- guide users through complex legal requirements, and
- provide context-sensitive help at each step.

While physical forms require manual calculations and the separate completion of related documents, automation platforms handle these tasks seamlessly. Integrating court rules and requirements into the underlying logic ensures that generated documents not only contain consistent information but also meet formatting requirements.

Modern document automation platforms represent a significant advancement in legal technology. Although document automation cannot replicate the comprehensive guidance provided by lawyers, it significantly reduces traditional barriers to access. These platforms represent a crucial development toward equalizing justice for individuals who cannot afford traditional legal representation.

8.4.2 *How Automation Reshapes Legal Tasks*

The development of legal consciousness, a critical first step in legal engagement, is enhanced by document automation's structured approach. Legal consciousness is discussed further in Section 3.2.1. These systems break down complex legal concepts into comprehensible components, helping users understand both the information they must provide and its legal significance. This systematic disaggregation of legal requirements helps bridge the considerable knowledge gap unrepresented litigants face.

The gathering of legal information becomes more systematic through integrated guidance. Instead of requiring users to identify relevant legal standards independently, these systems incorporate legal requirements directly into the interview. This integration ensures that users receive relevant legal information when needed, significantly reducing the risk that they will overlook parts of the form that are crucial to their legal case.

Document automation platforms excel at helping users distinguish legally relevant information. The technology structures the fact-gathering process through targeted inquiries, while save-and-return functionality acknowledges the often prolonged and interrupted nature of information collection. Field validation and error checking further ensure the completeness and accuracy of the collected information.

The filing process, traditionally a significant barrier for unrepresented litigants, becomes more manageable through automated generation of complete filing packages and, where available, integration with courts' electronic filing systems. These features can reduce procedural errors that often impede unrepresented litigants' cases, including errors in service.

Although preparation to appear in court is not directly automated, these systems support it by, for example, including hearing preparation materials and organizing exhibits. This documentation-based support empowers unrepresented litigants to present their cases more effectively in court.

8.5 CONCEPTUAL UNDERPINNINGS OF DOCUMENT AUTOMATION

A document is a written, printed, or digital record that captures information, agreements, or declarations. But its significance extends far beyond its physical or digital boundaries. It is a powerful instrument that creates binding relationships and obligations among parties. Think of a document like a bridge: while you can see its physical structure, its true importance lies in connecting people and enabling interactions that would not otherwise be possible. The "four corners" of a document contain the words, but the real power lies in how those words shape behavior, relationships, and obligations in the real world.

According to Yuval Noah Harari, "The written document was invented many times in many places" and "[s]ome of the earliest examples come from ancient Mesopotamia."[10] Additionally:

> [D]ocuments changed the method used for creating intersubjective realities. In oral cultures, intersubjective realities were created by telling a story that many people repeated with their mouths and remembered in their brains. Brain capacity consequently placed a limit on the kinds of intersubjective realities that humans created. Humans couldn't forge an intersubjective reality that their brains couldn't remember.
>
> This limit could be transcended, however, by writing documents. The documents didn't represent an objective empirical reality; the reality was the documents themselves …
>
> [W]ritten documents thereby provided precedents and models that would eventually be used by computers. The ability of computers to create intersubjective realities is an extension of the power of clay tablets and pieces of paper.[11]

In modern legal systems, changes in legal status are initiated and completed by means of legal documents. For example, a lawsuit or motion is typically initiated by a complaint or petition asserting a claim and is resolved by a document that embodies an order or decision affirming or rejecting the claim. Similarly, wills and contracts alter the legal relationships among individuals when they are embodied in documents containing legally effective language and are executed in the proper fashion. Harari explains:

> In human networks connected by written documents and bureaucratic procedures … society relies in part on the interaction between humans and documents. In addition to human-to-human and human-to-story chains, such societies are held together by human-to-document chains. When we observe a bureaucratic society at work … what we see is documents compelling humans to engage with other documents.[12]

A significant portion of the workload of attorneys and judges consists of drafting documents to achieve legal goals. Unsurprisingly, document drafting is a task for which unrepresented litigants often need assistance. Litigants, whether represented or unrepresented, must typically submit a document to a court to initiate or respond to legal actions.

[10] Yuval Noah Harari, Nexus: A Brief History of Information Networks from the Stone Age to AI 64 (2024) ("A cuneiform clay tablet dated to the twenty-eighth day of the tenth month of the forty-first year of the reign of King Shulgi of Ur (ca. 2053/4 BCE) recorded the monthly deliveries of sheep and goats.").

[11] *Id.* at 65.

[12] *Id.* at 74.

In formal, rule-governed fields like litigation, medicine, and engineering, documents are typically highly structured and standardized.[13] Even in routine documents, such as attendance records or employment applications, standardized formats simplify the process of recording and finding predictable information, such as names and addresses.

The Standard Generalized Markup Language ("SGML") was developed to allow documents to be created and stored in a form that is agnostic as to how the physical document will be printed.[14] The separation of content from presentation permits documents to be printed in different editions or publications, and enables pervasive changes, such as font changes, to be made easily and efficiently.[15] HyperText Markup Language ("HTML"), which largely overlaps SGML, extended this idea to the World Wide Web to permit a given set of text to be formatted appropriately for a variety of display engines.[16]

The semantic web extends the distinction between content and presentation. In the Semantic Web, the Resource Description Framework ("RDF"), represents content largely through "triples" functioning like a subject, predicate, and object.[17] The terms in the triples can themselves be defined through conventions, such as the Web Ontology Language ("OWL") or Extensible Markup Language ("XML"), which represent meaning through standardized relationships.[18]

Various projects have adapted Semantic Web concepts for the law. LegalRuleML is based on Rule Markup Language ("RuleML") to standardize and promote the use of legal rules in web-based applications.[19] Akoma Ntoso ("linked hearts" in the Akan language of West Africa) began as a project to standardize the structure and content of parliamentary, legislative, and judicial documents across different systems.[20] Akoma Ntoso has been endorsed by the United Nations Department of Economic and Social Affairs and has become a component in the e-government strategies of multiple governments.[21]

13 Mohammad Ahmadi Achachlouei et al., *Document Automation Architectures: Updated Survey in Light of Large Language Models*, ARXIV 1 (Aug. 18, 2023), https://perma.cc/L8F6-NGG8.

14 *Standard Generalized Markup Language (SGML)*, LIBRARY OF CONGRESS (Apr. 25, 2023), https://perma.cc/XQZ6-84XU.

15 Abel Gómez et al., *A Framework for Variable Content Document Generation with Multiple Actors*, 56 INFO. & SOFTWARE TECH. 1101 (2014).

16 Tim Berners-Lee, *Information Management: A Proposal*, W3 (Mar. 1989), https://perma.cc/CXM7-5YXH.

17 *Resource Description Framework*, SPHN, https://perma.cc/ZJ8K-HKGL.

18 *Id.*

19 Monica Palmirani & Guido Governatori, *LegalRuleML Core Specification Version 1.0*, OASISOPEN (Aug. 30, 2021), https://perma.cc/L2YY-MPLX.

20 Gioele Barabucci et al., *Multi-layer Markup and Ontological Structure in Akoma Ntoso*, *in* 6327 AI APPROACHES TO THE COMPLEXITY OF LEGAL SYSTEMS: COMPLEX SYSTEMS, THE SEMANTIC WEB, ONTOLOGIES, ARGUMENTATION, AND DIALOGUE 133 (Pompeu Casanovas et al. eds., 2009).

21 *Id.; see also, e.g., ISA² – Interoperability Solutions for Public Administrations, Businesses, and Citizens: Digitising EU Law Production*, EUR. COMM'N, https://perma.cc/447Q-XX2D.

8.6 DOCUMENT AUTOMATION IN PRACTICE

Now that we have examined the conceptual underpinnings of document automation, we can briefly review the history of these systems, some of the platforms that exist today to aid in their construction, and several examples of existing systems.

Document automation has existed for many years. As Marc Lauritsen has indicated, the initial document automation systems were based around word processing software. These programs contain functionalities allowing, for example, the search for and replacement of specific placeholders, the execution of macros, and mail-merge operations. By building on these features, it is possible to construct document automation tools.[22]

Since the 1970s and 1980s, a crop of specialized software has emerged, allowing for the easier creation of document automation tools.[23] Some of these platforms are open-source, such as Docassemble.[24] There is also a wealth of closed-source and commercial platforms, such as A2J Author,[25] HotDocs,[26] Contract Express,[27] LawDroid,[28] and Gavel.[29] While these platforms have different specific functionalities, they generally offer both an author interface, which allows authors to create new form templates, and a user interface, which allows users to complete and download their documents. These components can be installed as software or provided as cloud-based services that creators and users access via a web browser.

8.7 EXAMPLES OF DOCUMENT AUTOMATION PLATFORMS

As Lauritsen describes, document automation platforms are in use across a variety of actors in the legal system, with different target users.[30] The systems are often not limited to preparing documents; they can accompany a user through steps such as understanding their legal rights, attempting to negotiate their situation with the other party through online dispute resolution, and, if this fails, helping the user complete a form so they can take their claim to court.[31] This section explores a few

22 Marc Lauritsen, *Current Frontiers in Legal Drafting Systems* (2007) (11th Proc. Int'l Conf. AI & L Working Paper), https://perma.cc/HJ7Q-AJ8J.

23 *Id.*

24 DOCASSEMBLE, https://perma.cc/A5TZ-UZVF.

25 A2J AUTHOR, https://perma.cc/EXH9-JDCR.

26 *Mitratech HotDocs*, MITRATECH, https://perma.cc/V73Y-UWHE.

27 *Contract Express – Legal Document Automation Software*, THOMSON REUTERS, https://perma.cc/WK67-EPSN.

28 LAWDROID, https://perma.cc/NK4B-NAUP.

29 GAVEL, https://perma.cc/9RX6-JTU5.

30 Lauritsen, *supra* note 22.

31 Darin Thompson, *Creating New Pathways to Justice Using Simple Artificial Intelligence and Online Dispute Resolution*, 2015 INT'L J. ONLINE DISP. RESOL. 1, 4 (2015).

examples of existing document automation tools, based on the actors that provide them, including nonprofit legal service organizations, courts and other government institutions, commercial entities, and law firms.

Nonprofit legal service organizations, such as legal aid clinics,[32] provide a lot of document automation tools. These organizations can offer the public access to such systems, helping them navigate their interactions with the legal system. Many such systems exist across the world. One prominent example is LawHelp Interactive ("LHI") (profiled in Section 13.3.1). Based on the HotDocs platform, LHI provides approximately 5,000 modules across forty states and has been used to create millions of documents.[33] Examples in Canada include Community Legal Education Ontario, which offers the "Steps to Justice" system to help individuals complete forms in family, housing, immigration, and other areas of law.[34] Steenhuis describes two systems that help complete forms regarding tenant eviction defense in Massachusetts and immigration in Chicago, which can both speed up the process and catch errors early, saving thousands of hours for thousands of individuals.[35]

Courts and other government institutions may also directly provide document automation platforms, for example, to assist unrepresented litigants in finding and completing the correct forms.[36] For instance, the Boston Municipal Court and other courts in Massachusetts offer a guided interview to help litigants complete a small claims form, which can then be directly filed with the court.[37] Many other governmental institutions likewise allow online interaction and form completion, as part of what is known as e-government.[38]

Beyond helping people in their interactions with the court system, document automation can also support internal operations within these entities. For example, Westermann discusses the use of a tool that would prompt a judge to answer questions about their decision and then quickly generates a template for the judge to compete in order to render that decision. Thus, the structure of a decision document could be created quickly based on the judge's responses, while leaving placeholders for the judge to insert their reasoning.[39]

32 *Id.*
33 *Id.*; LawHelp Interactive, https://perma.cc/GBL9-KJCS.
34 Steps to Justice, https://perma.cc/GRR5-WRW9.
35 Quinten Steenhuis, *AI and Tools for Expanding Access to Justice*, *in* The Cambridge Handbook of AI in Civil Dispute Resolution (Amy J. Schmitz, Pietro Ortolani & Marco Giacalone eds., 2026).
36 Lauritsen, *supra* note 22.
37 *File a Small Claim in the Boston Municipal Court, District Court, or Housing Court*, Mass. Gov't, https://tinyurl.com/ypxc7cmx.
38 R Silcock, *What Is E-Government*, 54 Parliamentary Aff. 88 (2001).
39 Hannes Westermann, Using Artificial Intelligence to Increase Access to Justice 485 (Mar. 2023) (Ph.D. Dissertation, University of Montreal) (on file with the Cyberjustice Laboratory).

There are also *commercial entities* that offer document automation services to the public.[40] In the US, platforms such as Rocket Lawyer[41] and LegalZoom[42] help individuals complete forms and prepare documents in a wide variety of legal domains. An enormous market is the filing of taxes via platforms such as TurboTax,[43] which allow users to enter their information to create relevant tax documents.

Law firms are another user of document automation. They might use these tools to facilitate client intake, by using the software to elicit the initial information from the user, allowing them to start with data that has already been collected. They can also use document automation software internally, for example, to support the efficient reuse of documents and templates created in-house, or to purchase templates for specific document types to be used internally.[44]

8.8 PROMISES AND CHALLENGES

Document automation is a powerful approach that can address a number of important challenges related to access to justice. It provides a better, more efficient, and less error-prone way for litigants to locate and complete forms, or to draft other legal documents. With document automation, litigants receive better support in their interactions with the legal system. The support provided by the templates and the information in the system can save users a significant amount of time and money. Forms that are completed more accurately can increase litigants' likelihood of success in court or yield other favorable outcomes, such as a will being valid and precise or a license being granted. From the perspective of courts and government agencies, correctly completed forms reduce the need to request clarifications, ensuring time savings and a smoother overall process.

Document automation is thus a valuable tool that allows litigants to benefit from legal knowledge encoded in templates, enabling them to carry out tasks that they otherwise might have needed a lawyer for or failed to accomplish. Yet document automation is not a binary proposition: Litigants may, for example, use such systems to fill out forms that can then be reviewed in conjunction with a legal aid clinic, or even complete the forms with the direct assistance of clinic staff. In this way, the efficiency and consistency gains can be realized while maintaining a human in the loop to correct oversights or provide assistance when the user requests it.

At the same time, today's document automation platforms remain limited in several respects. First, creating the templates that underlie document automation

40 Lauritsen, *supra* note 22.
41 ROCKET LAWYER, https://perma.cc/3QSW-96M3.
42 LEGALZOOM, https://perma.cc/79XU-BZUP.
43 *TurboTax*, INTUIT, https://perma.cc/ACT4-RX9J.
44 Lauritsen, *supra* note 22.

platforms can take a significant amount of time,[45] and doing so requires legal expertise and a thorough understanding of the forms, which can become a bottleneck for implementing such systems in many domains. Second, there is no guarantee that document automation systems will be effective or helpful. If templates are not carefully designed and tested, users may encounter the same complexity and confusion they experience with traditional forms. Third, while these systems can assist with navigating a form's structure and performing certain logical steps (such as adding together values or skipping irrelevant sections based on information provided by the user), they are often unable to assist with substantive drafting, which can pose a significant challenge for laypeople. Some forms, for example, require individuals to explain which legally relevant events have occurred or what they want to claim, both of which may require legal knowledge.[46] Finally, the user of a document automation platform remains constrained by the fields and content of the form itself. For example, if the form is badly designed or does not properly cover the user's situation, those flaws will also be reflected in the document automation system.

In Section 8.9, we examine some approaches to address these challenges.

8.9 THE FUTURE OF DOCUMENT AUTOMATION SYSTEMS

As we have seen, document automation represents an important step toward increasing access to justice by helping laypeople navigate one of the most challenging areas of the judicial system. At the same time, several limitations remain with the current approaches. In this section, we explore how, for example, the integration of large language models ("LLMs") can enhance the current paradigm of document automation, thereby further expanding the use of this technology.

8.9.1 *Automatically Creating Document Automation Templates*

A severe limitation of current document automation approaches is the effort required to create the templates that underlie these systems. As shown in Section 8.3, for example, converting a form into an automation workflow typically involves manually transforming the form into an encoded template. This process requires deconstructing the entire form into discrete questions, logical connections between these questions, explanations to help the user answer them, and a template that indicates where the information should ultimately be placed.[47] The template must then be evaluated to ensure that it is correct. Creating templates for document automation requires experts who possess both legal expertise and

45 Quinten Steenhuis, David Colarusso & Bryce Willey, *Weaving Pathways for Justice with GPT: LLM-Driven Automated Drafting of Interactive Legal Applications*, ARXIV 3 (Dec. 14, 2023), https://perma.cc/M2W2-TFWT.

46 Salyzyn et al., *supra* note 8.

47 Steenhuis, Colarusso & Willey, *supra* note 45.

technical expertise in encoding information in a document automation platform. It can also require a significant amount of time – Steenhuis, Colarusso, and Willey note that this work can take hundreds of hours.[48] This template creation process can thus create a bottleneck for deploying new document automation tools for unrepresented litigants.

To overcome these challenges, AI could be used to automate steps in the template creation process. Such an approach was discussed by Steenhuis, Colarusso, and Willey.[49] They developed a tool called the Assembly Line Weaver, which takes as input a DOCX or PDF template, asks the user some questions, and outputs a basic Docassemble interview.[50] The authors then experimented with leveraging generative AI models such as GPT-3 and GPT-4 to automate parts of the process, such as automatically labeling variables from Word documents (i.e., finding fields such as {{ claimant_name }} in a document). The authors even explored whether LLMs could automatically generate an interview from an inserted PDF document, that is, finding fields in the PDF documents and automatically drafting relevant questions and interview logic. The initial results were promising, with 93% of the fields on certain forms being recognized and correctly implemented into the interview. However, for the worst form, the approach was successful in only 28% of the cases, underscoring the importance of including a human in the loop to review the outputs.[51] Integrating generative AI into the interview creation workflow thus appears to be a promising approach to addressing the deployment bottleneck.

A similar approach was explored in Janatian et al.,[52] where the authors investigated whether GPT-4 could automatically translate legislation into pathways for the JusticeBot system (profiled in Section 13.7). The JusticeBot is not directly focused on document automation; instead, it provides legal information. However, Westermann discusses the use case of using these pathways to generate legally relevant documents, such as letters, submissions, decision templates, and contracts.[53]

Janatian et al. found that GPT-4 was able to create decision pathways correctly in 40% of the cases, with 50% of the cases requiring only slight adjustments. Even more interestingly, the AI system often helped annotators identify errors in their own encoding of laws.[54] This again shows the power of using LLMs to assist experts in more quickly creating drafts of logical representations.

48 *Id.*

49 *Id.* at 1.

50 *Id.* at 2.

51 *Id.* at 8.

52 Samyar Janatian et al., *From Text to Structure: Using Large Language Models to Support the Development of Legal Expert Systems*, *in* 379 Legal Knowledge and Information Systems 167, 167 (Giovanni Sileno, Jerry Spanakis & Gijs van Dijck eds., 2023).

53 Westermann, *supra* note 39, at 482–88.

54 Janatian et al., *supra* note 52.

8.9.2 *Automatic Data Input*

Another expansion of document automation is the use of generative AI to intervene more directly in the drafting process, for example, by helping users automatically collect information. Most document automation frameworks today rely on users to locate and enter the correct information. In some cases, this may be easy – for example, people generally know their names and addresses. In other cases, providing such information can be more challenging. The information may be contained in complex letters or forms (such as a driver's license, lease contract, or government communication), requiring effort on the part of the user to locate it. Furthermore, users may make errors when entering data into the document automation system. Salyzyn et al. identified the need to cycle among documents to obtain the correct information as a source of distraction when completing court forms.[55]

Generative AI and LLMs can be integrated into the document automation process to assist users and a variety of projects have explored this approach. Westermann and Savelka examined whether LLMs can extract information from pictures of forms.[56] Instead of having to carefully read and then transcribe information, a user could simply take a picture of a form. The LLM would identify and extract the correct information and pass it to a document automation platform for further processing and integration into document templates. The authors investigated a variety of document formats (such as screenshots of PDFs, pictures of documents taken with a modern phone in good lighting conditions, and pictures taken with an older phone in poor lighting conditions), with more or less neat writing. The evaluation pipeline is illustrated in Figure 8.4. While the recognition accuracy was not perfect (ranging between 43% and 100%, depending on the format), the models were always able to

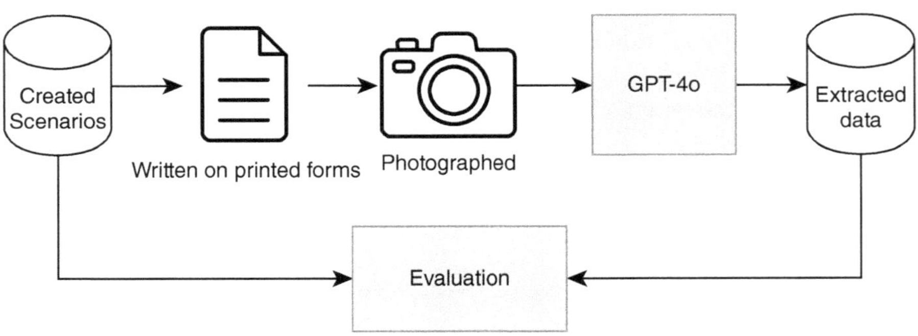

FIGURE 8.4 Pipeline for evaluating handwritten text extraction from completed forms. Printed with permission from Hannes Westermann and Jaromir Savelka.

[55] Salyzyn et al., *supra* note 8, at 284.

[56] Hannes Westermann & Jaromir Savelka, *Analyzing Images of Legal Documents: Toward Multi-Modal LLMs for Access to Justice*, ARXIV 1 (Dec. 16, 2024), https://perma.cc/9ES9-URYA.

locate the information correctly and showed promising performance in transcribing it.[57] This approach therefore shows promise in automatically extracting information from complex documents, especially when combined with a human in the loop to correct any inaccurate information.

8.9.3 *More Advanced Drafting*

Currently, most document automation tools rely on structural automation. They follow a logical template to decide where specific information should be placed and can perform calculations and logical reasoning to determine values based on the user's inputs. However, narrative descriptions and texts are left entirely to the user.[58] For example, if a user needs to justify why they believe their landlord has breached the lease, there may be various ways to phrase an answer, depending on the unique factual situation. Here, most template-based document automation tools can provide guidance on how to write such answers, but the user must determine which information is legally relevant and how to contextualize it to complete the field correctly. Crafting compelling narratives and aligning factual descriptions with legal criteria is one of the most challenging tasks in completing forms, as explored in depth by Karl Branting.[59] A recent line of research explores how LLMs can automatically ask users questions, analyze their responses in light of legal requirements, and then draft a narrative.

An example of such an approach lies in Document Automation, Large Language Model Assisted ("Dallma").[60] This project relies on the insight that legal documents are semi-structured. Certain elements, such as headings and explanations, are always required. Other sections are determined by logic, for example, whether a specific law applies or whether a particular section of a form must be completed. Yet some elements require user input or the drafting of complex narratives.

Dallma aims to bring these elements together by combining a traditional document automation approach, modeled after Docassemble, with LLMs. For each question, instead of asking the user to provide information directly, the template can designate an LLM as the target. The LLM will then read and analyze the relevant information and can, for example, draft narrative explanations and apply legal criteria. The LLM can also indicate that it does not have enough information and ask follow-up questions to gather more information from the user.

57 *Id.* at 5.

58 Steenhuis, Willey & Colarusso, *supra* note 2.

59 Branting et al., *supra* note 7; Karl Branting & Sarah McLeod, *Narrative-Driven Case Elicitation*, ICAIL Workshop AI for Access to Just. (2023); Salyzyn et al., *supra* note 8.

60 Hannes Westermann, *Dallma: Semi-Structured Legal Reasoning and Drafting with Large Language Models*, 2nd Workshop on Generative AI and Law (2024), https://perma.cc/9VHF-77N7.

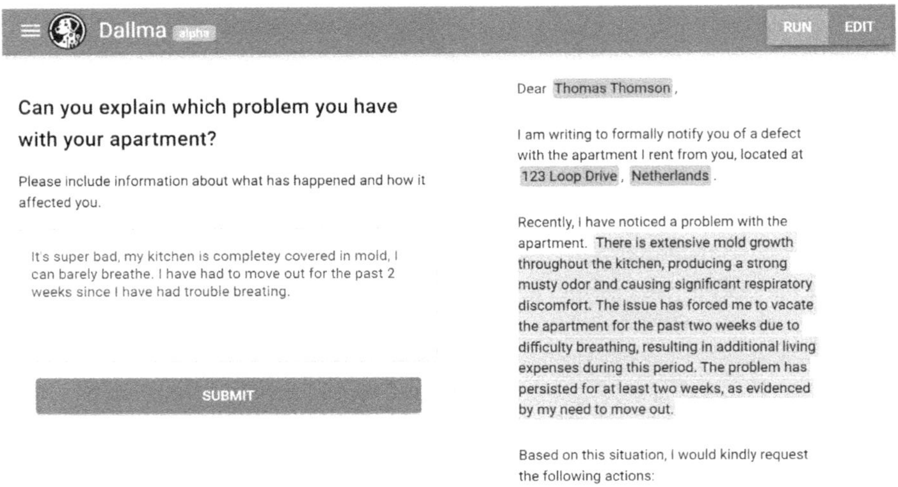

FIGURE 8.5 The Dallma system combines user input with template logic and text generated by an LLM.

Figure 8.5 illustrates an example of a completed Dallma template (on the right), in which the user provided their name and address and the LLM completed the issue description based on the user's input (on the left). The LLM can correct mistakes, improve the tone, and align the content of the user's input with the relevant legal requirements. For example, in Figure 8.5, the user entered "breating" in their input, and the LLM corrected it to "breathing." The different sources of text are integrated into a letter template to create the final letter. This approach has significant potential for augmenting document automation.

Multiple researchers have evaluated narratives produced by systems that integrate LLMs for narrative drafting. For example, Erik Bornmann sought to use GPT-4 and models from Anthropic to help draft narratives in family law, such as a legal description of a domestic abuse situation. As input, the researchers used a guided interview that collected specific facts from the user, which were then turned into a coherent narrative by an LLM. Based on an initial study of the results, they found that the LLM was able to generate promising affidavits.[61]

Lauritsen and Westermann also evaluated the capability of LLMs to correct text given specific instructions, with the aim of enhancing document automation platforms. The user would begin drafting a specific section, after which the AI would identify flaws and ask follow-up questions to obtain any missing information, and then incorporate that information into a new, corrected draft of the section. The reported performance was overall positive; however, the LLM displayed a few tendencies toward "over-enthusiasm,"

[61] Erik Bornmann, *CLEO's Narrative Generator Prototype: Using GenAI to Help Unrepresented Litigants Tell Their Stories*, JURIX AI & ACCESS TO JUST. WORKSHOP (2024).

that is, adding details that were plausible but not part of the provided information. Thus, this approach is promising but requires further work and evaluation.[62]

8.9.4 *Beyond the Form?*

Most of these document automation systems are guided by court forms. In many cases, however, the form is designed to elicit the required information directly from a user, in paper or digital form. The court creates the form to help the user demonstrate that they satisfy the underlying legal requirements to obtain a certain outcome. Yet because the form is bound by a fixed structure, this representation is likely lossy and may introduce complexity or even impose a structure that is not amenable to representing all cases covered by the law.

Likewise, courts rely on an often slow cycle of submission and evaluation, sometimes followed by feedback – such as notifying the litigant that certain information is missing – before rendering a decision.

Many of the constraints that informed the design of the paper form may no longer hold up, given the advent of technology and AI. Would these changes make it possible to design a format that supports a more active, collaborative approach? One could imagine a living storage space online where users submit documentation and answer questions about their cases, working in conjunction with AI systems, lawyers, court officers, or administrative entities. Instead of relying on a cycle of submission, evaluation, and return, the system could take a more active role, supporting the user in selecting, synthesizing, and presenting the information to help them interact with the government in a constructive manner. Rather than relying on forms as potentially inaccurate simplifications of the requirements set out in the law, such systems could instead rely directly on the requirements stated in the law, offering easier interactions and greater flexibility.

While there are risks with such an approach (e.g., regarding the neutrality of the institutions), it is worth considering what comes after the form, and how AI may help make it a reality. One alternative approach that might inform the creation of a novel document automation paradigm, not bound by the constraints of the form, is speech-act-oriented document automation.[63]

A document can be viewed as consisting of two components: (1) content – meaning the things that the document is intended to accomplish; and (2) the surface realization or presentation – the choice and arrangement of words expressing that content.[64]

62 Marc Lauritsen & Hannes Westermann, *In with the Old: Enhancing "Classical" Document Automation with Generative AI*, AI4A2J-ICAIL (2025).

63 *See generally* L. Karl Branting, James C. Lester & Charles B. Callaway, *Automating Judicial Document Drafting: A Discourse-Based Approach*, *in* Judicial Applications of Artificial Intelligence 7 (Giovani Sartor & Karl Branting eds., 1998); L. Karl Branting & James C. Lester, *A Framework for Self-Explaining Legal Documents*, JURIX 57, 77 (1996).

64 Daniel Jurafsky & James Martin, Speech and Language Processing (2d ed. 2008).

In computational linguistics, "content" typically refers to logical meaning and pragmatic goals, while "presentation" (usually termed "surface realization") encompasses the text itself, as well as any layout information.[65] A key insight of the computational linguistics community is that the content often consists of speech acts.

The philosophy of language community developed speech act theory to account for the fact that language is used for more than simply conveying information. In *How to Do Things with Words*, J. L. Austin coined the phrase *performative utterance* to describe sentences like "I pronounce you man and wife" or "I hereby sentence you to thirty days in jail" that are not statements of fact but are actions that have effects in the real world.[66] Austin elaborated on this idea by distinguishing three categories of acts that an utterance can accomplish: (1) locutionary – the act of saying something; (2) illocutionary – for example, requesting, refusing, declaring, asserting; and (3) perlocutionary – the effects of the act on the listener. Illocutionary acts are essentially equivalent to performative utterances, and the "illocutionary force" is the kind of speech act that the speaker intends to perform.

Speech act theory is essential for analyzing ordinary discourse. For example, "Can you reach the salt?" usually has the illocutionary force of a request – that the listener perform an action – and is not ordinarily a factual question. Similarly, "The last person who tried that got into trouble" usually has the illocutionary force of a warning, that is, not to try the same thing. In the movie *2001: A Space Odyssey*, HAL 9000 says, "I'm sorry, Dave. I'm afraid I can't do that." The viewer has no difficulty understanding that the illocutionary force of HAL's statement is a refusal – HAL is not sorry and can do that. These examples illustrate the importance of identifying the illocutionary content of ordinary utterances in order to comprehend them.

Speech act theory is also an important tool for understanding legal documents. As mentioned above, legal documents can initiate and effectuate changes in legal status, such as creating or removing rights or obligations, if they comply with certain requirements. Thus, a compliant document functions as a kind of performative utterance where its illocutionary force is the document's legal effect, for example, to create a binding contract, enact a statute, or rule in favor of a particular litigant.[67]

Moreover, the interpretation of statutory language, contracts, and other legal documents can be viewed through the lens of speech act theory. Here, the focus is on the intent behind the words and how they are supposed to function within a legal framework. Understanding illocutionary forces – what the utterances are meant to accomplish – can be crucial in legal interpretation. For instance, the word "shall" in

65 *See* Noam Chomsky, Aspects of the Theory of Syntax (MIT Press 1969).

66 John L. Austin, How to Do Things with Words (J. O. Urmson & Marina Sbisà eds., 2d ed. 1975). Much of the exploration of speech act theory was performed by John Searle. *See, e.g.*, John R. Searle, Speech Acts: An Essay in the Philosophy of Language (1970).

67 Barry Smith, *Document Acts*, *in* Institutions, Emotions, and Group Agents: Contributions to Social Ontology 19 (Anita Konzelmann Ziv & Hans Bernhard Schmid eds., 2014).

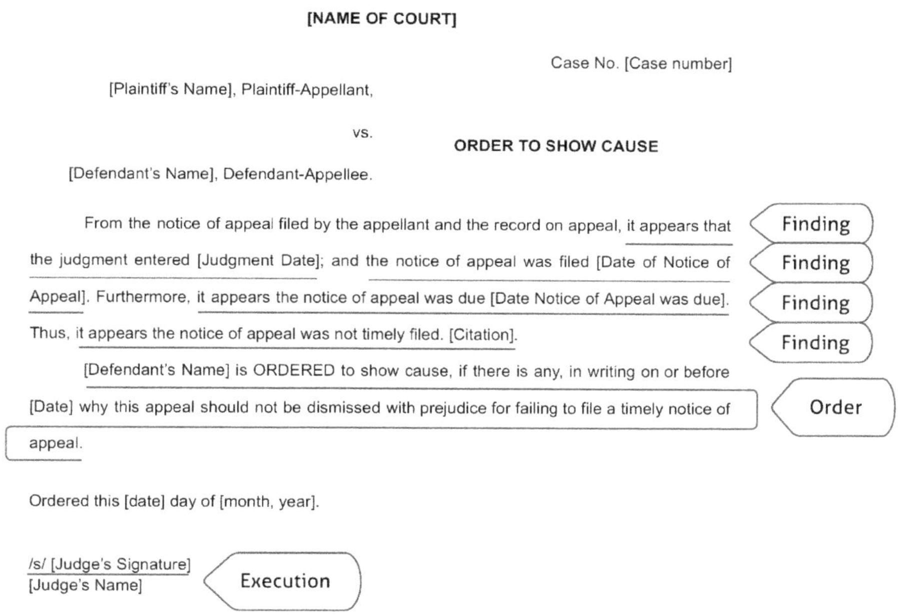

[NAME OF COURT]

Case No. [Case number]

[Plaintiff's Name], Plaintiff-Appellant,

vs.

ORDER TO SHOW CAUSE

[Defendant's Name], Defendant-Appellee.

From the notice of appeal filed by the appellant and the record on appeal, it appears that the judgment entered [Judgment Date]; and the notice of appeal was filed [Date of Notice of Appeal]. Furthermore, it appears the notice of appeal was due [Date Notice of Appeal was due]. Thus, it appears the notice of appeal was not timely filed. [Citation].

[Defendant's Name] is ORDERED to show cause, if there is any, in writing on or before [Date] why this appeal should not be dismissed with prejudice for failing to file a timely notice of appeal.

Ordered this [date] day of [month, year].

/s/ [Judge's Signature]
[Judge's Name]

FIGURE 8.6 Six speech acts in a sample US state appellate court order to show cause.

legislative texts is typically interpreted as mandatory, indicating an obligation rather than a suggestion, and reflecting its illocutionary force.

Legal scholars have applied speech act theory to various aspects of the law, arguing that many legal controversies can be resolved by closely analyzing the language used in statutes, regulations, and contracts.[68] This kind of analysis helps clarify ambiguities where the literal interpretation of a text might diverge from its intended function or the customary practices of its interpretation.

Speech act theory also sheds light on the performative nature of certain legal procedures. A performative utterance, a concept introduced by Austin, is an utterance that accomplishes what it describes simply by being spoken within the appropriate context, provided certain conditions (which Austin termed "felicity conditions") are met.[69]

The individual clauses of legal documents are often themselves performative. For example, Figure 8.6 displays a sample order to show cause from a US state appellate court whose content includes six speech acts: four findings, an order, and an execution. Taken together, these speech acts create a legal state in which the appeal will

[68] *See, e.g.*, Deborah Cao, *Legal Speech Acts as Intersubjective Communicative Action, in* INTERPRETATION, LAW AND THE CONSTRUCTION OF MEANING 65 (Anne Wagner et al. eds., 2007).

[69] AUSTIN, *supra* note 66.

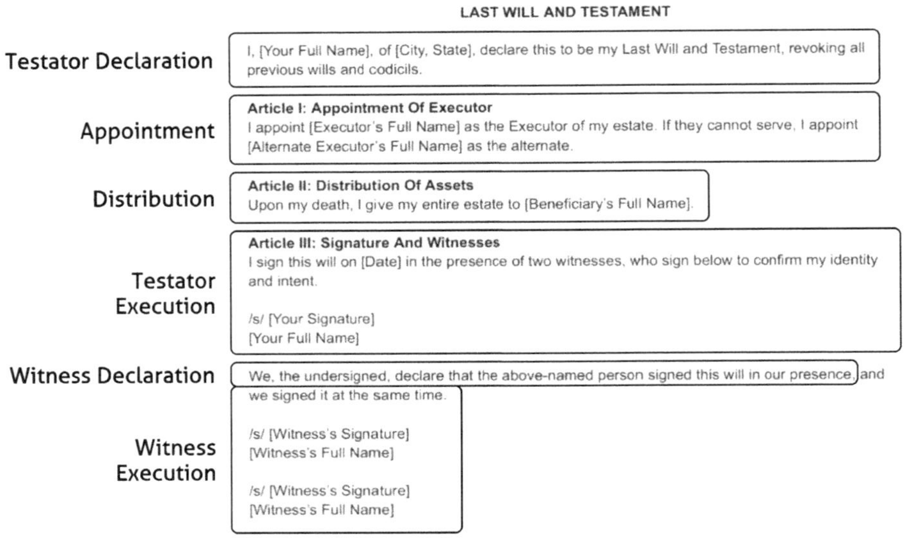

FIGURE 8.7 Sample last will and testament annotated with speech acts.

be dismissed unless the appellant convinces the court that a notice of appeal was filed in a timely fashion.

Speech acts are not the sole content of documents. The order to show cause in Figure 8.6, for example, includes a case caption identifying the court, parties, and case number. Presenting this content requires specifying the exact wording, ordering, and layout of the content, consistent with the rules and practices of the court.

For example, a will's validity might hinge on the proper performative utterances in the presence of required witnesses. The content of the last will and testament shown in Figure 8.7 includes a series of speech acts, including two declarations, an appointment, a distribution, and two executions.

Automating the creation of documents based on speech act theory requires one set of rules that specify the document speech acts necessary to achieve each legal goal and a separate set of rules that specify the surrounding standard text and layout necessary for a document to conform to the institution's stylistic requirements. For example, in most common law jurisdictions, the requirements for a valid last will and testament include that the document be in writing, that it be signed by a testator in the presence of witnesses, and that it specify the distribution of assets on the testator's death.[70]

An enforceable document must contain a clause for each of these requirements. From an AI perspective, identifying the set of clauses needed for a valid legal

[70] *See, e.g.*, Eric Dorsch & Alexander Lewis, United States International Estate Planning Guide, Int'l Bar Ass'n, https://perma.cc/Z6GW-G3GU.

document is similar to the computational logic process described in Chapter 6. In a legal advisory system, the system seeks to determine whether a given legal conclusion can be established under a given set of rules and facts, eliciting additional relevant facts from the user as needed. In a speech-act-based system, the rules apply to speech acts rather than individual facts.

There are several advantages to speech-act-based document automation. These include that the correctness of a document can be validated in terms of the rules that generated it, that the document drafting system can be easily updated when legal rules change simply by updating the corresponding speech act rules, and that the drafting system can explain the purpose of each provision. Despite these advantages and the advocacy of many scholars, speech-act-based document automation has never been widely adopted. The primary reason is that developing the rules for such systems requires a combination of skills and effort that are unavailable to most courts and law firms. Instead, the prevailing approach to legal document automation is conceptually centered on forms.

In conclusion, speech act theory offers a robust analytical framework for legal scholars and practitioners by emphasizing the active role of language in law. It illuminates how statutes, contracts, and judicial pronouncements perform actions and how these actions shape legal rights and duties. Understanding this interplay between language and legal action is indispensable for a nuanced interpretation and application of the law. Incorporating speech act theory into document automation to a greater extent could thus add a valuable perspective.

8.10 CONCLUSION

Document automation represents a crucial technological bridge in the ongoing effort to expand access to justice for unrepresented litigants. These systems have evolved from simple form-filling tools to sophisticated platforms that can guide users through complex legal procedures while ensuring consistency and compliance with court requirements. The transformation from traditional manual document preparation to automated systems marks a fundamental shift in how unrepresented litigants can engage with the legal system.

The power of document automation lies in its ability to address multiple barriers simultaneously. By breaking down complex legal documents into manageable, interview-style interactions, these systems make the intimidating process of legal form completion more approachable for those without legal training. The technology's capability to validate information in real time, perform automatic calculations, and generate multiple related documents from a single data entry point significantly reduces common errors and inefficiencies that often impede unrepresented litigants' cases.

However, current document automation systems also have limitations. Most platforms still rely heavily on manually created templates and predefined question sequences, requiring significant initial investment in setup and maintenance.

The rigid structure of many systems can struggle to adapt to complex questions and case types that fall outside standard short-form templates. Additionally, while document automation can guide users through form completion and into the courtroom, it cannot fully replace the strategic guidance and advocacy that attorneys provide.

Looking ahead, the integration of AI and machine learning holds considerable promise for advancing document automation capabilities. Future systems may be able to:

1. generate dynamic templates based on jurisdictional requirements without manual creation;
2. adapt questioning patterns in real time based on user responses;
3. provide more sophisticated legal guidance;
4. offer enhanced language accessibility through improved translation capabilities; and
5. better handle complex or unusual cases through more flexible document generation.

While document automation cannot solve all access to justice challenges, it can be a powerful tool for reducing barriers to court access for unrepresented litigants. As these systems continue to evolve, their role in democratizing access to legal remedies is likely to grow.

The future of document automation in access to justice will depend on continued innovation, collaboration among stakeholders, and a commitment to user-centered design. Maximizing its impact will require thoughtful implementation that balances technological capabilities with user needs, while maintaining focus on the ultimate goal: ensuring justice is equitable and accessible to all.

9

Interactive Legal Technologies

*Sarah McLeod**

9.1 INTRODUCTION

Advances in AI, particularly natural language processing ("NLP") and machine learning ("ML"), have improved the utility and robustness of decision-support tools and virtual assistants. Recent advancements in generative AI offer the potential to bridge the language gap addressed in Chapter 2 and to assist unrepresented litigants in discovering information to help them assert their legal rights. This chapter begins with a background and history of dialogue systems, including chatbots. Section 9.3 outlines some of the benefits of chatbots as legal AI assistants and highlights some tools currently available to increase access to justice. Section 9.4 describes the design decisions for interacting with unrepresented litigants as opposed to with lawyers and courts. Section 9.5 explores these considerations in the context of case elicitation, which is the key activity of eliciting facts relevant to a potential legal claim or defense. Section 9.6 highlights the potential for generative AI to improve access to justice.

9.2 WHAT ARE INTERACTIVE LEGAL TECHNOLOGIES?

A *dialogue system* is a computer system that enables automatic human–computer interaction through speech or text. These conversational agents use NLP techniques to understand input from a user and decide how to respond. The history of these systems includes technologies that exemplify the complexities of modeling realistic conversations. A few of the seminal systems are presented in this section to highlight how these systems have matured since their inception.

The first dialogue systems included the ELIZA[1] program and its successor, PARRY.[2] These systems were remarkably simple programs that used pattern-matching

* This chapter is published with the permission of the MITRE Corporation. I thank Kevin D. Ashley for his review of multiple drafts of this chapter.

[1] Joseph Weizenbaum, *ELIZA – A Computer Program for the Study of Natural Language Communication between Man and Machine*, 9 COMMC'NS ACM 36, 36–45 (1966).

[2] Kenneth Mark Colby, Sylvia Weber & Franklin Dennis Hilf, *Artificial Paranoia*, 2 A.I. 1, 1–25 (1971).

algorithms to process input and translate it into a relevant response. Both systems were built with a focus on clinical psychology: ELIZA was designed to simulate a Rogerian psychotherapist, and PARRY was designed to mimic a paranoid schizophrenic patient. ELIZA mimicked a therapist by identifying specific keywords in the utterances of her interlocutor and applying a set of transformation rules to formulate a response in the form of a question that would elicit more information. For example, if a patient said, "I am very unhappy," a rule would transform this into the system response, "How long have you been unhappy?" The ELIZA program was improved upon, and its successor, PARRY, included a model of its own mental state as well as variables to adjust the levels of anger and fear. Topics identified during a conversation would cause the agent's level of anger or fear to rise or fall, affecting the responses it gave. An interesting historical note: the PARRY system is the first known system to pass the Turing test;[3] at the time, psychiatrists could not distinguish text transcripts of interviews with PARRY from transcripts of interviews with real people with paranoia.[4]

Modern conversational systems are generally grouped into two categories based on their application:[5] goal-oriented systems or open-domain systems, often called chatbots.[6] Goal-oriented systems are also commonly referred to as task-oriented or task-based systems since they are designed for extensive interactions with a user where the goal is to complete a task within a specific domain, for example, booking a flight or making a restaurant reservation. Goal-oriented systems have specific measures of success that drive their actions. By contrast, open-domain systems are designed to engage with users in unstructured conversations that mimic casual and open-ended discussions observed in human-to-human communication. These systems are designed to interact with users in short conversations without domain or topic restrictions. In both cases, the system must understand the user, decide how to respond, and engage in turn-based interactions (i.e., taking turns) relevant to the conversational history. The goal is to interact with a user beyond simple question answering.

Typical approaches to goal-oriented systems treat response generation as a pipeline of four specialized components: natural language understanding ("NLU"), dialogue state tracking, policy learning, and natural language generation ("NLG"). This pipeline is shown in Figure 9.1. First, the NLU module parses the input from

3 Wikipedia, *Turing Test*, https://perma.cc/P7TV-RVXS.

4 Colby, Weber & Hilf, *supra* note 2.

5 Hongshen Chen et al., *A Survey on Dialogue Systems: Recent Advances and New Frontiers*, 19 ACM SIGKDD Explor. Newsl. 25, 25–35 (2017).

6 Historically, academic literature used the term chatbot to refer to open-domain conversational agents, to highlight the chit-chat conversational style that distinguished them from goal-oriented systems. As of 2024, most commercial products use the term chatbot to refer to any conversational agent regardless of the role it was designed for. In the remainder of this chapter, we adopt the recent usage of the term and use "chatbot" to refer to any conversation agent.

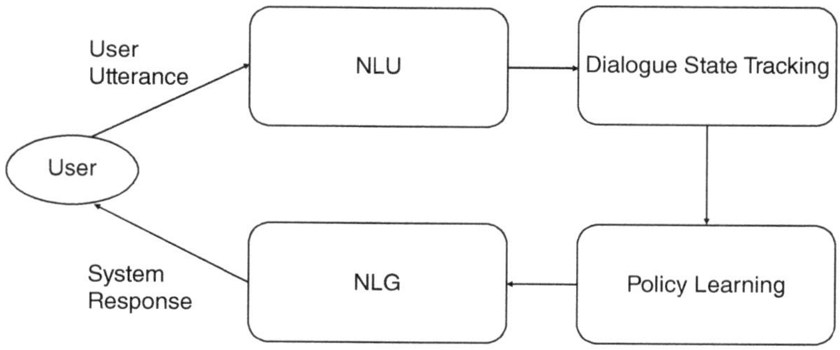

FIGURE 9.1 Goal-oriented dialogue system pipeline illustrating the processing flow from user utterance through NLU, dialogue state tracking, and policy learning to system response via NLG.

the human to detect the domain of the request, the intent of the utterance, and to identify information relevant to completing the task. For example, if the user were to say to the system, "Show me Thai restaurants near the Space Needle in Seattle," the system would construct the following knowledge structure (called a frame) by mapping words in the input utterance to semantic slots predefined according to different scenarios:[7]

- Domain: restaurant
- Intent: find restaurant
- Restaurant type: Thai
- Destination: Space Needle, Seattle

Next, this information is passed to the dialogue state tracking module. "Dialogue state" refers to the full representation of the user's goals and relevant facts at the current point in the conversation. To update the dialogue state information from the current turn, it combines information from previous turns, creating a condensed history of the conversation up to that point. Once the dialogue state is updated, it is fed into the policy learning module, which selects a response based on the entire conversation history (not just the most recent turn). The term "policy" comes from the area of ML called "reinforcement learning." In reinforcement learning, intelligent agents are trained to act in a dynamic environment in ways that maximize a reward signal. The process of learning the actions that maximize the reward signal is called "learning a policy." The learned policy is then used as a function that translates inputs into system responses. Chapter 7 provides an in-depth overview of ML, including reinforcement learning. Finally, the NLG module transforms the system's internal response into a natural language representation.

7 A task called slot-filling.

In contrast to goal-oriented systems, open-domain dialogue systems are designed to interact with users without topic restrictions. To achieve this, most modern open-domain systems learn to map a user message and dialogue history to an appropriate response from a set of pre-existing responses. Jinjie Ni et al. is an excellent resource for the curious reader interested in learning more about open-domain systems.[8]

In 1977, the influential Genial Understander System ("GUS")[9] for travel planning introduced the knowledge structures used in most modern goal-oriented dialogue systems. Since then, the evolution of these systems has followed advancements in statistical machine learning: from pattern matching and rule-based systems to neural models and deep learning. The 21st century saw an explosion of dialogue systems designed to be virtual assistants, including Apple Siri, Amazon Alexa, IBM Watson, Microsoft Cortana, and Google Assistant.

Since 2022, advancements in generative AI have resulted in models that seem to be skilled at general reasoning. While there is no consensus in the field on whether these models can perform general reasoning, proponents claim that reasoning is an emergent behavior of these models. Chapter 4 introduces generative AI and addresses this debate in greater detail. Arguments about the nature of cognition aside, what matters pragmatically is whether these models can be useful.

Current models, including instruction-finetuned large language models ("LLMs") like ChatGPT,[10] show promise; research suggests they are capable of understanding user needs and providing adequate responses.[11] ChatGPT and its contemporaries claim to be able to help users with writing essays, stories, emails, and content for sales and marketing; learning a new subject; searching the internet; coding autocomplete; improving personal productivity; and more. As of the time of this writing, popular models include Anthropic's Claude,[12] Google's Gemini (formerly Bard),[13] Jasper Chat,[14] Microsoft Copilot,[15] and Pi.[16] These models are not without their weaknesses, "hallucinations" being an obvious concern in contexts like the law.[17] For more on hallucinations, see Section 12.7.1 and Section 16.2.3. Nevertheless,

[8] Jinjie Ni et al., *Recent Advances in Deep Learning Based Dialogue Systems: A Systematic Survey*, 56 A.I. Rev. 3055, 3056 (2023).

[9] Daniel G. Bobrow et al., *GUS, A Frame-Driven Dialog System*, 8 A.I. 155, 155–73 (1977).

[10] ChatGPT, https://openai.com/chatgpt/ (last visited Jan. 11, 2025).

[11] Vojtěch Hudeček & Ondrej Dusek, *Are Large Language Models All You Need for Task-Oriented Dialogue?*, 24 Proc. Ann. Meeting Special Int. Grp. on Discourse and Dialogue 216, 216–28 (2023); Hannes Westermann, Jaromir Savelka & Karim Benyekhlef, *LLM Mediator: GPT-4 Assisted Online Dispute Resolution*, ICAIL Workshop A.I. for Access to Just. (2023).

[12] Claude, https://claude.ai/ (last visited Sep. 7, 2025).

[13] Google Gemini, https://perma.cc/ELH7-ZYG8.

[14] Jasper, https://perma.cc/9NT5-CDYD.

[15] Copilot,https://perma.cc/S5J6-UDG2.

[16] Pi, https://pi.ai/discover (last visited Sep. 7, 2025).

[17] *See, e.g.*, Mata v. Avianca, Inc., 678 F. Supp. 3d 443 (S.D.N.Y. 2023).

their potential as legal AI assistants expands opportunities for increasing access to justice (see Chapter 12).

Section 9.3 presents recent advances in legal chatbots and describes their significance as legal AI assistants. The following section discusses the important design decisions and human-centered approaches needed to empower unrepresented litigants to understand and assert their legal rights. The final section describes how these systems elicit information from unrepresented litigants and how recent advances in generative AI offer promising approaches to this task.

9.3 LEGAL CHATBOTS

Legal chatbots and generative AI virtual assistants are increasingly being improved and commoditized. New products are emerging every day. At the time of this writing, it is almost impossible to find a consumer-facing website that does not have an excited and persistent chatbot ready to greet users and attempt to answer questions the second they land on a webpage. As AI and machine learning systems have improved, they too have been adopted by the legal community, primarily as assistive tools for use by lawyers and courts. Chien and Kim note that "Efforts to address the justice gap through technology have generally followed the more general development of tools to increase lawyer efficiency, particularly in the areas of legal research and e-discovery."[18] A sample of popular commercial systems that help automate legal tasks includes the following:

- Juro's legal AI assistant[19] specializes in case management and helps automate routine contract procedures. Juro is built on ChatGPT and leverages AI to draft, review, and summarize contracts.
- Harvey AI,[20] the result of a partnership between the international law firm Allen & Overy and consulting firm PwC,[21] can automate routine legal tasks like due diligence, litigation, and legal document analysis.
- LawDroid Copilot[22] is a legal AI assistant that can draft emails, intake clients, summarize documents, analyze motions, research case law, and more.
- CoCounsel,[23] which was acquired by Thomson Reuters, is a generative AI chatbot powered by GPT-4 and Casetext's proprietary legal databases. It can assist with document review, deposition preparation, and database searches.

[18] Colleen V. Chien & Miriam Kim, *Generative AI and Legal Aid: Results from a Field Study and 100 Use Cases to Bridge the Access to Justice Gap*, 57 LOY. L.A. L. REV. 903, 915 (2025).

[19] JURO, https://perma.cc/Q8XL-XBVX.

[20] HARVEY, https://perma.cc/C6AW-GN8K.

[21] PRICEWATERHOUSECOOPERS LLP, https://perma.cc/PUW3-D2TC.

[22] LAWDROID, https://perma.cc/59C9-PEDQ.

[23] THOMSON REUTERS, *CoCounsel*, https://web.archive.org/web/20250127095538/https://casetext.com/cocounsel/.

In recent years, courts have seen an increase in unrepresented litigants.[24] This increase is due to many factors, from the growth of the consumer movement[25] to the fact that many people in need of legal assistance simply cannot afford a lawyer. In 2000, Branting noted that "domestic abuse victims were particularly likely to have few resources and little opportunity to obtain the services of a lawyer."[26] According to the US-based National Center for State Courts, 72% of family law cases have at least one unrepresented party.[27] The Legal Services Corporation estimates that 92% of low-income people in the US face substantial civil legal problems without sufficient legal assistance, 75% experience at least one such problem annually, and 39% face five or more.[28]

Unrepresented litigants have diverse backgrounds and reasons for proceeding without representation; however, they all share a common challenge. The unrepresented generally lack the necessary resources to represent themselves effectively and face disadvantages when the opposing side is represented by counsel.[29] Chapter 1 highlights the magnitude of the unmet global need for access to justice. At the same time, resources to help unrepresented litigants can be quite limited,[30] and law firms are unlikely to be interested in "low dollar one-shot litigants."[31]

As more people attempt to navigate justice systems on their own, fairness dictates that courts communicate about processes clearly and efficiently. At the same time, unrepresented litigants can present challenges to courts, such as creating administrative burdens and delays, and complicating efforts to maintain impartiality.[32] Branting argued that unrepresented litigants "frequently present staff and judges with a dilemma: providing too much help can constitute unauthorized practice of law (for court staff) or bias (for judges), but providing too little help can effectively deny pro se litigants access to the courts."[33]

24 *See, e.g.*, James E. Cabral et al., *Using Technology to Enhance Access to Justice*, 26 HARV. J.L. & TECH. 241, 247, 250, 271 (2012).

25 L. Karl Branting, *An Advisory System for Pro Se Protection Order Applicants*, 14 INT'L REV. L. COMPUTS. & TECH. 357, 358 (2000).

26 *Id.*

27 PAULA L. HANNAFORD-AGOR, FAMILY JUSTICE INITIATIVE: THE LANDSCAPE OF DOMESTIC RELATIONS CASES IN STATE COURTS, NAT'L CTR. FOR STATE CTS. 20 (2018), https://perma.cc/RQT6-VN4H.

28 LEGAL SERVS. CORP., THE JUSTICE GAP REPORT: THE UNMET CIVIL LEGAL NEEDS OF LOW-INCOME AMERICANS 8 (2022), https://perma.cc/LEC2-ZGKD.

29 Amy J. Schmitz & John Zeleznikow, *Intelligent Legal Tech to Empower Self-Represented Litigants*, 23 COLUM. SCI. & TECH. L. REV. 142, 146 (2021).

30 Aubrie Souza & Zach Zarnow, *Court Chatbots*, NAT'L CTR. FOR STATE CTS. 4 (2024) (on file with Mia Bonardi); Ayyoub Ajmi, *Revolutionizing Access to Justice: The Role of AI-Powered Chatbots and Retrieval-Augmented Generation in Legal Self-Help*, 53 THE BRIEF 1, 11 (2024).

31 Schmitz & Zeleznikow, *supra* note 29, at 145.

32 *Id.*

33 Branting, *supra* note 25, at 360.

To understand how best to assist unrepresented litigants, tool designers and developers must be aware of the specific needs of these users. In 2022, Ajmi conducted surveys in several US states and found that unrepresented litigants "prioritize access to court forms, clarity on court procedures, and understanding of court processes."[34] In addition, the civil problems most relevant to unrepresented litigants have a relatively stable set of relevant facts, procedures, and outcomes. Chatbots can be useful decision-support tools for navigating situations in which the legal rules governing relief are simple and highly consistent. These technologies can provide legal information and function as decision-support tools by helping users understand and navigate court procedures. Many court websites already provide information online; however, most do so by mirroring their internal organization structure.[35] If a litigant does not understand the distinction between departments in a court's organizational structure, they may not be able to find the resource they are looking for. Souza and Zarnow highlight many important ways courts and users can benefit from chatbots, including:

- Answering frequently asked questions, which can reduce the need for court staff or allow staff to focus on more complex tasks.
- Helping patrons ask better questions. Even if a question is not answered, the chatbot can direct patrons to the correct department and help them prepare more focused and relevant questions.
- Providing materials in multiple languages.
- Assisting users with case management and with completing tasks online, similarly to how law firms use chatbots to help with case management.
- Enabling remote access to court resources, which reduces the cost and time required to travel to court, thereby reducing the social costs associated with access to justice.

Legal AI chatbots that are designed for unrepresented litigants include:

- Rentervention[36] is a virtual assistant built by the Law Center for Better Housing to help Chicago tenants facing housing issues.
- JusticeBot[37] provides guidance to Quebec landlords and tenants regarding their rights and obligations in housing law.
- Nevada's Self-Help Chatbot[38] is available 24/7 and provides plain language guidance in multiple languages.

[34] Ajmi, *supra* note 30, at 11.
[35] Souza & Zarnow, *supra* note 30, at 8.
[36] Law Ctr. for Better Hous., *Rentervention*, https://lcbh.org/get-legal-help/#rentervention (last visited Sep. 7, 2025).
[37] JusticeBot, https://perma.cc/C8VM-UXU2.
[38] Nev. Self-Help Ctr., https://perma.cc/843K-23VS.

Each of these legal AI chatbots is profiled and described in more detail in Chapter 13.

Chatbots can be helpful for navigating a legal self-help environment; however, they come with inherent risks, similar to any software a court uses.[39] Chatbots require continued maintenance to keep the information current and are vulnerable to hacking and data theft.[40] If a chatbot provides personalized information, safeguards are needed to ensure that private information is shared only with the intended user. Importantly, chatbots can help court staff provide information to the public; however, a dialogue system cannot fully replace court staff. Additionally, legal AI assistants are more appropriate as decision-support tools for unrepresented individuals, than as autonomous systems that provide advice. This is particularly important because the distinction between legal information and legal advice is often unclear, and systems perceived as providing legal advice risk violating rules against the unauthorized practice of law ("UPL"). Chapter 14 discusses the ambiguity of the terms "legal information" and "legal advice," and the challenges related to UPL.

9.4 HUMAN–COMPUTER INTERFACE AND DIGITAL NUDGE

Legal AI assistants, including chatbots, hold promise for increasing access to justice by providing unrepresented litigants with tools to navigate and understand court resources and processes. These systems facilitate information gathering, help with questions and answers, and guide users through court resources, empowering unrepresented litigants to make informed and deliberate decisions to exercise and enforce their legal rights. When designing legal AI assistants for unrepresented individuals, it is important to develop systems that are useful, efficient, and transparent, with interfaces that are easy for any user to use and interpret. Chapter 6 on computational logic describes the important functions of a well-designed interface and outlines some of the design decisions relevant to unrepresented litigants. In the same vein, Schmitz and Zeleznikow highlight recent research into user-centric design principles and emphasize the importance of applying these principles to the design and evaluation of online dispute resolution ("ODR") software.[41] They list seven key recommendations identified by this research, including the need for robust and user-friendly tools; paperwork that is more visually clear, prioritized, and manageable; and warm, efficient welcoming experiences that encourage users to follow through with procedures.[42] The focus of their discussion is on

[39] Souza & Zarnow, *supra* note 30, at 10.
[40] *Id.*
[41] Schmitz & Zeleznikow, *supra* note 29, at 149–50.
[42] *Id.* at 149.

improving ODR; however, the design principles they outline can more generally be applied to any system designed for unrepresented litigants. Continuing the focus on user-centric design, Souza and Zarnow outline several design principles for building a chatbot that helps individuals understand and assert their legal rights.[43] They emphasize the importance of accessibility, regardless of education level or language spoken, and usability, including having a website chatbot that is easy to find and use.

As Schmitz and Zeleznikow note, "it is not sufficient that a system be easy to use, it must also provide what users need."[44] Usability, accessibility, and the ability to streamline task completion are important requirements when designing legal self-help tools; however, an important and often overlooked design decision is that the way information is presented to the user affects their decisions. Sela argues that research on user-interface ("UI") design for digital choice architectures[45] should inform the interface design for legal decision-support tools.[46] While their research centers on enhancing ODR systems, their recommendations can benefit any decision-support platform designed to assist unrepresented litigants.

Decades of research suggest that no self-guided interface in which a user needs to make choices to navigate can be neutral, which means the interface itself can (and will) influence the decisions the user makes.[47] This (intentional or unintentional) influence exerted by a choice environment is referred to as a "nudge." Thaler and Sunstein, who introduced the term "nudge," define it as "any aspect of the choice architecture that alters individuals' behavior in a predictable way without forbidding any options or significantly changing their economic incentives."[48] Within the context of software and UI design, digital nudging is "the use of user-interface design elements to guide people's behavior in digital choice environments."[49] Sela states, "Digital nudging works by modifying either *what* is presented (the content of a choice) or *how* it is presented (the visualization of a choice on the digital interface)."[50]

If digital nudging cannot be avoided, then the design of legal AI assistants must strike a balance between the inherent risks of digital nudging, particularly in a legal

43 Souza & Zarnow, *supra* note 30, at 11–25.

44 Schmitz & Zeleznikow, *supra* note 29, at 150.

45 Digital choice architecture is the practice of designing environments in which users make decisions and includes the design of online user interfaces.

46 Ayelet Sela, *E-Nudging Justice: The Role of Digital Choice Architecture in Online Courts*, 2019 J. Disp. Resol. 128, 128–29 (2019).

47 *Id.*

48 Richard H. Thaler & Cass R. Sunstein, NUDGE: Improving Decisions about Health, Wealth, and Happiness 85 (2009).

49 Shlomo Benartzi & Jonah Lehrer, The Smarter Screen: Surprising Ways to Influence and Improve Online Behavior 1–2 (2015).

50 Sela, *supra* note 46, at 142.

context, and the opportunities that can be gained by applying modern research on digital choice architectures. In many ways, "online courts are not different from digital choice environments that have been studied: they face an inherent risk of introducing bias, manipulating litigants' behavior, and negatively affecting the quality of their engagement with the process."[51]

At the same time, the goals of a digital nudge in commercial settings are very different from those in a legal setting.[52] Commercial websites are designed to steer users toward a particular action – for example, signing up for a service or spending more money on a website. In UI design, the term "dark patterns" refers to deliberately deceptive UI elements that design choices used to encourage users to make decisions they would not otherwise have made.[53] Many of these design "tricks" rely on known mechanisms triggered in choice environments. In contrast, Sela argues that the goal of online courts (and, by extension, any legal self-help tool) should be to "help litigants make informed and deliberate decisions that promote their self-determination and serve their own interests."[54] No interface can present options in a neutral way; however, by understanding the mechanisms that influence decision-makers, UI designers can use these mechanisms to "reduce bias and empower litigants to make informed and deliberate choices that best serve their own interests and promote their self-determination (while minimizing bias and maintaining the courts' impartiality)."[55]

If system designers want to avoid building a UI with unintentional bias, they must first understand the mechanisms that influence decision-makers. Sela summarizes decades of research by social psychologists and behavioral economists on the mechanisms that influence decision-making. This research suggests that seemingly minor variations in the context in which a decision is made can trigger processes that affect a user's decision-making.[56] This includes the social psychology theory that proposes that individuals use two distinct cognitive systems to access information and make decisions: an "automatic" system that is effortless and emotionally charged, and a "reflective" system that is reason-based, and therefore slower, effortful, and deliberately controlled.[57] There are also a number of overlapping and sometimes contradictory biases and mechanisms that interact with the cognitive systems employed when making decisions.[58] These include

[51] *Id.* at 137.
[52] *Id.* at 162.
[53] Harry Brignull et al., *Deceptive Patterns – User Interfaces Designed to Trick You*, Deceptive Design (Apr. 25, 2023), https://perma.cc/DW7C-JALW.
[54] Sela, *supra* note 46, at 137.
[55] *Id.* at 162.
[56] *Id.* at 139.
[57] *Id.*
[58] *Id.*

decoy effects,[59] status quo bias,[60] anchoring and adjustment effects,[61] priming effects,[62] loss aversion,[63] and scarcity effects.[64]

Even with careful and deliberate design, digital choice architectures cannot present options neutrally. This means any legal self-help tool will have an inherent bias, and, as Sela points out, "the use of nudges by public institutions raises a host of ethical concerns in-and-of-itself."[65] Common criticisms of digital nudging point to the obvious risk to autonomy and to how preventing individuals from making decisions entirely on their own reduces access to justice instead of improving it.[66] However, some conditions may satisfy the ethical use of nudging. Sela points to Sunstein, who suggests that nudges that "have the goal of increasing navigability – of making it easier for people to get to their preferred destination"[67] and "educative nudges … [aimed at] increasing people's own powers of agency"[68] may constitute ethical nudging. Sunstein continues that nudges that aim "to target, or to benefit from, behavioral biases tend to be more controversial, on ethical grounds, than efforts to appeal to deliberative capacities."[69]

This section has highlighted the factors necessary for designing efficient, usable, and fair legal AI assistants, and has underscored the importance of clear and consistent guidelines for ethical nudging in digital choice environments. Section 9.5 reviews systems that were designed with some of these user-centric principles in mind.

9.5 CASE ELICITATION

Legal case elicitation is a promising area of research that has the potential to increase access to justice by narrowing the language gap and helping laypeople determine the relevant facts needed to assert a claim or defense in court. Attorneys elicit case facts by starting with a general question (e.g., "How can I help you today?") and continuing with a series of follow-up questions that are used to determine which parts

59 A decoy effect occurs when the attractiveness of one option is increased by presenting it alongside an unattractive option that no one would reasonably choose (i.e., the decoy).

60 Status quo bias refers to the tendency to remain in the current state, since the disadvantages of leaving are perceived to be larger than the advantages associated with change.

61 Anchoring and adjustment effect occurs when a decision maker lacks information and therefore becomes biased toward any given starting values.

62 A priming effect describes the influence of introducing a topic or information before a decision is made, therefore increasing the likelihood that they will make a particular choice.

63 Loss aversion refers to the tendency for losses and disadvantages to have a greater impact on people's decision making than gains and advantages.

64 The scarcity effect describes the tendency for people to perceive scarce objects as more attractive or valuable than more readily available objects.

65 Sela, *supra* note 46, at 163.

66 *Id.*

67 THALER & SUNSTEIN, *supra* note 48, at 85.

68 *Id.*

69 Sela, *supra* note 46, at 163.

of the client's story can be presented in a compelling, coherent, and legally relevant way. This back-and-forth questioning and answering allows lawyers to elicit relevant facts and align them with the appropriate legal criteria.

This section highlights current research on decision-support tools designed to evaluate factual descriptions provided by unrepresented litigants. Systems that can evaluate a litigant's plain language description of a situation and provide relevant legal information play an important role in increasing access to justice. We end the section with a discussion of how generative AI has the potential to improve access to justice.

9.5.1 *Why Is Case Elicitation Necessary?*

Many technological innovations, including ODR, assist unrepresented litigants in asserting their rights, claims, or defenses. Branting developed an advisory system for pro se litigants in the domain of protection orders;[70] Thompson described the Justice Pathway Expert System ("JPES"), an expert system that provides support for unrepresented litigants within ODR;[71] Zeleznikow outlined the GetAid system, which helps lawyers determine whether an individual is eligible for aid;[72] and the Dutch platform Rechtwijzer,[73] which was designed to support separating couples, guides users toward appropriate resources based on information they provide about their situation. More recently, SPOT API can analyze a layperson's description of a situation and return a list of likely relevant legal issues.[74] One of the most widespread forms of legal self-help tools is document automation software.[75] Although widely used, a key limitation of document automation software is that it seldom assists users in formulating narrative statements of fact.[76] However, successful litigation requires aligning relevant facts with requirements for potential legal remedies while ignoring irrelevant facts. As Westermann et al. observed, "laypeople often tend to think of their situation in terms of what has happened (such as 'There is a water leak in my apartment')."[77] To assert their rights, unrepresented litigants must be able to determine how well facts fit the requirements for various legal remedies.

70 Branting, *supra* note 25, at 357–69; Figures 5.4–5.8.

71 Darin Thompson, *Creating New Pathways to Justice Using Simple Artificial Intelligence and Online Dispute Resolution*, 1 INT'L J. ONLINE DISP. RESOL. 5, 5 (2015).

72 John Zeleznikow, *Using Web-Based Legal Decision Support System to Improve Access to Justice*, 11 INFO. & COMMC'NS TECH. L. 15, 20–25 (2002).

73 Laura Kistemaker, *Rechtwijzer and Uitelkaar. Nl. Dutch Experiences with ODR for Divorce*, 59 FAM. CT. REV. 232, 232–43 (2001).

74 THE LEGAL INNOVATION & TECH. LAB'S SPOT API, https://perma.cc/6H3X-9DPG.

75 Karl Branting et al., *Induction of Narrative Models for Legal Case Elicitation*, PROC. 6TH WORKSHOP AUTOMATED SEMANTIC ANALYSIS INFO. L. TEXT 158, 158 (2023).

76 *Id.*

77 Hannes Westermann et al., *Bridging the Gap: Mapping Layperson Narratives to Legal Issues with Language Models*, PROC. 6TH WORKSHOP AUTOMATED SEMANTIC ANALYSIS INFO. L. TEXT 37, 37 (2023).

As discussed in Chapter 2, the language gap is a significant hurdle for unrepresented individuals who want to discover what legal remedies are available based on their situation. Unrepresented litigants may struggle to comprehend legal language and complex texts, as well as legal concepts and open-textured terms.[78] They may also not even be aware that their problem has a legal solution,[79] and when they do identify an appropriate legal remedy, they may not understand which forms to fill out[80] or which facts are relevant to their case.[81] Unrepresented litigants also face challenges in evaluating the quality of the information provided by self-help tools.[82]

9.5.2 *Current Research*

Recent research on case elicitation includes Westermann et al.[83] and Branting et al.[84] Westermann et al. describe a methodology to extend JusticeBot's capabilities (described in more detail in Chapter 12 and profiled in Section 13.7) with a system that maps layperson descriptions of factual events to legal issues using language models. JusticeBot is a decision-support tool that uses a hybrid case-based and rule-based reasoning system to provide users with legal information and references to previous similar cases based on their responses to questions about their situation. These questions and all their possible responses are collectively referred to as guided pathways, and their design was directly informed by the needs of unrepresented litigants.

The new JusticeBot feature maps a user's factual description of a situation to a database of example descriptions, which are linked directly to specific legal issues. To discover potentially relevant legal remedies, a user can create a description of their situation in plain language, and the system will map that text to database entries that describe the same or a similar situation. To test their methodology, Westermann et al. first needed to create a library of example descriptions aligned with specific legal issues. This library was created from descriptions drawn from two sources: examples written by the research team to capture the various ways a particular situation can be expressed and factual descriptions previously submitted by JusticeBot users. To map these examples to new factual descriptions, the examples must first be transformed into a

[78] Hannes Westermann, Using Artificial Intelligence to Increase Access to Justice 247 (Mar. 2023) (Ph.D. Dissertation, University of Montreal) (on file with the Cyberjustice Laboratory); Karl Branting et al., *Judges Are from Mars, Pro Se Litigants Are from Venus: Predicting Decisions from Lay Text, in* 334 Legal Knowledge and Information Systems 215, 215 (Serena Villata, Jakub Harašta & Petr Kremen eds., 2020).

[79] Westermann et al., *supra* note 77, at 37.

[80] *Id.*

[81] Branting et al., *Judges Are from Mars, Pro Se Litigants Are from Venus*, *supra* note 78, at 215.

[82] Westermann et al., *supra* note 77, at 246.

[83] *Id.* at 37–48.

[84] Branting et al., *Induction of Narrative Models for Legal Case Elicitation*, *supra* note 75, at 158–67.

mathematical representation, called a sentence vector. A sentence vector is a list of real-valued numbers, each of which captures a dimension of the sentence's meaning. For readers already familiar with sentence vectors, all example descriptions are vectorized with a multilingual universal sentence encoder. To achieve the mapping, new user sentences are vectorized with the same process (using a sentence encoder), and utterances are compared in mathematical space (also called embedded space). In the tool interface, the user is presented with the top three legal issues linked to database examples most similar to their factual description. The user is also presented with a description of the situation reflecting JusticeBot's understanding of the user's description, a suggested action, and a link to information about the relevant legal issues. This feature of JusticeBot remains in the research phase; however, it is a significant step toward further expanding access. A decision-support tool that interprets plain language descriptions of situations and provides information about potentially relevant legal remedies would play an important role in narrowing the gap between real and legal language.

Westermann et al. found that the system's ability to present the user with the correct relevant issue varied substantially depending on the type of issue and the dataset on which the model was trained.[85] They also note that whether the performance is adequate for a real-world system is still an open question. However, overall, the system showed promise in mapping user descriptions to relevant legal issues. As the authors note, the cost of failure for this technology is low because users can choose to ignore the system's suggestions and instead use the guided pathways within JusticeBot to continue their search for a relevant legal remedy. But when the system provides accurate and helpful information, access improves.

The ability to interpret text provided by a user is an important step in automatic case elicitation. Similar to Westermann et al., Branting and McLeod explored ways to analyze plain language texts provided by a user; however, their experimental methodology was informed by two complementary fields of prior work: investigations into the role of story understanding during legal client interviewing and induction of narrative schemas to support automated story understanding. Their work was based on empirical evidence suggesting that a coherent and legally relevant narrative is key to successful litigation.[86] During interviews, attorneys try to elicit "the causal and temporal connections that contribute to giving the events contextual meanings … within the aim of defining 'Who has done what, how, when, why and where?'"[87] This "account of the situation the client faces in light of the law" is sometimes termed a *case theory*,[88] and case theories "unite possible client narratives

[85] Westermann et al., *supra* note 77, at 46.
[86] Karl Branting & Sarah McLeod, *Narrative-Driven Case Elicitation*, ICAIL Workshop on A.I. for Access to Just. 1, 1 (2023).
[87] *Id.*
[88] *Id.* at 2.

with possible legal theories."[89] They observed that an attorney's narrative elicitation process is structured around their expectations about what constitutes a legally relevant story. They hypothesized that such expectations likely arise from hearing similar stories from numerous clients and argued that an automated narrative-driven case elicitation process must also represent generalizations from multiple relevant stories. The set of legal issues most common among unrepresented litigants is relatively stable; however, litigants can describe the same legal situation in various ways. A system that could analyze text from litigants in plain language and identify the set of legally relevant facts would play an important role in a decision-support tool designed to help unrepresented individuals understand how to satisfy the requirements of the legal remedies available to them.

Branting et al. introduced the Relevant, Irrelevant, Missing ("RIM") architecture for narrative-driven case elicitation. This architecture was designed to fill a gap in existing software – no software can currently interpret text provided by a user or assist a user in paraphrasing facts in a manner that is likely to communicate most effectively within court documents. A feature like this could help narrow the language gap by identifying legally relevant facts in users' descriptions and paraphrasing them in the manner required by a particular legal remedy.

The RIM architecture uses a model trained on legal narratives to guide interactions with a user aimed at distinguishing relevant case facts from irrelevant facts. Their approach has two components: an offline component in which narrative schemas are learned from data, and an online component in which schemas are used to guide interactions with litigants. These schemas consist of sequences of events that represent activities relevant to a particular situation and the order in which those activities typically occur. During offline learning, domain-specific narrative texts are converted to graphical event sequences.[90] The resulting graph representations of the sentences are then combined into domain-specific legal narrative schemas. To evaluate the approach, they experimented with two techniques for inducing legal narrative schemas: language models and event sequence alignment.[91] For the event sequence alignment technique, which was inspired by techniques used in molecular biology, multiple event sequences are aligned to identify the longest common subsequence.

Branting et al. evaluated the predictive models with the narrative cloze test, which estimates a model's ability to predict a missing (typically the next) event in a sequence. They noted that the cloze prediction accuracy observed for the language

[89] *Id.*

[90] Karine Megerdoomian, Karl Branting, Charles E. Horowitz, Amy B. Marsh, Nick Modly, Stacy J. Petersen, Eric O. Scott & Sujit B. Wariyar, *Automated Narrative Extraction from Administrative Records*, PROC. WORKSHOP A.I. & ADMIN. STATE 38, 38–48 (2019).

[91] Branting et al., *Induction of Narrative Models for Legal Case Elicitation*, *supra* note 75.

model approach is similar to that in previous narrative schema induction experiments. Whether performance is adequate for real-world implementation within the RIM architecture remains an open question that warrants investigation; the techniques show promise in distilling a human narrative into a succinct, relevant set of facts. Section 9.6 explores how generative AI could enhance the capabilities of these and other legal self-help tools.

9.6 GENERATIVE AI AND LEGAL AI ASSISTANTS

Generative AI has the potential to expand access to justice and is already being used in some areas of the law. CoCounsel, briefly described in Section 9.3, is a generative AI chatbot powered by GPT-4 and designed to help attorneys streamline legal research and document drafting.[92] Recently, LLMs have been shown to be a viable option for a task-oriented dialogue pipeline when combined with an in-domain state tracker.[93] This expands the possibilities for effective communication tools for legal AI assistants, including tools that help narrow the language gap.

LLM outputs rarely include legalese unless prompted to, making LLMs a potentially effective resource for explaining complex concepts in plain language. Chien and Kim conducted a pilot study with ninety-one legal aid attorneys to assess the usefulness of generative AI for common tasks, including document summarization, confirmatory or preliminary research, production of first drafts, and translation from legalese or English into more accessible formats.[94] At the end of the pilot, 90% of participants reported increased productivity, and 75% reported their intent to keep using the tools.[95] This suggests that generative AI may be a useful tool to augment the work of legal aid attorneys, an important step toward increasing access to justice.

Tan et al. investigated the ability of ChatGPT to provide legal information to laypeople.[96] Their research suggests that ChatGPT can understand users' needs; however, it is not yet accurate enough to provide reliable information to laypeople. They point to promising future work combining LLMs with rule-based systems, like JusticeBot. Related research includes LLMediator, which explores how models like LLMs may be used to support parties in arriving at a settlement during ODR.[97] The authors built an experimental platform that leverages GPT-4 to suggest reformulations of inflammatory messages from disputants and to draft messages for a mediator (or facilitators) to intervene efficiently in a discussion (see Figure 11.6).

[92] THOMSON REUTERS, *supra* note 23.
[93] Hudeček & Dusek, *supra* note 11, at 227.
[94] Chien & Kim, *supra* note 18.
[95] *Id.* at 5.
[96] Jinzhe Tan, Hannes Westermann & Karim Benyekhlef, *ChatGPT as an Artificial Lawyer?*, ICAIL WORKSHOP ON A.I. FOR ACCESS TO JUST. (2023), https://perma.cc/ZW7V-E66A.
[97] Westermann, Savelka & Benyekhlef, *supra* note 11.

In addition, the platform has an experimental feature that autonomously intervenes on behalf of a mediator to guide parties toward a settlement (see Figure 11.7).[98] A known strength of generative AI is its ability to identify multiple ways in which someone can express the same idea.[99] If generative AI can be shown to be reliable and accurate in a legal context, this will have tremendous implications for automated case elicitation.

Chapter 4 discusses generative AI in detail, including the opportunities and pitfalls associated with these technologies. Despite their ability to produce human-like text, these models cannot reliably generate accurate information. As of the time of this writing, there is no consensus on whether these models can truly reason over the data on which they are trained.[100] As Schilder points out, this leads to various risks, including reliability issues as well as ethical and bias concerns.[101] The tendency for LLMs to hallucinate is of particular concern, as these systems are being used by laypeople who may not be able to validate the information they receive (see Sections 12.7.1 and 16.2.3).[102] Current research suggests that generative AI is not yet accurate and reliable enough to support complex legal tasks; however, it holds promise when implemented as a legal AI assistant, particularly when combined with external reasoning components and knowledge sources.[103]

9.7 CONCLUSION

Dialogue systems, including those built with LLMs, provide a natural language interface that enables users to collaborate with technology in pursuit of a goal. The real-world systems and research outlined in this section show how chatbots can be helpful to both courts and unrepresented litigants. When designing a decision-support tool for unrepresented litigants, it is important to adopt a user-centric approach to increase the likelihood that the tool will meet their needs. It is also important to consider how, and in what contexts, options are presented to users to avoid unintended biases that may influence laypeople. Most legal AI assistants implement self-guided procedures, which comprise a series of steps in which litigants provide information and make choices to advance their cases to resolution. The design of these environments warrants careful review and clear, consistent guidelines, as

[98] *Id.*

[99] Tan, Westermann & Benyekhlef, *supra* note 96, at Section 2.

[100] GPT-4o claims reasoning and as of 2024 there are prompt-based reasoning engines. However, this is still an area of strong debate within generative AI.

[101] Frank Schilder, *Legal Expertise Meets Artificial Intelligence: A Critical Analysis of Large Language Models as Intelligent Assistance Technology*, PROC. 3RD INT'L WORKSHOP ON A.I. & INTELLIGENT ASSISTANCE FOR LEGAL PROS. DIGIT. WORKPLACE 4, 4–7 (2023).

[102] Tan, Westermann & Benyekhlef, *supra* note 96, at Section 5.

[103] Schilder, *supra* note 101; Tan, Westermann & Benyekhlef, *supra* note 96; Ajmi, *supra* note 30.

architectural decisions can shape users' decisions and actions, steering them toward certain behaviors, even inadvertently. Decision-support tools for case elicitation would benefit both lawyers and unrepresented litigants, thereby increasing access to justice in significant ways. Despite concerns, a strength of LLMs is their ability to translate complex language, enabling unrepresented litigants to articulate their needs and assert their claims and defenses, as well as to enforce their rights.

PART III

Promising Applications

10

Putting It All Together

*Mia Bonardi**

10.1 INTRODUCTION

From computational logic and machine learning ("ML") to generative AI and chatbots, each of these technologies has unique strengths and limitations in delivering legal help to unrepresented litigants. Yet no single approach on its own is currently sufficient to tackle the complexities of the legal system for unrepresented litigants. This chapter brings together the types of AI discussed in previous chapters and demonstrates how they can be combined to support unrepresented litigants navigating the legal system.

Facing the legal system without help is a daunting task for many. As discussed in Chapter 3, unrepresented litigants confront a range of challenges throughout all five stages of litigation: Recognition, Evaluation, Initiation, Litigation, and Resolution. They must engage legal consciousness,[1] gather both legal and factual information, weigh incentives and risks, draft proper documents, navigate filing and service procedures, appear in court effectively, communicate and negotiate with opposing parties, and continuously monitor case activity. Without the legal expertise and resources of a lawyer, these individuals often make mistakes and omissions that harm their cases, resulting in delays, unfavorable outcomes, or outright dismissal.[2] While the document automation and guided interviews discussed in Chapter 8 can assist people through much of the process on their own, even the most advanced AI tool currently cannot support unrepresented litigants through the entire process, from when the problem arises through to a legal resolution.

The limitations of one tool can be offset by the strengths of others by using multiple AI tools in one system. The goal is seamless support: a system that can handle the

* I thank Michelle Bernstein for her help with this chapter and for creating the figures included. I also thank Amy J. Schmitz for her review of multiple drafts of this chapter.

1 *See, e.g.*, Lynette J. Chua & David Engel, *Legal Consciousness Reconsidered*, 15 ANN. REV. L. & SOC. SCI. 335, 336–41 (2019) (defining and summarizing the literature on legal consciousness). Legal consciousness is discussed more in Section 3.2.1.

2 *See, e.g.*, Rebecca L. Sandefur, *Legal Advice from Nonlawyers: Consumer Demand, Provider Quality, and Public Harms*, 16 STAN. J. C.R. & C.L. 283, 299–300 (2020).

entire journey of a litigant. Comprehensive tools capable of addressing the diverse needs of litigants in an efficient and user-centric way are the ideal future of legal AI systems for litigants without lawyers. However, realizing this vision requires substantial financial investment and organizational capacity that many courts and legal aid organizations currently lack. While this chapter illustrates the potential of integrated systems, it is important to recognize the significant resource constraints that may limit their implementation.

In this chapter, we return to key insights from each previous chapter and illustrate them through a hypothetical tenant, Jaime. She navigates issues with her landlord concerning whether her home is safe and livable using an integrated AI legal system. Through Jaime's experience, we show how various AI technologies can collaborate to deliver comprehensive support. From initial case assessment to document preparation, we see how a chatbot using generative AI and computational logic provides Jaime with guidance at each step of the legal process. This narrative illustrates how a well-designed system can empower unrepresented litigants to understand their rights, gather relevant evidence, prepare legal documents, and ultimately find a resolution without extensive legal knowledge or expensive legal representation.

While showcasing the potential of integrated AI systems, this chapter also addresses important limitations and concerns. We examine how errors can compound across interconnected AI components, potentially leading to more significant problems than if the components were offered independently. The chapter explores how biases can accumulate across different AI tools and underscores the importance of integrating these technologies thoughtfully with existing human systems. By acknowledging these limitations alongside the benefits, we provide a balanced view of how integrated AI legal systems can be carefully designed and implemented to advance access to civil justice for unrepresented litigants.

10.2 THE POTENTIAL OF INTEGRATED APPROACHES

While no single AI technology can address all the needs of unrepresented litigants, combining different approaches offers the potential to create more comprehensive support systems. Each technology discussed in previous chapters has distinct strengths and limitations, but when thoughtfully integrated, they may complement each other to provide more effective assistance.

Chapters 2 and 4 discussed the language gap and introduced generative AI, explaining how it can create legal content and elicit legal information from a litigant that a court might need to make a decision. Generative AI systems that incorporate large language models ("LLMs") allow litigants to talk about their problems on their own terms. Generative AI can also turn that information into data that other systems can use. However, generative AI struggles to provide accurate legal information, interpretations, and arguments based on precedent (see Chapters 4, 12, and 16). For example, although models are continually advancing, they still may be unable to complete a court form reliably and accurately, warranting a human in the loop.[3] This is similar to the way that generative AI can be challenged by math.[4]

Chapter 6 introduced computational logic. With it, humans can build a logical flow that asks the right questions at the right times, helping litigants obtain or provide the correct information for their circumstances. Computational logic is adept at adhering to the legal rules, but it is rigid and struggles with situations that do not fit its logic. For example, it struggles with broader legal principles such as the "best interests of the child." At present, substantial human subject matter expertise is needed to construct such a system, so its development takes much longer. Depending on the complexity, most legal situations need their own customized code. However, research suggests that for some issues and case types, LLMs can build these initial pathways.[5]

Chapter 7 explored the evolution of ML in the legal domain, from early approaches to modern language models. While ML shows promise in document classification and outcome prediction, many models function as "black boxes," providing predictions without explanations. The chapter discusses how LLMs have advanced NLP capabilities and can generate fluent text, potentially offering guidance to litigants. However, it emphasizes that even these advanced models currently struggle with legal accuracy, jurisdiction-specific precedents, and the provision of reliable explanations for their predictions. For litigants, this creates significant limitations. ML systems, including LLMs, might effectively identify patterns in legal data but face challenges in delivering trustworthy, legally sound guidance. Without integration with systems that improve legal accuracy and interpretability, ML approaches alone cannot fully bridge the gap between prediction and the actionable support litigants need.

Chapter 8 on document automation showed how automated templates and guided interviews can help unrepresented litigants draft court forms and legal communications. This alone can assist people through much of the process on their own. However, because the vast majority of these automated templates rely on computational logic, they can be rigid without the support of other technologies.

Chapter 9 examined dialogue systems and chatbots for legal assistance. While these tools can help unrepresented litigants by processing natural language and providing legal information in plain language, they have significant limitations. Dialogue systems struggle to elicit case facts accurately, to bridge the language

[3] *See, e.g.*, Quinten Steenhuis, David Colarusso & Bryce Willey, *Weaving Pathways for Justice with GPT: LLM-Driven Automated Drafting of Interactive Legal Applications*, ARXIV 3 (Dec. 14, 2023), https://perma.cc/M2W2-TFWT.

[4] *See, e.g.*, Steve Lohr, *A.I. Can Write Poetry, but It Struggles with Math*, N.Y. TIMES (July 23, 2024), www.nytimes.com/2024/07/23/technology/ai-chatbots-chatgpt-math.html.

[5] Samyar Janatian et al., *From Text to Structure: Using Large Language Models to Support the Development of Legal Expert Systems*, 36 INT'L CONF. LEGAL KNOWLEGDE & INFO. SYS. (2023); Quinten Steenhuis, David Colarusso & Bryce Willey, *Weaving Pathways for Justice with GPT*, JURIX WORKSHOP ON AI AND ACCESS TO JUSTICE (2023).

gap consistently, and to avoid bias in interface design. These shortcomings explain why effective implementations typically combine dialogue systems with rule-based approaches and external knowledge sources.[6] Although valuable for information gathering and basic guidance, dialogue systems alone cannot provide litigants with the comprehensive, reliable support they need throughout the entire legal process.

Combining the unique strengths of these AI systems can make up for their weaknesses. This combination can make a system that is stronger than the sum of its parts. It can empower unrepresented litigants to engage with the legal system without exacerbating an already challenging situation.[7] While an integrated approach offers compelling advantages, achieving such comprehensive systems requires substantial financial investment and organizational capacity that may be beyond the reach of many courts and legal aid organizations currently serving unrepresented litigants. There are also risks in combining these technologies, which are discussed below. For more on this, see Chapter 15 on AI assurance.

10.3 MATCHING LITIGANTS' TASKS WITH TECHNOLOGY

As discussed in Chapter 3, unrepresented litigants confront a range of challenges. The AI and other technologies discussed previously – generative AI, computational logic, document automation, machine learning, dialogue systems, and more – have the potential to help litigants with the tasks they must complete, especially when combined in a modular way. Schmitz and Zeleznikow have suggested a similar modular approach in the online dispute resolution ("ODR") space, explaining: "It is modular in that all of the tools, or modules, are not necessary for every case."[8] Similarly, here we match the tasks required of civil litigants with the types of AI and other technologies discussed in other chapters.

We follow Jaime on her journey navigating unsafe and unlivable housing conditions with her landlord. The following scenario illustrates what comprehensive AI support could look like with sufficient resources and development. While technologically feasible, such a system would require significant investment that may be beyond the reach of many organizations currently serving unrepresented litigants.

–

Jaime rents an apartment in Maryland. A month ago, a pipe burst in her ceiling and water leaked onto her couch and table all day, ruining the furniture, carpet, and floor. She moved the furniture, but the pipe continued to leak. She has to keep

[6] *See, e.g.*, L. Karl Branting, *Data-centric and Logic-Based Models for Automated Legal Problem Solving*, 25 A.I. & L. 5, 25–27 (2017).

[7] *See* Aubrie Souza & Zach Zarnow, *Court Chatbots*, Nat'l Ctr. for State Cts. 5 (2024) (on file with Mia Bonardi).

[8] Amy J. Schmitz & John Zeleznikow, *Intelligent Legal Tech to Empower Self-Represented Litigants*, 23 Colum. Sci. & Tech. L. Rev. 142, 175 (2022).

a bucket under the leak and empty it when it fills. Jaime immediately asked her landlord to fix the pipe and the floor, but the landlord has not replied. Jaime has felt fatigued and congested for a while, and her doctor told her that she might be having an allergic reaction to the mold growing around the leak. Jaime has no legal representation and only limited knowledge of the legal system.

10.3.1 *Engaging Legal Consciousness*

Jaime knows her landlord should repair the leak and the resulting damage, but she is unsure whether she can compel her landlord to do so. A significant number of unrepresented litigants do not see their problems as "legal" in nature and instead turn to social support systems for help or resolution. The Public Understanding of Law Survey ("PULS") by the Victoria Law Foundation found that "Respondents handled 32% of problems on their own, only sought informal help from family and friends for 14%, obtained independent (but not legal) help for 29%, and got independent help from a legal service for 21% of problems."[9]

For those who identify their problem as legal, many attempt to contact multiple lawyers for help. They learn that few lawyers outside legal aid are willing to assist with these types of issues because they are not profitable. Even legal aid is limited in the cases it can take on due to resource constraints.

When Jaime first thinks about taking legal action, she has only a vague understanding of her rights as a tenant. Does Jaime have a case? Late at night, when Jaime is not working and is free to address this issue, she first visits the court's website, where she finds a chatbot.[10]

Figure 10.1 shows the legal AI chatbot using a combination of computational logic and generative AI to assist Jaime. This diagram illustrates the multi-layer processing that occurs when the chatbot handles Jaime's query. The system operates through three interconnected components. The *chatbot* on the left represents the user-facing conversation window where the user reports the initial problem. The *generative AI* on the right converts human language into data and, later, data into appropriate conversational responses. The *computational logic* sits between them, passing users' inputs to the generative AI. The generative AI is constrained by the computational logic and converts the user's inputs into data. For example, the computational logic offers only specific legal categories from which the AI can choose (e.g., "housing," "family," or "neither"). The computational logic pulls together all the data, then asks the generative AI to construct an appropriate conversational response based on that data. During this process, based on the user's inputs, the computational logic assigns

[9] *See, e.g.*, NIGEL J. BALMER ET AL., THE PUBLIC UNDERSTANDING OF LAW SURVEY: EVERYDAY PROBLEMS AND LEGAL NEED 16 (Victoria Law Found., 2023), https://perma.cc/F3JE-3D43; *see also* Amy J. Schmitz, *Access to Consumer Remedies in the Squeaky Wheel System*, 39 PEPP. L. REV. 279, 290 (2012) (discussing how "consumers lack information regarding their rights").

[10] Souza & Zarnow, *supra* note 7, at 4.

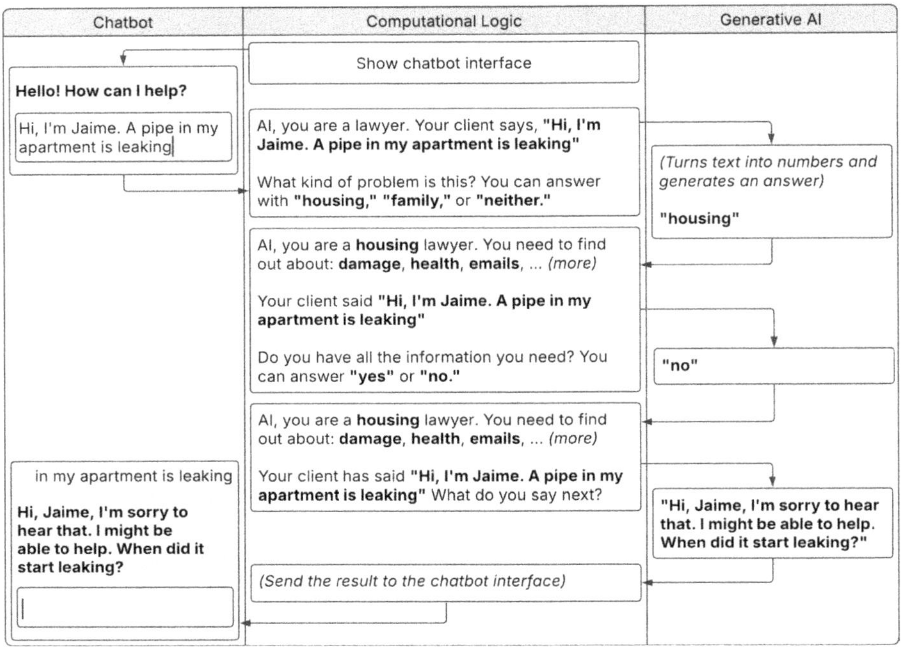

FIGURE 10.1 Legal AI assistant processing an initial request.

the generative AI roles to assume so that it can provide the most helpful responses. The flow demonstrates how a simple user input, such as "A pipe in my apartment is leaking," triggers a cascade of intelligent processing that mimics how a human professional would approach a client consultation: by understanding the domain, identifying legal requirements, assessing available information, and then asking targeted follow-up questions to gather the necessary details for providing effective assistance.

The chatbot uses generative AI to convert Jaime's answers into data and passes that data to the computational logic that the developers wrote for this particular set of laws. The tool still needs more information to help Jaime, but she at least begins to understand that this really could be a situation where the law could help.

10.3.2 *Gathering Factual Information*

Next, Jaime needs to identify and collect factual information related to her case. Jaime is unsure, though, which details will be important in court.[11] The same court-provided chatbot continues to assist her. The generative AI chatbot using narrative-driven case elicitation asks Jaime questions with a focus on "the life experiences

[11] *See* Karl Branting & Sarah McLeod, *Narrative-Driven Case Elicitation*, ICAIL Workshop AI for Access to Just. 1 (2023).

that give rise to legal claims," and Jaime writes her answers in her own words.[12] The generative AI formats Jaime's answers as structured data and transmits that data to a computational logic system.[13] This logic system uses rule-based algorithms to analyze the structured information and determine that Jaime needs to upload communications with her landlord.[14] The logic system then communicates back to the generative AI, specifying the data format it requires (such as JSON), and the generative AI provides the appropriately formatted response. The logic system validates this data and may repeat the process iteratively until it obtains the required information.[15]

The system, which combines generative AI with computational logic, asks Jaime specific follow-up questions to gather information. The computational logic component contains pre-programmed legal requirements and uses rule-based reasoning to determine what additional information is needed for Jaime's case type. It communicates these requirements to the generative AI, which then generates natural language questions tailored to Jaime's specific situation. For example, the system asks whether Jaime sent emails about the leak and whether she received any replies. It reminds her to check her email trash folder in case she missed any. The computational logic continuously evaluates Jaime's responses against its legal criteria and instructs the generative AI to ask follow-up questions until all necessary information is collected. Using this hybrid approach, the system guides Jaime through a structured questionnaire that provides the information she needs to decide whether to go to court.[16] However, the generative AI personalizes the interaction with Jaime, allowing her to tell her story.[17] The chatbot follows up to obtain the specific dates of the complaints Jaime has made to her landlord about the leaks and a description of how the repairs (or lack thereof) have affected her living conditions. The tool asks for additional documentation that might support Jaime's case, such as photos of the unrepaired damage and medical records,[18] since her health has been affected.

10.3.3 *Gathering Legal Information*

Jaime now needs to understand the specific laws governing tenant rights to present her case in court. However, she is not sure where to find the relevant laws.

[12] *Id.*

[13] *See* Westermann et al., *Bridging the Gap: Mapping Layperson Narratives to Legal Issues with Language Models*, Proc. 6th Workshop Automated Semantic Analysis Info. L. Text 37 (2023).

[14] *See id.*

[15] *See id.*

[16] *See* Steenhuis, Colarusso & Willey, *supra* note 3 ("Whether forms or narratives are the best presentation, ultimately, what decision makers need are the facts to make a decision.").

[17] Branting & McLeod, *supra* note 11 ("Clients' narratives are often 'redefined to be a legally relevant narrative' by counsel, a process that can sometimes diminish emotionally salient background information … [T]he achievement of a client's goals depends on the degree to which the client's story can be presented, whether in a written petition or to a judge or jury, in a compelling, coherent, and legally relevant way.").

[18] For a discussion on privacy and confidentiality issues, *see infra* Chapter 15 on AI assurance.

Jaime uses the chatbot to describe her situation, and by leveraging generative AI and computational logic, the tool uses machine learning systems to suggest resources to her, including organizations, articles, websites, and more. This system uses retrieval-augmented generation ("RAG") to pull from a curated legal database. It works by: (1) using natural language processing ("NLP") to extract key elements from Jaime's description, such as lease issues, location, and dispute type; (2) semantically matching her situation to relevant legal categories and jurisdictional requirements; (3) retrieving information from a curated database of verified Maryland legal resources, including pre-screened statutes, articles, and legal aid organizations; and (4) generating contextually appropriate explanations that translate complex legal text into understandable guidance. The system provides Jaime with jurisdiction-specific resources on tenant rights laws in Maryland and explanations of those laws.

10.3.4 *Weighing Incentives and Risks of Going to Court*

Filing a case requires both time and financial resources, and Jaime worries about the cost and stress of going to court. She seeks to understand the potential outcomes and weigh the risks involved before proceeding further. The generative AI has converted the information Jaime provided into data that the computational logic can understand. Based on tenant laws and Jaime's information, the computational logic goes through each legal factor to estimate how much money Jaime can expect to recover. For example, it calculates how long the plumbing has been broken and the cost of the furniture that the water ruined. It determines what the law requires the landlord to do and pay. It also calculates estimates for the costs that Jaime will incur in litigation. Some costs she may not be able to recover, such as the bus fare to get to the court, the potential cost and risk of the hours she will have to take off work, and the fees she might have to pay.

In Figure 10.2, the chatbot offers previous cases that are similar to Jaime's, as well as possible outcomes.[19] Figure 10.2 builds on Figure 10.1, retaining the original three components (chatbot, computational logic, and generative AI) and adding a specialized fourth component: *case comparison AI*. The system takes Jaime's housing case and systematically processes it through multiple layers: the computational logic identifies it as a housing matter and searches a database of 574 similar cases; the case comparison AI ranks relevant precedents (identifying cases in a standard court format such as H3D001, H3D305, and H3E112 as most similar); and the generative AI produces detailed summaries of each precedent case. This provides Jaime with a better understanding of the risks and benefits of going to court.

[19] *See* Hannes Westermann, Using Artificial Intelligence to Increase Access to Justice 258–59, 293–94, 339 (Mar. 2023) (Ph.D. Dissertation, University of Montreal) (on file with the Cyberjustice Laboratory); *see also infra* Section 13.7 for a profile of JusticeBot.

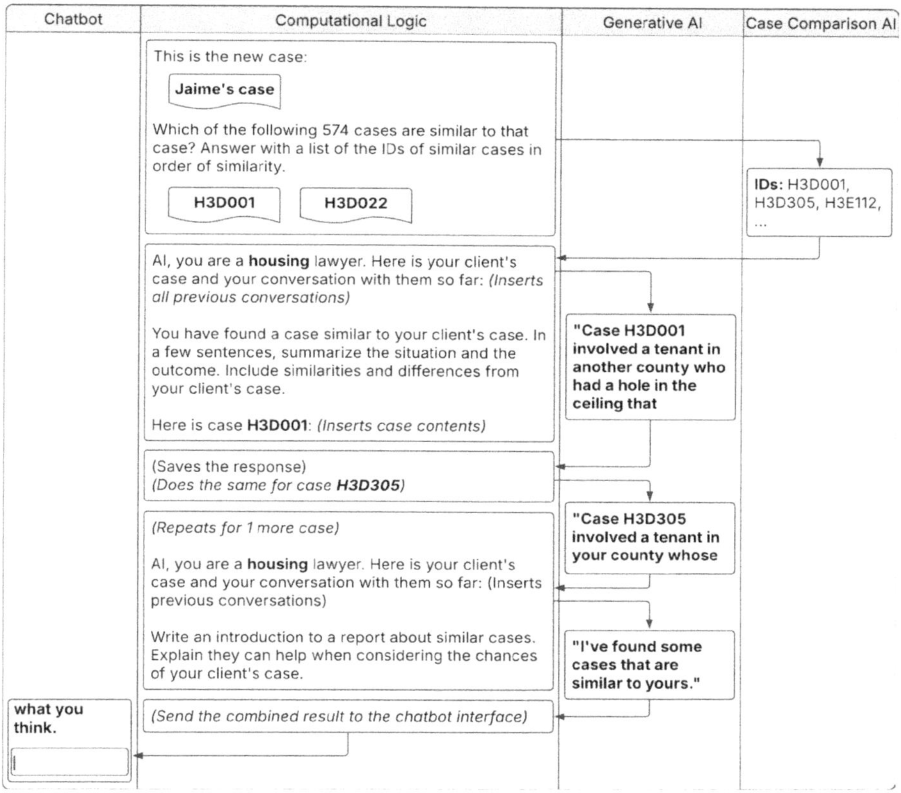

FIGURE 10.2 Legal AI assistant with case comparison AI for legal precedent research.

10.3.5 *Drafting Documents*

Having decided to go ahead with the case, Jaime now faces the task of drafting a complaint. With no experience in legal writing, she finds this process intimidating.

A document automation component simplifies this by leveraging the structured information that computational logic has collected through the intake and case assessment process (see Chapter 8). Document automation has evolved from traditional template-based approaches to more sophisticated AI-powered platforms (e.g., Dallma). Using Jaime's previous inputs, the document automation component generates a draft complaint that follows legal elements and pleading standards for tenant claims in Maryland as well as local court requirements.

As Jaime reviews the generated document, generative AI provides editing assistance. Meanwhile, the underlying computational logic identifies formatting issues and procedural requirements, highlighting errors and indicating where the document should be formatted differently to meet local court standards. With this integrated AI drafting support, Jaime can create a professional-looking document that makes it easier for the judge to identify relevant information, streamlining the process for both her and the court.

10.3.6 *Filing and Service*

Jaime must now properly file the complaint with the court and serve it on her landlord in accordance with specific procedural rules. Trying to follow this process without help could easily lead to costly mistakes, such as having her complaint dismissed for procedural errors and having to refile. Other mistakes can include failing to serve properly (or at all), serving the wrong person or entity, missing the statute of limitations, filing in the wrong court or jurisdiction, or failing to exhaust administrative remedies. Computational logic helps with procedural rules, such as filing deadlines, fees, and service methods.

Because Jaime is completing this work late at night while the court is closed, the tool files the form online the next day. It has already helped her identify the correct court for her case type and the court nearest to her. The tool also provides guidance on how to serve the complaint. Jaime has the option to save all her responses at any stage. She can also sign up for reminders about important dates related to her case, including her court date.

10.3.7 *Appearing in Court*

Jaime faces multiple challenges in preparing for her court appearance, ranging from logistical concerns about getting to court to apprehension about the legal proceedings. Beyond the stress of presenting her case, she must navigate practical barriers, including transportation costs, court schedules that conflict with her work hours, and unfamiliarity with court procedures.

The tool provides guidance for the hearing through a multi-component AI system that integrates geolocation services, image analysis capabilities, and cost calculation algorithms with an LLM and RAG. Building on the core chatbot interface and computational logic components in Figures 10.1 and 10.2, the system incorporates specialized services, including geolocation mapping that provides directions to the court, a bus fare calculation application programming interface ("API") for calculating transportation costs, and computer vision image analysis algorithms for assessing the technical quality of uploads. The system uses RAG to access court-specific requirements by retrieving information about court procedures, accepted file formats, and scheduling constraints from its legal knowledge base. When Jaime uploads evidence, computational logic coordinates between the image analysis component, which assesses quality, and RAG, which validates the evidence against court requirements. The LLM then synthesizes these technical assessments and generates personalized, actionable guidance in plain language.

Jaime receives a customized list of evidence to present in court, as well as guidance on how to take and upload high-quality photos. For instance, automated file format detection identifies that one of Jaime's images is in PNG format, while the RAG system confirms that the court accepts only JPEG formats. The computational logic triggers the LLM to explain this discrepancy to Jaime. The system also uses image analysis to help her submit high-quality images by assessing clarity, lighting, and readability.

Figure 10.3 builds on the core three components from prior figures by adding a fourth component: *image analysis AI*. When a user uploads a blurry photograph claiming to show mold on a wall, the system orchestrates a multimodal analysis: first, the computational logic assigns the AI to an investigative role to assess whether the image is useful; then the image analysis AI examines the photograph to determine whether it is useful, concluding that it is "too blurry"; finally, the system switches to a personal assistant role to provide constructive feedback to help Jaime take a better photo. The generative AI synthesizes these technical assessments into user-friendly language, explaining that the picture quality is insufficient and offering practical guidance on how to take and upload high-quality photos. Of course, Jaime can choose to override this feature and proceed with a photo that the system flags as unhelpful. This demonstrates comprehensive assistance that addresses both the technical adequacy of evidence and the practical needs of users seeking to document legal issues.

Figure 10.4 continues to build on this example and introduces a *geolocation service* for mapping and navigation, as well as a *bus fare AI* for calculating transportation costs. The generative AI synthesizes information from multiple components into coherent, actionable advice presented through the chatbot. It helps Jaime plan the logistics of attending court by calculating transportation costs between her address and the court. After determining that walking would take four hours while taking Bus 20E would require only forty-three minutes, the system provides a detailed cost analysis, including a $2 bus fare each way, $56 in court filing fees, and $20 in other anticipated expenses, totaling $80. It also manages scheduling around the possibility that court could take most of the

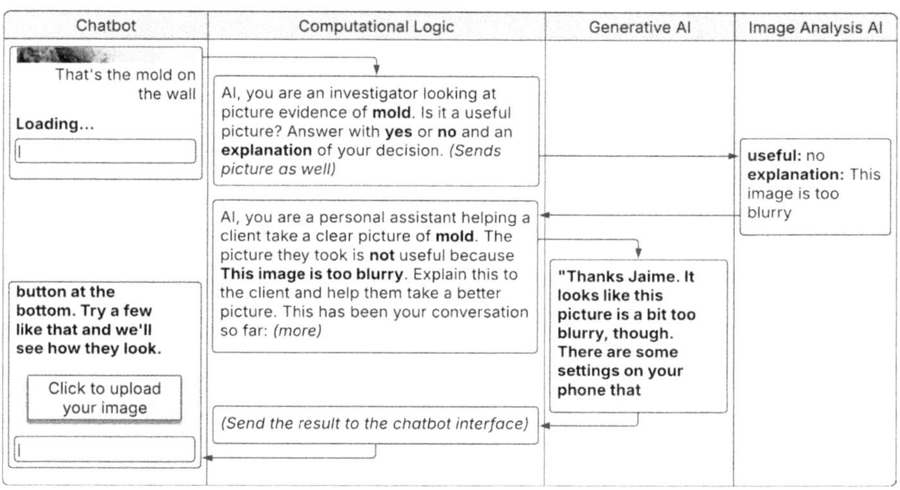

FIGURE 10.3 Legal AI assistant with an image analysis AI component for evidence gathering.

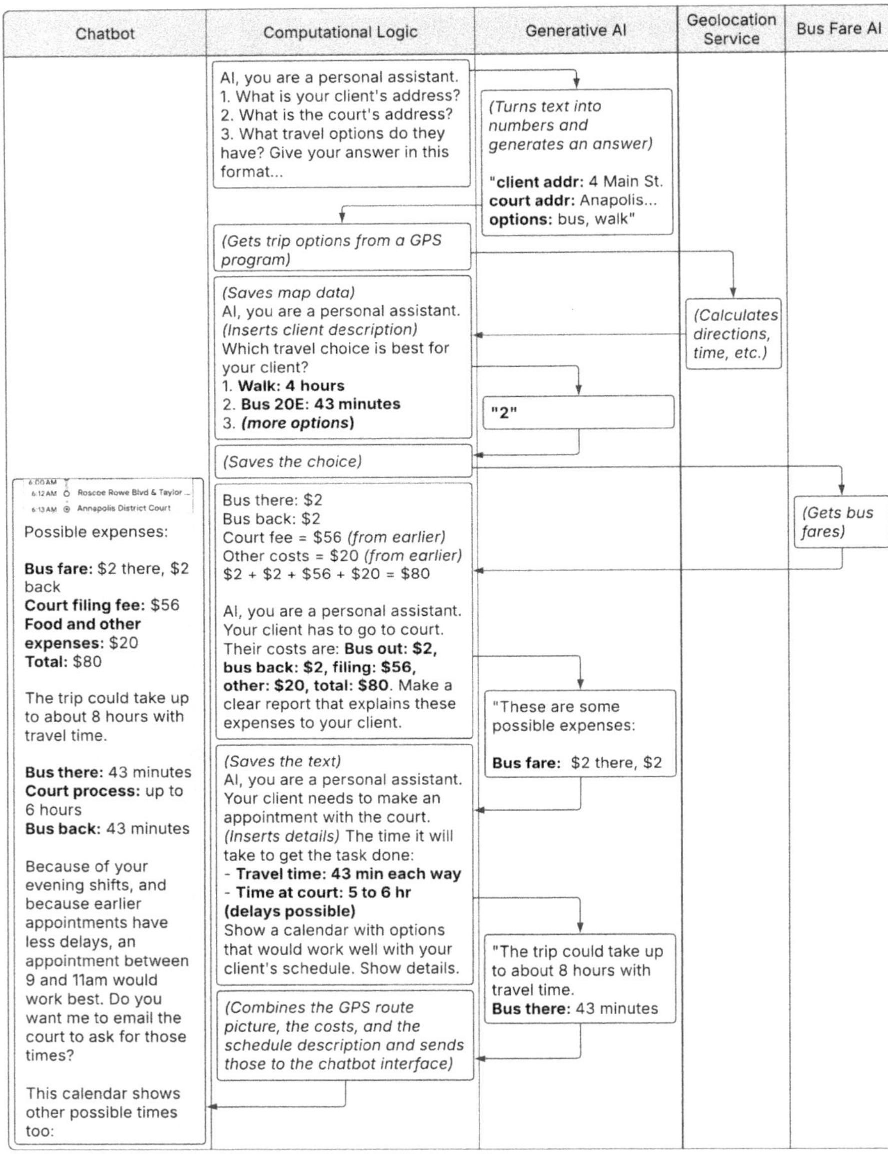

FIGURE 10.4 Legal AI assistant with geolocation service and bus fare AI components for logistics planning.

day, identifying optimal timing based on Jaime's work constraints. This is an example of how AI systems can coordinate multiple services to provide holistic assistance that addresses the legal, logistical, financial, and scheduling aspects of complex real-world situations.

Jaime is not just worried about getting to court; she is also nervous about appearing in court. She is unsure what to expect or how to present her case effectively. She worries about missing important points or being caught off guard by the judge's questions. While unauthorized practice of law ("UPL") restrictions prevent AI technologies from assisting unrepresented litigants in the courtroom,[20] a chatbot helps Jaime prepare by practicing with her. It pretends to be a judge and asks her questions that the judge might ask. Jaime practices her responses, receives feedback from the AI, and works to improve them. Through this preparation, she has the opportunity to learn courtroom procedures and become more comfortable presenting her case.

10.3.8 *Communicating and Negotiating*

Jaime has given the tool access to emails about her case. Before the case progresses too far, the tool alerts Jaime that the landlord has emailed an offer for a partial settlement. Figure 10.5 incorporates an email service component that provides automated monitoring capabilities for legal case management. The system continually checks Jaime's email inbox at regular intervals (10:25, 10:30, 10:35, and later 02:10), tracking the total number of emails as it increases from 303 to 305 messages and identifying new correspondence from various senders. The system distinguishes between routine emails and legally significant communications through a predefined alert list that flags specific contacts, such as "landlord." When an email arrives from alex@Rentals-R-Us.com – a sender identified as the client's landlord – offering a partial settlement of $150, the computational logic recognizes the legal significance, assumes the role of a housing lawyer, and triggers an automated alert. The generative AI then drafts an appropriate notification message with relevant context, illustrating how such systems can continually monitor cases and deliver professionally framed, time-sensitive updates. This email service component operates similarly to paid integration tools like Zapier, enabling users to connect various applications and automate tasks, such as sending emails based on specific triggers.

Jaime is very upset by the low offer from her landlord. She drafts an angry response. Before she sends it, the system detects problematic language and generative AI suggests alternatives.[21] The suggestions include explanations about why specific language changes might help her. She can choose to send her original message, accept the suggestion, or edit the revised version. Here, generative AI helps Jaime draft a

[20] *See* Complaint ¶¶ 25–27, In the Matter of DoNotPay, Inc., C-4812 (F.T.C. Jan. 14, 2025), https://perma.cc/F6TK-TR3K; *see also* Caitlyn Shelton, *"Robot lawyer" Set to Defend Human in U.S. Court*, FOX 8 (Jan. 12, 2023), https://perma.cc/7WB8-3TWL.

[21] *See* Hannes Westermann, Jaromir Savelka & Karim Benyekhlef, *LLMediator: GPT-4 Assisted Online Dispute Resolution*, ICAIL Workshop A.I. Access Justice (2023), https://perma.cc/S9WK-5G2U; Figure 11.6.

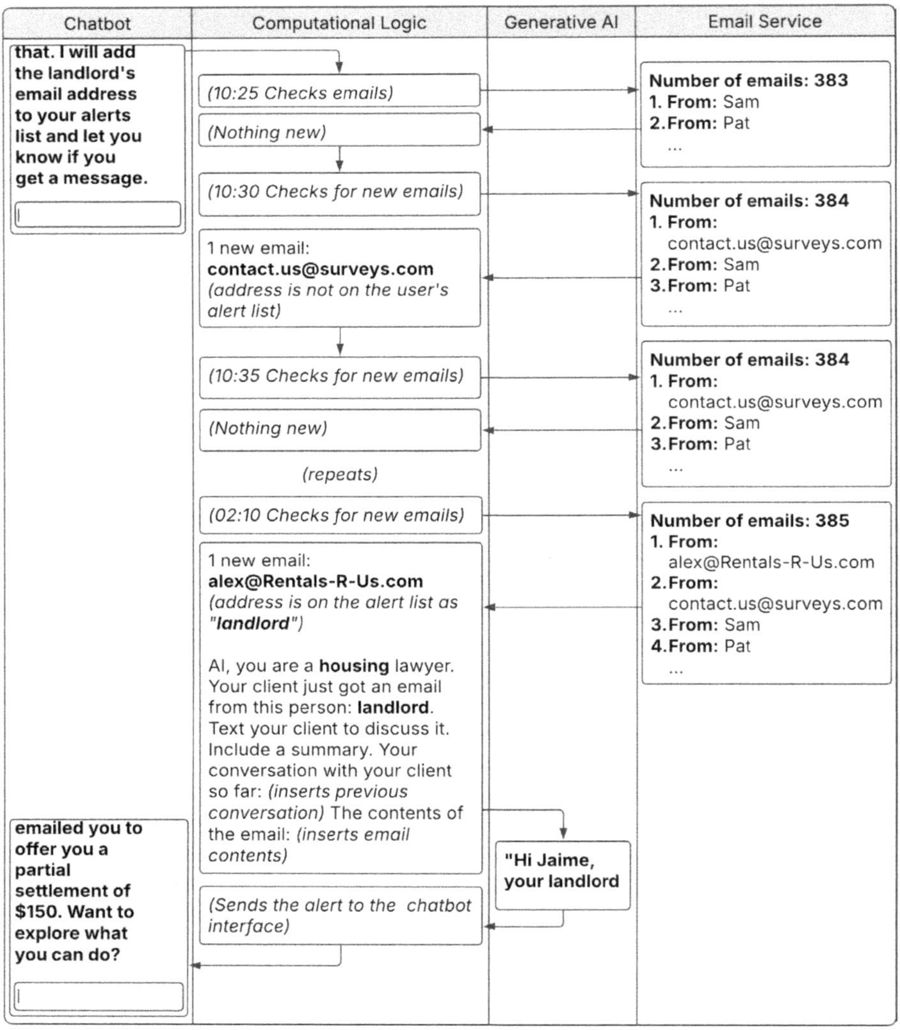

FIGURE 10.5 Legal AI assistant with an email service component for communications with the landlord.

response with a professional tone while expressing her willingness to negotiate if the offer were higher.

The AI may also help Jaime practice negotiating with her landlord, just as it helped her practice for court. This support helps Jaime communicate confidently and thoughtfully, balancing assertiveness with professionalism as she explores a potential settlement. Even though the landlord drags out the negotiation without giving a firm answer, the tool helps Jaime stay on top of court deadlines.

10.3.9 *Monitoring Case Activity*

As the case progresses, the tool helps Jaime monitor updates, including filings from the landlord and court notices. For instance, if the landlord files a motion claiming he never received Jaime's maintenance requests about the leaking pipe, Jaime has a limited number of days to respond by submitting copies of her repair requests. The machine learning systems track court databases and case management systems for new activity, such as the landlord filing a response or an upcoming hearing date. Jaime receives notifications whenever there is a new development in her case. Computational logic explains what each new filing means for Jaime's case and advises her on what she might need to do next. The tool continues to support Jaime until the end of the case.

–

This fictional case study following Jaime demonstrates how various types of AI can collaborate to assist an unrepresented litigant with legal tasks. Chatbots and dialogue systems, along with generative AI, communicate directly with Jaime, ML and computational logic provide crucial guidance on specific laws, and generative AI enhances Jaime's communication in her documentation and in court. This scenario demonstrates the potential for AI technologies to empower unrepresented litigants like Jaime to navigate the civil litigation process with greater knowledge and confidence.

Pairing AI tools with limited legal representation allows lawyers to intervene when legal expertise is needed while AI helps with routine tasks. In this model, lawyers assist on a limited basis at crucial junctures, benefiting from the work that Jaime had already completed using AI tools. If at any point Jaime's case becomes too complex, or issues arise that the system cannot handle, it directs her to a human legal professional for free legal assistance. Consider Rentervention, an AI-powered chatbot profiled in Section 13.8, which takes an "omnichannel" approach with support available through chatbot, phone, helpdesk, text message, and email.[22] For more complex cases, Rentervention connects tenants to a staff attorney.[23]

AI has significant potential to help courts and legal services provide more accessible, clear, and user-friendly pathways for unrepresented litigants.[24] However, realizing this vision will require not only technological development but also sustainable funding models and organizational capacity to support the creation and maintenance of such integrated systems. While the legal system could move toward a future in which every litigant has access to support regardless of resources or background, achieving this goal will require addressing the substantial resource constraints that currently limit widespread adoption of comprehensive AI assistance.

22 Video Interview by Mia Bonardi with Conor Malloy, Former Dir., Rentervention (July 17, 2024).
23 *Id.*
24 *See* Souza & Zarnow, *supra* note 7, at 4.

10.4 CONCERNS AND LIMITATIONS

Other chapters discuss the individual limitations of specific AI and other technologies, including generative AI's hallucinations in Chapters 12 and 16, computational logic's rigidity in Chapter 6, ML's "black box" problems in Chapter 7, and document automation's template constraints in Chapter 8. This section focuses on the limitations that arise when these technologies are combined into one integrated system.

10.4.1 *Integration Challenges*

When multiple systems are integrated, errors can be compounded and amplified. While generative AI's tendency to hallucinate is discussed in Section 12.7.1, and Section 16.2.3, these problems take on new dimensions in combined systems. In Jaime's case, if the generative AI component incorrectly calculates the statute of limitations for her habitability claim, this error ripples through the system. The computational logic module then uses this incorrect timeframe to determine Jaime's eligibility to file, and the document automation system prepares a complaint that appears valid on its face but may be dismissed by the court as untimely. In other words, each component might function correctly, but the final product is flawed because the generative AI confidently provided the wrong timeframe in the first instance. A potential solution could be to require the computational logic always calculate the timeframe.

Moreover, when multiple technologies are integrated, the interfaces between systems could introduce new vulnerabilities, and crucial information may be lost in translation. Each technology operates on fundamentally different principles: generative AI produces probabilistic outputs based on patterns in language, computational logic applies deterministic if–then rules, and document automation populates predefined templates with structured data.

Even when a tool uses RAG, accuracy is still a concern. Consider Figure 10.4, where the tool's accuracy is fundamentally constrained by the quality and currency of its external data sources. For example, if bus fare costs and travel time estimates are inaccurate at the source, they will also be inaccurate when the tool shows them to Jaime. Another example is court addresses and contact information. If courts do not update this information on their websites, then it will not be accurate when provided to Jaime.

10.4.2 *Humans Make Mistakes Too*

At the same time, humans make mistakes as well. Sometimes those mistakes can have a huge impact. In some contexts, digital systems are more accurate than humans; in others, they simply make different kinds of errors.

The user is also a component of these systems. Branting et al. highlight a fundamental challenge, noting that "pro se litigants seldom know what facts they need to establish or how to articulate and organize the facts in a manner that makes their claims amenable to evaluation."[25]

This limitation becomes particularly evident when examining current implementations. For instance, Westermann discusses how JusticeBot currently requires users to carry out legal assessments themselves to avoid violating UPL.[26] In one example, Westermann describes a landlord user who indicates their tenant is "frequently late" in rent payment – a characterization a judge might reject based on the actual frequency and circumstances.[27] As Westermann aptly points out, "the system thus relies on the layperson user to perform a step of legal reasoning," which may not always be accurate because it is a task in which they lack expertise.[28] Westermann also highlights how some systems, like FactorBot, make assumptions about their users – for example, that the user can prove the facts they provide and indeed know what a fact is in a legal sense.[29]

Some users' situations will require human legal assistance, and the system should recommend when this is the case. However, the traditional model of addressing the access to justice gap by matching each litigant with a lawyer has proven unsustainable. The sheer magnitude of need far exceeds available legal resources.[30] This reality forces us to confront difficult questions: Is imperfect assistance from AI systems better than the complete absence of guidance most unrepresented litigants currently face? What are the ethical implications when automated systems provide inaccurate legal information that worsens someone's situation? The old adage may apply here: perfect is the enemy of the good.

10.4.3 *Cumulative and Interacting Biases*

While Chapter 7 addresses bias in ML systems and Chapter 15 discusses AI assurance, integrated legal technologies introduce the problem of cumulative and interacting biases. Components may exhibit different biases that can reinforce each other or create entirely new patterns of discrimination when combined.

In Jaime's case, several biases across system components might interact in harmful ways. If the ML component analyzed housing case outcomes primarily from

[25] Karl Branting et al., *Judges Are from Mars, Pro Se Litigants Are from Venus: Predicting Decisions from Lay Text*, *in* 334 Legal Knowledge and Information Systems 215, 218 (Serena Villata, Jakub Harašta & Petr Kremen eds., 2020).

[26] Westermann, *supra* note 19, at 520–21.

[27] *Id.* at 521.

[28] *Id.*

[29] *Id.*

[30] World Just. Project, Measuring the Justice Gap: A People-Centered Assessment of Unmet Justice Needs Around the World 13 (2019), https://perma.cc/G2LY-DWBB.

jurisdictions with strong landlord protections, it might underestimate Jaime's chances of success and recommend an overly cautious approach.[31] The computational logic system might have been developed using legal expertise from large property management firms rather than tenant advocacy groups, encoding interpretations of habitability laws that favor landlords. Meanwhile, the document automation system might be built using templates originally designed for higher-value property disputes, prioritizing property damage documentation over health impact evidence that would be more relevant to Jaime's mold-related concerns.

None of these biases might be severe enough to completely undermine Jaime's case on its own. However, when combined, they could systematically disadvantage Jaime at every step: suggesting reduced compensation amounts, applying unfavorable legal interpretations, and producing documents that emphasize the least compelling aspects of her case. These interacting biases could create patterns of inequity that may be difficult to detect by testing any single component in isolation.

10.4.4 *Integrating with Human Systems*

The limitations of combined AI legal tools do not exist in isolation: they intersect with the human systems of courts, legal aid organizations, and support services. While individual AI components may perform well in controlled environments, their integration into existing legal infrastructures presents additional challenges.[32]

For Jaime, this might mean that while the AI system helps prepare a compelling case on paper, it fails to account for the specific procedural quirks of her local housing court or does not prepare her for interactions with court clerks who might have other submission requirements. The AI might not be aware of local tenant advocacy groups that could provide valuable support or recognize when Jaime's case has reached a point at which human legal assistance is essential.

Rather than viewing integrated AI as a complete replacement for human legal assistance, we should consider holistic models in which AI tools help streamline and organize information while human experts provide crucial oversight at key decision points. We should also consider more localized AI, of the sort that law firms and other corporations have adopted for internal use. Such systems could be developed for specific courts or jurisdictions, or even states. For Jaime, this might mean using AI to draft initial documents and identify relevant legal principles, followed by a brief consultation with a legal aid attorney before filing, to ensure the strategy is tailored to her specific situation.

[31] *See, e.g.*, Westermann, *supra* note 19, at 530.

[32] *See generally* Drew Simshaw, *Interoperable Legal AI for Access to Justice*, 134 YALE L.J. 795 (2025) (arguing for improved legal AI infrastructure and coordination across self-help platforms, legal aid organizations, and courts).

By acknowledging these complex, multilayered limitations while continuing to develop integrated AI assistants, we can work toward systems that meaningfully expand access to justice while maintaining the integrity and nuance that effective legal representation requires. This means designing systems with appropriate handoffs between AI and human support, clear indicators of uncertainty, and ongoing evaluation of outcomes for users like Jaime.

10.4.5 *Implementation Complexity and Resource Limitations*

While Jaime's experience illustrates the potential of integrated legal AI systems, it is crucial to acknowledge that building such comprehensive, seamless systems requires substantial resources, technical expertise, and time that many courts and legal aid organizations simply do not have. The system described above represents a significant technological undertaking that would demand coordinated development across multiple AI domains – a reality that may not align with the current capabilities or budgets of most organizations serving unrepresented litigants.

Creating an integrated system like the one supporting Jaime requires expertise spanning NLP, computational logic programming, ML, document automation, API integration, and user interface design. Each component must be carefully developed, tested, and maintained. For example, developing the computational logic component alone currently requires both subject matter legal experts and programmers who can translate complex legal rules into code. This is a time-intensive process that can take months or years to complete, even for a single area of law.

The ongoing costs extend far beyond initial development. Legal rules change, court procedures evolve, and technology requires regular updates. The system supporting Jaime would need continuous monitoring to ensure accuracy across all integrated components, regular updates to legal databases, and responsive technical support. This would require sustained funding and staffing commitments that many organizations cannot guarantee.

Many organizations serving unrepresented litigants operate with limited budgets and small staffs, prioritizing direct service provision over technology development. For these organizations, the choice often comes down to hiring an additional attorney or investing in complex AI development. Such a calculation often favors human resources, given the immediate, tangible impact on clients. The reality is that while integrated AI systems hold significant promise, they may remain out of reach for many organizations that could benefit most from their capabilities.

10.5 CONCLUSION

The future of legal AI systems lies not in isolated technologies but in thoughtfully integrated tools that combine the strengths of multiple approaches to support unrepresented litigants throughout their legal journey. As Jaime's case shows, different technologies can work together to address the various challenges faced by individuals navigating the legal system without representation. Chatbots provide accessible entry points and build initial confidence; machine learning systems offer precise document analysis and case tracking; computational logic ensures procedural accuracy; and generative AI enhances communication and document preparation.

The power of this integrated approach lies in its ability to create a seamless support system that adapts to users' distinct needs. By combining multiple technologies, the limitations of individual tools can be addressed while leveraging their unique strengths. Document automation becomes more intelligent when paired with generative AI, chatbots become more accurate when powered by computational logic, and machine learning systems become more practical when integrated with user-friendly interfaces.

However, realizing this vision requires confronting significant practical challenges. Beyond the technical considerations of bias mitigation, transparency requirements, and preserving human agency in legal decision-making, a substantial barrier is the resource investment required for development, implementation, and ongoing maintenance. Most courts and legal aid organizations currently lack the financial capacity and technical infrastructure needed to build and sustain such comprehensive systems.

As these technologies continue to evolve and improve, they have the potential to significantly reduce the barriers that currently prevent many individuals from effectively engaging with the legal system. Achieving this future will depend as much on developing sustainable funding models and organizational capacity as on continued technological innovation. Success will ultimately be measured not by what is technically possible, but by what can be practically implemented and maintained by the institutions and organizations best positioned to serve unrepresented litigants.

11

Online Dispute Resolution

*L. Karl Branting and Marco Giacalone**

11.1 INTRODUCTION

This chapter explores the evolution of online dispute resolution ("ODR") from its roots in alternative dispute resolution ("ADR") to its increasing role in modern legal systems. It examines ODR's ability to streamline dispute resolution through user-friendly, cost-effective, and time-efficient platforms, alleviating pressures on court dockets and enhancing access to justice. Integrating AI, including automated settlement proposals, negotiation analysis, and sentiment detection, is central to the discussion. The chapter highlights both the benefits, such as the reduction of geographical and financial barriers, and the challenges, notably the digital divide, algorithmic bias, and concerns regarding enforceability across jurisdictions. It underscores the significance of user-centered design, robust data protection measures, and the formalization of best practices, while continually prototyping emerging approaches to refine ODR technologies. The chapter concludes that well-implemented ODR platforms, supported by transparent standards and ethical AI, can contribute to making dispute resolution more equitable and responsive to societal needs.

11.2 WHAT IS ODR?

ODR emerged from the convergence of ADR practices and digital platforms, reflecting the need for more accessible and flexible mechanisms suited to an increasingly online world. ODR can be understood as "the use of Alternative Dispute Resolution techniques over the Internet," yet its scope now goes well beyond purely online transactions and often extends to offline disputes.[1] Rather than viewing ODR solely as an electronic extension of traditional mediation or arbitration, it is often

* We thank Marc Lauritsen for his review of this chapter.

[1] Marco Giacalone & Sajedeh Salehi, *Online Dispute Resolution: The Perspective of Service Providers*, *in* ALGORITHMIC CONFLICT RESOLUTION 77 (Francesco Romeo, Marco Dall'Aglio & Marco Giacalone eds., 2020).

recognized as its own paradigm, uniquely capable of handling modern cross-border commerce and large-scale caseloads (as exemplified by eBay's millions of disputes per year). In practice, ODR can complement or even replace face-to-face proceedings by offering secure messaging windows, automated workflows, and structured interfaces that guide users through negotiation and mediation from anywhere with an internet connection.

Much of ODR's appeal stems from reducing logistical burdens: virtual appearances spare disputants the cost and inconvenience of travel or time off work, and scheduling is streamlined since the asynchronous exchange of information can happen around the clock. Equally significant is ODR's potential to improve access to justice. By lowering cost barriers and simplifying legal processes, ODR can level the playing field between represented parties and those without counsel, easing the strain on court dockets. Yet as many scholars and practitioners stress, technology is no panacea: some disputes, particularly those involving deeply personal stakes or complex factual determinations, may still benefit from in-person interaction. Moreover, challenges such as the digital divide, algorithmic bias, and uneven adoption of enforceable standards across jurisdictions highlight the need for careful user-centered design, robust data protection, and transparent oversight of AI-driven ODR applications.

Nevertheless, as described throughout this chapter, well-structured ODR systems, particularly those designed with ethical AI principles and strong procedural safeguards, are increasingly seen as integral to the evolution of dispute resolution. Whether through automated blind bidding to settle small claims, text-based mediation for family disputes, or AI-assisted monitoring of negotiation dynamics, ODR platforms are poised to be a crucial resource in making legal remedies more accessible, streamlined, and responsive to the demands of digital-era dispute resolution.

11.2.1 *Definition and Evolution of ODR in the Legal Landscape*

ODR systems are communication platforms intended to permit disputes to be resolved without requiring the disputants to appear in court or even to be physically present in the same place.[2] Although ODR is not a form of AI, several components of ODR systems are amenable to AI techniques. Moreover, ODR systems can help reduce the imbalance between unrepresented litigants and those represented by attorneys in several ways. First, ODR can relieve litigants of the burden of traveling or taking time off work to appear in person at hearings during working hours. Second, ODR systems typically include a neutral facilitator or mediator whose function is to assist the parties in achieving a fair settlement. This neutral party can compensate for the handicap of lacking an attorney by promoting a settlement that

[2] NAT'L CTR. FOR STATE CTS., *Online Dispute Resolution*, https://perma.cc/FD5Y-UFLZ.

equally incorporates the interests of each party, regardless of whether they have an attorney. Finally, ODR can provide information about asserting legal claims and defenses to help litigants represent themselves more effectively, even if the case ultimately proceeds to trial.

ODR can be viewed as emerging from the absorption of ADR techniques into digital commerce.[3] The potential of the internet as a platform for resolving disputes more conveniently and less expensively than in traditional courts was recognized almost as soon as the internet came into existence.[4] However, the explosive growth of e-commerce was the driving force behind the widespread adoption of ADR into online digital systems. One of the earliest ODR implementations was eBay's mechanism for handling e-commerce disputes. Disputes among users began almost as soon as eBay was launched in 1995.[5] When eBay started developing its own in-house system for handling disputes in 2003, there were several million disputes per year; by 2011, eBay was handling over sixty million disputes per year.[6]

Without the impetus of exponentially growing numbers of disputes, courts were slower to adopt ODR. This held true despite its potential to reduce judicial caseloads, speed up decision times, and enhance laypersons' ability to understand and assert their rights and defenses. However, in light of these potential benefits, the European Union ("EU") promulgated the ADR Directive and the ODR Regulation in 2013, leading to the launch of the European ODR platform in 2016,[7] although it was later discontinued on July 20, 2025 following Regulation 2024/3228, and the United Nations Commission on International Trade Law promulgated guidelines on the use of ODR.[8]

Among the earliest court ODR initiatives was the eCourtroom launched by the Federal Court of Australia in 2001. This platform handles disputes, such as native title claims, where the parties are often widely separated geographically.[9] In the Netherlands, an online self-help tool to assist separating partners in negotiating divorce terms, the *Rechtwijzer uit elkaar*, became operational in 2014.[10] In North America, the first judicial ODR system was the British Columbia Civil Resolution Tribunal ("CRT"), which began public operations in 2016 and is profiled in

[3] For an introduction to ADR techniques, *see* Deborah R. Hensler, *Our Courts, Ourselves: How the Alternative Dispute Resolution Movement Is Re-Shaping Our Legal System*, 108 Penn St. L. Rev. 165 (2003).

[4] *See* M. Ethan Katsh, Law in a Digital World 42 (1995).

[5] M. Ethan Katsh & Orna Rabinovich-Einy, Digital Justice: Technology and the Internet of Disputes 31 (2017).

[6] *Id.* at 65, 35.

[7] Amy J. Schmitz, *Expanding Access to Remedies Through E-Court Initiatives*, 67 Buff. L. Rev. 89, 91, 137–38 (2019).

[8] United Nations Commission on International Trade Law, Rep. on the Working Group III (Online Dispute Resolution), U.N. Doc. A/CN.9/716, https://perma.cc/9JTL-VPB8.

[9] Katsh & Rabinovich-Einy, *supra* note 5, at 158–59.

[10] Laura Kistemaker, *Rechtwijzer and Uitelkaar.nl: Dutch Experiences with ODR for Divorce*, 59 Fam. Ct. Rev. 232 (2021).

Section 13.2.[11] The CRT was followed shortly by Utah,[12] with an Agent-based Intelligent Dispute Resolution ("AIDR") prototype, which may monitor ODR sessions and alert facilitators to potential issues, such as unproductive conflicts, delayed responses, or failure to resolve a dispute within the Utah Supreme Court's specified time limit.[13]

11.2.2 *The Role of ODR in Access to Justice*

Court ODR systems typically include an intake platform, a case management system, and a set of communication tools. Many court ODR systems require plaintiffs whose cases satisfy certain criteria (e.g., small claims or condominium claims) to file initially with the court's ODR system and permit such a case to be transferred to the court's regular docket only if the parties are unable to reach a negotiated agreement.

After the claim is filed in a typical system, the defendant is served with an ODR summons and claim. If the defendant responds to the summons, the parties communicate online with the assistance of a neutral party (facilitator or mediator).

Figure 11.1 shows the messaging window for the AIDR system,[14] displaying messages exchanged among the petitioner, respondent, and the facilitator. In some systems, parties initially negotiate directly, and a neutral party joins to help the negotiations only if they fail to do so (as in the CRT), while in other systems a neutral party may participate from the start (as in the Utah system).

Figure 11.2 shows a representative ODR case-management interface that displays situational information and suggestions for cases assigned to the neutral party (the facilitator, in this instance) handling the case. In the upper left of the window, the Status Updates panel displays alerts and updates for cases assigned to the facilitator. In this system, the status updates are categorized into Urgent Updates, such as time-sensitive alerts that require a facilitator's immediate attention, and Other Updates, such as document filings or suggested responses.

The Case Queue panel in the lower half of the window provides an overview of all the cases assigned to the facilitator, including the dates of the case initiation and the most recent activity. It also summarizes the most recent statuses and links to each case's messaging window.[15]

[11] Shannon Salter, *Online Dispute Resolution and Justice System Integration: British Columbia's Civil Resolution Tribunal*, 34 Windsor Y.B. Access Just. 112 (2017).

[12] Deno Himonas, *Utah's Online Dispute Resolution Program*, 122 Dick. L. Rev. 881 (2018).

[13] L. Karl Branting et al., *A Computational Model of Facilitation in Online Dispute Resolution*, 31 A.I. & L. 465 (2023).

[14] *Id.* at 481.

[15] *Id.*

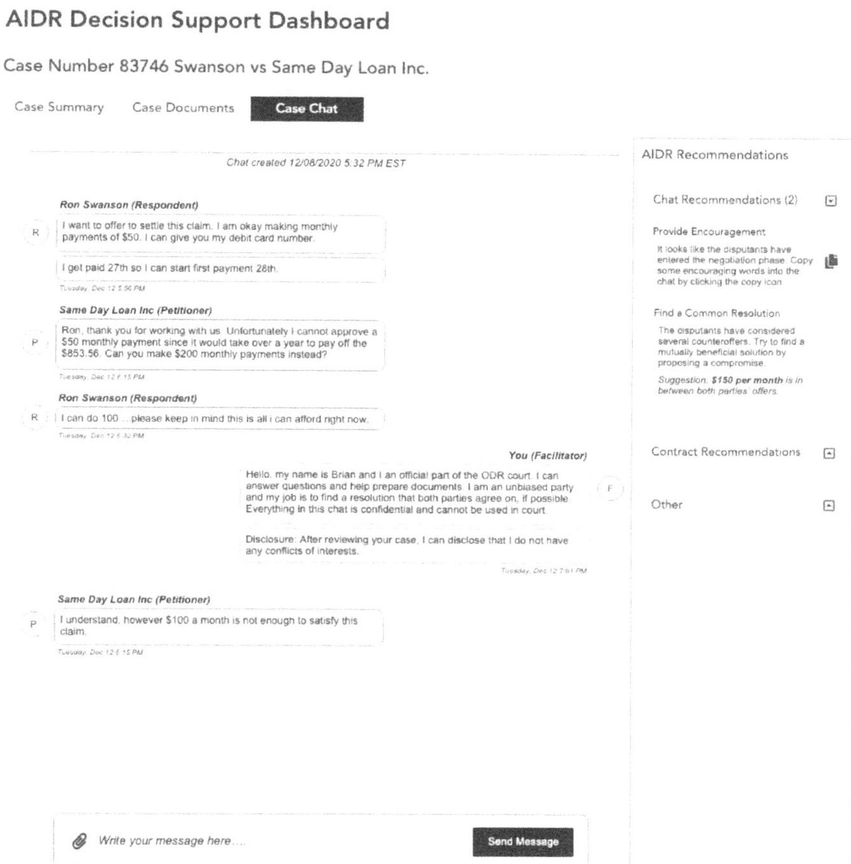

FIGURE 11.1 The messaging window for a typical ODR system shows exchanges among the petitioner, respondent, and the facilitator. Republished with permission from the MITRE Corporation.

If the parties settle the claim, the neutral party prepares an online settlement agreement, which the parties then execute. If the parties cannot reach a settlement, the ODR process is terminated, and the case is transferred to the court.

11.3 INTEGRATING AI INTO ODR

Several aspects of ODR processes are amenable to AI techniques, including devising fair settlement proposals, detecting and overcoming negotiation barriers, and providing decision support to neutral parties, such as summarizing the state of negotiations and suggesting appropriate messages to the disputants.

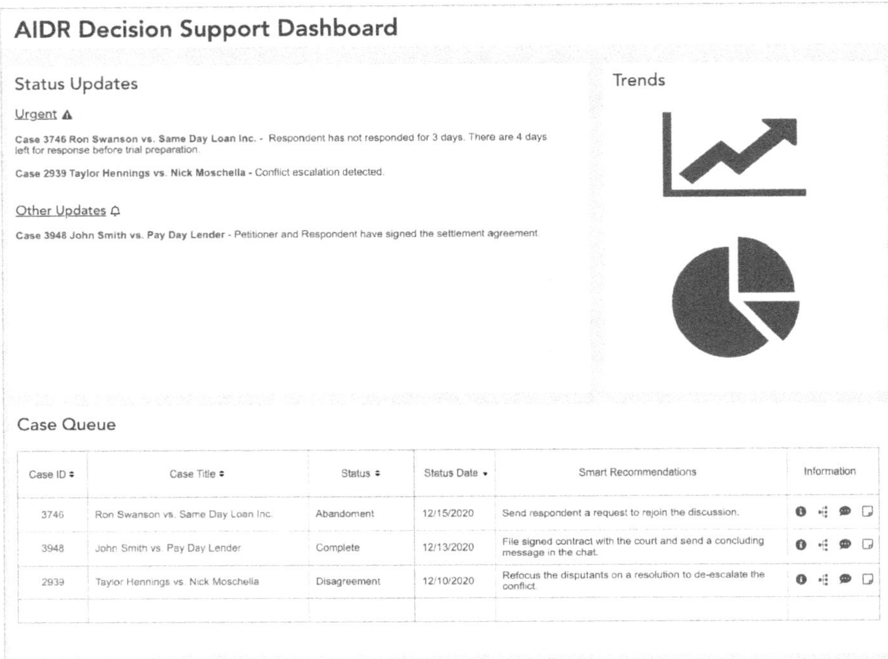

FIGURE 11.2 A representative ODR case-management interface. Republished with permission from the MITRE Corporation.

11.3.1 *Settlement Calculations and Proposals*

The field of alternative dispute resolution, which became ODR when practiced on the internet, was informed by the discipline of mediation, which seeks to systematize the process whereby a neutral party assists disputants in resolving conflicts.[16] A proposal that is acceptable to both parties must somehow make the best trade-off between each party's goals and priorities. Mediators typically try to arrive at such a proposal intuitively, but there are rigorous mathematical techniques for optimizing among competing goals, most notably utility theory[17] and game theory.[18] A number of research projects have explored automating mediation activities such as calculating the "best alternative

[16] Jay Folberg, *A Mediation Overview: History and Dimensions of Practice*, 1 MEDIATION Q. 3, 8 (1983).

[17] *See* George J. Stigler, *The Development of Utility Theory*, 58 J. POL. ECON. 307 (1950); Roberto Kuster, *Utility Function and Rational Choice as Support Mechanisms to Maximize Mediation and Legal Negotiation Settlement Output*, 17 PEPP. DISP. RESOL. L.J. 263 (2017).

[18] *See* John Nash, *Two-Person Cooperative Games*, 21 ECONOMETRICA 128 (1953); HOWARD RAIFFA, THE ART AND SCIENCE OF NEGOTIATION 7–9 (1982).

to a negotiated agreement" ("BATNA")[19] and applying game-theoretical principles to generate offers[20] or fair settlement proposals.[21]

Below, we examine several ODR systems and their game-theory-based methods for calculating settlements. For example, the SmartSettle system elicits the preferences of each party in the form of visible and secret bids. If the bids overlap, the system chooses a number in the "zone of possible agreement," that is, the middle of the settlement.[22] The Split-Up system used a simple neural network to learn optimal weights for the division of marital assets based on a small corpus of family law cases, together with a rule-based system to justify the proposed division.[23] Game theoretic techniques for proposal settlement were also incorporated into Family Negotiator, "a hybrid rule-based and case-based system which attempts to model Australian family law," and Family_Winner, which "uses both game theory and heuristics [to support] the process of negotiation by introducing importance values to indicate the degree to which each party desires to be awarded the issue being considered."[24] Other game-theoretic techniques are present in the Conflict Resolution with Equitative Algorithms ("CREA") platform,[25] where the users may choose between the Bid and the Rating methods.[26]

- *Rating Method*: Users express their preferences or utility for each good by rating each good using a 5-star system (scale 1 to 5 stars). The *rating weight* aims to evaluate the importance of each rating provided by the agents. The utility of a good for an agent is determined by the share of the good received by the agent, the effect of the rating given by the agent, and the market value of the good.

19 *See, e.g.*, Francisco Assis de Andrade et al., *Using BATNAs and WATNAs in Online Dispute Resolution*, *in* NEW FRONTIERS IN ARTIFICIAL INTELLIGENCE (JSAI-ISAI, LECTURE NOTES IN COMPUT. SCI. VOL. 6284) 5 (K. Nakakoji, Y. Murakami & E. McCready eds., 2010).

20 Ronghuo Zheng et al., *Multiagent Negotiation on Multiple Issues with Incomplete Information: Extended Abstract*, PROC. INT'L CONF. ON AUTONOMOUS AGENTS AND MULTI-AGENT SYS. 1279 (2013).

21 *See* Michal Chalamish & Sarit Kraus, *AutoMed: An Automated Mediator for Multi-Issue Bilateral Negotiations*, 24 AUTONOMOUS AGENTS & MULTI-AGENT SYS. 536, 538 (2012); Dave de Jonge et al., *Using Game Description Language for Mediated Dispute Resolution*, 34 AI & SOC'Y 767 (2019).

22 Arno Lodder & John Zeleznikow, *The Role of Artificial Intelligence in Online Dispute Resolution*, *in* ONLINE DISPUTE RESOLUTION: THEORY AND PRACTICE 102 (M. Wahab, E. Katsh, D. Rainey eds., 2012).

23 Andrew Stranieri et al., *A Hybrid Rule–Neural Approach for the Automation of Legal Reasoning in the Discretionary Domain of Family Law in Australia*, 7 A.I. & L. 153 (1999).

24 John Zeleznikow & Emilia Bellucci, *Building Negotiation Decision Support Systems by Integrating Game Theory and Heuristics*, PROC. IFIP INT'L CONF. ON DECISION SUPPORT SYS. 872, 874–75 (2004).

25 CREA PROJECT, https://perma.cc/UC2C-GNXQ.

26 *See* CREA PROJECT, CREA HANDBOOK 2–4, https://perma.cc/HDC3-6EN6.

- *Bid Method*: Users are allocated a virtual amount of money to distribute across the list of goods, allowing them to express their preferences for the goods. The bounds percent defines the effective interval of goods utilities, that is, the percent boundaries within which users can spread their virtual money over goods, regardless of their estimated values.

The use of game theory and other techniques for proposing equitable settlement proposals is a relatively straightforward application of well-understood quantitative techniques for balancing competing objectives. The larger challenge in implementing these systems is often designing preference elicitation interfaces that accurately and efficiently acquire the objectives to be balanced.[27]

11.3.2 *Negotiation Analysis and Support*

The effectiveness of ODR depends not only on providing an effective communication platform but also on assisting the disputants in negotiating a settlement that is acceptable to all. Various approaches have been explored for using AI to monitor the negotiation process and to provide assistance, either to a facilitator in the form of alerts or suggested messages or to the disputants in the form of messages autonomously generated by the ODR system.

To understand how AI can be helpful for negotiation analysis, it is useful to view negotiations as a form of discourse, that is, as a sequence of sentences related by meaning and by the goals of the speakers who uttered those sentences.[28] As depicted in Figure 11.3, the negotiation process can be divided into distinct phases as the disputants make, accept, reject, or counter offers until an offer is accepted or the negotiations come to an end.[29]

In addition to game-theory-based settlement calculations, certain discourse signals can also reveal whether a negotiation is progressing or has stalled. For instance, some simple discourse properties can indicate whether the negotiation is making progress or is floundering. An obvious example is that a long delay after one party posts an utterance in an ODR session may mean that the other party is neglecting or has abandoned the negotiations. A less obvious but potentially important aspect of

[27] *See, e.g.*, Fatemeh Salmanian, Hossein Jazayeriy & Jamal Kazemitabar, *User Preferences Elicitation in Bilateral Automated Negotiation Using Recursive Least Square Estimation*, 12TH INT'L CONF. ON INFO. & KNOWLEDGE TECH. 1 (2021).

[28] *See* DANIEL JURAFSKY & JAMES H. MARTIN, SPEECH AND LANGUAGE PROCESSING: AN INTRODUCTION TO NATURAL LANGUAGE PROCESSING, COMPUTATIONAL LINGUISTICS, AND SPEECH RECOGNITION 536 (2d ed. 2009). For a discourse view of negotiation, *see* Linda Putnam, *Negotiation and Discourse Analysis*, 26 NEGOTIATION J. 145 (2010).

[29] Figure 11.3 is based on the augmented transition network in ANNE VON DER LIETH GARDNER, AN ARTIFICIAL INTELLIGENCE APPROACH TO LEGAL REASONING 121 (MIT Press 1987); *see also* Mark D. Flood & Oliver R. Goodenough, *Contract as Automaton: Representing a Simple Financial Agreement in Computational Form*, 30 A.I. & L. 391, 392–93 (2022) (discussing the use of discrete finite automata to represent contractual structures).

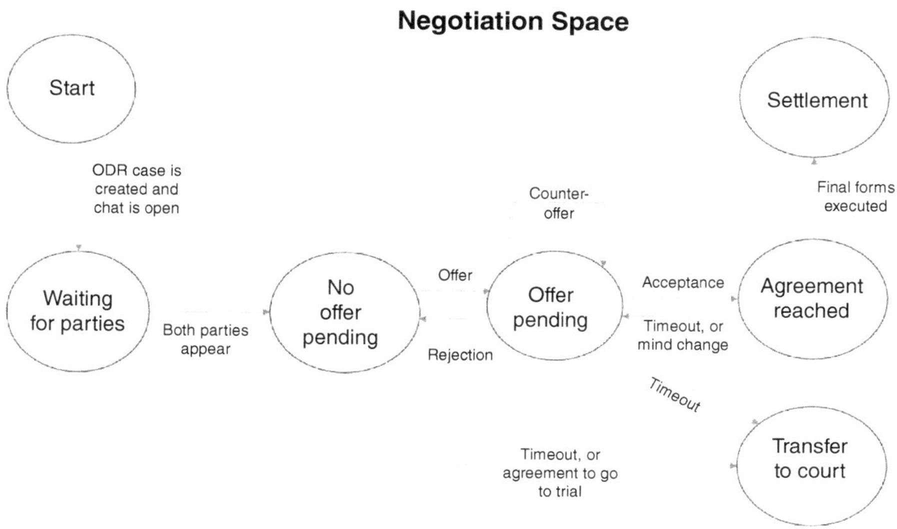

FIGURE 11.3 The stages of an ODR negotiation. Republished with permission from the MITRE Corporation.

discourse is the affect (emotional state) of the disputants, specifically whether negotiations are devolving into an unproductive, angry exchange. An intervention may be needed in either case, either to remind the non-responding party of the consequences of a default or to try to redirect the discussion in a more productive direction. A descent into angry exchanges can be detected using the AI technique of *sentiment analysis*.

11.3.3 *Sentiment Analysis in ODR*

Sentiment analysis is a computational linguistics technology developed to identify two aspects of the emotional content of a text passage: valence, that is, whether it is positive, negative, or neutral, and intensity, that is, how strongly the emotion is expressed.[30]

Figure 11.4 illustrates how words with emotional content can be arranged along axes representing intensity and the positivity or negativity of the emotion. Many other approaches to emotion detection in text and in facial expressions have been explored, particularly in educational software, where it is valuable for a system to adapt to the emotional state of the student user (e.g., providing enough challenge to

[30] Pradeep Nandwani & Ritu Verma, *A Review on Sentiment Analysis and Emotion Detection from Text*, 11 SOC. NETWORK ANALYSIS & MINING 1, 7 (2021).

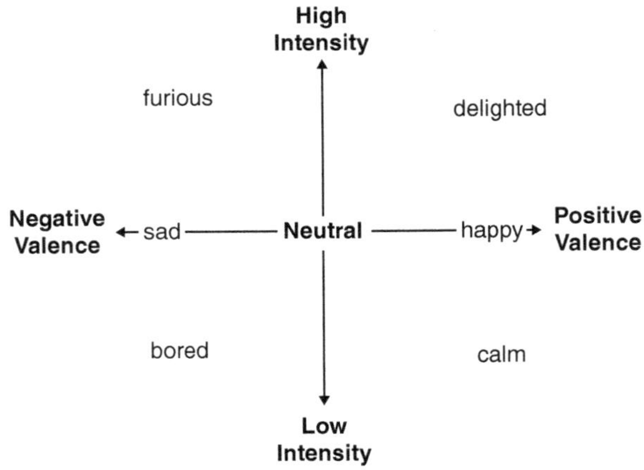

FIGURE 11.4 Emotion words arranged along valence and intensity dimensions. Republished with permission from the MITRE Corporation.

avoid boredom but not so much as to be frustrating).[31] However, sentiment analysis has a lengthy research and development history that has produced a variety of well-understood techniques, many of which are implemented in readily available open-source libraries. As a result, it is not difficult to estimate the valence and intensity of text passages.[32] The sentiment profiles of the facilitator, petitioner, and respondent in a typical ODR session are shown in Figure 11.5.

In Figure 11.5, each participant's sentiment fluctuates over the course of the session. The vertical axis represents sentiment scores, ranging from negative to positive, while the horizontal axis tracks the progression of the session. Although all three lines exhibit ups and downs, the facilitator's sentiment appears comparatively steady, whereas the petitioner and respondent show more pronounced swings between negative and positive values. These variations highlight the shifting emotional dynamics among the participants during the dispute resolution process.

There is some subtlety in determining whether an increase in negative affect in disputants' utterances indicates a sufficient risk of an unproductive conflict to justify intervening. Parties sometimes just want to feel heard and will negotiate more effectively after having had an opportunity to express some anger. In such situations, intervening would be counterproductive.

[31] William E. Villegas-Ch. et al., *Identification of Emotions from Facial Gestures in a Teaching Environment with the Use of Machine Learning Techniques*, 11 IEEE ACCESS 38010 (2023).

[32] *See, e.g.*, C.J. Hutto, *VADER (Valence Aware Dictionary and Sentiment Reasoner)*, https://perma.cc/RX4Z-UFMA. Ironic statements might appear to present a particular challenge to sentiment analysis since the intended sense of such statements is the opposite of their surface meaning, but irony detection is itself an area with extensive research. *See, e.g.*, Rolandos Alexandros Potamias et al., *A Transformer-Based Approach to Irony and Sarcasm Detection*, 32 NEURAL COMPUTING & APPLICATIONS 17309, 17310 (2020).

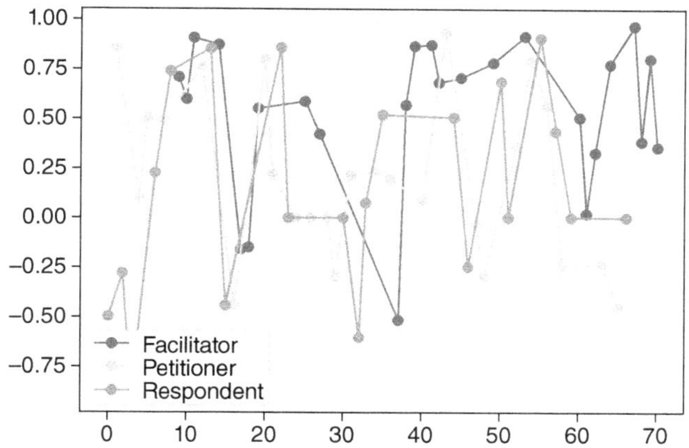

FIGURE 11.5 The sentiment profiles of the facilitator, petitioner, and respondent in a typical ODR session. Republished with permission from the MITRE Corporation.

One approach to detecting arguments is to average the most negative sentiment in each of several recent turns;[33] the average focuses on the most negative sentence of each turn because even a single highly negative sentence in a turn may indicate an elevated state of anger or contentiousness. In the recent AIDR prototype, an alert is sent to the facilitator, warning of a potential issue if the negativity of the last three turns exceeds a given threshold. This indicates that the disputants seem to be in a spiral of contentious, hostile utterances.[34]

A different approach to handling contentious language was prototyped in the LLMediator, which seeks to reformulate inflammatory messages before they can trigger an emotional interruption to the negotiations.[35] LLMediator uses a set of keywords to identify inappropriate or provocative words or phrases, then suggests less inflammatory alternatives. In the initial prototype, GPT-4 was prompted as follows:

> You are an ODR platform. You are given the chat message of a party. Reformulate the message to maintain the content but make it less confrontational and more encouraging for an amicable settlement. Respond directly with the reformulated message, do not explain.

As shown in Figure 11.6, the reformulated message is presented to the user with the option to send it instead of the original message.

[33] A "turn" consists of all the utterances by a party submitted at once in a chat field. A single turn often comprises multiple sentences.

[34] Branting et al., *supra* note 13, at 478.

[35] Hannes Westermann, Jaromir Savelka & Karim Benyekhlef, *LLMediator: GPT-4 Assisted Online Dispute Resolution*, ICAIL Workshop A.I. Access Just. § 7 (2023), https://perma.cc/S9WK-5G2U.

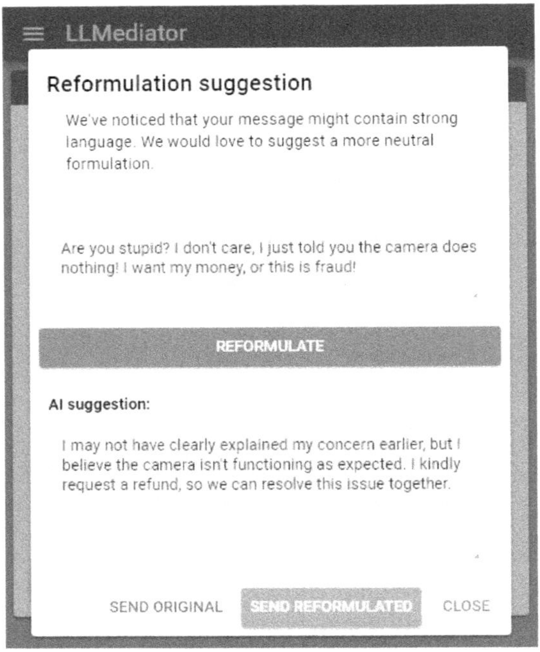

FIGURE 11.6 Example of a reformulated message in the LLMediator. Republished with permission from the Cyberjustice Laboratory.

11.3.4 *AI-Assisted Decision Support*

A more advanced way to use AI in ODR is to help the neutral party decide what actions to take, often sending specific messages but possibly drafting settlement agreements or forwarding the case to a court. In some designs, the AI could even perform these actions independently. A straightforward approach treats existing ODR session transcripts as a ready-made training set for supervised machine learning ("ML"). Each turn in the transcript becomes a chance for the model to determine whether the neutral party will act and, if so, to predict the action's content based on the preceding dialogue.

The AIDR system mentioned above relied on speech act theory, which posits that certain utterances do more than convey information; they actively create or alter the legal or social realities in which they occur (see Section 8.9.4 on speech-act-based document automation). By analyzing 6,802 transcripts from a US state court's ODR sessions, the system identified twenty-five distinct categories of facilitator actions (including taking no action). Each category corresponds to a particular type of illocutionary force – the functional aspect of what the utterance accomplishes – whether urging a disputant to reengage, declaring neutrality, or asking the parties to sign a settlement agreement. Grouping these variations together reflects the shared purpose behind each speech act rather than superficial differences in phrasing.

Rather than predicting the exact wording a facilitator would choose, AIDR first identifies which category of action is most likely. It then suggests the text the facilitator commonly uses for that action. Because AIDR relies on a large training corpus, it requires transcripts that often contain sensitive information and are not easy to obtain. Moreover, the model's accuracy hinges on having thousands of examples; smaller datasets are unlikely to provide reliable predictive power.[36]

Creating a corpus to train a model to predict facilitators' actions required devising the set of categories, manually labeling a representative set of sentences uttered by facilitators with those category labels, and then automatically labeling the many remaining facilitator sentences based on which labeled sentence they were closest to in semantic embedding space[37] (see Chapter 7 on ML). Once the category labels were assigned, a model was trained based on a set of features of the utterances that occurred leading up to the point when an action was to be predicted.[38] The resulting system accurately predicted when a facilitator would act and which of the twenty-five categories of actions would be taken.[39]

In a related study, Tan et al. evaluated GPT-4's potential to assume a mediator role in dispute scenarios, finding that large language models ("LLMs") sometimes outperformed humans in generating intervention messages.[40] This indicates that AI-driven mediation support may soon be both viable and robust.

11.4 CHALLENGES AND LIMITATIONS

While ODR offers significant advantages, several challenges and limitations must be addressed to realize its full potential in equalizing access to justice. One primary challenge is the issue of unequal access to technology, commonly referred to as the "digital divide."[41] Individuals without reliable internet access or the necessary devices

[36] Ryan Abbott & Brinson S. Elliott, *Putting the Artificial Intelligence in Alternative Dispute Resolution: How AI Rules Will Become ADR Rules*, 4 AMICUS CURIAE 685, 692 (2023).

[37] This procedure for bootstrapping a small number of manual annotations to an entire corpus, SCALE, is described in L. Karl Branting et al., *Scalable and Explainable Legal Prediction*, 29 A.I. & L. 213, 229 (2021).

[38] The following features were used for prediction: the speaker (i.e., the plaintiff, the defendant, or the facilitator) in the most recent utterance ("MRU") and in the immediately previous utterance; a semantic vector representation of the MRU; the number of turns since the beginning of the negotiation; the speech act categories of the most recent disputant utterance; the sentiment of the utterances in the most recent three turns in the negotiations; the word scores for pleasantness, activation, and imagery; and the duration since the MRU. *See* Branting et al., *supra* note 13, at 475.

[39] *Id.* at 477–78. Weighted f-measure (i.e., overall predictive accuracy) was 91.3 for predicting action vs. inaction and 79.9 for predicting the specific facilitator action.

[40] Jinzhe Tan et al., *Robots in the Middle: Evaluating LLMs in Dispute Resolution*, ARXIV 1, 4 (2024), https://perma.cc/GFB5-4PL2.

[41] *See generally* PIPPA NORRIS, DIGITAL DIVIDE: CIVIC ENGAGEMENT, INFORMATION POVERTY AND THE INTERNET WORLD-WIDE (2001).

may be excluded from participating, inadvertently leaving out vulnerable populations who might benefit most from accessible dispute resolution mechanisms.[42]

Concerns over fairness and impartiality present another significant challenge. There are risks of bias in AI algorithms used in ODR, which can affect the neutrality and fairness of the system.[43] Ensuring neutrality involves regularly auditing AI systems for biases, using diverse datasets for training, and maintaining transparency in algorithmic decision-making. These measures help uphold the integrity of automated systems and build trust among users.[44] For more discussion on this, see Chapter 15 on AI assurance.

Legal and regulatory issues also pose challenges. Questions about the enforceability of ODR outcomes and about navigating jurisdictional complexities in online environments can complicate the recognition and enforcement of agreements. Different legal systems and regulations can further complicate matters, especially in cross-border disputes. Addressing these issues requires international cooperation and the development of legal frameworks that support ODR across jurisdictions.[45]

It is natural to wonder whether generative AI, which can often be used without training in domain-specific examples, can provide an approach to facilitator decision support that obviates these challenges. The LLMediator system described earlier prototyped an approach in which a generative AI system was prompted with the last ten messages in the conversation and asked to:

> Respond to this communication between the parties. Stick to the role of the mediator, do not complete the parties' dialogue. Remain neutral, do not take the side of any party.[46]

As shown in Figure 11.7, the prototype demonstrated that plausible responses can be generated using this procedure. However, this prototype illustrates the challenge of replacing supervised learning models with generative AI: the absence of an annotated corpus means that evaluating the quality of the generated text is challenging. In AIDR, one can measure performance by comparing each predicted facilitator's action to the actual action taken, yielding a clear success rate. If accuracy is lacking, the training corpus can be refined or expanded, and the model can be retrained to improve performance systematically. Generative AI, on the other hand, operates with open-ended text generation rather than discrete prediction categories, so performance

[42] Katsh & Rabinovich-Einy, *supra* note 5, at 9.

[43] Ninareh Mehrabi et al., *A Survey on Bias and Fairness in Machine Learning*, arXiv 1, 2 (Jan. 25, 2022), https://perma.cc/6R4J-CBAY.

[44] Thomas Schulz, *Does Online Dispute Resolution Need Governmental Intervention – The Case for Architectures of Control and Trust*, 6 N.C. J.L. & Tech. 71, 97 (2004).

[45] *See, e.g.*, Leah Wing & Chris Draper, *Parameters of Online Dispute Resolution: Introducing a New Framework for ODR*, 2 Int'l J. Online Disp. Resol. 112 (2022) (introducing National Center for Technology and Dispute Resolution's ODR Framework).

[46] Westermann et al., *supra* note 35, at § 4.3.1.

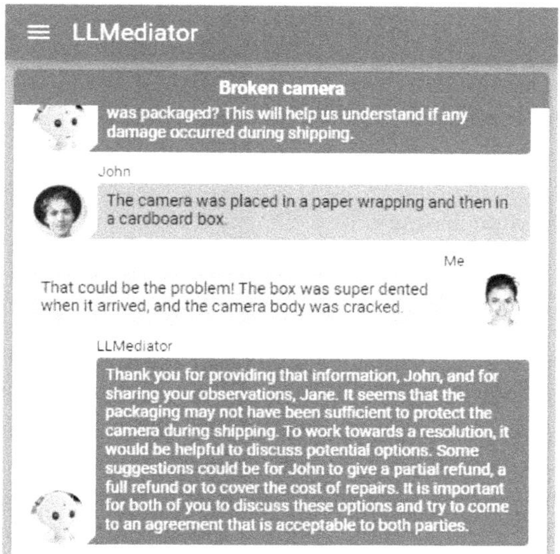

FIGURE 11.7 Example of a plausible response from the LLMediator. Republished with permission from the Cyberjustice Laboratory.

tuning relies on iteratively adjusting prompts. Yet assessing whether outputs meet a desired standard is more subjective, demanding external benchmarks or user feedback, typically in the form of human usability testing. While there are currently many uncertainties about the best way to use generative AI for ODR decision support, eliminating the problematic process of acquiring and annotating a corpus of transcripts creates a massive incentive for future research on the generative AI approach.

Nevertheless, the "hallucination" problem, in which LLMs produce convincing but false information, remains a concern, underscoring the need for rigorous human oversight in any AI-mediated dispute resolution context (see Sections 12.7.1 and 16.2.3).[47]

11.5 POTENTIAL APPLICATIONS OF ODR FOR ACCESS TO JUSTICE

ODR has the potential to significantly equalize access to justice by using technological advancements to overcome traditional barriers in the legal system. Emerging technologies such as blockchain, virtual reality, and advanced AI algorithms could substantially enhance ODR platforms by making them more accessible, efficient, and user-friendly. For instance, blockchain technology can provide secure, transparent, and immutable record-keeping. By utilizing decentralized ledger systems, blockchain ensures that all parties can access tamper-proof records of proceedings

[47] Tan et al., *supra* note 40, at 7.

and agreements.[48] This increased security and transparency can enhance trust in the ODR process, which is crucial for accepting and enforcing online resolutions.[49]

Virtual reality can simulate in-person mediation by creating immersive virtual spaces that replicate physical presence, thereby enhancing communication and fostering better mutual understanding in dispute resolution.[50] This technological application can be particularly beneficial in complex cases where nonverbal cues and personal interaction are important.

Advanced AI, especially in natural language processing ("NLP") and ML, can improve the efficiency and user experience of ODR platforms. AI algorithms can analyze large datasets of case law and past resolutions to provide insights and predict potential outcomes. This predictive capability can inform parties about the strengths and weaknesses of their positions, facilitating more informed decision-making.[51] AI can also automate administrative tasks, such as scheduling and document management, allowing human mediators to focus on substantive issues.

Integration with mobile platforms is another critical development that can expand the reach of ODR services. With the widespread use of smartphones globally, optimizing ODR platforms for mobile devices ensures that a broader population can access dispute resolution processes. Mobile applications can offer features like push notifications, real-time messaging, and user-friendly interfaces catering to individuals who may not have access to traditional computers or stable internet connections.[52]

The future of ODR is intertwined with the integration of other AI-powered legal tools, creating comprehensive support systems for litigants. This convergence can enhance the capabilities of ODR platforms and provide holistic assistance to users, particularly those without legal representation.[53]

AI-driven document automation tools guide users through creating legal documents by asking pertinent questions and automatically populating forms with

48 Marco Giacalone & Gioia Arnone, *Dispute Resolutions for Digital Assets in a Decentralized Virtual World*, 2024 European J. Privacy L. & Techs. 1, 13 (2024). *See also* Yann Aouidef, Federico Ast & Bruno Deffains, *Decentralized justice: A Comparative Analysis of Blockchain Online Dispute Resolution Projects*, 4 Frontiers in Blockchain 1, 3 (discussing the use of blockchain technology in decentralized justice platforms) (2021); Mayu Watanabe & Colin Rule, *ODR in the Metaverse*, 9 Int'l J. Online Disp. Resol. 21, 30 (discussing the potential of metaverse technologies in enhancing ODR's accessibility and transparency) (2022).

49 Schulz, *supra* note 44, at 72.

50 Béatrice S. Hasler et al., *Virtual Reality-Based Conflict Resolution: The Impact of Immersive 360° Video on Changing View Points and Moral Judgment in the Context of Violent Intergroup Conflict*, 23 New Media & Soc'y 2255, 2257 (2021).

51 Kevin D. Ashley, Artificial Intelligence and Legal Analytics: New Tools for Law Practice in the Digital Age 11–13 (2017).

52 Marta Poblet, *Introduction to Mobile Technologies, Conflict Management, and ODR: Exploring Common Grounds*, in Mobile Technologies for Conflict Management, vol 2 (2011).

53 David Freeman Engstrom & Jonah B. Gelbach, *Legal Tech, Civil Procedure, and the Future of Adversarialism*, 169 U. Pa. L. Rev. 1001, 1013 (2021).

appropriate information (see Section 8.9.3 about more advanced drafting). These tools utilize expert systems and legal databases to ensure compliance with relevant laws and regulations. Automating document drafting reduces the risk of errors and omissions, which is especially beneficial for unrepresented litigants unfamiliar with legal formalities.

Chatbots equipped with AI and NLP provide real-time assistance to users navigating ODR platforms. They answer frequently asked questions, explain legal terminology in plain language, and guide users through procedural steps (see Section 9.6 on generative AI and legal AI assistants). By simulating human-like interactions, chatbots make the ODR process more approachable and can operate 24/7, offering support outside traditional business hours.[54]

AI-powered legal research tools help users identify relevant statutes, case law, and regulations pertinent to their disputes. ML algorithms analyze vast legal databases to retrieve information tailored to the specifics of a case. Predictive analytics assesses likely outcomes based on historical data, providing parties with a better understanding of the strengths and weaknesses of their positions. This knowledge empowers users to make informed settlement decisions or to pursue further legal action.[55]

11.6 AI, ETHICS, AND ACCESS

ODR represents a significant advancement within the broader movement to harness AI and technology for equal justice. By addressing systemic barriers such as cost, complexity, and geographical limitations, ODR platforms contribute to a more inclusive legal system. The integration of AI into ODR enhances the efficiency and effectiveness of dispute resolution and sets a precedent for modernizing legal services.[56]

The potential for AI to democratize access to justice extends beyond ODR. Integrating ODR with other legal technologies such as online legal education platforms, virtual courtrooms, and AI-assisted legal aid services creates a comprehensive ecosystem. In this ecosystem, the ethical implementation of AI in legal contexts is paramount.[57]

Future research and development in ODR should prioritize critical areas to enhance its effectiveness and fairness. One essential focus is algorithmic fairness, for which developing methodologies to detect and mitigate biases in AI systems is

[54] Amy J. Schmitz & Colin Rule, The New Handshake: Online Dispute Resolution and the Future of Consumer Protection 21 (2017).

[55] Dominique Garingan & Alison Jane Pickard, *Artificial Intelligence in Legal Practice: Exploring Theoretical Frameworks for Algorithmic Literacy in the Legal Information Profession*, 21 Legal Info. Mgmt. 97 (2021).

[56] Katsh & Rabinovich-Einy, *supra* note 5, at 51.

[57] Luciano Floridi et al., *AI4People – An Ethical Framework for a Good AI Society: Opportunities, Risks, Principles, and Recommendations*, 28 Minds & Machs. 689 (2018).

crucial to ensure equitable treatment of all users. Studies have highlighted the risks of algorithmic bias in legal technologies, emphasizing the need for transparency and fairness-aware AI models to prevent perpetuating systemic inequalities.[58]

Data privacy and security also demand significant attention. Implementing robust safeguards to protect sensitive user data within ODR platforms is imperative, especially given increasing concerns over data breaches and unauthorized access. Regulations like the EU's General Data Protection Regulation ("GDPR")[59] and the recent EU Artificial Intelligence Act[60] set high standards for data protection, influencing global practices in safeguarding user information and ensuring users' trust in digital platforms (see Chapter 15 on AI assurance).

Another critical area is user-centered design. Involving end-users in the design process is vital to creating intuitive and accessible platforms that meet the needs of diverse populations. Recent research underscores the importance of participatory design approaches in developing legal technologies that are both effective and user-friendly, ensuring that technological advancements remain aligned with those they aim to assist.[61]

By emphasizing innovation and ethical considerations in these areas, ODR can play a pivotal role in transforming the justice system into a more responsive and equitable one. Integrating advanced technologies into ODR platforms promises to advance the long-standing goal of equal justice for all, making legal remedies accessible regardless of socioeconomic status or location.[62]

11.7 CONCLUSION

ODR stands at the intersection of technological innovation and legal practice, offering a pathway toward a more inclusive and efficient justice system. By integrating advanced AI tools, such as negotiation analysis, automated settlement proposals, and sentiment analysis, ODR platforms can help equalize access to justice by assisting unrepresented litigants with substantive and procedural requirements. To realize this potential, it is essential to formalize and disseminate best practices and evaluation standards for well-established ODR technologies while simultaneously prototyping and testing emerging applications.

58 Woodrow Barfield, *Towards a Law of Artificial Intelligence*, *in* Research Handbook on the Law of Artificial Intelligence 2, 29–30 (Woodrow Barfield & Ugo Pagallo eds., 2018).

59 Regulation 2016/679, 2016 O.J. (L 119) 1.

60 Regulation 2024/1689, 2024 O.J. (L 114) 1.

61 Donald A. Norman, Design for a Better World: Meaningful, Sustainable, Humanity Centered 179–81 (2024); Luke Thomas, Sarah Kaur & Simon Goodrich, *Making ODR Human: Using Human-Centred Design for ODR Product Development*, 5 Int'l J. Online Disp. Resol. 146, 147–48 (2018).

62 As highlighted in the United Nations' Sustainable Development Goals, particularly Goal 16, access to justice is fundamental to promoting peaceful and inclusive societies and building effective, accountable institutions at all levels. *See* G.A. Res. 70/1, U.N. Doc. A/RES/70/1, Goal 16 (Oct. 21, 2015).

Despite these technological strides, the principal obstacles to widespread adoption often prove to be cultural or institutional rather than technical. Legal professionals and justice institutions may be cautious about adopting novel tools that challenge familiar procedures, underscoring the need for collaborative efforts to demonstrate reliability, transparency, and ethical compliance. By addressing these barriers and fostering a culture receptive to data-driven decision-making, ODR can serve as a vital catalyst for modernizing dispute resolution processes and ensuring that the benefits of AI are equitably distributed across diverse populations.

12

Applications of Generative AI for Access to Justice

*Hannes Westermann and Marco Giacalone**

12.1 INTRODUCTION

As we discussed in Chapter 4, generative AI systems represent a major revolution in the development of AI. Their unparalleled textual drafting capabilities and flexibility in adapting to new tasks based on prompts make them well suited to tasks in the legal domain. Their uses have been extensively explored in academia, including answering bar exam questions,[1] performing statutory reasoning,[2] annotating court opinions[3] and other legal documents,[4] and even identifying themes and patterns in legal documents.[5]

In the legal industry, the adoption of generative AI is growing. In 2023, OpenAI invested in Harvey, a startup developing AI tools for legal professionals. Harvey's platform uses GPT-4 to assist with legal tasks such as drafting documents, conducting

* We thank Michael Livermore for his review of multiple drafts of this chapter.

1 Daniel Martin Katz et al., *GPT-4 Passes the Bar Exam*, 382 PHIL. TRANSACTIONS ROYAL SOC'Y 1 (2023); OpenAI, *GPT-4 Technical Report*, ARXIV 1 (Mar. 15, 2023), https://perma.cc/A24F-RYD9.

2 Andrew Blair-Stanek, Nils Holzenberger & Benjamin Van Durme, *Can GPT-3 Perform Statutory Reasoning?*, ARXIV 1 (May 10, 2023), https://perma.cc/9WE3-R977; Ha-Thanh Nguyen et al., *Black-Box Analysis: GPTs Across Time in Legal Textual Entailment Task*, ARXIV 1 (Sep. 11, 2023), https://perma.cc/9JQY-ZP4H.

3 Jaromir Savelka et al., *Can GPT-4 Support Analysis of Textual Data in Tasks Requiring Highly Specialized Domain Expertise?*, PROC. 6TH WORKSHOP AUTOMATED SEMANTIC ANALYSIS INFO. L. TEXT 1 (2023); Morgan A. Gray et al., *Empirical Legal Analysis Simplified: Reducing Complexity through Automatic Identification and Evaluation of Legally Relevant Factors*, 382 PHIL. TRANSACTIONS ROYAL SOC'Y 1 (2024).

4 Jaromir Savelka, *Unlocking Practical Applications in Legal Domain: Evaluation of GPT for Zero-Shot Semantic Annotation of Legal Texts*, 19 PROC. INT'L CONF. A.I. & L. 447 (2023); Jaromir Savelka & Kevin D. Ashley, *The Unreasonable Effectiveness of Large Language Models in Zero-Shot Semantic Annotation of Legal Texts*, 6 FRONTIERS IN A.I. & APPLICATIONS 1 (2023).

5 Jakub Drapal, Hannes Westermann & Jaromir Savelka, *Using Large Language Models to Support Thematic Analysis in Empirical Legal Studies*, 379 LEGAL KNOWL. & INFO. SYS. 197 (2023); Morgan Gray et al., *Using LLMs to Discover Legal Factors*, ARXIV 1 (Oct. 10, 2024), https://perma.cc/AXX2-2L68.

research, and analyzing contracts.[6] Major law firms have begun integrating generative AI into their operations. For instance, Allen & Overy, an international law firm, announced the use of an AI chatbot based on GPT-4 to assist over 3,500 lawyers with tasks such as contract analysis and due diligence.[7]

Of course, legal reasoning and drafting are also key components in addressing the issue of access to justice. As explored in Chapter 3, many of the gaps in effective access to justice incorporate aspects of legal understanding or legal reasoning. For example, laypeople may not be aware of how legal rules affect them or of how to enforce their rights. Given the capability of large language models ("LLMs") to analyze and draft texts, exploring their use in this area is of great interest. At the same time, it is important to remain aware of their limitations, such as issues of hallucination, bias, and privacy.

In this section, we explore some uses of LLMs for the specific goal of increasing access to justice. Illustrative examples from academic research demonstrate the potential of these models and provide a basis for discussing the merits of this approach. Then, we discuss some of the overall opportunities and limitations that stem from using LLMs in access to justice.

12.2 PROVIDING LEGAL INFORMATION

A key issue in access to justice is the language gap between a layperson's understanding of a situation and its legal significance (see Chapter 2). People may conceptualize their issue in terms of what has happened or what they want to achieve, and have difficulty linking this with the legal concepts that might open the door to using the legal system to resolve their issue.[8] For example, a tenant may not make the connection between their heating not working (a factual situation) and their landlord's failure to meet their obligation to provide a livable environment (a legal situation).

A lack of understanding of their legal rights is a key reason laypeople do nothing in response to a legal problem, and more and better legal information is often cited as a key opportunity to improve legal outcomes.[9] A few projects have aimed to use generative AI to bridge this language gap and provide legal information.

6 *Harvey*, OpenAI, https://openai.com/index/harvey/ (last visited June 18, 2025).

7 *A&O Announces Exclusive Launch Partnership with Harvey*, A&O Shearman (Feb. 15, 2023), https://perma.cc/U4JJ-7CCH.

8 Hannes Westermann, Using Artificial Intelligence to Increase Access to Justice (Mar. 2023) (Ph.D. Dissertation, University of Montreal) (on file with the Cyberjustice Laboratory); Karl Branting et al., *Judges Are from Mars, Pro Se Litigants Are from Venus: Predicting Decisions from Lay Text*, *in* 334 Legal Knowledge and Information Systems 215, 215 (Serena Villata, Jakub Harašta & Petr Kremen eds., 2020).

9 Westermann, *supra* note 8, at 102; Ab Currie, *The Legal Problems of Everyday Life*, *in* 12 Sociology of Crime, Law and Deviance 1, 56 (Rebecca L. Sandefur ed., 2009).

12.2.1 *Can ChatGPT Answer Legal Questions?*

One straightforward approach to obtaining legal information from generative AI is to ask legal questions directly to ChatGPT. For example, a user could describe a certain situation and ask ChatGPT to provide legal information for a specific jurisdiction. This approach was explored by Tan et al.[10] The authors asked questions of ChatGPT and evaluated the responses against those of an expert system relying on deterministic, symbolic AI (see Chapter 4). The responses were assessed along axes such as language comprehension, accuracy, completeness, and trustworthiness, as well as how harmless and user-friendly they were. Overall, the authors found that ChatGPT offered a user-friendly interaction mode and was able to understand the user's factual situation well, but suffered from the accuracy of the responses, frequently hallucinating answers to questions.[11]

Hallucination is thus an important limitation to overcome in using LLMs to provide legal information, particularly to unrepresented litigants who may not have the legal skills to verify the output of the model. Similar results were reported by Dahl et al., who found hallucinations when asking a model to provide information about a federal case. For some of the models, such hallucinations occurred in more than 70% of the cases.[12]

As we can see, directly asking LLMs for legal information carries some risks. However, there may be other ways of leveraging LLMs to bridge the language gap while avoiding these risks, for example, by combining the models with other AI systems, as we will explore later.

At the same time, the inherent legal information and reasoning capabilities of LLMs should not be discounted. To evaluate the capabilities of LLMs to perform such tasks, a group of researchers assembled the LegalBench dataset, which contains 162 tasks from 36 data sources.[13] These tasks cover areas such as issue spotting, rule recall, rule application, rule conclusion, interpretation, and rhetorical understanding.[14] The authors evaluated a variety of models on these tasks, some of which showed strong performance.[15] Moreover, the models have advanced significantly

[10] Jinzhe Tan, Hannes Westermann & Karim Benyekhlef, *ChatGPT as an Artificial Lawyer?*, ICAIL Workshop A.I. for Access to Just. 1 (2023), https://perma.cc/ZW7V-E66A.

[11] *Id.* at 5–6.

[12] Matthew Dahl et al., *Large Legal Fictions: Profiling Legal Hallucinations in Large Language Models*, arXiv 1 (June 21, 2024), https://perma.cc/WV8V-DCYZ.

[13] Neel Guha et al., *Legalbench: A Collaboratively Built Benchmark for Measuring Legal Reasoning in Large Language Models*, 36 Advances in Neural Info. Processing Sys. 2 (2024), https://perma.cc/4Y8U-J3HY.

[14] *Id.* at 4.

[15] *Id.* at 9.

even since the study was conducted in 2024. The study reveals both the potential of LLMs and the importance of reliable metrics for objectively comparing LLMs across different legal tasks.

12.2.2 *Combining LLMs and Information Retrieval*

Retrieving relevant information from a set of data, such as retrieving web pages based on a search query, is the well-studied field known as information retrieval ("IR").[16] One approach to enhance the quality of legal information provided by LLMs is retrieval-augmented generation ("RAG"),[17] which combines IR with LLMs. In this approach, a question is first used to find relevant documents from a corpus. However, unlike most IR approaches, the documents are not shown to the user directly but instead passed to an LLM as part of the prompt.[18] Rather than asking the LLM to answer a question based on its general knowledge (which may risk hallucinations), the LLM is asked to answer a specific question based on a number of provided sources. Thus, the answer can be grounded in relevant and up-to-date legal information.

In the legal field, knowledge is often spread over several textual sources, such as laws, case law, and firm documents, including contracts, licenses, emails, and documentation. The use of RAG in the legal field is therefore highly relevant and has been explored in both commercial and academic settings.

One key use of RAG in the legal field is to provide relevant and proven questions with legal answers, based on retrieved legislation. Louis et al. explored this use case.[19] They used a so-called retriever model (which can retrieve documents from a corpus) to identify relevant sources from Belgian legislation, based on queries such as "Can I continue to work if I am retired?" These sources were then given to several LLMs to generate an answer. While the approach worked relatively well, the authors found that issues of hallucination could not be fully overcome.[20] Other works have described the integration of RAG pipelines for legislation in various

[16] Christopher D. Manning, Hinrich Schütze & Prabhakar Raghavan, Introduction to Information Retrieval (2008).

[17] Grégoire Mialon et al., *Augmented Language Models: A Survey*, arXiv 1, 11 (Feb. 15, 2023), https://perma.cc/Y9BR-PYCM; Patrick Lewis et al., *Retrieval-Augmented Generation for Knowledge-Intensive NLP Tasks*, 33 Advances in Neural Info. Processing Sys. (2020), https://perma.cc/WVM3-5HEW.

[18] Lewis et al., *supra* note 17, at 2.

[19] Antoine Louis, Gijs van Dijck & Gerasimos Spanakis, *Interpretable Long-Form Legal Question Answering with Retrieval-Augmented Large Language Models*, 38 Proc. AAAI Conf. on A.I. 22266 (2024).

[20] *Id.* at 22272.

contexts, including Moroccan labor law,[21] criminal laws in Armenia,[22] German federal law,[23] food safety laws in India,[24] and automobile insurance in Quebec.[25]

RAG has also been explored as a means to provide better legal interpretations by retrieving case law, for example in work by Savelka et al.[26] They explored the use of LLMs to explain legal terms, such as "navigational equipment." The installation of navigational equipment is regulated by the American law governing vessel traffic, but the specific meaning of the term has only been defined through court cases. The researchers found that the models were much better at explaining the meaning of terms established by courts when combined with a traditional IR tool, which retrieved relevant cases explaining the terms and injected them into the prompt. The explanations generated using this method were preferred over those without it, and there were no hallucinations.[27]

At the same time, even RAG systems can fail occasionally. A study of commercial RAG models offered by legal publishers found that such models hallucinated less frequently than, for example, ChatGPT, but still provided factually incorrect or incomplete responses between 17% and 33% of the time.[28] As with all AI systems, understanding their performance before deployment is crucial for RAG systems as well. Pipitone and Amali introduce a benchmark (LegalBench-RAG) specifically designed to evaluate RAG systems.[29]

12.2.3 *Combining LLMs and Expert Systems*

Another interesting approach is to use LLMs not to interact directly with the layperson user, but rather to combine the generative AI component with a traditional

[21] Samir Amri, Saida Bani & Rkia Bani, *Moroccan Legal Assistant Enhanced by Retrieval-Augmented Generation Technology*, 7 Proc. Int'l Conf. Networking, Intelligent Sys. & Security 1 (2024).

[22] Armine Papikyan, Khoren Movsisyan & Vahan Petrosyan, *Using RAG to Build a Conversational Model on the Criminal Code of the Republic of Armenia*, American University of Armenia, https://perma.cc/2ZWS-H2CQ.

[23] Jérôme Agater & Ammar Memari, *SLANGO – The Initial Blueprint of Privacy-Oriented Legal Query Assistance: Exploring the Potential of Retrieval-Augmented Generation for German Law Using SPR*, 44 A.I. XLI 208 (2025).

[24] Karthick K et al., *Interactive Legal Assistance System Using Large Language Models*, 8 Int'l Conf. on I-SMAC 931 (2024).

[25] David Beauchemin, Zachary Gagnon & Richard Khoury, *Quebec Automobile Insurance Question-Answering with Retrieval-Augmented Generation*, arXiv 1 (Oct. 12, 2024), https://perma.cc/U43C-2F9D.

[26] Jaromir Savelka et al., *Explaining Legal Concepts with Augmented Large Language Models (GPT-4)*, arXiv 1 (June 22, 2023), https://perma.cc/2DUR-KV2X.

[27] *Id.* at 11.

[28] Varun Magesh et al., *Hallucination-Free? Assessing the Reliability of Leading AI Legal Research Tools*, arXiv 1 (May 30, 2024), https://perma.cc/QPC3-VWW6.

[29] Nicholas Pipitone & Ghita Houir Alami, *LegalBench-RAG: A Benchmark for Retrieval-Augmented Generation in the Legal Domain*, arXiv 1 (Aug. 19, 2024), https://perma.cc/37CU-89X6.

AI system, such as symbolic AI. In this way, the advantages of various AI approaches can be combined, leveraging the strengths of various types of AI systems.

Such integrations have been explored in the context of the JusticeBot project, which is profiled in Section 13.7. The JusticeBot allows individuals to better understand their legal situation by posing questions, analyzing the responses, and providing legal information.[30] While the JusticeBot itself relies on symbolic logic – avoiding issues with hallucinations or incorrect outputs – various approaches have been used to enhance the system with language models.

For example, researchers explored whether LLMs can assist in the creation of new JusticeBot tools. A JusticeBot system relies on encoded legal pathways that capture the criteria that need to be applied to determine whether a legal right exists. Figure 12.1 shows an example of such a pathway, covering landlord–tenant disputes in Quebec, which can be created and edited in the JusticeCreator interface.[31] Figure 12.2 shows a view of a translated version of a pathway informing a lessor whether they may terminate a lease, based on frequent lateness of rent. Creating such pathways can be arduous, as legal experts must read case law and legislation to capture the logical structure of the rules.

Thus, Janatian et al. investigated whether LLMs can be used to encode rules automatically into a logical format.[32] Here, legal experts could more efficiently develop JusticeBot systems in new domains. At the same time, the legal expert remains in control and can correct any errors the LLM makes in understanding the applicable law. Experiments conducted by Janatian et al. found that 90% of generated pathways were either logically perfect or only required slight adjustments to serve as the basis for a JusticeBot system.[33] Later research also explored whether LLMs could help with creating summaries of legal cases for use in the JusticeBot or similar systems.[34] Westermann et al. found that the LLM Claude 3.5 was able to assess whether a judge found a criterion to apply or not in 97% of cases, as well as generating helpful and concise summaries of why.[35] Language models thus offer promising ways to facilitate the creation of expert systems, which could expand their impact on access to justice.

[30] Hannes Westermann & Karim Benyekhlef, *JusticeBot: A Methodology for Building Augmented Intelligence Tools for Laypeople to Increase Access to Justice*, 19 PROC. INT'L CONF. A.I. & L. 351 (2023); Westermann, *supra* note 8.

[31] Westermann, *supra* note 8, at 338.

[32] Samyar Janatian et al., *From Text to Structure: Using Large Language Models to Support the Development of Legal Expert Systems*, *in* 379 LEGAL KNOWLEDGE AND INFORMATION SYSTEMS 167, 167 (Giovanni Sileno, Jerry Spanakis & Gijs van Dijck eds., 2023).

[33] *Id.*

[34] Olivier Salaün et al., *Conditional Abstractive Summarization of Court Decisions for Laymen and Insights from Human Evaluation*, *in* 362 LEGAL KNOWLEDGE AND INFORMATION SYSTEMS 123 (Enrico Francesconi, Georg Borges & Christoph Sorge eds., 2022); Hannes Westermann, Vern R. Walker & Jaromir Savelka, *Automated Mapping of Legal Criteria to the Texts of Adjudicatory Decisions Using LLMs*, 20 PROC. INT'L CONF. A.I. & L. 219 (2026).

[35] Westermann, Walker & Savelka, *supra* note 34.

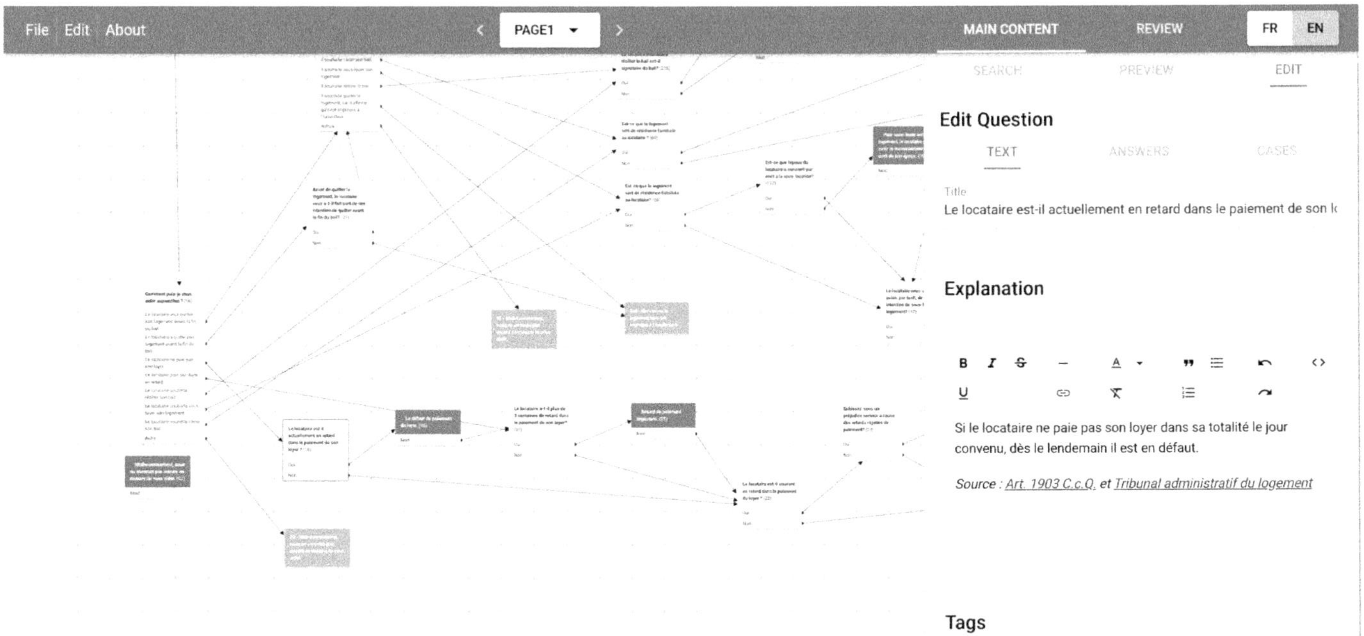

FIGURE 12.1 JusticeCreator interface. Republished with permission from the Cyberjustice Laboratory.

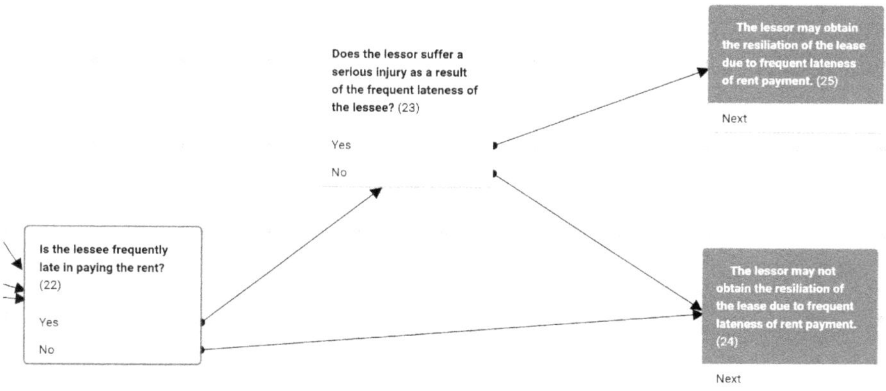

FIGURE 12.2 JusticeBot pathways determining lease resiliation due to lateness of rent payment. Republished with permission from the Cyberjustice Laboratory.

Another integration point between LLMs and expert systems lies in facilitating user interaction with an expert system. As described in Chapter 2, the language gap might prevent users from recognizing their rights. This could be the case even with the help of legal expert systems, as exhaustively listing all possible factual situations that could violate a legal right is not feasible. LLMs may offer options here, for example by suggesting relevant legal problems to a user based on a factual description of their situation. Such an approach was explored in Westermann et al.[36] The researchers found that the suggestions provided by the system often surfaced the relevant legal pathways, with 93.5% of the relevant issues appearing in the top three results.[37]

As we can see, LLMs hold significant promise in helping people understand their legal situation. Next, we explore whether these capabilities can also be leveraged by, for example, legal aid clinics to accelerate legal intake.

12.3 LEGAL INTAKE

Intake is an important barrier to effective access to justice. Legal aid clinics are required to spend a significant amount of time and human resources on intake, that is, determining whether a new case is eligible for legal support under a legal aid scheme, rather than actually assisting affected individuals. For unrepresented

[36] Hannes Westermann et al., *Bridging the Gap: Mapping Layperson Narratives to Legal Issues with Language Models*, PROC. 6TH WORKSHOP AUTOMATED SEMANTIC ANALYSIS INFO. L. TEXT 37 (2023).

[37] *Id.* at 8.

litigants, this can mean waiting in phone queues for many hours before being told whether they can obtain help.[38]

Generative AI has been used to try to address these issues. In Steenhuis et al., the authors explored the use of LLMs to apply intake rules to layperson descriptions of factual situations.[39] They created a dataset of descriptions of factual situations, as they would be expressed by laypeople. Then they provided real-world intake rules from three jurisdictions (i.e., Eastern Missouri, Mid-Missouri, and Western Missouri) to various LLMs as plain text, together with the factual situations, and asked the models to determine whether the situation would be eligible for legal aid or would require additional information. Overall, the best-performing model achieved a weighted precision of 86% – a strong result. Furthermore, the model took a cautious approach, preferring to request additional information rather than deny a situation if the answer was unclear.[40]

Such a system could serve as a first step in legal intake, allowing the pre-selection of cases that seem eligible and thus freeing up time in legal aid clinics.

12.4 FILLING OUT FORMS

Another important step in interacting with the legal system is filling out forms. Such forms lie at the source of many procedures in the justice system. However, forms are often complex and can be overwhelming.[41] Unrepresented litigants struggle to identify which forms they should use and to complete them correctly.[42] A root problem for this issue may lie in the fact that laypeople do not know which facts they need to establish or how to organize those facts to support their claims.[43]

Expert systems provide promising ways to fill out forms by asking the user specific questions and using that information to complete forms. This task, known as document automation, is explored in depth in Chapter 8. However, encoding forms in the required computer-readable template to enable document automation can involve significant effort, potentially taking hundreds of hours per form.[44] Once

[38] Quinten Steenhuis & Hannes Westermann, *Getting in the Door: Streamlining Intake in Civil Legal Services with Large Language Models*, ARXIV 1 (Oct. 2, 2024), https://perma.cc/FK2A-DKLN.

[39] *Id.*

[40] *Id.* at 7.

[41] Quinten Steenhuis, Bryce Willey & David Colarusso, *Beyond Readability with RateMyPDF: A Combined Rule-Based and Machine Learning Approach to Improving Court Forms*, 19 PROC. INT'L CONF. ON A.I. & L. 287 (2023).

[42] Westermann, *supra* note 8, at 107; JULIE MACFARLANE, THE NATIONAL SELF-REPRESENTED LITIGANTS PROJECT: IDENTIFYING AND MEETING THE NEEDS OF SELF-REPRESENTED LITIGANTS 8–9 (2013), https://perma.cc/V4TF-76L8.

[43] Branting et al., *supra* note 8, at 218.

[44] Quinten Steenhuis, David Colarusso & Bryce Willey, *Weaving Pathways for Justice with GPT: LLM-Driven Automated Drafting of Interactive Legal Applications*, ARXIV 1, 3 (Dec. 14, 2023), https://perma.cc/M2W2-TFWT.

more, LLMs have been investigated as a potential aid. Steenhuis et al. looked at how LLMs can generate such templates, finding that they are useful for creating drafts that can then be reviewed by human experts.[45] For a more in-depth discussion of this task, see Section 8.9.1.

On the other end of the process, generative AI may also be able to help users directly with the task of filling in forms. As already discussed in Section 8.9.3, laypeople struggle with drafting narratives, for example, showing why their factual situation leads to certain legal criteria being fulfilled. LLMs, with their ability to draft compelling texts, could be used to assist in such situations. Westermann presented such an approach in Dallma, a framework to conduct semi-structured reasoning with LLMs.[46] This system can ask specific questions of the user using symbolic logic and then use LLMs to decide how this information should be phrased when integrated into a specific field in a form. Furthermore, if the system determines that it lacks sufficient information, it can ask follow-up questions of the user to gather additional information.[47] While still early research, combining legal expert knowledge, user input, and LLMs seems like a promising approach for helping users complete forms. For a more in-depth exploration of this topic, see Section 8.9.3.

Most current approaches rely on the user to find and enter the relevant information into a digitized form. For example, a system could ask the user to enter information about their lease so that the system can complete a claims form. This task may pose difficulties for some users, as they might not know where to find such information in the lease, since it is often scattered across complex paper documents and forms. LLMs might also work as a tool here. Westermann et al. explored an approach that uses the new multimodal capabilities of LLMs to extract structured data automatically from pictures of filled-out forms. While not perfect, the results show promise in automatically extracting text even from blurry pictures or sloppy writing.[48] This research is explored in Section 8.9.2.

Overall, LLMs seem to offer promising capabilities in assisting users with the complex task of filling out forms, which has important implications for access to justice.

12.5 MEDIATION

Of course, improving access to justice also includes supporting individuals in resolving their disputes once they have understood their legal rights and potentially completed the

[45] Steenhuis, Colarusso & Willey, *supra* note 44.

[46] Hannes Westermann, *Dallma: Semi-Structured Legal Reasoning and Drafting with Large Language Models*, GENLAW CTR. (2024), https://perma.cc/T37U-NVBH.

[47] *Id.*

[48] Hannes Westermann & Jaromir Savelka, *Analyzing Images of Legal Documents: Toward Multi-Modal LLMs for Access to Justice*, ARXIV 1 (Dec. 16, 2024), https://perma.cc/9ES9-URYA.

necessary forms. Approaches such as alternative dispute resolution ("ADR"), including negotiation, mediation, and arbitration, and online dispute resolution ("ODR") play an important role in this, offering cost-effective and constructive ways to resolve disputes.[49] Bottlenecks in such systems can involve the cost of the process being higher than the dispute value or there not being enough mediators in a certain area.[50]

LLMs have interesting uses in mediation. Mediation is a conflict resolution method that uses a neutral third party (mediator) to guide parties to resolve their issues.[51] With their sophisticated language understanding, LLMs could support the parties and the mediator in several ways.

Integrating LLMs into mediation was explored in the scope of the LLMediator project,[52] described in Chapter 11. Westermann et al. presented a system that leverages LLMs for several purposes. First, it automatically detects inflammatory messages in a negotiation, such as messages that insult the other party and thus derail the dispute resolution process. Once detected, the system proposes another way to formulate the same message so that it is less inflammatory.[53] Figure 12.3 shows an example of a message that was reformulated.

Second, the system can support the mediator in formulating interventions. Here, the system reads the discussion between the parties and drafts a message to help the parties understand each other's views and find a settlement. This message can then be sent, edited, or discarded by the mediator.[54] Potentially, after a thorough investigation, it could also be sent directly to the parties in certain situations, although this, of course, carries additional risks.[55]

Tan et al. explored the quality of the messages generated by such a system. When compared with messages generated by humans without specific mediator training, they found that blind evaluators largely preferred both the types of interventions and the chosen interventions written by LLMs.[56] While they discussed caveats regarding, for example, the non-expert nature of the evaluators and the difficulty of evaluating nuanced content such as intervention messages,[57] the result does highlight the potential for such models to be used in mediation.

[49] Karim Benyekhlef et al., eAccess to Justice (2016).

[50] Karl Branting et al., *A Computational Model of Facilitation in Online Dispute Resolution*, 31 A.I. & L. 465 (2022).

[51] Leonard L. Riskin, *Understanding Mediators' Orientations, Strategies, and Techniques: A Grid for the Perplexed*, 1 Harv. Negot. L. Rev. 7 (1996); Tony Whatling, Mediation Skills and Strategies: A Practical Guide (2012).

[52] Hannes Westermann, Jaromir Savelka & Karim Benyekhlef, *LLMediator: GPT-4 Assisted Online Dispute Resolution*, ICAIL Workshop on A.I. for Access to Just. (2023), https://perma.cc/C5GX-VKA9.

[53] *Id.* at 4–6.

[54] *Id.* at 6.

[55] *Id.* at 6–7.

[56] Jinzhe Tan et al., *Robots in the Middle: Evaluating LLMs in Dispute Resolution*, arXiv 1 (Oct. 9, 2024), https://perma.cc/4UK5-ZSZ8.

[57] *Id.* at 9.

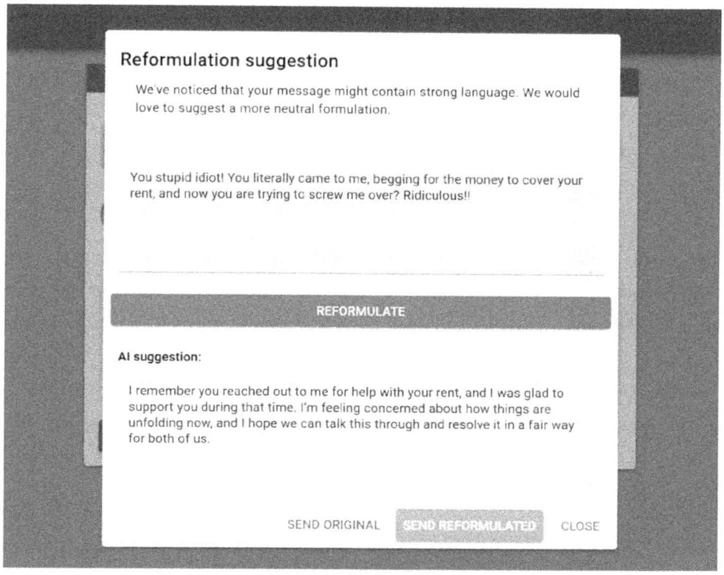

FIGURE 12.3 LLMediator reformulation of inflammatory message. Republished with permission from the Cyberjustice Laboratory.

Another example of using generative AI to facilitate ODR comes from the Conflict Resolution with Equitative Algorithms ("CREA") project.[58] Co-funded by the European Commission and developed by a consortium of universities and stakeholders, CREA employs AI to assist in asset divisions among parties across six EU countries.[59] The process begins with an open-source chatbot that provides comprehensive information about asset-division procedures, timelines, and costs, guiding users through the dispute resolution process using game-theoretical algorithms to help ensure equitable outcomes. The platform includes a "digital journey" tool, which is a trustworthy chatbot that offers precise and reliable legal information and redirects parties to legal professionals such as notaries, mediators, and lawyers when necessary.[60] LLMs such as Llama can be used to provide guidance to the dispute resolution process in the scope of this system.[61]

–

As we have seen, generative AI has a variety of use cases in access to justice, only some of which we have exemplified here. There are likely many more. Furthermore,

58 Marco Giacalone & Sajedeh Salehi, *CREA: An Introduction to Conflict Resolution with Equitative Algorithms*, *in* ALGORITHMIC CONFLICT RESOLUTION 1 (Francesco Romeo, Marco Dall'Aglio & Marco Giacalone eds., 2019).

59 *CREA Project*, CREA (2023), https://perma.cc/3LY4-CYF2.

60 F. Amato et al., *An Intelligent Conversational Agent for the Legal Domain*, 14 INFORMATION 307 (2023).

61 *Id.* at 12.

the results here should improve further with newer, more powerful reasoning models. However, some of the projects also highlight potential limits and issues with using current generative AI for access to justice tasks. Next, we explore both the opportunities and challenges of using such models.

12.6 OPPORTUNITIES

As the previous section has shown, generative AI holds significant potential to enhance access to justice and address several crucial barriers across the various interaction points between people and the legal system. LLMs can contribute to access to justice in exciting ways, as illustrated by the various approaches discussed previously. We tease out several underlying opportunities from these projects, including (1) crossing the language gap, (2) providing legal information, (3) drafting legal documents, (4) resolving legal disputes in novel ways, (5) supporting legal professionals, and (6) creating efficiency and entirely new tasks.

12.6.1 *Crossing the Language Gap*

As discussed in Chapter 3, crossing the language gap presents an important opportunity for using LLMs in the legal field. The systems described earlier show the capabilities of LLMs in linking factual descriptions to legal issues. This capability goes far beyond most symbolic AI systems, which need to rely on specific rules encoded into it. Generative AI, on the other hand, benefits from the understanding of language that stems from its training on enormous corpora of texts, to "intelligently" detect potential legal problems raised by factual situations.[62] Generative AI systems could thus act as intelligent translators, helping laypeople identify that their problem has a legal nature and that legal avenues may be available to them. Surveys show that people who do not attempt to address a legal problem are often not aware of their rights,[63] which means that this functionality can make an important contribution to access to justice.

12.6.2 *Providing Legal Information*

Of course, after identifying the legal issues affecting laypeople, the next step is to provide the user with relevant legal information, informing them of their rights and the avenues available for resolving their disputes. LLMs are also an important part of the picture here. While legal websites and symbolic systems can be a powerful way to convey legal information, they can be time-consuming to create and may not be

[62] Westermann et al., *supra* note 36; Steenhuis & Westermann, *supra* note 38.
[63] Currie, *supra* note 9.

fully tailored to a user's specific situation. Generative AI can offer personalized legal guidance by interpreting a user's situation and providing tailored, plain-language information based on techniques such as RAG. LLMs can be asked to explain or simplify legal jargon. Furthermore, they can be prompted to, for example, interact in various languages or adapt their writing style to the user's reading comprehension level,[64] which could help explain the law and a legal situation to a wide range of users. LLMs, therefore, have the potential to interact in a more in-depth manner than many traditional approaches. As we saw, the systems likewise do not need to be fully based on LLMs but rather can combine generative AI and other approaches to take advantage of the various approaches.

12.6.3 *Drafting Legal Documents*

LLMs can also be helpful in drafting documents. Writing legal documents and completing forms can be daunting for individuals without legal expertise.[65] Interactive drafting tools, such as Dallma,[66] can guide users through document preparation with context-specific prompts. Such systems can support users in document drafting in various ways, including pre-filling certain fields, providing real-time suggestions, highlighting inconsistencies or missing information, adjusting sections to ensure they meet standards and regulations, and even integrating information from documents uploaded by the user. Educational components, such as explanations of legal terms and access to additional resources, can further empower users.[67]

12.6.4 *Resolving Legal Disputes in Novel Ways*

Finally, generative AI opens the door to new ways of resolving disputes. Tools such as the LLMediator can intervene in an intelligent manner even before a message is sent, encouraging a user to maintain a positive tone in their interactions. This type of direct, real-time intervention before the other party sees the message could be tricky to accomplish with an in-person mediator, since LLMediator relies on being able to intervene before a communication is transmitted to the other party. There are many more ways of integrating LLMs into mediation to support the parties in the dispute, such as monitoring emotions, suggesting further steps, or highlighting previous outcomes.[68]

64 Chieh-Yang Huang, Jing Wei & Ting-Hao "Kenneth" Huang, *Generating Educational Materials with Different Levels of Readability Using LLMs*, ARXIV 1 (June 18, 2024), https://perma.cc/5E86-3HXQ.

65 Branting et al., *supra* note 8.

66 Westermann, *supra* note 46.

67 Henry Prakken, *Komt de Robotrechter Er Aan?*, 2018 NEDERLANDS JURISTENBLAD 269 (2018).

68 *See supra* Chapter 11, *Online Dispute Resolution*.

12.6.5 *Supporting Legal Professionals*

Beyond these steps, which focus directly on the layperson, generative AI can also be used to support legal professionals. Studies have shown that generative AI can deliver significant productivity enhancements to professionals on various tasks.[69] Whether assisting legal aid clinic employees, lawyers, judges, mediators, or other legal professionals with tasks such as document and intervention drafting or assessing legal aid eligibility, AI can allow legal professionals to accomplish their work faster and potentially with better quality, enabling them to help more people in better ways. Targeting legal professionals instead of laypeople further alleviates issues of hallucinations, since legal professionals are better placed to verify the output of the AI system. Of course, care still needs to be taken so that legal professionals are in the loop and able to have real insight into the process (see Section 12.7.1).

12.6.6 *Creating Efficiency and Entirely New Tasks*

Overall, the benefits of AI can be categorized into multiple areas, including making certain tasks more efficient to perform and enabling entirely new tasks.[70] This also applies to the use of generative AI in access to justice. By making tasks more efficient, the threshold for interacting with the legal system can be lowered. Laypeople without the resources to consult a lawyer could obtain legal information, gain access to better on-ramps to lawyers and the court system, and receive help navigating these processes through drafting assistance or dispute resolution support.

A lot of promise also lies in using LLMs to accomplish completely new tasks. Although less research has been conducted in this area, some integrations into areas such as mediation demonstrate the potential for these approaches. As the capabilities of LLMs to analyze, synthesize, translate, and generate data grow, we believe that many promising new approaches will be identified that can further impact the field of access to justice. For example, researchers have recently turned their focus toward agentic AI, which consists of various LLMs carrying out complex workflows in an active manner,[71] such as handling complex software development

[69] Erik Brynjolfsson, Danielle Li & Lindsey R. Raymond, *Generative AI at Work* 1 (Nat'l Bureau of Econ. Rsch., Working Paper No. 31161, 2023), https://perma.cc/ZJ5W-H85G; Jakob Nielsen, *AI Improves Employee Productivity by 66%*, NIELSEN NORMAN GRP. (JULY 16, 2023), https://perma.cc/FZ5L-B9XC.

[70] *See, e.g.*, Erik Brynjolfsson & Tom Mitchell, *What Can Machine Learning Do? Workforce Implications*, 358 SCIENCE 1530 (2017).

[71] Mark Purdy, *What Is Agentic AI, and How Will It Change Work?*, HARV. BUS. REV. (Dec. 12, 2024), https://perma.cc/6WJ4-FY66.

tasks, including planning, coding, error-checking, and iterative improvement.[72] Leveraging such approaches in access to justice could be very exciting.[73]

12.7 CHALLENGES

There are also some important challenges that need to be addressed for the optimal use of generative AI in access to justice. Various approaches to overcoming these challenges were presented in previous sections. It should be noted that generative AI systems can differ greatly in their implementations and purposes. Different use cases, targeted users, and individual LLMs have different risk profiles, making it difficult to discuss these issues as a whole. Let us nonetheless draw out some general challenges, including (1) hallucinations and errors, (2) bias, (3) evaluation, (4) transparency, (5) data privacy, and (6) conceptual issues.

12.7.1 *Hallucinations and Errors*

Perhaps the most important challenge of using LLMs is their tendency to hallucinate information. This can lead laypeople to make misguided and harmful decisions. While hallucinated information can be reduced with RAG approaches as well as approaches that integrate symbolic AI, even such approaches may not be a silver bullet for fully eliminating hallucinations.[74] LLMs may also make inaccurate legal assessments, leading to the presentation of information that is simply wrong.

Addressing the risk of hallucination is important for many legal use cases. Various approaches were explored in Sections 12.2–12.5. First, benchmarks such as LegalBench and LegalBench-RAG provide an important element, enabling a quantitative understanding of how often hallucinations and incorrect information are provided. At the same time, benchmark results might not paint a full picture of the real-world performance and impact of AI systems.[75]

It should also be emphasized that the impact of hallucinations and errors largely depends on how the system is framed and the type of users it targets. First, when a system provides results directly to a layperson, that individual might not be well placed to detect and overcome a hallucination. One way to address this issue is to frame the AI tool as "augmented intelligence," which supports users in their tasks rather than

[72] Sean Michael Kerner, *GitHub Copilot Previews Agent Mode as Market for Agentic AI Coding Tools Accelerates*, VENTUREBEAT (Feb. 7, 2025), https://perma.cc/486L-9K5P.

[73] *See, e.g.*, Catherine Gage O'Grady & Casey O'Grady, *Agentic Workflows in the Practice of Law – AI Agents as Ethics Counsel*, 39 GEO. J. LEGAL ETHICS 247 (2025).

[74] Magesh et al., *supra* note 28.

[75] Harini Suresh & John V. Guttag, *A Framework for Understanding Unintended Consequences of Machine Learning*, ARXIV 1 (Dec. 1, 2021), https://perma.cc/CS6C-XZ3G; Joy Buolamwini & Timnit Gebru, *Gender Shades: Intersectional Accuracy Disparities in Commercial Gender Classification*, 81 PROC. MACH. LEARNING RSCH. 15 (2018).

aiming to replace decision-making. For example, when LLMs are used to suggest the rephrasing of a form field (see Section 12.4)[76] or to suggest a reformulated message (see Section 12.5),[77] the user can verify that the rephrased text is factually accurate.

Second, there could be cases where certain types of errors are less harmful than others and might be tolerable. For example, when using LLMs as a first filter for legal aid intake, a false negative (i.e., telling an eligible user that they are not eligible) can have harmful impacts, while a false positive (i.e., telling a non-eligible user that they are eligible) would simply cause the user to go ahead in the process and be told that they are ineligible later.[78] Thus, tuning the system to favor false positives in this case could reduce the negative impact of potential errors.

Third, the intended user can play a big role in the risk of hallucinations. Legal professionals, for example, can probably verify and correct legal hallucinations better than can laypeople without legal training. Framing an AI system as one that creates a draft, which is then passed to legal professionals for verification and further iteration, could be a powerful collaboration paradigm, as implemented in several of the aforementioned projects.[79] At the same time, one has to be careful of the risk of so-called automation bias: when interacting with AI systems, people often stop sufficiently monitoring the output of the systems, sometimes due to complacency.[80] Furthermore, even if a tool only offers a "suggestion," the effect may be a shift of accountability, where overriding the suggestion might carry legal risk.[81] AI does not absolve lawyers of their responsibility to provide competent representation; instead, they must understand the capabilities and limitations of these tools to use them effectively and ethically.[82]

Overall, addressing the risks of hallucination is a complex topic that will not be solved in the scope of this section. However, as the technology of generative AI continues to advance, deciding on ways of understanding, measuring, alleviating, and limiting the impact of hallucinations will likely continue to be an important topic.

12.7.2 *Bias*

Bias is another important issue regarding LLMs in access to justice (see Chapter 15 on AI assurance). As LLMs are trained on enormous text corpora, they may absorb

[76] Westermann, *supra* note 46.

[77] Westermann, Savelka & Benyekhlef, *supra* note 52.

[78] Steenhuis & Westermann, *supra* note 38.

[79] Westermann, Savelka & Benyekhlef, *supra* note 52; Janatian et al., *supra* note 32.

[80] Kate Goddard, Abdul Roudsari & Jeremy C Wyatt, *Automation Bias: A Systematic Review of Frequency, Effect Mediators, and Mitigators*, 19 J. AM. MED. INFORMATICS ASS'N 121 (2012).

[81] Harry Surden, *Ethics of AI in Law: Basic Questions*, *in* OXFORD HANDBOOK OF ETHICS OF AI 719, 734 (Markus D. Dubber, Frank Pasquale & Sunit Das eds., 2020).

[82] MIREILLE HILDEBRANDT, SMART TECHNOLOGIES AND THE END(S) OF LAW: NOVEL ENTANGLEMENTS OF LAW AND TECHNOLOGY (2016).

biases in the texts.[83] This could lead to, for example, toxicity or the perpetuation of stereotypes.[84] Bias is a complicated and tricky topic when it comes to AI and can appear based on a variety of choices made when such systems are built.[85]

Such issues can pose risks when applied in legal contexts, where the decisions rendered can have important implications for the individual. AI models trained on historical data may perpetuate existing biases, resulting in unfair outcomes and disproportionately affecting marginalized groups.[86] For instance, if an AI model is trained on legal decisions that contain implicit biases, it may reproduce those biases in its predictions or recommendations, thereby undermining principles of equality and justice. Dressel and Farid (2018) emphasize that algorithmic predictions in criminal justice can be biased, affecting the fairness and accuracy of judicial decisions.[87]

Biases can also appear in other forms. For example, while legal decisions are published online and thus likely used to train LLMs, these decisions represent a minority of actual case outcomes, as most cases tend to settle. By being primarily exposed to court cases, AI systems may learn biases toward the court system, which could push users toward engaging in litigation instead of finding an amicable resolution.[88]

In developing LLM-driven access to justice tools, mitigating bias will be a crucial topic. To minimize this risk, robust validation frameworks should be developed, and legal experts should be involved in their development and oversight. Continuous monitoring and auditing are essential, including implementing bias detection and mitigation strategies.[89]

12.7.3 *Evaluation*

Building on the previous sections, a crucial step in applying LLMs to access to justice is the evaluation of these models. Technical methods for evaluating AI applications for legal tasks are addressed in Chapter 16. Understanding their performance and accuracy will inform how and where they are deployed. Traditionally, in machine learning ("ML"), evaluation is done in a quantitative manner, by portioning a part of the dataset to use as test data and reporting metrics of performance

[83] Emily M. Bender et al., *On the Dangers of Stochastic Parrots: Can Language Models Be Too Big?* 🦜, Proc. ACM Conf. Fairness, Accountability & Transparency 610 (2021), https://perma.cc/SKW5-ULCR.

[84] Boxin Wang et al., *DecodingTrust: A Comprehensive Assessment of Trustworthiness in GPT Models*, arXiv 1 (Feb. 26, 2024), https://perma.cc/4HZF-R5Y7.

[85] Suresh & Guttag, *supra* note 75.

[86] Ninareh Mehrabi et al., *A Survey on Bias and Fairness in Machine Learning*, 54 ACM Comput. Surv. 1 (2022).

[87] Julia Dressel & Hany Farid, *The Accuracy, Fairness, and Limits of Predicting Recidivism*, 4 Sci. Adv. 1 (2018).

[88] Westermann, *supra* note 8, at 147.

[89] Eirini Ntoutsi et al., *Bias in Data-driven Artificial Intelligence Systems – An Introductory Survey*, 10 WIREs Data Mining and Knowledge Discovery 1 (2020).

on these results.[90] This paradigm does not fully translate to LLMs. As Kapoor et al. point out, the capability of LLMs to perform tasks that to some extent require creativity and judgment makes them much harder to evaluate.[91] Similar results were found by Tan et al., where an assessment of mediator messages was performed. The authors discussed the difficulty of evaluating such messages, which often require subjective and nuanced decisions. Today, LLMs can perform such tasks without any obvious flaws, making it very difficult to assess how "good" a message is.[92] Ma et al. discuss observing annotated legal data as a survey of individual complementary viewpoints, rather than a single objective "truth."[93]

Fully understanding the impact of generative AI in the access to justice field will require an evaluation that goes beyond the model's performance to also look at how the system interacts with human users and the legal system as a whole. For more on technical methods for evaluating legal AI applications, see Chapter 16. To ensure the practical usability of such systems, user-centric design and testing are crucial. Engaging with diverse populations through focus groups and user testing can identify common comprehension challenges.[94] Interdisciplinary collaboration among technologists, legal scholars, and ethicists can facilitate the development of nuanced evaluation metrics and ethical impact assessments.[95]

12.7.4 *Transparency*

Transparency and explainability are also critical issues (see Chapter 15 on AI assurance). The "black box" nature of deep learning models makes it difficult to understand how decisions are made, conflicting with the legal profession's need for transparency and accountability.[96] In legal contexts, practitioners must comprehend the rationale behind AI systems' recommendations to ensure they align with legal reasoning and ethical standards.[97] This opacity challenges the fundamental legal principle that

[90] Westermann, *supra* note 8.

[91] Sayash Kapoor, Peter Henderson & Arvind Narayanan, *Promises and Pitfalls of Artificial Intelligence for Legal Applications*, ARXIV 1 (Jan. 10, 2024), https://perma.cc/M4W2-LHZ5.

[92] Tan et al., *supra* note 56, at 9.

[93] Megan Ma, Brandon Waldon & Julian Nyarko, *Conceptual Questions in Developing Expert-Annotated Data*, PROC. 19TH INT'L CONF. ON A.I. & L 427 (2023).

[94] Andrew Blair-Stanek, Nils Holzenberger & Benjamin Van Durme, *Can GPT-3 Perform Statutory Reasoning?*, ARXIV 1 (May 10, 2023), https://perma.cc/9WE3-R977.

[95] Claudio Novelli et al., *Generative AI in EU Law: Liability, Privacy, Intellectual Property, and Cybersecurity*, ARXIV 1 (Mar. 15, 2024), https://perma.cc/Y8EC-BDMZ; Kapoor, Henderson & Narayanan, *supra* note 91.

[96] *See generally* FRANK PASQUALE, THE BLACK BOX SOCIETY: THE SECRET ALGORITHMS THAT CONTROL MONEY AND INFORMATION (2015).

[97] Francesco Contini, Alessandra Minissale & Stina Bergman Blix, *Artificial Intelligence and Real Decisions: Predictive Systems and Generative AI vs. Emotive-Cognitive Legal Deliberations*, 9 FRONTIERS SOCIO. 1 (2024).

justice must not only be done, but must also be seen to be done. Završnik highlights that AI might not adequately protect defendants' rights, particularly in the areas of evidence evaluation and the opportunity for cross-examination.[98]

There are several pathways to address this issue. In Section 12.2.3, we saw approaches that combined explainable symbolic reasoning with LLMs.[99] Such systems could leverage LLMs to perform, for example, open-textured reasoning and argumentation, while still supporting the explainability of defined rules. That said, the free-text reasoning still relies on LLMs and may thus lack explainability. Models with reasoning capacity, such as OpenAI o1[100] and DeepSeek-R1,[101] can further provide a limited explanation of how they planned to draft the text, which can help the user understand their reasoning process to some extent.

Even so, it is important to consider the level of transparency required for different tasks. For tasks where an AI system makes a decision, understanding the reasons behind the decision is often crucial for fairness. However, when generative AI assists a user in preparing the narrative portion of a legal form, transparency may play a lesser role because the user can verify and correct the text they ultimately submit. Thus, understanding *why* the LLM arrived at a certain formulation may be less important. Once more, framing the system as augmented intelligence may be helpful.

12.7.5 *Data Privacy*

Data privacy and confidentiality present another challenge (see Chapter 15 on AI assurance). Handling sensitive legal information requires strict adherence to data protection regulations such as the General Data Protection Regulation ("GDPR"), ensuring client confidentiality.[102] Legal professionals must ensure that their AI tools comply with these regulations to protect client data from unauthorized access or breaches. Furthermore, legal professionals must verify that AI tools comply with professional ethical obligations, including competence, supervision, and client confidentiality, as outlined by organizations such as the European Commission for the Efficiency of Justice[103] and the American Bar Association.[104]

[98] Aleš Završnik, *Criminal Justice, Artificial Intelligence Systems, and Human Rights*, 20 ERA Forum 567 (2020).

[99] Janatian et al., *supra* note 32; Westermann, Savelka & Benyekhlef, *supra* note 52.

[100] *OpenAI o1 System Card*, OpenAI (Dec. 5, 2024), https://perma.cc/5PH7-7PFM.

[101] DeepSeek-AI et al., *DeepSeek-R1: Incentivizing Reasoning Capability in LLMs via Reinforcement Learning*, arXiv 1 (Jan. 22, 2025), https://perma.cc/5YD8-E6PG.

[102] Paul Voigt & Axel von dem Bussche, The EU General Data Protection Regulation ("GDPR") (2017).

[103] Eur. Comm. for the Efficiency of Just., *European Ethical Charter on the Use of Artificial Intelligence in Judicial Systems and Their Environment*, Eur. Parl. (2019), https://perma.cc/3XFG-W3AR.

[104] *ABA Releases 2019 TECHREPORT and Legal Technology Survey Report*, Am. Bar Ass'n. (Oct. 23, 2019), https://tinyurl.com/5n6nscuk.

Many commercial models today offer guarantees for data protection in their contracts, and open-source models are allowing capable models to run on local computers, which may address some of the issues with data privacy and protection. Understanding the implications of various models and systems for lawyers and access to justice practitioners will be an important step toward their safe adoption.

12.7.6 *Conceptual Issues*

The technology of LLMs is constantly evolving. Soon, the question might arise as to the extent to which such models can be used in place of human advisors or even judges in certain situations.

Discussing these questions requires the assessment of important conceptual issues underlying the use of AI for legal tasks. Providing personalized legal advice involves more than regurgitating legal information; it requires interpreting specific legal issues, applying laws to individual circumstances, and considering nuances that AI systems may not fully capture. AI models may lack the contextual understanding for nuanced legal interpretation and cannot empathize with clients or comprehend the emotional aspects of legal issues. Ethical considerations also arise concerning the unauthorized practice of law (discussed in depth in Chapter 14) and confidentiality when AI provides legal advice without appropriate human supervision.[105]

The notion of AI functioning as judges introduces even more profound challenges. Some jurisdictions have explored the concept of "AI judges." For example, the Hangzhou Internet Court, established in China in 2017, handles internet-related cases such as online shopping disputes and copyright infringement using AI technologies, giving rise to discussions relating to the use of AI in delivering judgments.[106]

Such a use of AI would push many of the questions raised previously (regarding bias, transparency, automation bias, etc.) to their limits.[107] Furthermore, it raises philosophical questions about the ethics of automated decision-making (which is inherently backward-looking, by relying on previous data for training)[108] and the philosophical foundations of judicial decision-making. As a society, we have chosen to assign the accountability of judgment to judges. This choice may be affected by the integration of AI systems into the process.[109] Today, building systems that serve

105 Masha Medvedeva, Michel Vols & Martijn Wieling, *Using Machine Learning to Predict Decisions of the European Court of Human Rights*, 28 A.I. & L. 237 (2020).

106 Changqing Shi, Tania Sourdin & Bin Li, *The Smart Court – A New Pathway to Justice in China?*, 12 Int'l J. Ct. Admin. 4 (2021).

107 *Id.*

108 *See, e.g.*, Sonja B Starr, *Evidence-Based Sentencing and the Scientific Rationalization of Discrimination*, 66 Stan. L. Rev. 71 (2014).

109 Surden, *supra* note 81, at 734.

as an aid rather than a replacement for humans for such tasks is likely the more productive and usable approach.[110]

In any case, when implementing technology in the judicial sector, it is crucial to understand that such a development is likely not neutral but rather affects how justice is rendered.[111] Involving stakeholders, through public engagement and education, plays a critical role in shaping the adoption of AI in the legal domain. Conducting public forums and educational campaigns can inform citizens about AI's role and limitations in justice, build trust, and ensure that implementation aligns with societal values and expectations. Calo discusses the importance of public understanding and the need for a roadmap in AI policy to address legal and ethical challenges.[112] Furthermore, addressing underlying conceptual challenges requires developing ethical guidelines, legal frameworks, and theoretical models that define AI's appropriate role in legal advice and judgments.[113]

12.8 CONCLUSION

We have examined the use of generative AI to increase access to justice. Such models offer tremendous advances in the ability of computers to interact with texts. As such, these models are showing promise in addressing the needs of civil litigants, including identifying legal issues, providing information, drafting documents, facilitating legal intake, and offering mediation. We examined various academic projects that showcase and evaluate these approaches, highlighting the ability to build many such systems without the need to collect specific training data. Based on this research, it seems we are at a stage in technological development where AI can meaningfully contribute to addressing the important issue of access to justice.

However, it is essential to exercise caution when creating such systems. Issues such as hallucination, overestimation of capabilities, bias, and privacy concerns can manifest in the creation of such tools. Involving stakeholders and legal aid practitioners as well as holistically evaluating the impact of such systems is crucial to

[110] Ben Shneiderman, *Human-Centered Artificial Intelligence: Reliable, Safe & Trustworthy*, 36 INT'L J. HUM.–COMPUT. INTERACTION 495 (2020).

[111] Nicolas W. Vermeys & Karim Benyekhlef, *Best Practices in the Field of Cyberjustice*, SEMINAR ON RECENT TRENDS AND GOOD PRACTICES IN THE APPLICATION OF ELECTRONIC TECHNOLOGY TO JUDICIAL PROCESSES (E-JUSTICE) (2011), https://perma.cc/2GQX-U42V.

[112] Ryan Calo, *Artificial Intelligence Policy: A Primer and Roadmap*, 51 UC DAVIS L. REV. 399 (2017).

[113] *Recommendation of the Council on Artificial Intelligence*, OECD (2019), https://perma.cc/98VY-G2BZ; High-Level Expert Group on AI, *Ethics Guidelines for Trustworthy AI*, EUR. COMM'N (2019), https://perma.cc/B5VK-5NM3; Raja Chatila & John C. Havens, *The IEEE Global Initiative on Ethics of Autonomous and Intelligent Systems*, *in* ROBOTICS AND WELL-BEING 11 (Maria Isabel Aldinhas Ferreira et al. eds., 2019); UNESCO, *Recommendation on the Ethics of Artificial Intelligence* (2022), https://perma.cc/V2EW-XZR9.

ensuring that LLMs contribute to the field, rather than introducing another pathway to obtain incorrect or misleading information.

Simultaneously, one may want to consider the alternatives available to many people today. People often struggle to understand their legal rights, and many lack access to professional legal assistance. If the alternative to an AI system is no access to legal information and help, even imperfect AI systems may offer better outcomes and empowerment to individuals than no help at all. Finding the right balance where the integration of generative AI into the legal system is both ethical and safe, while positively affecting society, is an important task from technological, legal, and policy perspectives.

PART IV

Today's Access to Justice Systems

13

Today's Access to Justice Systems

*Kiernan Moran and Mia Bonardi**

13.1 INTRODUCTION

Every day in courts, clinics, and communities across the country, the gap between those who need legal help and those who can access it is painfully clear. The access to justice crisis affects millions of people across socioeconomic classes worldwide. Traditional legal processes often remain expensive, time-consuming, and inaccessible to many individuals. The range of civil legal needs is vast, from navigating bankruptcy proceedings and small-claims court to addressing housing disputes and seeking protection from abusers. Chapter 1 discusses four factors that exacerbate the global access to justice crisis: (1) growing societal complexity, (2) overprofessionalization, (3) bias toward institutional plaintiffs, and (4) the language gap. At its core, the crisis reflects a persistent structural market failure – one in which legal services, shaped by traditional profit incentives, constrained public funding, and restrictive regulatory schemes like unauthorized practice of law ("UPL") rules, fail to provide the support needed for people without the financial means to meaningfully access the justice system.

Recognizing opportunities to bridge the justice gap with emerging technologies, attorneys, technologists, and justice advocates are developing increasingly creative ways to help people gain entry to the legal system. This chapter explores innovative tools that are transforming the way people interact with the justice system. These legal tech innovators have taken distinct approaches in pursuit of the same goal: leveraging technology to make justice accessible to all.

From online tribunals that handle civil disputes to AI-powered chatbots providing legal guidance, these pioneering initiatives represent a fundamental shift in how legal assistance is delivered. The tools range from simple online forms and

* At the time of writing, Kiernan Moran is employed at Quest for Justice and Mia Bonardi previously contributed to Suffolk University Law School's Document Assembly Line Project. Both Quest for Justice and Suffolk's Document Assembly Line Project are profiled in this chapter.

All data, dates, opinions, laws, figures, and other information in this chapter are current as of June 2025.

automated guidance to sophisticated AI systems that assist users in navigating complex legal procedures in discrete areas. These initiatives are designed with the end user in mind, ensuring that legal processes, which can be intimidating and complex, are simplified and made more accessible.

The initiatives profiled include British Columbia's Civil Resolution Tribunal, Pro Bono Net's LawHelp Interactive and Justicia Lab, and Kansas's Protection Order Portal; AI-powered tools like Upsolve's bankruptcy tool, JusticeBot, Rentervention, Suffolk University Law School's Document Assembly Line Project, and Nevada's Self-Help Chatbot; and paid tools such as Hello Divorce, Courtroom5, and Quest for Justice. Each initiative shares common goals despite its distinct approaches. They aim to simplify legal processes, provide accessible information in plain language, reduce costs, and ultimately empower individuals to navigate the legal system effectively.

While the potential for AI tools to enhance access to justice is great, these innovations often arise in response to overwhelming circumstances that strain traditional court systems. The COVID-19 pandemic, for example, highlighted the dire need for digital access as courts became overwhelmed with backlogs, leaving many people unable to obtain timely resolution for their cases.

The development of these legal tech tools is not a static process but one that requires constant iteration. Technologists and lawyers must collaborate closely, continually refining their platforms based on user feedback and evolving legal needs. This process is akin to "building a plane while flying it," a mantra of several of the initiatives we highlight. This is a challenging task that requires flexibility, creativity, and an unwavering focus on the end user.

As these systems continue to evolve and expand, they offer promising models for addressing the justice gap through innovation while raising critical questions about the intersection of technology, legal practice, and equitable access to justice. Their successes and challenges offer valuable insights for future developments in the evolving field of providing legal help to those who need it most.

13.2 BRITISH COLUMBIA CIVIL RESOLUTION TRIBUNAL

The British Columbia Civil Resolution Tribunal ("CRT") is revolutionizing the way legal disputes are resolved by offering a fully remote online dispute resolution ("ODR") system for litigants. Established in 2016 to address the backlog in multi-unit property dispute cases (cases brought between tenants, owners, and landlords of condominiums) and mounting delays in small claims court, the CRT brings dispute resolution into the digital age. What sets the CRT apart is its ability to offer a fully remote, technology-driven process in which individuals can upload evidence, attend hearings, and file forms, all from the comfort of their homes. In just a few short years, the CRT has successfully handled more than 52,000 claims, making dispute resolution more accessible, affordable, and efficient.

The CRT's mission was laid out in the 2012 Civil Resolution Tribunal Act, which established the framework for the newly formed tribunal's responsibilities, powers, and authorities. The goal of the CRT is to provide legal guidance that:

1. is accessible, speedy, economical, informal and flexible;
2. applies principles of law and fairness, and recognizes any relationships between parties to a dispute that will likely continue after the tribunal proceeding is concluded;
3. uses electronic communication tools to facilitate resolution of disputes brought to the tribunal; and
4. accommodates, so far as the tribunal considers reasonably practicable, the diversity of circumstances of the persons using the services of the tribunal.[1]

Since its launch, the CRT's jurisdiction has steadily expanded beyond its original focus on multi-unit property disputes. It now includes small claims, societies and cooperative associations cases, vehicle accidents, and disputes involving intimate images. As Canada's first online tribunal, the CRT has become a model for future small claims tribunals and a torchbearer for harnessing technology to facilitate access to justice.

The CRT allows unrepresented individuals to litigate entire cases remotely. As Shelley Lopez, CRT Chair explained,

> The goal was to provide twenty-four-seven access to anyone from their home as and when it suits them ... It allows people to participate on their smartphone, on their tablet, on their laptop. For instance, you take your kids to school and then draft a bit of your submissions, and then you put your kids to bed, and you can come back and finish up.[2]

However, a party can still request an oral hearing (which would be by video), and a CRT tribunal member can then decide if that is appropriate.

The CRT's process is streamlined into four key stages, illustrated in Figure 13.1. First, litigants access the online portal to either apply for relief through the CRT or respond to a claim. At this stage, litigants are given the option to serve the opposing party personally or to use the CRT to effectuate service. Second, the parties negotiate through a secure platform to explore potential settlements. Third, if the negotiation fails, a facilitator or case manager helps the parties work toward a resolution. Finally, if the dispute remains unresolved, an independent tribunal member issues a binding decision on the parties. To prepare for this stage, participants are told they can gather evidence that supports their position (even expert evidence) and upload it to the secure platform. The evidence is then shared with the opposing parties and

[1] Civil Resolution Tribunal Act, S.B.C. 2012, c. 25 § 2 (Can.).

[2] Video Interview by Mia Bonardi with Shelley Lopez, Chair, B.C. Civil Resolution Tribunal (Nov. 7, 2024).

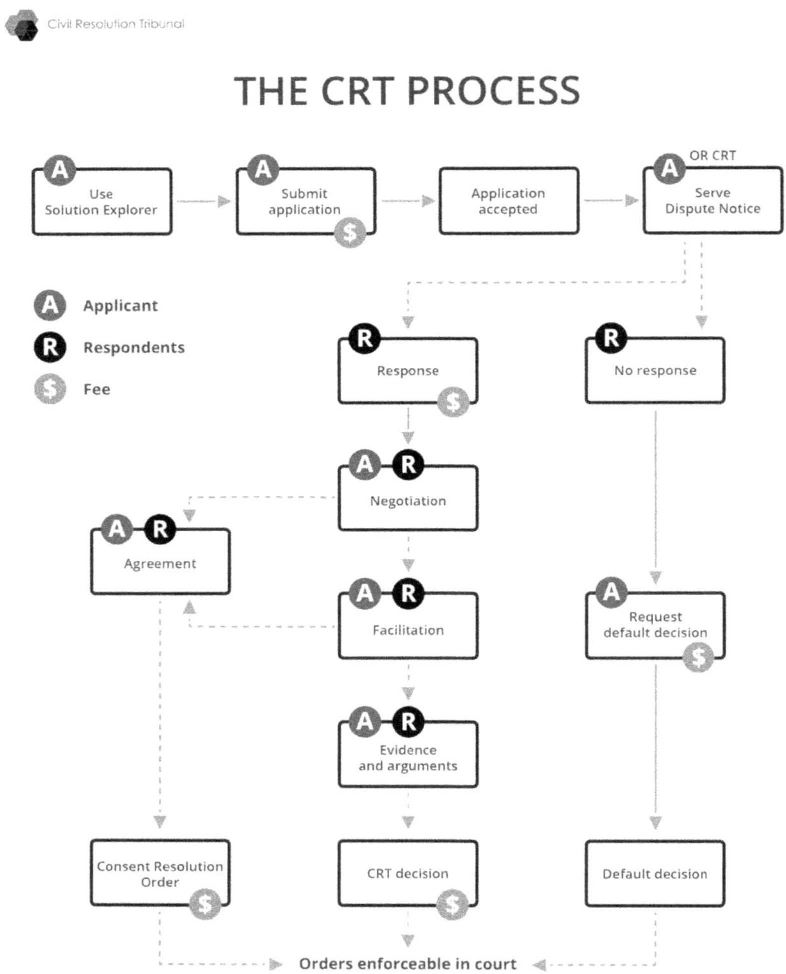

FIGURE 13.1 The Civil Resolution Tribunal Process (as of March 2025, and can change without notice).

the tribunal in a round-robin setting, and the participants are provided with a neutral evaluation by the arbiter.

The CRT takes necessary steps to ensure the process is seamless and straightforward. For individuals with limited digital literacy, the CRT offers in-person and phone support to help users navigate the CRT platform. The CRT emphasizes the importance of clear communication and plain language, typically at a sixth to eighth grade reading level, and a user-focused design. By providing concise information, guided pathways, and potential legal consultations, the CRT ensures that litigants can navigate the process with confidence.

By June 2017, the Civil Resolution Tribunal Act was amended to allow the CRT to handle cases beyond the small claims threshold of $5,000 CAD, offering an affordable alternative to traditional litigation. The CRT also strives to keep costs for litigants as low as possible. Ms. Lopez explained, "We have a generous fee waiver program. There's an intake fee, and then only if you don't settle do you pay a tribunal decision fee. And the fees are very low, and they're really not meant to be a cost recovery."[3] With a focus on providing convenience, affordability, and fairness, the CRT platform has become a resounding success for its users. Despite the fact that litigation, negotiation, and lawsuits rarely leave anyone satisfied, between 2023 and 2024, 92% of its users felt the CRT was respectful during the process, and 83% felt they were treated fairly.

Despite its successes, the CRT continues to face challenges in scaling its services. Ms. Lopez reflected, "What made good sense for the CRT in 2016 when we had one area [of jurisdiction] … doesn't make sense necessarily anymore with six areas of jurisdiction."[4] Rolling out new features and expanding into additional areas of law requires significant effort, as forms and processes must be tailored to each jurisdiction type. Despite extensive consultations with stakeholders, ultimately, the platform is for the users, so the CRT needs to consistently evolve its processes. Ms. Lopez likened this to "building the plane as you're learning to fly it."[5]

Another challenge faced by the tribunal is the variation in time required to resolve different types of cases. For example, multi-unit strata property cases with no monetary limit require significantly more time for tribunal members to adjudicate than other cases. Ms. Lopez emphasized that "getting at the data is huge" and that "having data that you can actually track [helps] figure out whether processes need to change and how they should change."[6] Reflecting on the platform's design, Ms. Lopez noted, "When you design the platform upfront, you don't always know what data you want to collect until you're seeing trends later."[7]

Looking ahead, Ms. Lopez envisions leveraging new technologies to further streamline and enhance services for users. While the tribunal sees great potential in using AI to summarize decisions and explain complex legal concepts, progress has been slower due to budget constraints and concerns over the reliability of large language models ("LLMs"). Nevertheless, Ms. Lopez acknowledges that users may choose to use AI on their own, noting, "If a participant at the CRT decides to use a third-party AI service to help with their submissions, and they are fully

[3] *Id.*
[4] *Id.*
[5] *Id.*
[6] *Id.*
[7] *Id.*

informed about the risks [around reliability and accuracy], that's perfectly fine. However, parties cannot submit fake cases, which we have learned often happens with AI-generated submissions, and we expect to soon have a rule expressly to that effect."[8] The CRT respects users' autonomy in seeking outside assistance as long as it does not undermine the principle of fairness. In encouraging other jurisdictions to adopt similar ODR models, Ms. Lopez offers a simple yet powerful piece of advice: "Don't be afraid."[9]

13.3 PRO BONO NET

In the pre-internet era, legal aid was more constrained by burdensome paper processes and a lack of scalable tools. Recognizing this problem, Mark O'Brien and Michael Hertz co-founded Pro Bono Net, a trailblazing technology nonprofit dedicated to supporting access to justice. The catalyst for Pro Bono Net came from a 1993 immigration crisis when a ship named the *Golden Venture* carrying nearly 300 Chinese asylum seekers ran aground in New York. Mr. O'Brien recalled that the sudden arrival and dispersal of the asylum seekers into detention centers across the country created a crisis within the legal aid system, revealing deep gaps in coordination, subject-matter expertise, and large-scale mobilization of lawyers across multiple jurisdictions.[10] From this incident, Pro Bono Net's founders recognized how the internet could enable such coordination by providing a centralized infrastructure that could mobilize lawyers, streamline information sharing, and scale up pro bono capabilities.

Since then, Pro Bono Net has developed, managed, and provided a range of legal technology tools to support legal aid organizations and unrepresented litigants across various areas of law. According to Brescia, "the Pro Bono Net constellation of sites has served millions of consumers in its decades of operation."[11] Figure 13.2 features some of these sites, several of which we highlight later, including LawHelp Interactive and Justicia Lab, as well as a tool developed by Justicia Lab, Citizenshipworks.

At Pro Bono Net, innovation is less about disrupting the legal system and more about adapting it: meeting people where they are with tools that make the law more navigable. Sam Harden, former Senior Innovation Manager at Pro Bono Net, observed, "A lot of the secret sauce that lawyers have is just from seeing the same thing over and over. It's not something that you learn in law school or because you're smart. It's just pattern recognition."[12] This insight reflects a broader design

8 *Id.*
9 *Id.*
10 Video Interview by Kiernan Moran with Mark O'Brien, Co-Founder, Pro Bono Net (Oct. 25, 2024).
11 Ray Brescia, Lawyer Nation: The Past, Present, and Future of the American Legal Profession 180 (2024).
12 Video Interview by Kiernan Moran & Mia Bonardi with Sam Harden, Former Senior Innovation Manager, Pro Bono Net (Mar. 17, 2025).

FIGURE 13.2 The Pro Bono Net (2025). Printed with permission from Pro Bono Net.

principle at Pro Bono Net: that recognizing patterns is not just a lawyer's skill, but something that can help simplify and streamline the legal process for unrepresented litigants. Pro Bono Net's innovations remind us that access to justice is not a lofty policy goal but begins by dismantling everyday obstacles, such as complexity and repetition, that make the legal system feel impenetrable.

13.3.1 *LawHelp Interactive*

One of Pro Bono Net's most transformative projects was the result of its acquisition of LawHelp Interactive ("LHI") in 2005. Launched in the early 2000s, LHI provides guided interviews that help individuals complete legal forms. Within five years, Pro Bono Net scaled LHI from completing 20,000 forms per year to more than one million.

A major factor in LHI's success was its early collaboration with courts. California, where self-help services were already particularly robust, became one of LHI's first large-scale adopters. California courts adopted LHI's document automation tool to streamline the process of completing legal forms. The tool asks users to enter their information once and then automatically populates it across all necessary forms. This eliminated repetitive tasks and reduced errors. It also enabled litigants to focus on the key aspects of their cases rather than getting bogged down in procedural nuances.

In Los Angeles, for instance, LHI was deployed to help streamline form completion in areas of law that frequently involve unrepresented litigants, such as divorce and family law. Divorce in California historically required litigants to complete twenty forms across three phases of the case. California Judicial Council Managing Attorney Bonnie Hough oversaw LHI's implementation in California courts and recalled that, before LHI, self-help centers in Los Angeles served up to 300 unrepresented litigants a day. Ms. Hough explained that unrepresented litigants would first sit through a lengthy orientation on the required paperwork, fill out the forms on their own, and only then receive one-on-one help to correct mistakes.[13] According to Ms. Hough, the LHI tool reduced the time spent by self-help center staff assisting litigants with form preparation from 2–4 hours per person to just 15–30 minutes per person.[14] Ms. Hough viewed the adoption of access to justice technology as beneficial for both litigants and the courts: "I think there's a real unity of interest between the public and the courts … having the papers legible and complete is really helpful for the court … It allows the judge to ask questions and get any additional information they need to make a decision."[15] LHI demonstrates how simple, well-designed tools can drive an outsized impact in expanding access to justice.

13.3.2 *Justicia Lab*

Building on the momentum of LHI's success, Pro Bono Net broadened its access to justice mission beyond automated forms. In 2007, it launched the Immigration Advocates Network to support the legal needs of immigrants to the US. Under the leadership of Director Rodrigo Camarena, this initiative evolved into Justicia Lab, an incubator for developing technology to assist individuals navigating immigration to the US. Drawing on his experience running a nonprofit that connected Spanish-speaking immigrants to essential services, Mr. Camarena combined a human-centered design approach and systems thinking in the lab: "We really get into a problem space. We work directly with impacted individuals, with advocates, with lawyers and non-lawyer advocates … to understand potential solutions and innovate … not just helping an individual or organization, but to help the field overall."[16]

One notable project developed by Justicia Lab is Citizenshipworks, a platform that reduces language barriers and simplifies the naturalization and citizenship process by offering translations of forms in Chinese and Spanish. According to Citizenshipworks, the platform has guided more than 50,000 immigrants through the naturalization process and supports a network of more than 200 nonprofit partners nationwide.[17]

13 Video Interview by Kiernan Moran with Bonnie Hough, Managing Att'y, Cal. Jud. Council (Mar. 11, 2025).

14 *Id.*

15 *Id.*

16 Video Interview by Kiernan Moran with Rodrigo Camarena, Dir., Justicia Lab (Apr. 9, 2025).

17 Citizenshipworks, *Who We Are*, https://perma.cc/6PUN-C6LD.

The same commitment to usability shapes Justicia Lab's newest project. In 2024, Justicia Lab joined the Google.org AI for Social Impact Accelerator, and the team launched iMMPATH AI, pairing optical-character recognition ("OCR") with multimodal AI to provide multilingual, step-by-step guidance for anyone with a smartphone to respond to immigration correspondence from the government.[18] The user simply takes a picture of the Notice to Appear form and iMMPATH securely extracts the critical data, translates the text, and then presents a plain-language roadmap of the legal process for the user.[19] As Mr. Camarena explains, the tool "does more than translate – it pulls out the key values and breaks the whole process into clear, actionable steps immigrants can actually follow."[20] The app also provides optional notifications and reminders for key deadlines and next steps.[21]

–

Two of Pro Bono Net's pillars, LawHelp Interactive and Justicia Lab, illustrate the organization's larger vision: deploying adaptable technology to widen the doors of justice for people who must navigate the system without a lawyer. From self-help forms to AI-powered document interpretation, Pro Bono Net's tools carry the same core philosophy: justice should not depend on the representation someone can afford.

However, the real test for access to justice tools is sustainability, which involves carrying each tool beyond its initial launch and evolving it to account for changing user needs and to incorporate new technologies. Mr. O'Brien explains, "It's easy to get money to build the first iteration, but very difficult to build version 2.0 and 3.0 by integrating new technologies."[22] Recognizing the need to reach beyond traditional legal aid funding sources, Pro Bono Net sought support from national funders, such as the Open Society and Gates foundations, and implemented a fee-for-service model to facilitate ongoing investment from courts, private law firms, and nonprofit organizations that use its services.

In July 2025, Zach Zarnow was appointed the new executive director of Pro Bono Net after nearly six years with the National Center for State Courts.[23] While Mr. Zarnow noted, "We're working toward a rebrand and restructuring," he emphasized that the recognizable pillars of Pro Bono Net, including LHI and Justicia Lab, will remain.[24] Mr. Zarnow explained that Pro Bono Net will continue to use AI and other advanced technology tools but will focus on selecting

18 Video Interview with Rodrigo Camarena, *supra* note 16.
19 *Id.*
20 *Id.*
21 *Id.*
22 Video Interview with Mark O'Brien, *supra* note 10.
23 Emily Sawicki, *New Pro Bono Net Director on Obstacles, Opportunities at 25*, Law360 (July 11, 2025), https://perma.cc/JF4M-KV9J.
24 Video Interview by Mia Bonardi with Zach Zarnow, Exec. Dir., Pro Bono Net (Aug. 1, 2025).

the right tool for the task. He recommends, "Start by figuring out what problem you're trying to solve and what your goals are and working backward from there to select the best tool."[25] Mr. Zarnow emphasized that whether help comes from "AI or a community justice worker, or whatever else, we're going to use the right tool for the situation."[26]

13.4 UPSOLVE

In the US, millions of people face crushing debt. Medical bills, layoffs, and predatory loans often force individuals into dire financial situations; however, the complexity of bankruptcy proceedings can make this powerful debt relief tool inaccessible to those who need it most. Upsolve, a groundbreaking 501(c)(3) nonprofit, is transforming access to bankruptcy protection through free digital tools and personalized legal assistance. Since 2018, the platform has helped eliminate more than $783 million in debt for more than 13,000 people.[27] Upsolve's success can, in part, be attributed to its unusual blend of funders, including the Legal Services Corporation, the Robin Hood Foundation, the Hewlett Foundation, and the New York Bar Foundation, as well as individual donors.[28]

Upsolve offers a range of debt management tools and educational resources to help users better manage their finances. Through its platform, users can access customized recommendations for debt relief and rate each option's effectiveness with a thumbs-up or thumbs-down based on their financial situation. The AI-powered chatbot offers step-by-step guidance for individuals filing for bankruptcy, assisting them in gathering necessary financial information, completing required forms, and understanding the key stages of the process. Following the platform's process, users can typically discharge their debts within four months.

Upsolve was founded by Rohan Pavuluri, Jonathan Petts, Ben Jackson, and Mark Hansen.[29] During his first year at Harvard University, Mr. Pavuluri encountered a stark reality: while technology was revolutionizing countless industries, few focused on building tools for low-income families and marginalized communities.[30] As a research assistant at Harvard Law School's Access to Justice Lab, Mr. Pavuluri witnessed firsthand the potential of leveraging technology to mitigate the access to

25 *Id.*

26 *Id.*

27 Upsolve, *Eliminate Your Debt with Bankruptcy*, https://perma.cc/4V73-GHZC.

28 Upsolve, *How Is Upsolve Free?* (July 8, 2025), https://perma.cc/HT9E-YJDY.

29 Video Interview by Mia Bonardi with Jonathan Petts, Co-Founder & Chief Exec. Off., Upsolve (Sep. 18, 2024).

30 Upsolve, *Is Upsolve Real? Is This a Legitimate Service?* (May 7, 2025), https://perma.cc/WHK3-Y4JR.

justice crisis, in which basic civil rights remained available only to those who could afford legal representation.[31]

Bankruptcy emerged as a crucial focus area. Despite its potential to stop wage garnishments, improve credit, and increase job prospects, the system was designed in a way that made it nearly impossible for individuals to navigate without expensive legal help.[32] This realization led Mr. Pavuluri to start Upsolve with attorneys Mr. Petts and Mr. Jackson and technologist Mr. Hansen.[33]

The organization's early days were marked by humble beginnings and uncertainty. Mr. Petts explained, "Just getting started was the biggest challenge. It was the fear of starting something so speculative and risky and seemingly destined to fail."[34] The team began with a basic system: transferring questions from a one-hundred-page bankruptcy form into an Excel spreadsheet. Low-income Brooklyn residents seeking pro bono bankruptcy assistance would fill out a Google form, and the team would then manually input their responses into the full set of official bankruptcy forms. Once completed, they would print the document and instruct the individuals to bring it to the bankruptcy court. Mr. Petts recalled, "I just remember thinking what a terrible idea this was, and how totally unscalable it was. But it was just a really important problem."[35]

Despite initial obstacles, the team persevered, focusing on user-first design principles. They recognized that their target users, many of whom had lived in poverty their entire lives, needed an intuitive platform that transcended legal jargon and financial complexity. Through constant iteration and refinement, Upsolve evolved into a sophisticated yet accessible digital tool, as illustrated by its chapter 7 Bankruptcy Checklist in Figure 13.3.

Upsolve has also sought recourse in the courts, with varying results. Upsolve has volunteers without law licenses provide limited verbal legal advice to help "New Yorkers fill out checkboxes on a one-page answer form provided by the State, in the hopes that more people will avoid defaulting outright in such actions."[36] New York law includes several statutes that prohibit UPL, which generally prevent people who are not lawyers from providing legal advice.[37] Upsolve

[31] *Id.*

[32] Video Interview with Jonathan Petts, *supra* note 29.

[33] Upsolve, *supra* note 30.

[34] Video Interview with Jonathan Petts, *supra* note 29.

[35] *Id.*

[36] Upsolve, Inc. v. James, 604 F. Supp. 3d 97, 103 (S.D.N.Y. 2022); Upsolve, Inc. v. James, No. 22-1345, 2025 WL 2598725 (2d Cir. Sep. 9, 2025), *petition for cert. filed*, No. 25-948 (Feb. 6, 2026); Phillip Suderman, *Appeals Court Blocks Innovative Program Helping New Yorkers Fight Debt Collection Lawsuits*, Inst. for Just. (Sep. 9, 2025), https://tinyurl.com/bdea5u5s.

[37] *See* N.Y. Jud. Law §§ 476-a, 478, 484, 485 (McKinney 2024). A court may also hold a non-lawyer who practices law in civil or criminal contempt. *See id.* §§ 750, 753. The Attorney General is authorized to sue "any person, partnership, corporation, or association" who engages in the unauthorized practice of law." *Id.* § 476-a.

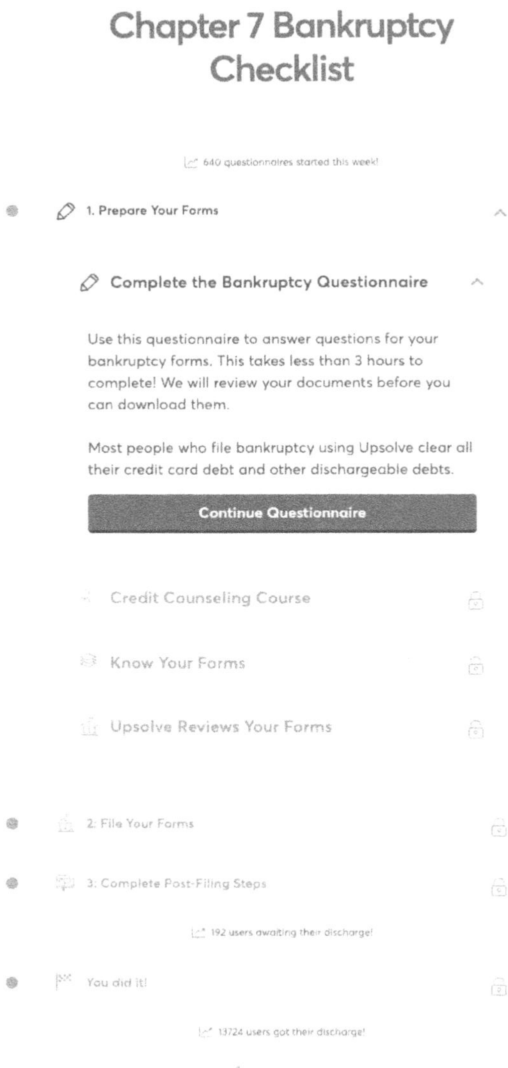

FIGURE 13.3 Upsolve's step-by-step checklist to guide users through the bankruptcy process (2025). Printed with permission from Upsolve.

challenged the enforcement of these statutory restrictions, seeking a preliminary injunction on First Amendment grounds. The organization argued that its volunteers were offering speech, not conducting legal actions like court representation. After the federal district court granted the preliminary injunction, the United States Court of Appeals for the Second Circuit later vacated and remanded this decision, and Upsolve has filed a petition for certiorari with the United States Supreme Court.[38]

Looking ahead, Upsolve recently launched an in-app AI support agent.[39] This tool can respond dynamically to what users see on their screens, troubleshoot errors, and guide them through complex steps in real time.[40] It leverages retrieval augmented generation ("RAG") to draw on eight years of expert-created content from Upsolve, providing context-specific help as users navigate the app.[41] Upsolve aims to develop AI-powered tools that will help users navigate the complex decision-making process of choosing among seven available options for discharging unsecured debt. Upsolve's technology-driven approach promises to make financial decision-making more accessible and informed for those who need it.

13.5 KANSAS PROTECTION ORDER PORTAL

In 2020, as the COVID-19 pandemic disrupted daily life, domestic-abuse victims became trapped in isolation with their abusers. Although Kansas courts continued to accept and process protection order filings as emergency matters, filings still declined over time: over three years, protection order case filings decreased by 15.7%, from 13,545 cases filed in 2019 to 11,423 in 2021.[42] The Kansas Judicial Branch secured COVID-relief grants and hired the University of Missouri–Kansas City School of Law ("UMKC") and Professor Ayyoub Ajmi of CiviLaw.Tech to implement its Kansas Protection Order Portal ("KSPOP").

In just three years, KSPOP has improved access to protection orders, conducting more than 92,000 eligibility reviews and facilitating the filing of more than 30,000 protection orders.[43] The online tool enables petitioners to prepare and electronically submit their protection order petitions without needing to print or hand-deliver paper forms.

When users visit KSPOP, they first complete an eligibility review that explains the different types of Kansas protection orders and helps them determine which one fits their situation. Once eligibility is confirmed, KSPOP uses Jotform Enterprise to collect answers, pairs them with the statutorily required Kansas

[38] *See supra* note 36.

[39] Claire Robinson, *What We're Trying with AI Support (and Why It Feels Different)*, AGENTS OF CHANGE (Apr. 17, 2025), https://perma.cc/9VHJ-9J46.

[40] *Id.*

[41] *Id.*

[42] KAN. BUREAU OF INVESTIGATION, DOMESTIC VIOLENCE, STALKING, AND SEXUAL ASSAULT IN KANSAS 45 (2023), https://perma.cc/7DEC-RLQM.

[43] Video Interview by Kiernan Moran & Mia Bonardi with Ayyoub Ajmi, Prof., UMKC Sch. of L. & Founder, CiviLaw.Tech (Sep. 26, 2024).

Judicial Council forms, and transmits the finished packet to the court's e-filing system via a secure dashboard.

KSPOP emphasizes its use of practical, plain-language information. From the outset, the team recognized that navigating the legal system could be intimidating, especially for individuals in crisis. Rather than leaving users to decipher long, open-ended statutory questions on their own, KSPOP retains the statutory questions but supplements them with both contextual guidance and targeted follow-up prompts to help users provide complete and accurate answers. For example, KSPOP asks users to describe the most recent incident of abuse, where and when it happened, and who witnessed it. Throughout the interview, the portal provides plain-language tips on what to expect in the case and includes a one-click "safe exit" button that instantly redirects users to Google if they need to leave the screen quickly.[44] When the questionnaire is complete, users can file their petitions directly from the portal, eliminating the need to file in person at the clerk's office.

The spark for KSPOP came in early 2019 when Kansas 10th Judicial District Judge Keven O'Grady approached UMKC about teaching students document automation. When the pandemic struck in March 2020, the Office of Judicial Administration ("OJA") expedited the concept and, with Supreme Court approval, secured grant funding to transform it into a statewide system. Judge O'Grady reached out to UMKC once again, urgently looking to apply document automation to the escalating challenges in processing protection orders during the pandemic. Professor Ajmi and his team at the law school embarked on a mission to solve the problem.

Guided by the OJA, Professor Ajmi and a team of staff and students at UMKC interviewed clerks, judges, and victim advocates to pinpoint pain points in the paper process. They concluded that transparency, step-by-step education, and one-stop electronic filing were essential. Although the prototype questionnaire was sketched quickly, implementation exposed practical hurdles. Building a truly accessible protection order tool required a mobile-friendly interface that could handle up to fifty pages of documents, all while maintaining enterprise-grade security and access to the court's e-filing system. Until that interface was ready, petitions were routed to a secure court email inbox.

KSPOP is the product of broad collaboration among OJA, Supreme Court justices, judges, clerks, legal aid organizations, UMKC faculty and students, and vendors, all working together and contributing their expertise. Kansas Legal Services played a key role in the project's design phase, while law school research assistants worked on technical and legal aspects of the portal. Buy-in from both the Kansas Supreme Court and the OJA was critical: it lent the project credibility, ensured broad adoption, and secured the ongoing commitment of resources for content updates, staff training, user support, and technical enhancements.[45]

[44] *Id.*
[45] *Id.*

The pandemic's disruption of traditional court operations was a catalyst for rethinking existing systems. Professor Ajmi opined, "If we didn't have COVID, we would not be able to have this project, as sad as that is."[46] Without the shift in demand for protection orders caused by the pandemic, the project might not have gained the traction it needed. Although the Court had been considering pro se e-filing options prior to COVID-19, Professor Ajmi notes that the pandemic "created the urgency and the funding to move quickly."[47] Accelerating adoption, the Kansas Supreme Court further formalized the new workflow by authorizing petitions filed through KSPOP to be accepted as originals.[48]

KSPOP empowers Kansans who might otherwise lack the time, resources, or legal knowledge to seek vital protections. This system not only enhances access to legal remedies but also ensures that critical protections are available to those who are most vulnerable. Although the portal currently relies on traditional software rather than generative AI, Professor Ajmi stresses that "the real barrier isn't technology, it's having the courage to build the tool."[49]

13.6 SUFFOLK UNIVERSITY LAW SCHOOL'S DOCUMENT ASSEMBLY LINE PROJECT

As the constable began removing the tenant's belongings from their home, time was running out. In what would prove to be a pivotal moment, the tenant was able to file a motion online to stay the eviction. This motion not only halted the process but ultimately led to the tenant winning their appeal. This tenant's victory over an illegal eviction was not just a personal triumph; it represented the success of an innovative project that facilitated access to justice during one of the most challenging periods in modern history.

Suffolk University Law School's Legal Innovation and Technology ("LIT") Lab made this life-changing intervention possible through its Document Assembly Line Project. The initiative, which simplified access to legal documents and the court system, emerged in response to the COVID-19 pandemic. With the courts shut down, there was an urgent need for the legal system to adapt. Using Docassemble, the Document Assembly Line Project developed CourtFormsOnline.org, a platform that expedites the drafting and, in some cases, filing of a variety of legal forms in Massachusetts and other jurisdictions. Users simply select the appropriate category for their court filing, such as family law, landlord–tenant, or employment; enter the necessary information on a smartphone or computer through a step-by-step guided

[46] *Id.*
[47] *Id.*
[48] Order Auth. Acceptance of Documents Submitted Through the Marriage License Portal and Prot. Order Portal, 2021-RL-033 (Kan. 2021).
[49] *Id.*

interview of the required forms; and then, in some cases, submit the completed form electronically to the court.

The catalyst came from former Massachusetts Supreme Court Chief Justice Ralph Gants, who issued a powerful call to action to the state bar. He challenged attorneys to serve the most vulnerable during this unprecedented time, acknowledging that while offerings might not be perfect, the necessity for immediate action outweighed the fear of failure: "Sure, we will make mistakes, but if we have the agility and wisdom to learn from those mistakes, we will fail, and fail again, until we succeed. If we stand strong, resilient, and adaptive, and work together as judiciary and bar to find 'duct tape' solutions to immediate problems that otherwise might take years to solve, we will leave this crisis with a better, more resilient system of justice. And perhaps, if we do our jobs well, a future generation will say of us, 'This was their finest hour.'"[50]

The crisis particularly affected unrepresented litigants facing high-stakes challenges. Professor David Colarusso, Co-Director of Suffolk's LIT Lab with Professor Quinten Steenhuis, reflected, "There were people who were in lockdown with their abusers. They needed a way to deal with that. We wanted them to have access to the courts."[51] Many individuals lacked basic resources, including computers, technical knowledge, or the ability to navigate e-filing systems. For them, physically closed courts represented insurmountable obstacles.

Suffolk's LIT Lab mobilized a global response, attracting more than 200 volunteers from eleven time zones and five continents. This diverse coalition of attorneys, subject-matter experts, technical professionals, and law students worked at the seemingly impossible, often "building the plane while flying it," as team members would say. The project's success demonstrated how a crisis can catalyze innovation. Professor Colarusso said, "Massachusetts asked for help, and the people of the world stepped up."[52]

Using open-source tools as well as agile project management and development techniques, the team automated court forms for CourtFormsOnline.org,[53] making both form completion and e-filing possible via smartphone. The technical implementation, however, proved to be the easier part of the equation. "The challenges the Assembly Line faced were never technical," Professor Colarusso noted. "There were always problems with adoption. Change is change, and especially for people working in a place where mistakes matter, you don't want to make mistakes."[54]

[50] Letter to the Bar from Mass. Sup. Jud. Ct. Chief Just. Ralph D. Gants, MASS.GOV (Mar. 19, 2020), https://tinyurl.com/58t767uc.

[51] Video Interview by Kiernan Moran with David Colarusso, Co-Dir., Suffolk Univ. L. Sch. Legal Innovation & Tech. Lab (Oct. 30, 2024).

[52] *Id.*

[53] CT. FORMS ONLINE, *Free DIY Legal Help for Massachusetts*, https://perma.cc/8KLF-2CNT.

[54] Video Interview with David Colarusso, *supra* note 51.

A crucial breakthrough came when the team secured a memorandum of understanding with Massachusetts's trial courts in just six weeks, an unprecedented timeline for such an agreement, according to Professor Colarusso.[55] This partnership enabled seamless integration with court procedures and proved instrumental to the project's success. The impact was immediate: the first user accessed the system just thirteen minutes after its launch, at 12:13 AM.[56]

As former Chief Justice Gants had hoped, the team's willingness to innovate and adapt led to tools that might otherwise have taken years to develop. In answering his call – "failure is not an option" – they created not just a temporary fix but a blueprint for transforming access to justice through technology and collaboration.[57] The Document Assembly Line Project proved that when faced with seemingly insurmountable challenges, innovation and determination can create, in the words of former Chief Justice Gants, "a better, more resilient system of justice."[58]

13.7 JUSTICEBOT

JusticeBot, a product of the Cyberjustice Laboratory and hosted by the Administrative Housing Tribunal in Quebec, presents a compelling case study on how AI can help bridge the justice gap and enhance equitable access to legal assistance. JusticeBot is a free, innovative tool offered in French that uses a combination of natural language processing ("NLP") and machine learning ("ML") to provide laypeople with legal information about landlord–tenant issues. JusticeBot has been used more than 40,000 times.

The user interacts with JusticeBot by answering questions and navigating through a guided pathway designed by legal experts. For each question, the user is provided with a plain language explanation of the issue, along with relevant explanatory legal cases, as illustrated in Figure 13.4. At the end of the interview, JusticeBot provides the user with relevant legal information and a list of previous cases similar to their own, along with the case outcomes. JusticeBot also provides the user with a list of possible options to pursue in resolving their issue.

A crucial part of the JusticeBot system is the JusticeCreator, the back-end program that provides a tool for creating legal decision-making support tools across various fields. Illustrated in Figure 13.5, JusticeCreator enables legal experts to use a no-code tool to graphically design and edit decision trees that connect the questions asked by JusticeBot users to potential legal outcomes. Because the JusticeCreator was built for experts with little to no technical experience, it has the potential to increase the impact of tools like JusticeBot.

55 *Id.*
56 *Id.*
57 Letter to the Bar from Mass. Sup. Jud. Ct. Chief Just. Ralph D. Gants, *supra* note 50.
58 *Id.*

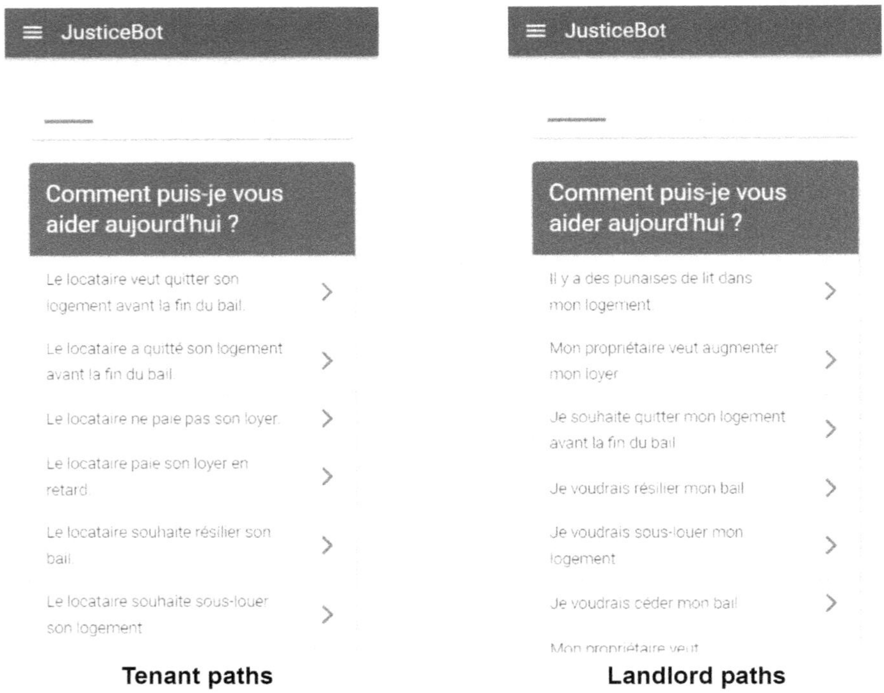

FIGURE 13.4 JusticeBot's landlord and tenant pathways (2025). Printed with permission from the Cyberjustice Laboratory.

The Cyberjustice Laboratory, founded in 2010 by Professor Karim Benyekhlef at the University of Montreal, is a pioneering research hub dedicated to partnering with public institutions to design and develop technology to fulfill public needs in the justice system. Professor Valentin Callipel, Head of Mission at the Cyberjustice Laboratory, explained that while other tools offered in the private sector aim to increase access to justice by focusing on the individuals, "Our approach is to work for the public sector, like tribunals, to help them deliver better justice."[59]

JusticeBot was born out of a collaboration between the Cyberjustice Laboratory and Concordia University's exploratory work in ML, which ultimately led to the foundational ideas for JusticeBot. Professor Callipel noted, "We had a very strong interest in enhancing the way lay people could access the justice system … the key for us was to be able to develop a tool that can provide useful information for the public."[60] The Cyberjustice Laboratory's access to a vast dataset of more than one million publicly available housing cases from the Administrative Housing Tribunal in

[59] Video Interview by Karl Branting & Mia Bonardi with Karim Benyekhlef, Founder & Dir., & Valentin Callipel, Head of Mission, Cyberjustice Lab'y (Apr. 4, 2024).
[60] *Id.*

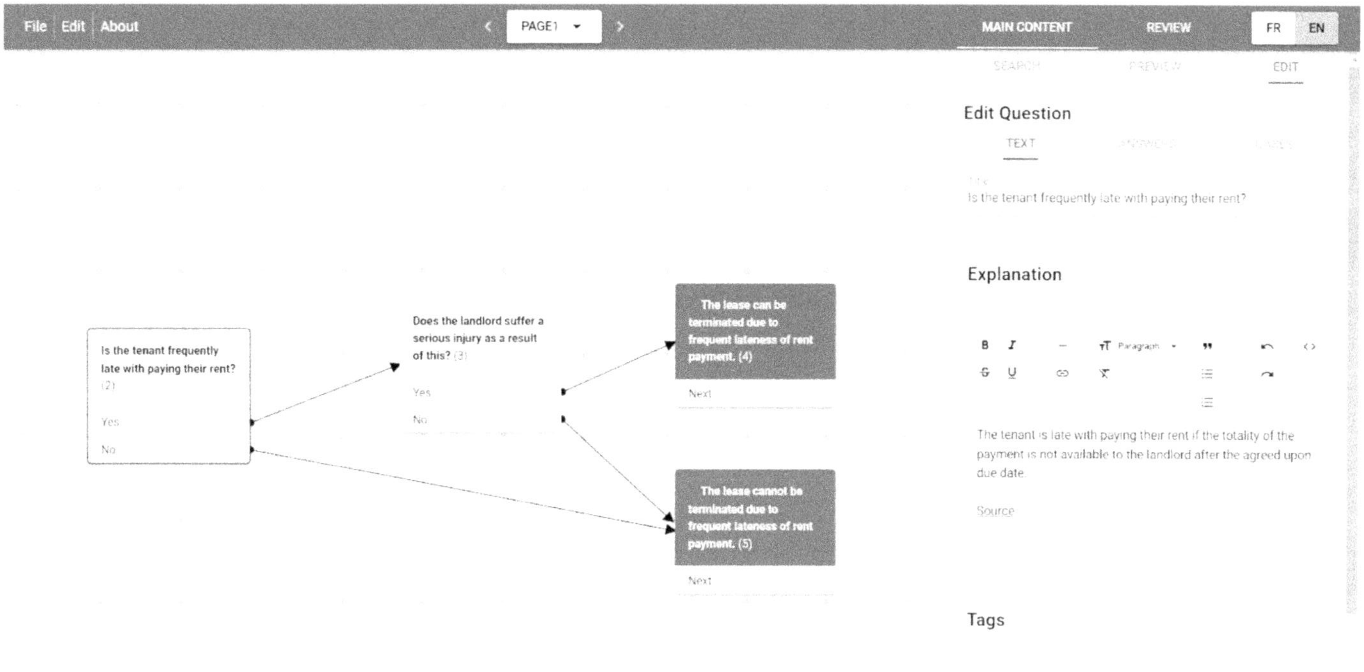

FIGURE 13.5 Legal expert's interface for building decision trees in the JusticeCreator (2025). Printed with permission from the Cyberjustice Laboratory.

Quebec was a game-changer for developing JusticeBot. The original team, primarily composed of computer science experts without legal expertise, envisioned JusticeBot as a predictive tool to help laypeople understand the outcome of their cases.

However, annotating cases for ML predictions seemed nearly impossible due to the variability and nuance in legal texts and pertinent case-by-case facts. The complexity and variability inherent in legal reasoning, coupled with the ethical implications of providing predictive outcomes to laypeople, necessitated rethinking JusticeBot's design.

A pivotal moment came in February 2017 during the Cyberjustice Laboratory's "Hack Justice" event. Then a student, Hannes Westermann won the event with his design of a democratic participation tool and was encouraged to pursue a Ph.D. at the University of Montreal, where he was offered the opportunity to contribute to the JusticeBot project. Now Assistant Professor of Law and Artificial Intelligence at Maastricht University, Professor Westermann was deeply interested in JusticeBot's potential to make a difference in people's lives. He explained, "Since so many people face these cases, you can have a big numerical impact on people who don't often have access to lawyers."[61]

While still a Ph.D. student, Professor Westermann assumed the role of lead researcher for JusticeBot in 2018. In what he considers a critical transition of his Ph.D. thesis, the team shifted JusticeBot toward being a tool that provides information and context, rather than making predictions about legal case outcomes. Professor Callipel explained that the team "deviated our work toward the more traditional expert system approach to make sure that we were able to offer a tool that could be used by a public institution."[62] This shift helped JusticeBot make significant progress toward becoming a live and useful tool.

From the outset, the JusticeBot team designed the platform with the goal of supporting public-sector use, particularly through partnerships with courts and other legal institutions. However, developing legal AI tools for public institutions is challenging, and JusticeBot faced significant hurdles in its initial development. Professor Benyekhlef noted, "There is always a big, legitimate fear from public institutions that the tool could give false information."[63] JusticeBot provides general legal information, leaving analysis and decision-making to the user. The system is explicitly designed to communicate this approach to the user, both to prevent them from overestimating the system's capabilities and to encourage them to draw their own conclusions regarding their situation.

"Putting it online and getting the feedback and seeing people actually interact with it, of course, has been very informative and really shows the potential," Professor

[61] Video Interview by Karl Branting with Hannes Westermann, Assistant Prof. of L. & Intel., Maastricht Univ. (Mar. 28, 2024).

[62] Video Interview with Karim Benyekhlef & Valentin Callipel, *supra* note 59.

[63] *Id.*

Westermann said.[64] JusticeBot's evolution, from ML experiment to trusted public-facing expert system, demonstrates how academic innovation, ethical foresight, and public-sector collaboration can provide legal assistance in tangible, measurable ways. As the Cyberjustice Laboratory expands into new domains, like consumer and data protection law, JusticeBot's success in democratizing landlord–tenant law offers a compelling model for future AI-driven tools designed to serve the public good.

13.8 RENTERVENTION

Since its launch in 2019, Rentervention has transformed access to legal housing assistance in Chicago, serving more than 50,000 residents through its AI-powered platform. Developed by Chicago-Kent's Law Center for Better Housing, Rentervention demonstrates AI's potential to help democratize legal knowledge and address the critical gap in housing legal services.

Rentervention uses AI to provide free and accessible legal guidance to Chicagoans facing housing issues. It provides housing assistance through a combination of digital tools and human support. In 2023, Rentervention won the Chicago Innovation Award, which is presented to organizations that have developed innovative products addressing challenges faced by Chicago's neighborhoods and residents.[65]

Upon visiting Rentervention's website, users are greeted by "Renny," a virtual, AI-powered legal chatbot. Powering Renny is an AI-driven platform that uses a combination of generative AI and RAG techniques to provide tailored legal assistance beyond scripted responses. This technology enables Renny to pull pertinent legal information from a repository of legal knowledge and case law and provide customized responses based on the specific questions users ask. Renny can inform tenants of their rights, addressing issues such as landlord retaliation and property maintenance. Parts of Renny are built using an open-source chatbot framework with a low-code interface, enabling individuals without technical backgrounds, such as new attorneys and interns, to contribute to the development of the tool. As former Director Conor Malloy put it, this approach "democratizes the process of development," making it easier for legal professionals to build and refine self-help tools without needing to code.[66]

Although about 90% of Rentervention users interact with Renny, the platform offers several ways tenants can seek legal assistance, including by phone, help desk, text message, and email.[67] For more complex cases, Renny connects tenants to the staff attorney. If the situation remains unresolved, the staff attorney connects the

[64] Video Interview with Hannes Westermann, *supra* note 61.

[65] Law Ctr. for Better Hous., *Rentervention Named Winner at 22nd Annual Chicago Innovation Awards* (Nov. 17, 2023), https://tinyurl.com/4hhaneux.

[66] Video Interview by Mia Bonardi with Conor Malloy, Former Dir., Rentervention (July 17, 2024).

[67] Peter Riley, *A Pathway to Justice: AI and the Legal Aid Intake Problem*, Medium (Mar. 25, 2025) https://perma.cc/XB5B-ZN7Y.

individual to a volunteer attorney. Mr. Malloy described this approach as "applying appropriate human interventions, like bringing humans into the loop, and intelligently applying human resources to connect with people."[68] With only one paralegal and one staff attorney, Renny has empowered the Rentervention team to handle many more cases while expending fewer resources.

Mr. Malloy observed that the traditional model of "scaling up" legal aid – merely adding more staff – was not a sustainable or cost-effective option due to the sheer volume of legal need.[69] By leveraging emerging technologies, he aimed to "democratize legal knowledge," providing a more scalable and accessible approach to legal assistance.[70]

While Rentervention has been a resourceful tool for many, one challenge it faces is language accessibility. The platform's chatbot struggles to provide effective assistance in Spanish and other languages. This gap in service highlights the broader issue of providing equitable access to legal support across diverse populations. Rentervention continues to work on integrating Spanish-language capabilities into its chatbot, texting, and voice services.

The platform's goal is to continuously improve Renny, maximizing its reach and the quality of its information to empower tenants to assert their housing rights. Mr. Malloy explained, "I want every tenant talking to Renny all the time."[71] Looking forward, Rentervention aims to expand its capabilities and services to more Chicagoans by partnering with local organizers and developing new tools for other areas of law. Future developments include refining its AI capabilities to provide even more personalized legal guidance, exploring additional languages, and expanding modes of communication.

13.9 THE NEVADA SELF-HELP CHATBOT

In 2020, the Supreme Court of Nevada partnered with CiviLaw.Tech, a legal tech company founded by University of Missouri–Kansas City School of Law Professor Ayyoub Ajmi, to develop a groundbreaking generative AI-powered chatbot that provides legal guidance to the general public. Since its launch in June 2022, the Nevada Self-Help Chatbot has assisted more than 4,000 unique users, recording more than 5,000 sessions with an average session length of two minutes.[72]

During the discovery phase, Professor Ajmi conducted extensive surveys with hundreds of members of the public, judges, clerks, and advocates.[73] These efforts helped identify user needs and laid the groundwork for the Nevada Self-Help Chatbot.

[68] *Id.*
[69] *Id.*
[70] *Id.*
[71] *Id.*
[72] Video Interview by Kiernan Moran & Mia Bonardi with Ayyoub Ajmi, Prof., UMKC Sch. of L. & Founder, CiviLaw.Tech (Nov. 13, 2024).
[73] *Id.*

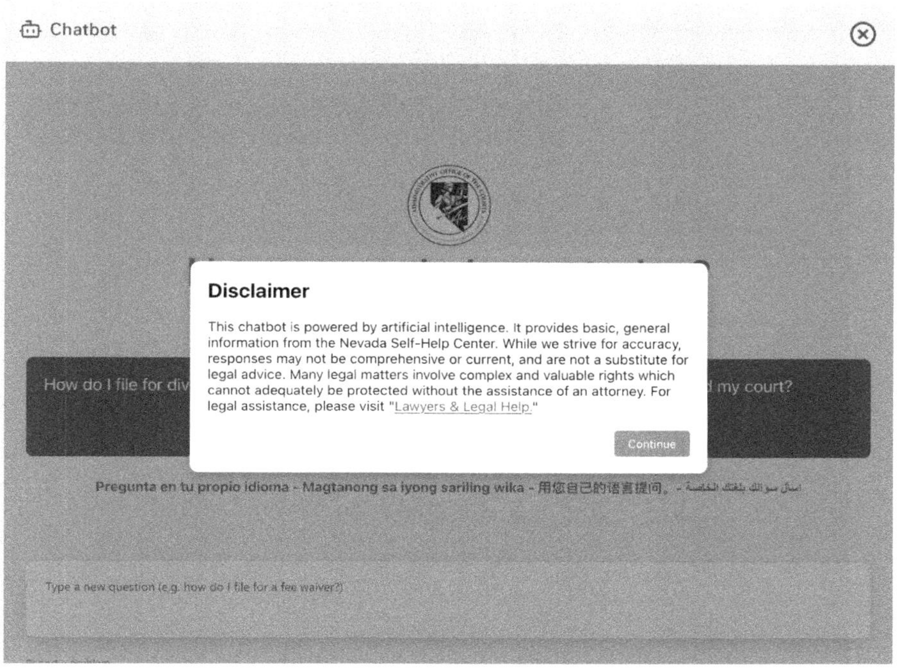

FIGURE 13.6 Nevada Self-Help Chatbot disclaimer (2025). Printed with permission from the Supreme Court of Nevada.

The Nevada Self-Help Chatbot was developed to make legal processes more accessible by using RAG to ensure responses are grounded in Nevada law and procedure. Initially, the chatbot was built on Microsoft Azure, combining decision-tree frameworks and AI-based language understanding.[74] However, as Professor Ajmi and his team continued their work, they realized that these tools were insufficient for handling complex user inquiries. The breakthrough came when they transitioned to OpenAI's GPT model.[75] According to Professor Ajmi, this shift enabled the chatbot to deliver more humanlike responses, enhancing its conversational capabilities.[76] While the chatbot offers conversational support, it also makes the user aware of its limitations, as illustrated in Figure 13.6.

The chatbot also offers multilingual support. According to Professor Ajmi, "the GPT model is already trained to handle multiple languages, up to fifty languages, and can probably do more. Since we didn't instruct the model to limit the language, it can answer in any language the user wants."[77] As shown in Figure 13.7,

74 *Id.*
75 *Id.*
76 *Id.*
77 *Id.* (citing Alec Radford et al., *Robust Speech Recognition via Large-Scale Weak Supervision*, ARXIV 1 (Dec. 6, 2022), https://perma.cc/Y5PP-7XSM).

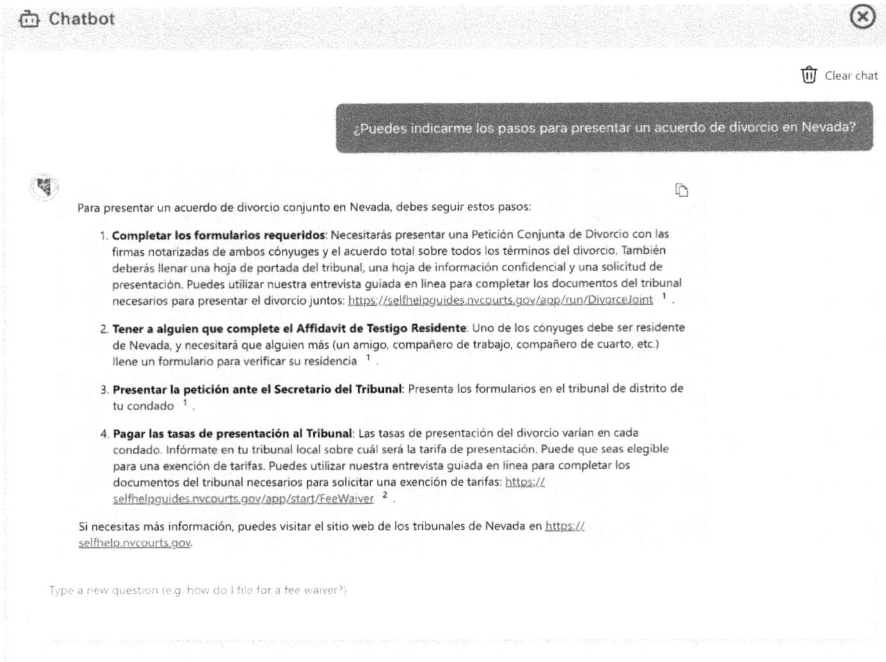

FIGURE 13.7 Nevada Self-Help Chatbot delivering divorce-related legal information in Spanish (2025). Printed with permission from the Supreme Court of Nevada.

the chatbot delivers step-by-step guidance in the same language used in the user's original inquiry.

Professor Ajmi collaborated closely with legal professionals to ensure the chatbot's accuracy and effectiveness. He explained, "The chatbot is supposed to make the delivery of legal guidance more effective. It's not about replacing people; it's about scaling assistance to meet the overwhelming demand."[78] The chatbot expanded accessibility and extended assistance beyond regular court hours, overcoming the limitations of in-person or phone-based support.

A notable success was the chatbot's ability to guide users through legal processes such as expunging criminal records. This required collaboration with legal experts to develop clear, step-by-step instructions. The result was a tool that provides users with a straightforward and intuitive way to complete complex tasks.

One of the strategic decisions made early on to achieve this success was to build upon the already popular Nevada Self-Help website, SelfHelp.NVCourts.gov,[79] which had strong analytics and high search engine rankings. The website provided

[78] *Id.*
[79] NEV. SELF-HELP CTR., https://perma.cc/843K-23VS.

a ready audience for the chatbot, which is included as a pop-up on every page, along with video explainers and links to guided interviews tailored to specific areas of law. A DIY section consolidates all relevant links, so users can navigate available resources. A user feedback feature, which collects data through a thumbs-up or thumbs-down system, has been instrumental in refining the tool.

Looking ahead, Professor Ajmi believes that generative AI will fundamentally change how people access legal information: "I think ChatGPT is the end of websites."[80] Professor Ajmi envisions a future where legal services in the US are as accessible as smartphone applications, eliminating the need for static web pages. However, he also acknowledges the challenges of regulating such rapidly advancing technology. He predicts that UPL restrictions and other regulations will need to evolve to keep pace with the capabilities of AI.

Professor Ajmi foresees other jurisdictions developing similar chatbots, advocating for generative AI as a transformative tool for access to justice.[81] For Professor Ajmi, the chatbot represents more than just a technological achievement; it is a blueprint for innovation in access to justice. His advice to others in the field is simple: "Pick your group, set a plan, and stick to it. Launch as soon as you can, and then test, test, and test."[82]

By combining court support at the highest level with cutting-edge technology, Professor Ajmi hopes the Nevada Self-Help Chatbot will inspire similar initiatives. As he continues to push the boundaries of what is possible, one thing is clear: the future of access to justice is digital, dynamic, and driven by court collaborations with people like Professor Ajmi.

13.10 COMMERCIAL AND FEE-BASED LEGAL HELP TOOLS

In recent years, private companies have come to recognize what legal aid organizations have long understood: millions of people fall into the justice gap. There is a large group of potential consumers who are "too poor" to hire counsel yet "too rich" to qualify for free legal aid. The unmet demand, combined with technological advancements, has sparked a new wave of legal innovation in the private sector. To serve this overlooked middle, a new cohort of justice-tech companies is stripping overhead, automating routine tasks, and guiding users through legal procedures at consumer-friendly prices. Companies like Courtroom5, Hello Divorce, and Quest for Justice are betting that well-designed software can ease court burdens while delivering meaningful legal assistance to those the traditional bar has failed to serve. If these technology-driven models can deliver high-quality legal services that are

80 Video Interview with Ayyoub Ajmi (Nov. 13, 2024), *supra* note 72.
81 *Id.*
82 *Id.*

both affordable and accessible, these companies could not only ease the burden on legal aid and the courts but also help expand access to justice for millions.

13.10.1 *Courtroom5*

Courtroom5 is a justice-tech platform built to support self-represented litigants navigating debt collection, foreclosure, family disputes, and other serious legal issues. It offers a structured path to legal self-representation through litigation training, document automation, AI-powered guidance, and community support. The platform's core innovation is the *Personal Practice of Law*, a structured methodology that empowers pro se litigants to handle their cases step by step. Its automated assistants guide users through complex workflows in plain language.[83] On AI integration, Courtroom5 Co-Founder and CEO Dr. Sonja Ebron explained that "AI plays a central role in helping users determine next steps in their cases, understand legal procedures, analyze fact patterns, perform accurate legal research, and generate persuasive filings."[84] Built around the *Personal Practice of Law* curriculum, automated assistants break down legal complexity into plain-language checklists and auto-populate filings to keep pro se litigants on track.[85]

13.10.2 *Hello Divorce*

Hello Divorce is a venture capital-backed platform that helps primarily self-represented individuals navigate divorce through automation and expert, step-by-step guidance. The platform combines a hybrid of self-guided tools, legal document automation, on-demand strategy sessions, and full-service divorce plans, available in all fifty states. Since its launch in 2018, the platform has served more than 50,000 people across the US.[86] As of June 2025, Hello Divorce is beta testing an "AI Divorce Assistant" designed to further streamline the process.[87] According to Co-Founder and CEO Erin Levine, the AI assistant "guides users through forms, explains legal concepts, and helps identify next steps."[88] Behind the scenes, the same technology triages customer inquiries, accelerates expert review, and, in Ms. Levine's words, "supercharge[s] some of our experts and deliver[s] faster support to more users."[89] Yet Hello Divorce integrates AI with deliberate care. "Divorce isn't a nice-to-have

83 E-mail Interview by Kiernan Moran with Sonja Ebron, Co-Founder & Chief Exec. Off., Courtroom5 (May 22, 2025).
84 *Id.*
85 *Id.*
86 E-mail Interview by Kiernan Moran with Erin Levine, Co-Founder & Chief Exec. Off., Hello Divorce (May 15, 2025).
87 *Id.*
88 *Id.*
89 *Id.*

problem – it's high-stakes and deeply personal," Ms. Levine said. "One wrong answer from a chatbot can create real harm. That's why we're solving for real pain points, testing heavily, and avoiding hype."[90]

13.10.3 *Quest for Justice*

Quest for Justice ("Q4J") is a legal technology company that owns and operates JusticeDirect Law Firm and JusticeDirect Law Firm DC, both alternative business structure law firms based in Arizona and Washington, DC, respectively. Arizona is one of the few states that allows complete nonlawyer ownership of law firms, a model known as an alternative business structure ("ABS").[91] See Chapter 14 for more on UPL and ABS. This regulatory flexibility enables Q4J to integrate software engineers, designers, and attorneys within a single business entity. Q4J and JusticeDirect offer unrepresented litigants a range of services, including limited-scope representation, small claims court assistance, demand letter generation, attorney consultations, and attorney document review. The company's mission is to address "middle cases": situations where individuals have cognizable legal claims but cannot secure representation because their case cannot be taken on contingency – where the lawyer only gets paid if they win – or they cannot afford full legal services through litigation. Currently, the platform uses guided interviews and generative AI to help individuals draft the legal documents necessary for litigating small claims cases. The company offers limited-scope legal services powered by technology and automation, where attorneys use generative AI to support, research, draft, and edit, enabling timely, flat-fee assistance. Co-Founder and CEO Binh Dang noted that "AI-driven technology enables attorneys to maximize efficiency and practice at the top of their license," in other words, focusing on high-level strategy.[92] As Mr. Dang put it, "AI reduces the cost of human labor … allow[ing] attorneys to deliver more affordable and accessible legal services to a broader market."[93]

–

For all three companies, their for-profit incentives align closely with public purpose. As Courtroom5's Dr. Ebron said, "courts and legal aid organizations have unparalleled reach and credibility. Private companies bring agility and innovation. Together, we can create referral systems, improve user education, and streamline

[90] *Id.*

[91] Ariz. Jud. Branch, *Alternative Business Structure: Expanding Access to Legal Services*, https://perma.cc/F6T2-MGCE.

[92] E-mail Interview by Kiernan Moran with Binh Dang, Co-Founder & Chief Exec. Off., Quest for Justice (May 6, 2025).

[93] *Id.*

legal processes to make them more inclusive."[94] Hello Divorce CEO Ms. Levine likewise stated: "Courts don't have the resources to solve the access crisis alone. Private companies bring speed, user experience, and innovation. Courts bring trust, accountability, and reach."[95] When these platforms help litigants file accurate paperwork or settle disputes early, court clerks handle fewer rejections and judges engage with better-prepared parties.

Yet a revenue-first model may also steer firms toward matters their users cannot afford, risking continued neglect of the very poorest litigants. Professor Claudia Johnson, one of the first architects of Pro Bono Net's LawHelp Interactive, reflected, "I'm not against technology, but I am against the closed conversation happening among the people making money from it ... The priorities must come from the client communities, not the system."[96]

Nevertheless, the founders of these commercial platforms echoed a core concern long voiced by creators of free tools: that the greatest barrier to expanding access to justice is not technological capability, but the legal system itself. These companies, like many nonprofit organizations, explained that the law has failed to keep pace with technological innovation. Q4J's Mr. Dang explained, "The root cause of limited access to justice stems primarily from judicial actions rather than legislative ones."[97] Hello Divorce's Ms. Levine called for "regulatory clarity that allows legal professionals to work in new, scalable ways."[98] Dr. Ebron, meanwhile, urged states to clarify that an AI guide for pro se users is not unauthorized practice: "We don't necessarily need new laws; we need clearer and broader interpretations of existing ones."[99] Mr. Dang cautioned that jurisdictions clinging to twentieth-century rules "will inevitably stagnate, freezing their available legal services in place, like artifacts preserved in amber."[100] UPL issues are discussed further in Chapter 14.

If the regulatory thicket clears, each of these companies believes that AI has the potential to fundamentally transform access to justice. "I believe we are only beginning to realize the potential that AI technology holds for transforming the legal services market," said Mr. Dang.[101] Dr. Ebron agreed: "AI promises the delivery of expert-level support at scale and at a fraction of traditional costs."[102] Ms. Levine emphasized that scalability does not mean sloppy: "Used responsibly, AI helps us scale expert-backed support. But it must be paired with up-to-date data, rigorous

94 E-mail Interview with Sonja Ebron, *supra* note 83.
95 E-mail Interview with Erin Levine, *supra* note 86.
96 Video Interview by Kiernan Moran with Claudia Johnson, Lecturer in L., Univ. of Penn. Carey Sch. of L. (Oct. 28, 2024).
97 E-mail Interview with Binh Dang, *supra* note 92.
98 E-mail Interview with Erin Levine, *supra* note 86.
99 E-mail Interview with Sonja Ebron, *supra* note 83.
100 E-mail Interview with Binh Dang, *supra* note 92.
101 *Id.*
102 E-mail Interview with Sonja Ebron, *supra* note 83.

testing, and human oversight – especially in areas where small errors can have big consequences."[103] The justice gap will not close overnight, but these commercial and fee-based tools demonstrate that a viable market can exist where public interest and private incentive finally align.

13.11 CONCLUSION

The innovations explored in this chapter represent a pivotal shift in how legal help is delivered to those who need it most. Many of these legal technologists intervened during times of crisis, providing crucial support when traditional systems faltered. Despite emerging out of necessity, these innovations have demonstrated the impact of technology in expanding the reach of scarce legal resources and addressing the market failure of access to justice in the civil justice system. This concluding section draws together several key takeaways from these projects, including: (1) how technology can be used to scale legal assistance beyond traditional staffing approaches; (2) the centrality of user-centered design, multilingual access, and multichannel delivery; (3) the challenges of sustainability, funding, and post-crisis implementation; (4) the ethical and regulatory tensions posed by AI and UPL rules; and (5) the critical role of institutional willingness to adopt and support innovation.

Unlike criminal cases, where the Supreme Court's decision in *Gideon v. Wainwright*, 372 U.S. 335 (1963) guarantees legal representation for defendants who cannot afford it, civil litigants are left to navigate the legal system alone. This limitation means that legal aid for civil litigants is reserved for only those in the most dire circumstances. The traditional model of "scaling up" by simply adding more human professionals to fill the gap has proven insufficient to address the overwhelming need. Baron and Bibas argue that "[t]he more lawyers for everyone solution is a dead end" and "Civil Gideon is a distraction. Time spent pursuing it through litigation or legislation is time not spent on better and more workable solutions."[104]

Instead, these initiatives have built tools that scale differently, leveraging technology to amplify human expertise, allowing each small team to assist thousands or even tens of thousands of individuals in just a few years. Their work has had a direct, life-changing impact: helping domestic abuse survivors seek protection during pandemic lockdowns, preventing illegal evictions as families faced housing insecurity, guiding individuals through bankruptcy to escape crushing debt, and enabling countless others to access justice who would otherwise have been left without recourse. These victories span volunteer-driven nonprofits and private justice-tech firms, showing that both free and paid models can save homes, protect families, vindicate cognizable legal claims, and discharge overwhelming financial obligations.

[103] E-mail Interview with Erin Levine, *supra* note 86.

[104] Benjamin H. Baron & Stephanos Bibas, Rebooting Justice: More Technology, Fewer Lawyers, and the Future of Law 101, 103 (2017).

One thing that connects these tools is their user-centered approach. From the CRT to Upsolve's bankruptcy filing tool and Hello Divorce's AI Divorce Assistant to Nevada's Self-Help Chatbot, each initiative, whether grant-funded, institutionalized, volunteer-based, or revenue-driven, prioritizes accessibility, simplicity, and practicality. They share a common understanding that legal processes must be reimagined from the perspective of those navigating them without professional guidance. "We're building tools for pro se litigants by experienced pro se litigants. That's how real change happens," observed Courtroom5's Dr. Ebron, underscoring the importance of designing *with* end users, not just *for* them.[105]

Still, challenges remain. Access to justice technology requires safeguards. Unlike attorneys who can fact-check AI systems, unrepresented litigants often lack the resources or expertise to verify the information they receive. This reality underscores the importance of robust testing, transparent design, and continuous improvement informed by user feedback. As several projects acknowledged, they had to "build the plane while flying it," constantly refining their approaches based on real-world challenges.[106] As Professor Johnson said, "We can no longer just have attorney–client ethics; we need embedded ethics."[107]

The digital divide also poses a significant barrier. Many projects have recognized that digital access alone is insufficient; users need support across multiple channels, including phone, text, and in-person assistance. Rentervention exemplifies this "omnichannel" approach with support available through chatbot, phone, helpdesk, text message, and email.[108]

Language translation presents another hurdle, with many platforms struggling to provide equally robust service in languages beyond English. Leveraging GPT's capacity to generate text in more than fifty languages, the Nevada Self-Help Chatbot claims that multilingual support is possible. However, Rentervention reports that extending service beyond English, particularly into Spanish, can erode answer quality, so language accessibility remains an ongoing technical and resource challenge. As these technologies evolve, ensuring equitable access across languages, technical literacy, and abilities remains critical.

Funding presents another persistent challenge. Many of these innovations emerged from crisis responses, volunteer efforts, or academic initiatives. As Professor Ajmi, a developer of KSPOP, observed, "If we didn't have COVID, we would not be able to have this project, as sad as that is."[109] This reality highlights how crises often catalyze innovation but also raises questions about sustainability once the initial urgency passes. Suffolk University Law School's Document Assembly Line Project

[105] E-mail Interview with Sonja Ebron, *supra* note 83.
[106] *See, e.g.*, Video Interview with Shelley Lopez, *supra* note 2.
[107] Video Interview with Claudia Johnson, *supra* note 96.
[108] Video Interview with Conor Malloy, *supra* note 66.
[109] Video Interview with Ayyoub Ajmi (Sep. 26, 2024), *supra* note 43.

exemplifies this phenomenon, mobilizing more than 200 volunteers from eleven time zones and five continents in response to the pandemic's strain on the court system.[110]

Similarly, Mr. Malloy's insights on Rentervention demonstrate how technology can help legal aid organizations do more with limited resources: "The traditional model of 'scaling up' legal aid – merely adding more staff – was not a sustainable solution for addressing the sheer volume of legal needs in a cost-effective manner."[111] Transitioning to sustainable models while maintaining accessibility requires creative approaches and institutional support from courts, legislatures, universities, and legal foundations. A hybrid service model that combines grant dollars for high-need users with flat-fee or subscription revenue for the middle market offers a complementary, long-term path to sustainability for justice tools that cannot depend on justice grants alone.

Moreover, these innovations must navigate complex regulatory environments, including UPL restrictions that can hamper their reach, as discussed more in Chapter 14. Upsolve has filed a petition for certiorari with the United States Supreme Court, challenging the Second Circuit's decision that New York's restrictions on providing legal advice are content-neutral under the First Amendment.[112] The JusticeBot team addressed UPL concerns by clearly designing their system to provide general legal information while leaving the analysis and decision-making authority to the user.[113] For-profit justice-tech companies argue that modernized rules would enable them to scale responsibly without compromising consumer safeguards.

Similarly, Professor Ajmi, reflecting on the Nevada Self-Help Chatbot's future, predicted that UPL restrictions and other regulations will need to evolve to keep pace with AI's capabilities.[114] The tension between innovation and regulation remains a central challenge, with Professor Ajmi noting also that often "it is not the technology that we need; it is the courage for people to build the tools because there is a lot of politics going on that prevents those systems from being made."[115] As AI and other technologies advance, courts and bar associations will increasingly need to reconsider how UPL regulations apply to AI-driven legal information systems designed to serve those who cannot afford traditional legal representation.

The future of access to justice depends not just on technological innovation but on the willingness of institutions to embrace change. This sentiment echoes that of former Massachusetts Supreme Court Chief Justice Gants, who called for innovative

[110] Video Interview with David Colarusso, *supra* note 51.
[111] Video Interview with Conor Malloy, *supra* note 66.
[112] *See supra* note 36.
[113] Video Interview with Karim Benyekhlef & Valentin Callipel, *supra* note 59; Video Interview with Hannes Westermann, *supra* note 61.
[114] Video Interview with Ayyoub Ajmi (Nov. 13, 2024), *supra* note 72.
[115] Video Interview with Ayyoub Ajmi (Sep. 26, 2024), *supra* note 43.

action during the pandemic, despite the risks of failure.[116] As Professor Colarusso noted, "the challenges the Assembly Line faced were never technical … there were always problems with adoption."[117] CRT Chair Ms. Lopez advised other jurisdictions considering similar innovations: "Don't be afraid."[118]

Ultimately, these initiatives remind us that the essence of access to justice is human dignity and empowerment. Technology serves not as an end in itself but as a means to ensure that legal rights are meaningful for all, not just those who can afford traditional representation. By putting the needs of users first and leveraging technology to meet them where they are, these innovators are not just building better tools; they are helping to build a more just society.

Whether the interface is free at the point of use or costs a modest fee, the underlying objective remains the same: put actionable legal power directly in people's hands. As these technologies continue to evolve and expand, they offer promising models for addressing the justice gap through innovation while raising critical questions about the intersection of technology, legal practice, and equitable access. Their successes and challenges offer valuable insights for future developments in the changing landscape of legal assistance. The measure of success will always be whether these tools truly empower those who need them most, ensuring that justice is not just a principle but a reality accessible to all.

116 Letter to the Bar from Mass. Sup. Jud. Ct. Chief Just. Ralph D. Gants, *supra* note 50.
117 Video Interview with David Colarusso, *supra* note 51.
118 Video Interview with Shelley Lopez, *supra* note 2.

PART V

Barriers and Risks

14

The UPL Barrier

*Mia Bonardi, L. Karl Branting, and Sateesh Nori**

14.1 INTRODUCTION

The legal profession stands at a critical juncture: How can we harness AI to expand access to justice while protecting vulnerable consumers from harm? This question demands moving beyond reflexive opposition or uncritical embrace toward a rigorous examination of how emerging technologies can be responsibly deployed to serve those our current system abandons. In the US, where 92% of low-income individuals cannot access adequate legal help,[1] rigid adherence to century-old unauthorized practice of law ("UPL") restrictions has become its own form of consumer harm, sanctioning exclusion through artificial scarcity. Meanwhile, the innovations that could address this scarcity remain stunted by UPL uncertainty, as developers avoid creating targeted legal assistance tools rather than risk violating rules that provide no clear boundaries. This chapter examines how we can move beyond this paradox to create frameworks that serve both innovation and protection.

The human impact of this regulatory paralysis plays out daily. Consider this typical situation: A tenant sits in a hallway inside a housing court, clutching a stack of papers she barely understands. Her landlord is trying to evict her family of four, claiming she has violated her lease, but she does not understand exactly why. The legal documents are incomprehensible to her. Although she qualified for a free attorney from a local legal services organization, she was told that they did not have enough resources to take on her case. She could not afford to hire a private attorney. Even the $300 consultation fee was more than she had in her bank account. The court offers self-help services for unrepresented litigants, but there were more than thirty people in line for them that morning.

In an act of desperation, she opens her smartphone and types into ChatGPT: "My landlord says I broke my lease because I got a roommate to help pay rent. Can they evict me for this in California?"

* We thank Marc Lauritsen for his review of multiple drafts of this chapter.

[1] Legal Servs. Corp., The Justice Gap: The Unmet Civil Legal Needs of Low Income Americans 48 (Apr. 2022), https://perma.cc/K2WZ-NUKB.

ChatGPT provides a detailed response about California tenant rights, subletting rules, and potential defenses – guidance that helps her defend against her eviction.[2] Yet if a legal technology company, a nonprofit organization, or a legal aid organization had designed a specialized AI tool to help tenants like this one navigate housing court, that same assistance might have triggered unauthorized UPL sanctions. In short, it is illegal in most states for people without a law license to provide legal advice. However, OpenAI, the owner of ChatGPT – like Google, Reddit, Twitter, and TikTok – is unlikely to face prosecution for delivering such legal advice. Notably, a July 2025 report by the Institute for the Advancement of the American Legal System ("IAALS") noted that "any meaningful response to regulating AI legal tools must consider Big Tech's influence in some way."[3]

This dilemma lies at the heart of a crisis in access to justice. As noted above, 92% of low-income people in the US cannot access adequate legal help, and millions of people represent themselves in court each year.[4] In 76% of civil cases in US state courts, at least one party is unrepresented, usually the defendant.[5] Despite this, the legal profession maintains a strict barrier around how people receive legal assistance. UPL restrictions are maintained under the guise of consumer protection,[6] yet they now prevent the very innovations that could expand access to legal guidance.

Every day, unrepresented litigants lose their homes, custody of their children, and their financial security, not because they lack legal rights, but because they cannot afford to understand or exercise them. AI-powered tools offer unprecedented potential to bridge this knowledge gap, providing instant, affordable guidance tailored to individual circumstances. Yet these same AI-powered tools face a regulatory landscape designed for a bygone era, in which legal advice can be provided only by licensed attorneys charging hundreds of dollars per hour or by legal aid organizations serving those who qualify for their help.

This chapter builds on Chapter 13 and features interviews with leaders of access to justice innovations and their comments on navigating UPL restrictions. We examine how UPL restrictions have become a primary barrier to AI and other technologies expanding access to justice. As Engstrom and Stone argue, "the present-day

2 Mia Bonardi, ChatGPT "My landlord says I broke my lease because I got a roommate to help pay rent. Can they evict me for this in California?" (July 20, 2025).

3 Jessica Bendarz & Ericka Byram, Regulating AI in the Delivery of Consumer-Facing Legal Services: Unlocking Legal Regulation, Inst. for the Advancement of the Am. Legal Sys. 13 (July 2025), https://perma.cc/ZKC5-MLBC.

4 Legal Servs. Corp., *supra* note 1; *see, e.g.*, Jud. Council of Cal., Statewide Action Plan for Serving Self-Represented Litigants (Feb. 2004), https://perma.cc/6HKH-9UKH; *Just the Facts: Trends in Pro Se Civil Litigation from 2000 to 2019*, U.S. Courts (Feb. 11, 2021), https://perma.cc/D7TN-XMA5.

5 Paula Hannaford-Agor, Scott Graves & Shelley Spacek Miller, Civil Justice Initiative: The Landscape of Civil Litigation in State Courts, Nat'l Ctr. for State Cts. iv (2015), https://papers.ssrn.com/sol3/papers.cfm?abstract_id=2700745.

6 Nora Freeman Engstrom & James Stone, *Auto Clubs and the Lost Origins of the Access-to-Justice Crisis*, 134 Yale L.J. 123, 133, 192 nn.331–32 (2024).

access-to-justice crisis – a crisis that dooms most Americans to navigate complex legal processes without any expert assistance – is not a product of inattention or inertia. The crisis was, rather, constructed by the legal profession of which we are a part."[7] We explore the legal profession's inability to define "the practice of law," which creates uncertainty that stifles innovation; examine how three companies have navigated UPL restrictions; and highlight the absurd reality that general-purpose AI systems routinely provide legal guidance, while specialized legal aid tools remain stunted. While the focus of this chapter is on UPL, Chapter 17 addresses institutional recommendations more broadly.

The evidence reveals a system in contradiction: major technology companies avoid UPL enforcement, while purpose-built legal aid innovations face regulatory scrutiny; unrepresented litigants turn to unreliable sources for guidance they desperately need; and courts increasingly encounter people who have already received AI assistance, despite professional prohibitions. The legal profession faces a choice: adapt these century-old restrictions to the technological reality or risk becoming increasingly irrelevant as AI assistance proliferates beyond regulatory reach.

The question is not whether AI will transform legal services; it already has. The question is whether the legal profession will embrace reforms that ensure this transformation serves justice. In this chapter, we examine the current state of UPL, the evolution of these restrictions, efforts to challenge UPL, and recent reforms, including regulatory sandboxes and why they should be expanded to other jurisdictions.

14.2 THE CURRENT STATE OF UPL

UPL generally refers to unlicensed individuals providing legal services. These restrictions somewhat arbitrarily distinguish between "legal information" and "legal advice," which can be difficult to differentiate in practice. *Legal information* is typically understood as general knowledge about the law and court processes, while *legal advice* involves guidance tailored to an individual's specific circumstances.[8] This ambiguity complicates the development and deployment of AI tools intended to assist unrepresented litigants because developers must often navigate vague and inconsistent UPL standards to avoid liability.

Conduct that constitutes the "practice of law" lacks definitional clarity. In 2003, the American Bar Association ("ABA") Task Force on the Model Definition of the Practice of Law concluded that it could not define the practice of law and that each state should develop its own definition.[9] Despite the proclaimed importance

7 *Id.* at 123.

8 *See, e.g.*, John M. Greacen, *Legal Information vs. Legal Advice*, 106 JUDICATURE 48, 49–54 (2022); NAT'L CTR. FOR STATE CTS., *Legal advice vs. Legal Information*, https://perma.cc/B6VB-2ZHP.

9 AM. BAR ASS'N TASK FORCE ON THE MODEL DEFINITION OF THE PRAC. OF L., REPORT 13 (Aug. 2003), https://tinyurl.com/495pub64; *see generally* Appendix A: State Definitions of the Practice of Law, AM. BAR ASS'N (2003), https://perma.cc/3MQ2-SD4B.

of UPL restrictions in protecting consumers and regulating legal practice, there is no clear, uniform definition of what actually constitutes "practicing law." This creates significant uncertainty for both practitioners and innovators in the legal services market.

Some jurisdictions provide a narrow definition of the practice of law, some a quite broad one, and some provide no definition at all.[10] As an example of a jurisdiction with "no precise definition," on April 6, 2024, the New York State Bar Association's ("NYSBA") Task Force on AI released a report and recommendations to the NYSBA's House of Delegates and offered an obfuscating note on the practice of law: "[W]ithout a uniform definition and precise meaning of the practice of law, we fall upon the adage: 'You know it when you see it.'"[11] This formulation essentially admits that regulators are relying on subjective, ad hoc determinations rather than clear, informed standards. Sam Harden, former Senior Innovation Manager at Pro Bono Net, explains how "we've siloed the legal industry [where] you can't practice law if you're not a lawyer – and we're not going to tell you what the practice of law actually is. A kind of weird, weird regulatory scheme."[12]

Despite this ambiguity, UPL restrictions generally apply broadly to activities such as document preparation, legal advice, court representation, and out-of-state practice, albeit with notable exemptions for self-representation, government employees, supervised law students, and certain professionals performing incidental legal work.[13] This definitional uncertainty is particularly problematic because UPL violations can carry serious civil and criminal penalties.[14] Without clear boundaries for what constitutes legal practice, it is challenging for anyone, including lawyers, to determine when AI tools provide assistance that crosses the line.

Although Figure 14.1 does not detail all possible categories of UPL or UPL exemptions, it illustrates the current state of UPL regulations, specifically for technology that can assist unrepresented litigants, and categorizes them by risk of UPL violation. The three zones – "Safe," "Gray," and "Danger," – are based

[10] Bendarz & Byram, *supra* note 3, at 8; *see* Julian Moradian, *A New Era of Legal Services: The Elimination of Unauthorized Practice of Law Rules to Accompany the Growth of Legal Software*, 12 Wm. & Mary Bus. L. Rev. 247, 251 (2020).

[11] N.Y. State Bar Ass'n, Report and Recommendations of the New York State Bar Association: Task Force on Artificial Intelligence 31 (Apr. 6, 2024), https://perma.cc/W2TK-W4XV.

[12] Video Interview by Kiernan Moran & Mia Bonardi with Sam Harden, Former Senior Innovation Manager, Pro Bono Net (Mar. 17, 2025).

[13] Restatement (Third) Of Law Governing Lawyers § 4(c) cmt. A (A.L.I. 2000).

[14] *E.g.*, Conn. Gen. Stat. §§ 51-88, 53a-35a(8), 53a-41(a) (2024) (designating UPL as a class D felony, which may result in up to five years' imprisonment and up to a $5,000 fine); Fla. Stat. § 454.23 (2024) (cross-referencing Fla. Stat. §§ 775.082–084 to impose five-year term of imprisonment and/or $5,000 fine as a third degree felony, where the term of imprisonment may increase for habitual offenders); Miss. Code Ann. § 97-23-43 (2024) (permitting a fine up to $5,000 and up to five years' imprisonment for habitual offenders).

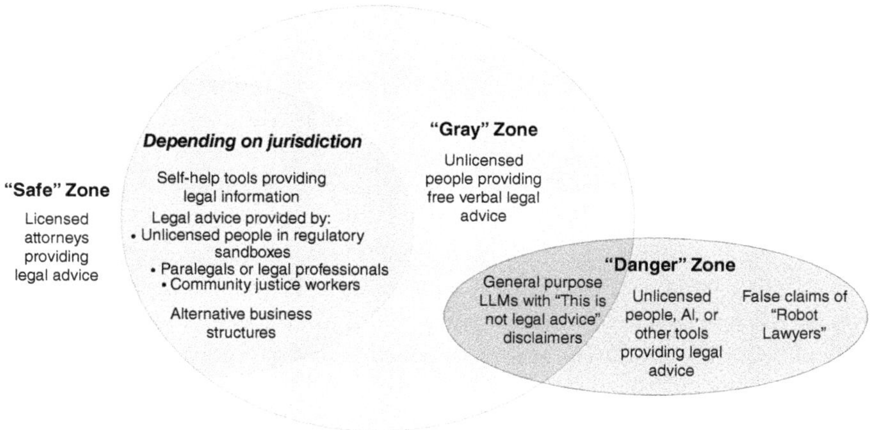

FIGURE 14.1 The current state of UPL regulations, specifically for technologies that assist unrepresented litigants, ranging from licensed attorneys in the "Safe" Zone to unlicensed providers giving legal advice in the "Danger" Zone.

on licensing status, exemptions, and potential risks. The "Safe" Zone contains licensed attorneys providing traditional legal advice. The "Gray" Zone encompasses unlicensed people offering legal information or services, depending on the jurisdiction, including self-help tools, paralegals, and community justice workers. The "Danger" Zone includes unlicensed individuals, AI systems, or other tools that provide legal advice without proper disclaimers, as well as false claims that tools are "robot lawyers." Often, legal tools avoid even the appearance of providing personalized guidance, since imprecise and subjective UPL definitions can push these technologies from the "Safe" or "Gray" Zones to the "Danger" Zone, as depicted in Figure 14.1. The overlapping zones demonstrate how the boundaries of modern UPL regulations are blurred and intersecting. These converging zones also show how the distinction between "Safe" and "Danger" Zones might be indistinguishable – eliminating the "Gray" Zone – depending on jurisdiction or legal activity.

Some AI-powered tools provide "gray advice," not to be confused with the "Gray" Zone, which Porcaro defines as "interactive advice software that presents as self-help, but that offers personalized assistance related to someone's well-being or livelihood, and that serves as a limited-scope stand-in for professional help."[15] At present, gray advice actually lies within the "Danger" Zone when it contains legal advice, which can be difficult to distinguish from other forms of assistance. Consider the contrasting fates of different AI-powered legal assistance technologies.

[15] Keith Porcaro, *Gray Advice*, 25 DUKE L. & TECH. REV. 48, 50 (2024).

The chilling effect of UPL is visible in the choices developers are forced to make. In developing the chatbot "Roxanne AI,"[16] Sateesh Nori's team chose to focus the tool on housing conditions rather than evictions, due to the risk of error in eviction cases triggering UPL scrutiny. This choice was made because the failure of the chatbot to give proper guidance in an eviction case, although low, would likely have been highly scrutinized in the press and in public opinion around the use of AI tools. Such a failure, in a field in which legal services lawyers are often in favor of UPL, would reinforce the justification for UPL as a consumer protection tool.

In another project, "Depositron,"[17] a chatbot that helps tenants prepare letters to request the return of their security deposits, Nori was reluctant to add the functionality of preparing and serving court papers on behalf of users for fear of triggering UPL sanctions.

Yet general-purpose AI systems, like OpenAI's ChatGPT, Anthropic's Claude, or Google's AI Search Overview, routinely provide substantive legal guidance while purportedly maintaining regulatory immunity through broad disclaimers.[18] Sam Harden observes this contradiction: "ChatGPT is not supposed to give legal advice, you know. If you ask it, 'Give me legal advice,' it says, 'I'm not a lawyer. I can't give you legal advice.' But then if you start asking it enough questions, it really does – you know, in my view, because nobody knows what legal advice is."[19]

This raises a provocative question: why do state bar associations not pursue UPL actions against major technology companies whose AI systems regularly provide personalized legal guidance?[20] The answer may reveal fundamental weaknesses in traditional UPL enforcement that could signal its eventual obsolescence. Two factors likely explain this enforcement gap: (1) jurisdictional complexity and (2) strategic vulnerability.

First, traditional UPL enforcement assumes that local practitioners are operating within defined geographic boundaries, but AI systems operate globally and simultaneously across jurisdictions.[21] We must consider when a tool or activity that falls within the "Safe" or "Gray" Zones in some jurisdictions is or could be in the "Danger" Zone in others. Determining which state bar has the authority to pursue enforcement, and under which state's UPL statutes, presents challenges that

[16] Hous. Ct. Answers, *AI Assistant for NYC Housing Repairs*, https://perma.cc/VKP7-HUQY.

[17] Depositron, *Get Your Deposit Back!*, https://perma.cc/D9R8-ZEBS.

[18] *E.g.*, Sam Harden, *Hey Look Another Survey about AI and Legal Advice*, Substack (Aug. 20, 2024), https://samharden.substack.com/p/hey-look-another-survey-about-ai (showing Google's AI Search Overview providing specific legal advice).

[19] Video Interview with Sam Harden, *supra* note 12.

[20] *See, e.g.*, Bendarz & Byram, *supra* note 3, at 13 ("Big Tech is, many noted, too big to regulate."); Harden, *supra* note 18 ("Please don't misunderstand me here – I genuinely don't want, at any professional level, Google or some other tech company to get hauled in front of a state bar committee on unlicensed practice … [I]t'd probably end in more pointless regulation that ultimately harms the public and enriches lawyers.").

[21] *See, e.g.*, Bendarz & Byram, *supra* note 3, at 13.

existing regulatory frameworks are ill-equipped to handle. Professor Ayyoub Ajmi describes this jurisdiction challenge as "the genie [being] out of the bottle, and there is no stopping it."[22]

Second, and more fundamentally, the prospect of major technology companies mounting vigorous defenses of their AI systems could expose fundamental inconsistencies and weaknesses in UPL restrictions. A well-funded challenge to existing UPL restrictions might force courts to confront difficult questions about what constitutes legal advice, whether traditional competency requirements make sense in the digital age, and whether UPL restrictions serve their stated protective purposes or merely preserve professional monopolies.

This regulatory asymmetry also creates perverse incentives that undermine UPL restrictions. Companies developing tools specifically to democratize legal access face heightened scrutiny from state bars and other regulators, while those offering legal guidance as an ancillary feature of general-purpose products operate largely unimpeded. The result is a two-tiered system in which direct legal aid innovations are discouraged, and indirect legal advice proliferates unchecked.[23]

Only through thoughtful UPL reform that creates clear regulatory pathways for specialized legal AI tools, while maintaining meaningful consumer protections, can we enable the development of legal assistance technologies that genuinely serve the public interest rather than merely protecting professional prerogatives.

14.3 THE ENFORCEMENT PARADOX

Current UPL enforcement reveals a fundamental paradox: the very restrictions maintained to protect consumers from unqualified legal advice now prevent the development of sophisticated tools that could provide better guidance than the general-purpose AI systems people already use. This paradox reflects deeper tensions within the legal profession about the role of technology in legal services and the meaning of professional competence in the digital age. As AI capabilities evolve, these tensions are increasingly unsustainable, forcing a reckoning with fundamental assumptions about how legal knowledge should be transmitted and by whom.

14.3.1 *AI Assistants in the Courtroom*

The courtroom is traditionally viewed as the most protected space, where inaccurate legal guidance can result in irreversible harm, including loss of housing

[22] Video Interview by Kiernan Moran & Mia Bonardi with Ayyoub Ajmi, Prof., UMKC Sch. of L. & Founder, CiviLaw. Tech (Nov. 13, 2024).

[23] *See* Drew Simshaw, *Access to A.I. Justice: Avoiding an Inequitable Two-Tiered System of Legal Services*, 24 Yale J.L. & Tech. 150, 174–77 (2022); Porcaro, *supra* note 15.

or liberty, or financial ruin. Until recently, UPL rules have generally prohibited litigants from receiving legal advice in the courtroom except from licensed attorneys who demonstrated competency through bar examinations, took an oath of professional responsibility, and remained subject to ethical oversight.

As discussed further in Section 14.5.3, DoNotPay faced multiple state bar investigations, class-action litigation, and Federal Trade Commission fines after marketing itself as "the world's first robot lawyer" and attempting to provide targeted legal services.[24] The company's plan to provide AI guidance to a defendant wearing smart glasses during live court proceedings prompted threats of criminal prosecution, and its founder, Joshua Browder, abandoned the effort entirely.[25]

The reality of modern legal practice often leaves a chasm between the ideal of universal legal representation and the practical availability of affordable counsel. Into this representation gap, AI and other tools have emerged as accessible alternatives, offering immediate guidance, even during live court proceedings.

Extract 14.1 illustrates this phenomenon through a simulated interaction in which Anthropic's Claude provided real-time courtroom guidance to someone facing an eviction hearing.[26] Claude distinguished between AI-provided legal advice and legal information, even when providing it to a litigant inside a courtroom. Although Claude explicitly disclaimed providing legal advice and characterized its guidance as "general information about court procedures," the substance of its recommendations reveals the inadequacy of the distinction between "legal information" and "legal advice." Claude provided scripts for the litigant to address the judge, strategic timing suggestions, and tactical advice about presenting defenses, which bear a striking resemblance to what a practicing attorney might offer.

EXTRACT 14.1 Claude providing real-time courtroom guidance to someone in a simulated eviction hearing while disclaiming that it is not providing legal advice.

> M I'm in court for an eviction hearing. My landlord is asking the judge for summary judgment because I didn't file an answer to their complaint. I didn't respond because I don't know how/ I don't think I should be evicted. What can I do and what should I say? The judge is looking at me funny.

You need to speak up immediately. Here's what to say and do:

[24] Complaint, In re DoNotPay, Inc., C-4812 (F.T.C. Jan. 14, 2025), https://perma.cc/MW42-D8DD.

[25] Bobby Allyn, *A Robot Was Scheduled to Argue in Court, then Came the Jail Threats*, NPR (Jan. 25, 2023, 6:05 PM EST), https://perma.cc/YKX5-UCLG; Kerry L. Alvarez, *Sue Anyone with a Click of a Button? FTC Cracks Down on DoNotPay's Misleading AI Claims*, J. OF HIGH TECH. L. (Nov. 19, 2024), https://perma.cc/292R-3DSJ.

[26] Mia Bonardi, Claude Sonnet 4, "I'm in court for an eviction hearing ..." (July 30, 2025) (see Extract 14.1).

Say this to the judge right now: "Your Honor, I request permission to file a late answer to the complaint. I did not respond because I was unaware of the proper procedures and did not have legal representation. I have defenses to this eviction that I believe are valid, and I respectfully request the opportunity to present them."

Key points to mention if the judge asks:

- You didn't understand the legal process or requirements for filing an answer
- You have legitimate defenses to the eviction (be ready to briefly state what they are)
- You're not trying to delay proceedings unfairly – you genuinely want to respond to the allegations
- You're willing to file your answer immediately or within a short timeframe the court sets

What might happen:

- The judge may allow you to file a late answer and continue the case
- They might ask you to briefly state your defenses on the record
- They could reschedule the hearing to give you time to properly respond

If the judge seems hesitant: Ask if you can have a brief continuance to obtain legal assistance or file a proper answer. Many courts have self-help resources or legal aid available.

Important: Be respectful, speak clearly, and don't argue with the judge. Focus on your willingness to participate properly in the legal process rather than making excuses for not responding initially.

The key is acting immediately – don't wait for the judge to rule on summary judgment without speaking up.

M Is this legal advice?

No, this is not legal advice. I'm providing general information about court procedures and suggestions for what you might say, but I'm not a lawyer and cannot provide legal advice.

What I shared are general guidelines about how eviction proceedings typically work and common ways people address procedural issues like failing to file timely responses. However, every situation is different, and local laws and court rules vary significantly.

For actual legal advice specific to your situation, you would need to consult with a qualified attorney who can review the details of your case and local laws. Many areas have legal aid organizations that provide free or low-cost assistance for housing matters.

If you're currently in court, you might also ask the judge if the court has any self-help resources available or if there's a way to get legal assistance before proceeding.

The real-time nature of this interaction, which occurred during court proceedings, further complicates the arbitrary distinction between legal information and legal advice. When an AI system provides case-specific, strategic guidance tailored to immediate and ongoing court proceedings, the functional difference from attorney representation becomes minimal, regardless of disclaimers about the nature of the service.

Ultimately, as Professor Ajmi explains,

> Unless you're going to stop the LLM itself, you're not going to stop unrepresented people from going to the LLM. You can tell them they are not allowed to use it, but you can't really enforce that. They can still use it. They can still get help. They can still write letters. They can still get help understanding legal processes.[27]

The solution lies not in prohibiting what cannot be stopped, but in creating regulatory pathways that allow specialized legal AI tools to emerge with robust consumer protections, ensuring that those who need legal guidance most can access reliable, accountable assistance.

14.4 THE EVOLUTION OF UPL RESTRICTIONS

UPL restrictions are not unique to the US.[28] However, the US's approach to regulating UPL is distinguishable in its scope, enforcement mechanisms, and historical development, creating a regulatory landscape unlike any other in the world.[29]

Engstrom and Stone locate the origins of UPL in the US in the early 1900s when auto clubs offered a wide array of free legal services to their members, which was a "prime benefit" of membership.[30] They argue:

> The bar's triumphant campaign against the clubs' legal services – driven mainly, we argue, by a spirit of protectionism induced by the Great Depression – would reverberate far beyond the auto clubs themselves. It would obliterate then-burgeoning group-legal-service providers of every stripe, stamping out a unique and socially valuable mechanism to deliver affordable legal services at scale. It would fundamentally alter the balance of power held by legislatures and courts when it came to defining and policing law practice. And it would plant other doctrinal seeds that eventually sprouted and grew into the country's current, profound access-to-justice crisis.[31]

27 Video Interview with Ayyoub Ajmi (Nov. 13, 2024), *supra* note 22.

28 *See* Mia Bonardi & L. Karl Branting, *Certifying Legal AI Assistants for Unrepresented Litigants: A Global Survey of Access to Civil Justice, Unauthorized Practice of Law, and AI*, 26 COLUM. SCI. & TECH. L. REV. 34, 87 (2025).

29 *Id.*; *see* Laurel S. Terry, *Putting the Legal Profession's Monopoly on the Practice of Law in a Global Context*, 82 FORDHAM L. REV. 2903, 2904–05 (2014); Gillian K. Hadfield & Deborah L. Rhode, *How to Regulate Legal Services to Promote Access, Innovation, and the Quality of Lawyering*, 67 HASTINGS L.J. 1191, 1192–95 (2016).

30 Engstrom & Stone, *supra* note 6, at 144.

31 *Id.* at 127.

Similarly, Brescia argues that what a "lawyer of 1945 who could peer into the future would see is a profession that closely resembles the image the profession's leaders envisioned for it in the 1920s."[32] Binh Dang, Co-Founder and CEO of Quest for Justice, similarly argues that "Jurisdictions that cling to outdated, overly restrictive regulations will inevitably stagnate, freezing their available legal services in place like artifacts preserved in amber."[33]

UPL rules are maintained under the guise of consumer protection but are inherently protectionist.[34] The legal profession's ability to guard against competition by ambiguously defining what constitutes the "practice of law" is a significant barrier to the innovative delivery of legal services.[35] The tension between consumer protection and the legal profession's preservation continues to shape debates about UPL reform, particularly as new technologies and service models challenge traditional assumptions about the delivery of legal services.

14.5 NAVIGATING UPL RESTRICTIONS

Companies have developed distinct strategies for navigating UPL restrictions, each offering insights into potential paths forward. The experiences of Upsolve, LegalZoom, and DoNotPay illustrate three different approaches, respectively: (1) a First Amendment challenge, (2) an antitrust strategy, and (3) testing it on the margins.

14.5.1 *First Amendment Challenge*

Upsolve is the largest nonprofit organization specializing in bankruptcy services in the US, and it aims to "ensure that all Americans can access their legal rights."[36] Upsolve and its free bankruptcy filing tool are profiled in Section 13.4.

In 2022, Upsolve successfully sought action on First Amendment grounds against the New York State Attorney General to prevent the enforcement of UPL restrictions on its American Justice Movement ("AJM") program.[37] However, in September 2025, the United States Court of Appeals for the Second Circuit vacated and remanded this decision, and Upsolve has filed a petition for certiorari with

32 Ray Brescia, Lawyer Nation: The Past, Present, and Future of the American Legal Profession 101 (2024).

33 E-mail Interview by Kiernan Moran with Binh Dang, Co-Founder & Chief Exec. Officer, Quest for Just. (May 6, 2025).

34 Brescia, *supra* note 32, at 133, 192 nn.331–32.

35 *See, e.g.*, N.Y. State Bar Ass'n, *supra* note 11, at 31.

36 Ben Jackson, *How Bankruptcy Changed My Life – And Why I'm Helping Others: The Story Behind Upsolve*, Upsolve (May 21, 2025), https://perma.cc/S8Y5-T5DL; Complaint at 2 ¶ 3, Upsolve, Inc. v. James, 604 F. Supp. 3d 97 (S.D.N.Y. 2022) (No. 1:22-cv-00627-RMB).

37 Complaint, *supra* note 36, at 1–4; Upsolve, Inc. v. James, 604 F. Supp. 3d 97, 102–03, 120–21 (S.D.N.Y. 2022).

the United States Supreme Court.[38] The AJM program trained people without law licenses to give free verbal legal advice on how to respond to a debt collection lawsuit.[39] The legal advice was limited to helping clients fill out a one-page answer form provided by New York State.[40] The federal district court explained that Upsolve's challenge was distinct from prior cases where courts typically held that "UPL statutes regulate professional 'conduct' and merely burden a non-lawyer's speech incidentally" and that Upsolve's complaint was "novel" because it was "(1) an as-applied challenge to a UPL statute where (2) a plaintiff sought to give pure verbal speech."[41] On appeal, the Second Circuit held that "the UPL statutes are content neutral and thus subject only to intermediate scrutiny."[42] Institute for Justice Deputy Litigation Director Robert McNamara, who argued the case on behalf of Upsolve, explained that the Second Circuit's decision "suggest[s] that occupational-licensing laws give the government special powers to censor speech. They don't, and we look forward to the Supreme Court explaining that fact."[43]

Jonathan Petts, Co-Founder and CEO of Upsolve, explains:

> UPL is a constant thing to navigate whenever you're delivering legal services online, even for free, which is sad, because I think it stifles innovation. But we don't let that stop us from acting. Fear of someone's overbroad – in our view, erroneous – application of state UPL law won't cause us to stop trying to innovate to provide free legal help, free legal information, and free legal forms to low-income folks who can't afford lawyers.[44]

14.5.2 *Antitrust Strategy*

LegalZoom, founded over twenty years ago "on the idea of equal access and opportunity, emerged as one of America's most recognized pioneers in online legal services."[45] LegalZoom's approach fundamentally challenged traditional legal service delivery by making legal document preparation more affordable and accessible to consumers. LegalZoom is an example of a company that "turn[ed] the relationship between service and client on its head: they match the service to

[38] Upsolve, Inc. v. James, No. 22-1345, 2025 WL 2598725 (2d Cir. Sep. 9, 2025), *petition for cert. filed*, No. 25-948 (Feb. 6, 2026); Phillip Suderman, *Appeals Court Blocks Innovative Program Helping New Yorkers Fight Debt Collection Lawsuits*, Inst. For Just. (Sep. 9, 2025), https://tinyurl.com/bdea5u5s.

[39] Complaint, *supra* note 36, at 1–4.

[40] *Id.* at 10 ¶ 34, Ex. A.

[41] *Id.* at 18–19.

[42] *Upsolve*, No. 22-1345, 2025 WL 2598725.

[43] Suderman, *supra* note 38.

[44] Video Interview by Mia Bonardi with Jonathan Petts, Co-Founder & Chief Exec. Off., Upsolve (Sep. 18, 2024).

[45] LegalZoom, *About Us*, https://perma.cc/B92A-3A7P.

the client rather than the client to the service."[46] However, this democratization of legal services placed the company squarely within contested UPL territory, operating in the "Gray" Zone depicted in Figure 14.1.

Beginning around 2008, LegalZoom faced significant regulatory challenges from multiple state bar associations, which alleged that it was engaged in the unauthorized practice of law.[47] One consequential case emerged in a Missouri class action, where a federal district court in *Janson v. LegalZoom.com, Inc.* found that LegalZoom's services went "beyond self-help because of the role played by its human employees" who intervened at various stages of document preparation.[48] Notably, the court reasoned that human involvement was central to its conclusion, stating that

> LegalZoom's branching computer program is created by a Legal-Zoom employee using Missouri law. It is that human input that creates the legal document. A computer sitting at a desk in California cannot prepare a legal document without a human programming it to fill in the document using legal principles derived from Missouri law that are selected for the customer based on the information provided by the customer.[49]

This reasoning reflects technological limitations in 2011, before the emergence of mainstream generative AI capable of applying legal principles without pre-programmed decision trees.

In 2015, LegalZoom filed a $10.5 million antitrust lawsuit against the North Carolina State Bar after years of regulatory disputes.[50] This action proved successful; the parties reached a consent agreement allowing LegalZoom to operate in North Carolina, and the state legislature subsequently codified provisions that permit online document preparation services with appropriate consumer protections.[51]

LegalZoom's journey from UPL defendant to antitrust plaintiff created a new precedent that benefits the entire legal technology industry. Perhaps more importantly for our discussion, the technological assumptions underlying earlier decisions like *Janson* – that computer-generated legal documents required extensive human programming – highlight how evolving AI capabilities are outpacing traditional regulatory frameworks.

46 BRESCIA, *supra* note 32, at 177–78.

47 *See* Isaac Figueras, *The LegalZoom Identity Crisis: Legal Form Provider or Lawyer in Sheep's Clothing?*, 63 CASE W. RSRV. L. REV. 1419, 1419–22 (2013).

48 Janson v. LegalZoom.com, Inc., 802 F. Supp. 2d 1053, 1064 (W.D. Mo. 2011).

49 *Id.* at 1065.

50 Complaint, LegalZoom.com, Inc. v. N.C. State Bar, No. 1:15-cv-00439 (M.D.N.C. June 3, 2015); *see generally* Rebecca Haw Allensworth, *Antitrust Scrutiny for the Occupations: "North Carolina Dental" and Its Impact on U.S. Licensing Boards*, 4 PAZMANY L. REV. 169 (2016).

51 Daniel Fisher, *LegalZoom Settles Fight with North Carolina Bar Over Online Law*, FORBES (Oct. 23, 2015, 9:40 AM EDT), https://perma.cc/EUT9-2JLM; Barry Smith, *Legislation Settles Lengthy Dispute between State Bar, LegalZoom*, CAROLINA J. (June 20, 2016), https://perma.cc/LZN3-ZNTG; N.C. GEN. STAT. § 84-2.2 (2016).

14.5.3 *Testing It on the Margins*

DoNotPay is a legal-tech platform that previously claimed to be "the world's first robot lawyer" and an "AI lawyer," until it was investigated and fined by the Federal Trade Commission for "making deceptive claims about the abilities of its AI chatbot."[52] DoNotPay now advertises itself as "Your AI Consumer Champion."[53] Founded by entrepreneur Joshua Browder in 2015, DoNotPay initially gained attention by automating consumer-focused tasks, such as disputing parking tickets.[54] Since then, it has expanded into consumer rights generally, claiming it uses AI to help consumers "fight big corporations, protect [their] privacy, find hidden money, and beat bureaucracy."[55]

In 2023, DoNotPay planned for its AI tool's legal advice to enter the courtroom, seeking to operate squarely in the "Danger" Zone, as illustrated in Figure 14.1. Apparently, "[t]he person challenging a speeding ticket would wear smart glasses that [would] both record court proceedings and dictate responses into the defendant's ear from a small speaker. The system relied on a few leading AI text generators, including ChatGPT and DaVinci."[56] "Multiple state bars" contacted DoNotPay about its intent to enter the courtroom, and Mr. Browder was quoted explaining, "the threat of criminal charges was enough to give it up."[57]

DoNotPay has also faced class-action litigation and regulatory scrutiny in several jurisdictions, accusing it of unlawfully practicing law.[58] Such litigation underscores the complexities inherent in adapting century-old UPL frameworks to rapidly advancing technology.

–

The divergent paths taken by Upsolve, LegalZoom, and DoNotPay reveal three distinct strategies for navigating UPL restrictions. Each company faced regulatory uncertainty precisely because there is no uniform definition of the "practice of law." In the absence of reform, each developed strategies to navigate the UPL barrier.

52 *FTC Finalizes Order with DoNotPay That Prohibits Deceptive "AI Lawyer" Claims, Imposes Monetary Relief, and Requires Notice to Past Subscribers*, FED. TRADE COMM'N (Feb. 11, 2025), https://perma.cc/XR4N-8UXE; *see* Complaint, *supra* note 24.

53 DONOTPAY, https://perma.cc/DU4V-76Y8.

54 Samuel Gibbs, *Chatbot Lawyer Overturns 160,000 Parking Tickets in London and New York*, GUARDIAN (June 28, 2016, 6:07 AM EDT), https://perma.cc/4GDX-PNYZ.

55 DONOTPAY, *supra* note 53; RJ Vogt, *DoNotPay Founder Opens up on "Robot Lawyers,"* LAW360 (Feb. 9, 2020, 8:02 PM EST), https://perma.cc/PC89-XMTW ("[O]ur bread and butter is consumer rights.").

56 *See* Allyn, *supra* note 25.

57 *Id.*

58 Stephanie Pacheco, *Analysis: DoNotPay Lawsuits: A Setback for Justice Initiatives?*, BLOOMBERG L. (Mar. 28, 2023, 2:00 AM PST), https://tinyurl.com/5n7y99cs; Sara Merken, *Legal AI startup DoNotPay reaches settlement in consumer class action*, REUTERS (June 6, 2024), www.reuters.com/legal/legalindustry/legal-ai-startup-donotpay-reaches-settlement-customer-class-action-2024-06-06/.

14.6 SCALING UPL REFORM

A "regulatory sandbox" is a formal framework established by legal regulatory authorities that allows law firms, legal technology companies, and legal service providers to test innovative services or technologies under relaxed rules for a defined period, while maintaining consumer protections and regulatory oversight.[59] Utah's model is a traditional regulatory sandbox, creating UPL allowances for approved entities under specific conditions.[60] Instead of sandboxing, Arizona removed its rules that prohibited nonlawyer ownership of law firms and its model is known as alternative business services or ABS.[61]

The reforms established in Utah and Arizona have catalyzed a growing interest in UPL reform across multiple jurisdictions.[62] Similar legal regulatory sandboxes exist in British Columbia, Manitoba, Ontario, Saskatchewan, England, and Wales.[63] Bednarz and Jolivette conclude that "several Canadian provinces have now shown through their work that the access to justice crisis can be mitigated through such a framework, paving the pathway to success for US states wh[ich] are gearing up to follow."[64] A June 2025 Rhode Center report explains that the reform landscape reveals both successes and setbacks, with Utah scaling back its program from 39 entities in 2022 to just 11 as of April 2025, while Arizona has expanded from 19 to 136 approved entities.[65] The report notes that "[t]he current state of reforms in Arizona and Utah reflects two different state responses to challenges to policy reform agendas."[66] It explains, "the situation remains in a state of flux, making it hard to predict any future path. What is clear is the intuitive notion that politics will shape the trajectory of particular reform efforts ..."[67]

Interest in the sandbox model is spreading, with several US states developing or proposing their own regulatory sandbox programs, including Washington, Indiana, and Minnesota.[68] In December 2024, the Washington Supreme Court approved a

59 *See, e.g.*, Jessica Bednarz & Krista Jolivette, *Utah Sandbox Inspires Similar Regulatory Initiatives in Canada and other States*, INST. FOR THE ADVANCEMENT OF THE AM. LEGAL SYS. (Nov. 20, 2024), https://perma.cc/255G-EZ83.

60 DAVID FREEMAN ENGSTROM, NATALIE A. KNOWLTON & LUCY RICCA, LEGAL INNOVATION AFTER REFORM: FIVE YEARS OF DATA ON REGULATORY CHANGE, STAN. L. SCH. DEBORAH L. RHODE CTR. ON THE LEGAL PRO. 3 (2025), https://perma.cc/6CLF-36B8.

61 *Id.*; ARIZ. CTS., *Alternative Business Structures (ABS) Frequently Asked Questions*, https://perma.cc/XS7E-2F76.

62 Bednarz & Jolivette, *supra* note 59; ENGSTROM, KNOWLTON & RICCA, *supra* note 60, at 6.

63 *See* Bonardi & Branting, *supra* note 28, at 87; Bednarz & Jolivette, *supra* note 59.

64 Bednarz & Jolivette, *supra* note 59.

65 ENGSTROM, KNOWLTON & RICCA, *supra* note 60, at 1, 16–17.

66 *Id.* at 18.

67 *Id.*

68 *Id.* at 14–15.

regulatory sandbox, based on the Utah model, that will allow successful applicants to practice law under limited exemptions from court rules and statutes.[69] Indiana's Supreme Court approved the concept of a sandbox program in October 2024, previously citing the state's lawyer shortage as an "existential threat to the legal profession and those we serve."[70] Meanwhile, the Minnesota State Bar Association created an AI Working Group and adopted its recommendations to establish a generative AI regulatory sandbox.[71] The newly formed AI Standing Committee is still studying the proposals and developing its own recommendations.[72]

The choice between sandboxes and permanent reform requires strategic consideration of political realities. A 2024 IAALS report advocates that the "[e]limination of, waivers of, or changes to unauthorized practice of law and ethics rules are generally going to be more successful than pilot projects in the regulatory reform space."[73] While the permanent elimination of UPL restrictions would be preferable to sandboxes, as "entities that are targeted by these reforms are less likely to invest in a pilot project than a permanent program," sandboxes remain valuable because they provide an opportunity to initiate a permanent program.[74] Including "at least one, but ideally as many as possible, representatives from the state's supreme court on any regulatory innovation task force" is recommended.[75]

The success of scaling reform will ultimately depend on careful attention to design principles, measurable outcomes, and realistic assessment of political and professional resistance. As Sandefur and Denne emphasize, "The ability of members of the public to resolve their justice problems lawfully is the critical data point for evaluating the access to justice impacts of regulatory reforms."[76] Sandefur and Ricca note, however, "People-centered justice solutions often de-center lawyers, and

[69] Order, *In re Matter of the Adoption of a Pilot Project to Test Entity Regulation Using the Practice of Law Board's Framework for Legal Regulatory Reform*, No. 25700-B-721 (Wash. Dec. 5, 2024); *Innovation in Law*, Wash. State Bar Ass'n (Updated Dec. 31, 2024), https://perma.cc/NP69-2T9H.

[70] Order on Interim Recommendations Made by the Commission on Indiana's Legal Future, Cause No. 24S-MS-116 (Ind. Oct. 3, 2024); Interim Recommendations, Comm'n on Ind.'s Legal Future, Interim Recommendations 3 (July 30, 2024), https://perma.cc/6DG7-RJRZ.

[71] Minn. State Bar Ass'n Working Grp. on AI, Implications of Large Language Models (LLMs) on the Unauthorized Practice of Law (UPL) and Access to Justice (June 2024), https://perma.cc/HWG5-XP9N; Damien Riehl, *AI + MSBA: Building Minnesota's legal future*, Minn. State Bar Ass'n (Oct. 1, 2024), https://perma.cc/KV42-2TYV.

[72] *Artificial Intelligence Committee*, Minn. State Bar Ass'n, https://perma.cc/47HD-8EF9.

[73] Jessica Bednarz, Unlocking Legal Regulation: Lessons Learned and Recommendations for the Future, Inst. for the Advancement of the Am. Legal Sys. 9 (Aug. 2024), https://perma.cc/26MZ-6X5X.

[74] *Id.*; *see* Bendarz & Byram, *supra* note 3, at 16–17, 21.

[75] *Id.* at 8.

[76] Rebecca L. Sandefur & Emily Denne, *Access to Justice and Legal Services Regulatory Reform*, 18 Ann. Rev. L. Soc. Sci. 27, 37 (2022).

so may face resistance from lawyers who fear losing their place as gatekeepers of justice."[77] Zach Zarnow, Executive Director of Pro Bono Net, compares regulation in the medical field to the legal field: "They have decades and decades and decades of proven ability to provide services to people across different skill sets and licenses and liabilities and insurances and all sorts of things that protect people, ensure proper training, and ultimately get people the help they need. It's entirely doable to have that same system replicated in the legal world."[78] Ultimately, the path forward demands bold leadership from supreme courts willing to embrace innovation, sustained advocacy from access to justice organizations, and continued investment in programs that demonstrate the potential of reform to transform legal services delivery while protecting consumers. Given the persistent access-to-justice crisis documented in Chapter 1, jurisdictions can no longer justify maintaining antiquated restrictions that deny legal assistance to millions of people when proven alternatives exist.

14.7 THE CHILLING EFFECT

UPL restrictions present significant barriers to the development and deployment of AI-powered legal tools designed to help unrepresented litigants. While these restrictions are maintained to protect consumers,[79] they often have the unintended consequence of stifling technological innovation that could expand access to justice.[80]

AI tools that could assist unrepresented litigants are frequently held back or forced to adopt overly cautious designs due to UPL concerns.[81] Tech and AI-driven legal services designed for unrepresented litigants focus on guiding users through legal procedures, generating forms, or explaining legal concepts. But these tools must limit their functions to avoid crossing the line into activities that might be construed as legal advice. Marc Lauritsen argues, "UPL is a blunt instrument that is wholly unsuited to regulating automated legal advice systems."[82] For example, companies developing legal chatbots and document automation tools face regulatory challenges and risk legal penalties if their products are interpreted as providing unauthorized legal advice. Such tools are subject to standards that are ill-defined and subjective.[83]

An essential debate within the legal community is whether states should loosen UPL restrictions to foster innovation or strictly enforce existing rules to maintain

77 Rebecca L. Sandefur & Lucy Ricca, *Outside the Box: How States Are Increasing Access to Justice Through Evidence-Based Regulation of the Practice of Law*, 108 JUDICATURE 59, 63 (2024).

78 Video Interview by Mia Bonardi with Zach Zarnow, Exec. Dir., Pro Bono Net (Aug. 1, 2025).

79 Engstrom & Stone, *supra* note 6, at 133, 192 nn.331–32.

80 *See, e.g.*, BENDARZ & BYRAM, *supra* note 3, at 10.

81 *See, e.g.*, *id.*

82 Marc Lauritsen, *Guest Post: Unauthorized Help – A Contrarian UPL Analysis*, LAWSITES (July 31, 2024), https://perma.cc/A8QX-9WMS.

83 *See, e.g.*, N.Y. STATE BAR ASS'N, *supra* note 11.

high standards for legal services. Proponents of deregulation argue that these tools democratize legal assistance, enabling consumers to access justice affordably and quickly.[84] Conversely, opponents worry that unchecked technological tools could create lasting harm by providing substandard, inaccurate legal assistance.[85] Proponents rebut that the rigid enforcement of UPL restrictions may stifle innovation, keep legal services unaffordable for many, and sustain barriers to justice.[86] For example, Hadfield writes:

> By defining legal practice as only those economic inputs that include a large individual human capital component, professional regulation of legal markets inhibits, for example, the extension into legal markets of the largescale information processing that underlies much of the revolution in the modern economy.[87]

Conversely, opponents often warn that a too lenient stance could expose vulnerable consumers to potential harm through unqualified or misleading legal services.[88] Professor Claudia Johnson, one of the first architects of Pro Bono Net's LawHelp Interactive, focuses on the risks to low-income clients: "We need to have contestability. We need due process. We need to think about the implications: If someone gets bad advice from AI, how do they challenge it? How do you cross-examine it? How do you appeal?"[89]

Some argue that the wrong type of deregulation could be harmful. As Drew Simshaw argues, without proper regulatory reform, AI development risks creating inequitable two-tiered systems where the poor receive inferior AI assistance while premium law firms harness advanced capabilities, or where AI fails to meaningfully disrupt, or even expands, existing access barriers.[90] Simshaw advocates embracing regulatory reforms to prevent these outcomes and to facilitate equitable AI access across the legal landscape.[91]

Additionally, while Marc Lauritsen says that standards and even certifications may be "highly desirable," he explains that any pre-certification "regime chills beneficial innovation," and "[c]ertification proposals for legal self-help software give oxygen to the idea that the lawyer monopoly extends by default to all forms

84 *See, e.g.*, Stephanos Bibas, *Lawyers' Monopoly and the Promises of AI*, 134 YALE L.J. 920, 930–31 (2025).

85 *See* Video Interview by Kiernan Moran with Claudia Johnson, Lecturer in L., Univ. of Penn. Carey Sch. of L. (Oct. 28, 2024).

86 *See, e.g.*, BENDARZ & BYRAM, *supra* note 3, at 10; Lauritsen, *supra* note 82.

87 Gillian Hadfield, *"Legal Barriers to Innovation,"* 60 STAN. L. REV. 101, 138 (2008).

88 *See, e.g.*, Brief of Amici Curiae Consumer Law Experts, Civil Legal Services Organizations, And Civil Rights Organizations in Opposition to Plaintiffs' Motion for a Preliminary Injunction at 20, *Upsolve, Inc. v. James*, 604 F. Supp. 3d 97 (S.D.N.Y. 2022) (No. 1:22-cv-00627-RMB) ("The consequences of receiving incorrect or inadequate legal advice can be disastrous for low-income New Yorkers.").

89 Video Interview with Claudia Johnson, *supra* note 85.

90 Simshaw, *supra* note 23, at 156–57, 180, 216.

91 *Id.*

of legal help."[92] Bonardi and Branting proposed a model to work within the current UPL barrier and demonstrated that legal AI assistants could be certified for their accuracy under a model similar to current sandboxes.[93] In a July 2025 report, IAALS suggested both proposals could be potential approaches "to regulating AI in consumer-facing legal services."[94]

The path forward requires neither wholesale deregulation nor rigid enforcement of outdated restrictions. A balanced approach would create a framework in which innovation can flourish within appropriate boundaries, ensuring that AI tools designed to democratize legal access receive the regulatory clarity they need while maintaining meaningful consumer protections. The alternative of continued regulatory paralysis serves neither consumer protection nor access to justice goals.

14.8 A MODERN VIEW ON RISK AND ACCESS

The emerging evidence challenges many assumptions underlying current UPL enforcement. Walters argues, "Any discussion of protecting consumers must begin with the fact that so few Americans get help from lawyers with their legal issues."[95] Notably, "[t]he vast majority of UPL lawsuits filed against online services are brought not by consumers but by lawyers or unauthorized practice committees, and generally settle without examples of harm."[96] A June 2025 Rhode Center report on the regulatory sandboxes in Utah and Arizona found "little to no evidence of consumer harm."[97]

Yet the access crisis continues. Professor Ajmi explains, "We need to talk about regulating AI, while also building it. We cannot just stop and wait until we talk about it and then decide what to do. Because we have 92% of low-income American adults who don't have sufficient legal help. And they are not going to be waiting for us to talk about how to regulate AI."[98] AI tools, although not a replacement for licensed attorneys, can significantly benefit unrepresented litigants by assisting them in understanding complex court forms and navigating procedural requirements.[99] Brescia argues, "To the extent that the information provided to the individual is accurate and assists the individual in navigating

[92] Lauritsen, *supra* note 82; *see generally* Marc Lauritsen, *Liberty, Justice, and Legal Automata*, 88 CHI.-KENT L. REV. 945 (2013).

[93] *See* Bonardi & Branting, *supra* note 28.

[94] BENDARZ & BYRAM, *supra* note 3, at 18, 22.

[95] Ed Walters, *Re-Regulating UPL in an Age of AI*, 8 GEO. L. TECH. REV. 316, 328 (2024).

[96] Deborah L. Rhode, *What We Know and Need to Know about the Delivery of Legal Services by Nonlawyers*, 67 S.C.L. REV. 429, 433 (2016).

[97] ENGSTROM, KNOWLTON & RICCA, *supra* note 60, at 32–33.

[98] Video Interview by Kiernan Moran & Mia Bonardi with Ayyoub Ajmi, Prof., UMKC Sch. of L. & Founder, CiviLaw.Tech (Sep. 26, 2024).

[99] *See, e.g.*, BRESCIA, *supra* note 32, at 190 ("There is no question that technology can bring critical legal resources to those who might otherwise not have access to them.").

through their legal issue in a competent fashion, the only threat to the legal profession is that this service might undermine the lawyer monopoly."[100] Prioritizing protectionism over access is antithetical to the *Basic Principles on the Role of Lawyers*.[101]

Traditional legal services, though often of higher quality, remain out of reach for many unrepresented litigants due to cost and availability constraints.[102] While AI tools like chatbots may sometimes provide incomplete or inaccurate guidance,[103] they offer an alternative to no assistance at all. The one-to-one approach of trying to connect every unrepresented litigant with a legal professional is simply impossible given the sheer volume of need.[104] Moreover, Baron and Bibas explain, "the evidence that lawyers are necessary to justice in all cases is surprisingly weak. This is particularly true for simpler disputes with lower stakes. Even if lawyers are desirable, they are not essential across the board."[105]

There are various proposed approaches to regulating AI in legal services, but these efforts may be overtaken by technological reality. Walters argues that "state legislatures should re-evaluate laws that govern the practice of law by software providers that are not licensed to practice, with the explicit goal of expanding legal assistance to more people."[106] Ebron argues, "We don't necessarily need new laws; we need clearer and broader interpretations of existing ones."[107] Brescia argues, "the profession should embrace technological and other innovations for the ways they can further the values of professionalism, access, and inclusion in the broadest sense."[108] Sandefur and Denne explain:

> Contemporary regulatory reform projects replace professionalism with other logics, such as market discipline, competition, or innovation. Some are expressly intended to expand access to justice by permitting new kinds of legal services that may be cheaper or otherwise more accessible than services from fully licensed lawyers (e.g., Utah Work. Group Regul. Reform 2019). *Sometimes discussed as acts of deregulation, most are actually projects of reregulation*.[109]

[100] *Id.*

[101] Basic Principles on the Role of Lawyers, Adopted by the Eighth United Nations Congress on the Prevention of Crime and the Treatment of Offenders, Havana, Cuba (Sep. 7, 1990), https://tinyurl.com/ycjbj54s.

[102] *See* Legal Servs. Corp., *supra* note 1, at 43–55.

[103] Aubrie Souza & Zach Zarnow, *Court Chatbots*, Nat'l Ctr. for State Cts. 4 (2024) (on file with Mia Bonardi).

[104] Benjamin H. Baron & Stephanos Bibas, Rebooting Justice: More Technology, Fewer Lawyers, and the Future of Law 99 (2017).

[105] *Id.* at 99–100.

[106] Walters, *supra* note 95, at 319.

[107] E-mail Interview by Kiernan Moran with Sonja Ebron, Co-Founder & Chief Exec. Officer, Courtroom5 (May 22, 2025).

[108] Brescia, *supra* note 32, at 198.

[109] Sandefur & Denne, *supra* note 76, at 29 (emphasis added).

Legal reform advocates propose various regulatory reforms that may be characterized as "acts of reregulation."[110] However, some observers suggest a fundamentally different scenario may emerge where technology outpaces regulatory capacity entirely. As Sam Harden observes, "I think we may see deregulation by default, almost where it just kind of happens."[111] Similarly, Connor Malloy explained, "I think that technology will overtake the ethical constraints and put us all in kind of a pickle for a moment."[112] Ultimately, the legal profession faces a critical juncture where the choice may not be between different regulatory frameworks, but between proactive adaptation and reactive scrambling in the wake of technological disruption that renders century-old regulatory boundaries obsolete.

14.9 CONCLUSION

UPL restrictions are a primary barrier preventing AI and other technologies from expanding access to justice to those who need it most. While 92% of low-income people in the US cannot access adequate legal help, the very innovations that could bridge this gap face regulatory uncertainty that stifles development.[113] General-purpose AI systems routinely provide legal guidance with impunity, while specialized tools designed specifically for vulnerable populations remain stunted by UPL concerns.

The path forward requires abandoning the fiction that century-old professional boundaries can address twenty-first century technological capabilities. State bar associations and legislatures should establish clear safe harbors for AI tools designed to assist unrepresented litigants, particularly those developed by nonprofit organizations and legal aid providers, such as exemptions from UPL liability or affirmative permissions to use AI tools in specified circumstances.[114] Regulatory sandboxes, such as those pioneered in Utah and Arizona, provide a framework for testing innovative legal services while maintaining adequate consumer protections.[115] Such reforms should be scaled and made permanent. Regulators should focus on AI assurance standards (see Chapter 15) and ensure AI tools clearly disclose their limitations while meeting measurable standards for accuracy (see Chapter 16).[116]

At this point, anything must be better than the status quo for those denied justice, and if new approaches prove inadequate, the data will reveal this, allowing us

[110] *See, e.g.*, Bonardi & Branting, *supra* note 28; *see generally* BENDARZ & BYRAM, *supra* note 3.

[111] Video Interview with Sam Harden, *supra* note 12.

[112] Video Interview by Mia Bonardi with Conor Malloy, Former Dir., Rentervention (July 17, 2024).

[113] *See* LEGAL SERVS. CORP., *supra* note 1, at 43–55.

[114] *See* Bonardi & Branting, *supra* note 28, at 45–47, 51–52; Walters, *supra* note 95, at 319. *See generally* BENDARZ & BYRAM, *supra* note 3; Ashley Krenelka Chase & Sam Harden, *Through the AI-Looking Glass and What Consumers Find There*, 29 J. TECH. L. & POL'Y 1, 2–3 (2025).

[115] ENGSTROM, KNOWLTON & RICCA, *supra* note 60.

[116] *See* Bonardi & Branting, *supra* note 28, at 45–47, 51–52.

to correct course. But maintaining the current system helps no one except those who benefit from the lawyer monopoly. The legal profession stands at a crossroads. It can continue enforcing restrictions that preserve professional monopolies while the justice gap widens, or it can embrace reforms that harness AI's potential to expand access to justice. As courts increasingly encounter litigants who have already received AI guidance despite UPL restrictions, the legal profession must confront this reality. Regarding UPL reform, Zach Zarnow remarks, "I think we're just right on the cusp of some big changes happening."[117] The reason is clear, as Professor Ajmi explains: "The genie is out of the bottle."[118] The question is whether the legal profession will lead this transformation or be swept aside by it.

[117] Video Interview with Zach Zarnow, *supra* note 78.
[118] Video Interview with Ayyoub Ajmi (Nov. 13, 2024), *supra* note 22.

15

AI Assurance

*Neel Guha and Izak C. Rosenfeld**

15.1 INTRODUCTION

AI assurance is the process of ensuring that intelligent systems are valid, accurate, complete, comprehensible, and free from bias.[1] This chapter explores the concept of "AI assurance" in the context of access to justice and AI systems designed for unrepresented litigants. The notion of AI assurance is not new or unique to legal applications. Virtually every application of AI – spanning transportation, healthcare, hiring, and more – has raised questions about how developers and other stakeholders can ensure that AI systems meet minimum performance and quality standards. Within the field of AI, there is an entire subfield of "evaluation" dedicated to questions of measurement and quality assurance. AI assurance is an essential component of AI governance and responsible AI practices.

This chapter examines two dimensions of assurance: (1) reliability and (2) privacy and accountability. Although AI assurance broadly construed might also encompass other aspects of AI systems and their deployment,[2] these dimensions hold particular importance for legal AI applications targeted at unrepresented litigants and thus merit special attention. Section 15.2 examines reliability, focusing on different definitions and technical methodologies. Section 15.3 examines privacy and accountability, considering the intersection of data privacy, the impacts of AI on user protections, and the regulatory landscape that arises from different legal frameworks across the globe.

* This chapter is published with the permission of the MITRE Corporation. We thank L. Thorne McCarty for his review of this chapter.

1 Mia Bonardi & L. Karl Branting, *Certifying Legal AI Assistants for Unrepresented Litigants: A Global Survey of Access to Civil Justice, Unauthorized Practice of Law, and AI*, 26 COLUM. SCI. & TECH. L. REV. 34, 87 (2025). For a slightly broader formulation, *see* Feras A. Batarseh, Laura Freeman & Chih-Hao Huang, *A Survey on Artificial Intelligence Assurance*, 8 J. BIG DATA 60, 61 (2021).

2 For work defining other dimensions of assurance, *see* Percy Liang et al., *Holistic Evaluation of Language Models*, ARXIV 1 (2023), https://perma.cc/S8NN-48JN.

15.2 RELIABILITY

The first dimension is reliability: in simple terms, whether a particular AI system *actually works*. This section focuses on how reliability is defined, why it matters, and how to measure it.

15.2.1 *Defining Reliability*

The definition of reliability often depends on the type of AI system and the specific task the system is purported to perform. Because reliability is a function of AI outputs, the appropriate definition of reliability flows from the form and purpose those outputs serve.

For instance, consider an AI system used to determine whether provisions in a lease agreement may be enforceable under local housing law.[3] This is a predictive AI system specialized for a particular jurisdiction. The system's input is a provision from a lease. Its output is either "enforceable" or "unenforceable," depending on whether the provision is enforceable under local housing law.

Reliability for this system might correspond to whether its outputs are accurate. In other words, if the system is given a provision that legal experts recognize as enforceable, does the system output "enforceable?" Similarly, if the system is given a provision that legal experts recognize as unenforceable, does the system output "unenforceable?"

Reliability might also encompass whether the system's outputs are calibrated. Many predictive systems associate outputs with probabilities, which can be interpreted to assess the system's confidence – for instance, whether a system is highly certain or relatively uncertain in its prediction. To be calibrated, the system's communicated certainty should also be "correct." When the system is confident, its predictions should be mostly correct, and when it lacks confidence, its predictions should be less accurate.

Reliability might also demand that a system be robust and that small, meaningless changes to the inputs not alter its outputs. For instance, typos in a lease agreement, whether present in the original text or introduced through a digitization process, should not alter the system's predictions.[4] And when predictions concern individuals, reliability might also require that a system be unbiased and produce similar performance for different subgroups.

Many of these notions of reliability also apply to generative AI systems, which produce unstructured text instead of class predictions. For instance, consider a generative AI system that provides legal help to unrepresented litigants by answering

[3] For a larger discussion motivating the considerations of this task, *see* David Hoffman & Anton Strezhnev, *Leases as Forms*, 19 J. EMPIRICAL L. STUD. 90 (2022).

[4] Though robustness may seem like a given, modern deep learning systems can struggle with robustness, due to their construction. *See* Andrea Tocchetti et al., *A.I. Robustness: A Human-Centered Perspective on Technological Challenges and Opportunities*, 57 ACM COMPUT. SURV. 141, at 1 (2025).

questions about what the law says or how it might apply to their specific issues.[5] The potential for such chatbot systems has generated significant excitement about their ability to expand access to legal information and help remedy access to justice gaps.

The reliability of this system might also correspond to whether its outputs are accurate, calibrated, robust, and unbiased. Accuracy here captures whether the system's text is correct in its assertions, sound in its logic, and free of factual misstatements. Calibration concerns whether the system appropriately expresses uncertainty. The law is full of "close calls" and "gray areas," and the system's responses should reflect this. Robustness concerns whether the system's answers are consistent across different phrasings of identical questions, or when questions contain typos.[6] Bias relates to whether the system offers similar performance across different types of users, who may come from different demographic groups or geographies.[7]

Reliability for generative AI might also encompass additional criteria. For instance, a legal chatbot should produce answers that are helpful, in that they offer useful or actionable information to users.[8] A system might produce answers that are free of misstatements or errors but at such a high level of generality, or so lacking in detail, that they provide little value.[9] Reliability might also concern the tone of the system's responses. Serious legal questions demand serious answers: a system's responses should not contain flippant language, humor, or other tonally inappropriate sentiments.

15.2.2 *Why Does Reliability Matter?*

Reliability is significant given the sensitive settings in which unrepresented litigants might use legal AI systems. AI systems might provide advice that unrepresented litigants rely on when deciding whether to initiate or sustain legal processes. They may use AI systems to craft legal documents that are relied upon in formal legal proceedings. When AI systems produce faulty or incorrect outputs, litigants

5 Margaret Hagan, *User Research Report into AI for Access to Justice: Legal Question & Answers*, MEDIUM (Mar. 20, 2024), https://perma.cc/ZU4Y-TGX7.

6 Again, a notable challenge is that Generative AI systems tend to be sensitive to small choices regarding how questions are asked (i.e., how they are *prompted*). Jingming Zhu et al., ProSA: Assessing and Understanding the Prompt Sensitivity of LLMs, *in* FINDINGS OF THE ASSOCIATION FOR COMPUTATIONAL LINGUISTICS: EMNLP 2024 1950 (Yaser Al-Onaizan, Mohit Bansal & Yun-Nung Chen eds., 2024), https://perma.cc/5HC3-GULP.

7 Researchers have found that Generative AI systems can provide different answers based on demographic identity. *See* Alejandro Salinas, Amit Haim & Julian Nyarko, *What's in a Name? Auditing Large Language Models for Race and Gender Bias* ARXIV 1 (Jan. 24, 2025), https://perma.cc/CNV7-GU6A.

8 Yuntao Bai et al., *Training a Helpful and Harmless Assistant with Reinforcement Learning from Human Feedback* ARXIV 1 (Apr. 12, 2022), https://perma.cc/KW6V-T59U. *See* Margaret Hagan, *Measuring What Matters: Developing Human-Centered Legal Q-and-A Quality Standards through Multi-Stakeholder Research* (Dec. 1, 2024), https://tinyurl.com/mv6b9pdy.

9 *See supra* note 8.

may be exposed to additional liability, fail to receive the appropriate remedy, or waste valuable resources.

Reliability is also crucial because unrepresented litigants rarely can verify AI outputs. When the individual using a legal AI system is legally trained – for example, a lawyer at a firm, in-house counsel at a company, a judge in a court, or a government administrator – that individual can exercise oversight over the system's outputs. They can verify AI outputs for correctness, fact-check assertions, and determine when AI predictions should be ignored or overruled. But the presumption in the access to justice setting often is, and should be, that the unrepresented litigant relying on the AI system has no expertise or training in the law.

This raises the stakes. Because unrepresented litigants cannot be relied upon to oversee and correct AI system outputs, developers must ensure that such systems meet higher standards for reliability. Mistakes ordinarily caught by legal professionals are unlikely to be caught by unrepresented litigants. Thus, developers must ensure those mistakes do not occur, or are extremely unlikely to occur, in the first place.

Finally, assuring reliability for AI systems can be analogized to the protections the legal system offers represented litigants concerning the quality of the legal representation they receive. Lawyers are subject to a licensing scheme, which can be understood as seeking to ensure minimum standards of competency and knowledge. They are also subject to ethics requirements, with violations policed by local authorities. And in extreme situations, harmed clients may obtain recompense through legal malpractice claims.

Such protections do not extend to unrepresented litigants relying on AI because they are unrepresented, and there is no client–lawyer relationship. However, many of the policy goals motivating the measures we take to ensure adequate legal representation nonetheless persist in the context of unrepresented litigants and AI. We want unrepresented litigants to receive correct legal information and guidance so that they may appropriately navigate the legal system and receive the remedies they are owed.[10] Ensuring reliable AI systems is how we realize this goal.[11]

15.2.3 *How Can Reliability Be Measured?*

Developers measure the reliability of AI systems through a suite of techniques commonly known as *evaluation*.[12] For predictive AI systems, evaluation follows

[10] At present, there is substantial uncertainty about *who* should be responsible for ensuring that AI systems for unrepresented litigants meet minimum reliability standards. While developers will ideally engage in some level of self-assessment, it is unclear who should define and enforce those standards – courts, novel regulatory bodies, or litigants themselves.

[11] *See generally* Laura Freeman, Abdul Rahman & Feras A. Batarseh, *Enabling Artificial Intelligence Adoption through Assurance*, 10 Soc. Scis. 322 (2021).

[12] Moritz Hardt & Benjamin Recht, Patterns, Predictions, and Actions: A Story about Machine Learning 1, 10 (Oct. 26, 2021), http://arxiv.org/pdf/2102.05242.

a structured process: First, developers construct a dataset consisting of inputs to feed into the AI system, with corresponding correct *targets* that the system should ideally produce.[13] They then feed the inputs into the AI system and compare its outputs to the targets in the dataset. By quantifying how the outputs compare to the targets across the dataset, developers can produce empirical measures of reliability.

Recall the example of the predictive AI system for determining whether a lease provision is enforceable (see Section 15.2.1). To evaluate this system, developers would construct an evaluation dataset by collecting different lease provisions for a particular jurisdiction. These would be the inputs. Relying on legal expertise, they would then annotate each provision according to whether it is enforceable under that jurisdiction's housing law. These enforceability annotations would be *targets*. Developers would then feed all the provisions into the AI system, collect its outputs, and count the number of provisions for which the output and target are identical. This would correspond to measuring the *accuracy* of the system: the fraction of time the system's prediction was correct.[14]

Generative AI systems are evaluated slightly differently. Developers still begin by constructing a dataset of inputs to feed into the AI system. But because generative models produce long-form text sequences, and many different generations may be equally correct, developers typically rely on some type of manual assessment of AI outputs. That is, they feed inputs from the dataset into the AI system and manually grade the AI outputs according to specified criteria.[15]

For instance, in the context of the legal chatbot discussed above, developers would first collect different queries that unrepresented litigants might ask the chatbot. These would be the inputs. They would then feed these inputs into the AI system and collect the responses. Then, developers would have legal experts assess these outputs according to a grading rubric that captures the reliability criteria discussed previously. The scores produced by this grading process would then be aggregated to produce an overall score for the system.[16]

[13] *Id.* at 146.

[14] Accuracy is merely one metric, and developers might additionally compute other metrics. *See* Oona Rainio, Jarmo Teuho & Riku Klén, *Evaluation Metrics and Statistical Tests for Machine Learning*, 14 SCI. REP. 6086 (2024).

[15] Varun Magesh et al., *Hallucination-Free? Assessing the Reliability of Leading AI Legal Research Tools* ARXIV 1 (May 30, 2024), https://perma.cc/63M5-6S99. Because manual grading is so expensive – and developers must repeat it with every tweak to the AI system they make – recent work has explored automated forms of grading, which might rely on other AI systems. *See* Lianmin Zheng et al., *Judging LLM-as-a-Judge with MT-Bench and Chatbot Arena* ARXIV 1 (Dec. 24, 2023), https://perma.cc/HH4Q-BM9X.

[16] An important consideration for both the predictive and generative setting is ensuring that the data used to measure model performance has not been used to train the model. If so, measured results can be uninformative, because models often memorize the data they are trained on – a situation known as *data contamination*. *See* Bonardi & Branting, *supra* note 1, at 99.

When considering how this evaluation process might apply to AI systems used by unrepresented litigants, several aspects are worth highlighting. The first relates to the types of inferences a particular evaluation allows. For instance, if the dataset used to evaluate the lease prediction system relies on provisions (and annotations) from one jurisdiction, then the evaluation can provide information only about reliability with regard to that jurisdiction.[17] Evaluation does not support drawing inferences about how reliable that system may be for a different jurisdiction.[18] Similarly, if the legal chatbot is only evaluated with questions about housing, then the evaluation offers little information about the reliability of that system for other issues.[19] Recognizing that an evaluation's information is constrained by dataset composition matters for broader considerations around unrepresented litigants' use of AI. Stakeholders must be certain that the usage context of an AI system (the types of inputs fed into it) aligns with how that system was evaluated.

Second, and relatedly, it is essential that the datasets used for evaluation contain data that is representative of the actual usage. If developers are assessing the reliability of the lease prediction system for a particular jurisdiction, they should use actual clauses from that jurisdiction, provided to the system just as potential unrepresented litigant users might. For instance, if developers envision unrepresented litigants feeding the system lease text produced by applying Optical Character Recognition ("OCR") to scanned documents, then the datasets used for evaluation should be constructed similarly. And if developers expect that unrepresented litigants' questions to the chatbot will contain false presumptions about the law or be poorly worded, then evaluation datasets should reflect these properties. Research has shown that AI performance can be extremely sensitive to these nuances.[20] If evaluation datasets do not reflect these nuances, then the information produced will fail to capture the reliability of systems in practice.

15.3 PRIVACY AND ACCOUNTABILITY

The second dimension of AI assurance we cover is privacy and accountability, which includes how AI tools handle user data, the extent to which such interactions are regulated, and when individual users' data may call for a higher standard of care from AI systems. This section focuses on crucial considerations at the intersection of AI and privacy, key regulatory frameworks, and why accountability matters.

17 *Id.*

18 For instance, scholars have noted performance variations across jurisdictions. Matthew Dahl et al., *Large Legal Fictions: Profiling Legal Hallucinations in Large Language Models*, 16 J. LEG. ANALYSIS 64 (2024).

19 Bonardi & Branting, *supra* note 1, at 98–99.

20 Magesh et al., *supra* note 15.

15.3.1 *Protecting Confidential, Personal, or Sensitive Data*

One of the greatest concerns around the use of AI tools in the modern era is the handling and processing of data that is confidential, personal – also known as personally identifiable information ("PII") – or sensitive. Typical examples include biographical data, contact information, banking or financial data, medical information – often separately referred to as personal health information ("PHI") – and visual or biometric data (including facial identification and fingerprints).

From a privacy perspective, there are certain minimum standards and expectations an individual should have regarding how their data is handled or processed. In the EU, for example, the General Data Protection Regulation (or "GDPR")[21] identifies specific rights to which all individuals (also known as data subjects) are entitled, such as the right to have their data deleted (known as the right to be forgotten) by a data controller or processor.[22] To establish accountability, the GDPR also provides obligations for parties who process, store, or handle the data (also known as data processors and data controllers) from individuals.[23] These are in addition to the fundamental principles, including having a legitimate lawful purpose to collect data,[24] obtaining informed consent to process data,[25] and even ensuring data is stored or handled in a safe and reasonable manner.[26] In line with "the Brussels effect,"[27] many jurisdictions have followed the GDPR, with some replicating its provisions in their entirety (see, e.g., Australia,[28] Brazil,[29] India,[30] Nigeria,[31] South Africa,[32] Switzerland,[33] and Thailand[34]). Even in the US, where no federal privacy law exists, many states have attempted to mirror the effects of the GDPR by carving out specific rights and protections for data users,[35] with California being the first to

21 Regulation 2016/679, of the European Parliament and of Council of 27 April 2016 on the Protection of Natural Persons with Regard to the Processing of Personal Data and on the Free Movement of Such Data, and repealing Directive 95/46/EC, 2016 O.J. (L 119) 1 [hereinafter GDPR].

22 *Id.* art. 17.

23 *Id.* arts. 24–43.

24 *Id.* art. 6(1).

25 *Id.* art. 7(3).

26 *Id.* art. 32.

27 Anu Bradford, The Brussels Effect: How the European Union Rules the World (2020).

28 Privacy Act 1988 (Cth) (Austl.); Privacy Amendment (Notifiable Data Breaches) Act 2017 (Cth) (Austl.).

29 Lei Geral de Proteção de Dados (Decreto No. 13.709, de 14 de Agosto de 2018) (Braz.).

30 Digital Personal Data Protection Act, 2023 (India).

31 Nigeria Data Protection Act (2023) (Nigeria); Nigeria Data Protection Regulation (2019) (Nigeria).

32 Protection of Personal Information Act 4 of 2013 (S. Afr.).

33 Federal Act on Data Protection, SR 253.1 (2020) (Switz.).

34 Personal Data Protection Act 2019 (Thai.).

35 Int'l Ass'n of Privacy Pros., *U.S. State Privacy Legislation Tracker*, https://perma.cc/U5EP-8GZC.

do so through its implementation of the California Consumer Privacy Act.[36] This patchwork of regulations represents a global landscape of privacy regulation and accountability for parties developing and operating systems that interact with data.

The effectiveness of most AI tools is based on the vastness of the dataset on which the tool has been trained.[37] Large language models ("LLMs") touted as successful often have the greatest volume of background data. The ability of an AI tool, especially generative AI, to produce optimal outputs is fundamentally attributable to the extent to which that tool has been trained on existing data (and how well it can identify similarities, differences, equivalences, and interactions between data points). When viewed from the perspective of access to justice and equalizing engagement with legal systems, the nature of the data needed to train an AI tool is most significant. An effective AI tool that can truly assist individuals seeking legal recourse must have sufficient background data connected to both successful and failed attempts at achieving justice.[38] It is understandable that, to learn from the past and provide the highest level of accuracy in supplying information or generating content for those seeking justice, these AI tools require access to as much data as possible. While this is a logical conclusion, it also triggers a significant privacy risk: if AI tools require access to historical data associated with the events and outcomes of criminal and civil legal matters, then the personal, confidential, sensitive, and potentially gruesome details of an unknown number of individuals will be used by these technologies.

This raises the question: how will those who own the technology behind these AI tools balance the need for data to train the tool with the fundamental privacy rights of the individuals whose data is being used in this way? It is hard to canvass the entire spectrum of privacy risk and potential digital harms that may come to those individuals, but one can imagine that the unfettered deployment of AI tools at a large scale could create a seemingly infinite list of opportunities for an individual's data to be disclosed, processed, or handled without their express knowledge or consent. This is not a challenge unique to AI tools. Most prominent social media platforms, cloud-based tools, and mobile software have been forced to tread the fine line between maximizing the utility of their system and complying with their obligations to users under privacy laws and regulations (such as the GDPR). However, a key distinguishing factor is the material reliance of generative AI and LLMs on large quantities of data, far greater than that of historical behemoths supplying technologies to the masses.

[36] CAL. CIV. CODE §§ 1798.100–99 (West 2018).

[37] *Communication from the Commission to the European Parliament, the Council, the European Economic and Social Committee and the Committee of the Regions*, A *European Strategy for Data*, COM/2020/66 final, at 2–3 (Feb. 19, 2020) ("The availability of data is essential for training artificial intelligence systems, with products and services rapidly moving from pattern recognition and insight generation to more sophisticated forecasting techniques and, thus, better decisions.").

[38] Lauren Naudts & Anton Vedder, *Fairness and Artificial Intelligence*, *in* THE CAMBRIDGE HANDBOOK OF THE LAW, ETHICS AND POLICY OF ARTIFICIAL INTELLIGENCE 95–98 (Nathalie A. Smuha ed., 2025).

One potential way to mitigate this harm is for AI systems to present their users (particularly, in the legal context, unrepresented litigants) with clear, plain-language policies that articulate the ways in which data is collected, used, and stored. As many scholars have identified, the use of complex legalese or technical jargon often obscures crucial privacy information that users should understand before accepting the terms that bind them.[39] Given the potentially sensitive and high-risk environments in which they operate, AI tools for unrepresented litigants should be especially upfront and transparent about how user data is stored, processed, and protected. This practice, paired with regulatory oversight, should create a greater degree of accountability for the parties providing legal AI tools in the context of access to justice.

15.3.2 *Regulation of AI in the Context of Privacy*

Although not alone in the quest to establish comprehensive regulations to protect the privacy rights of individual users, the EU has become synonymous with the forefront of digital governance under the law. Since the GDPR, the EU has taken significant steps toward extending privacy controls and legal guardrails to AI. The introduction of the EU AI Act[40] in 2023 (becoming law in 2024) was the first move on this front. In addition to the extensive rights and obligations identified under the GDPR, the EU AI Act aims to bring large-scale data processing by LLMs and generative AI systems into line. Key aspects of the EU AI Act include the classification of AI according to risk,[41] the prohibition of AI systems that are considered to have an unacceptable level of risk,[42] and the imposition of requirements on providers of AI models.[43] These requirements include:

1. Preparing documentation on training and testing processes and evaluation results;
2. Identifying capabilities and limitations so AI providers can comply with privacy requirements;
3. Establishing a policy to comply with EU copyright laws; and
4. Publishing a detailed summary of the content used for training the AI model.[44]

[39] Woodrow Hartzog, *The Inadequate, Invaluable Fair Information Practices*, 76 Md. L. Rev. 952 (2017); Adam S. Chilton & Omri Ben-Shahar, *Simplification of Privacy Disclosures: An Experimental Test* 1 (Coase-Sandor Working Paper Series in Law and Econ. No. 737, 2016).

[40] Regulation 2024/1689, of the European Parliament and of the Council of 13 June 2024 Laying Down Harmonised Rules on Artificial Intelligence and Amending Regulations (EC) No 300/2008, (EU) No 167/2013, (EU) No 168/2013, (EU) 2018/858, (EU) 2018/1139 and (EU) 2019/2144 and Directives 2014/90/EU, (EU) 2016/797 and (EU) 2020/1828 (Artificial Intelligence Act), 2024 O.J. (L 212) 1.

[41] *Id.* art. 6.

[42] *Id.* art. 5.

[43] *Id.* art. 53.

[44] *Id.*

Notwithstanding the implementation of the EU AI Act, several GDPR provisions are specifically relevant to AI, including AI providers' obligations around fair processing,[45] data minimization,[46] and conducting data privacy impact assessments when engaging in high-risk processing activities.[47]

Many criticize the EU AI Act as failing to set a standard as high as the EU did with the introduction of the GDPR in 2018.[48] However, a parallel line of criticism stems from the high compliance costs and the risks of stifling innovation that arise from the EU AI Act, especially for start-ups or smaller developers of AI technologies.[49] In the US, as of 2024, sixteen states provide a right to opt out of the processing of personal data for purposes of profiling in furtherance of decisions that produce legal or similarly significant effects concerning a consumer. These effects include decisions that result in the provision or denial of financial and lending services, housing, insurance, education enrollment or opportunity, criminal justice, employment opportunities, healthcare services, or access to essential goods or services.[50]

With advancing regulatory oversight in the AI context, it will become increasingly difficult to navigate the suitability guidelines for specific AI mechanisms, which may, in turn, limits individuals' access to the tools that would otherwise facilitate their pursuit of justice. This represents a fundamental challenge in balancing privacy regulation, individual protection, and accountability.

Separately, there are strict rules around treating information subject to attorney–client privilege.[51] Unrepresented litigants and providers of AI tools must consider whether the AI tools they employ could be considered a "legal representative," as this may present a variety of challenges, including bringing specific data shared with those tools into the purview of legal privilege or wading into the territory of the unauthorized practice of law (as discussed in Chapter 14). While legal disclaimers may serve to clarify the role of AI tools (e.g., a notice that the information provided by the AI tool is not to be considered "legal advice"), this still presents a challenge of enforceability for the disclaimer itself and the reasonable expectations of the prospective "client."[52] Additionally, if an AI mechanism is considered to be engaging

45 GDPR, *supra* note 21, art. 5(1)(a).

46 *Id.* art. 5(1)(c).

47 *Id.* art. 35.

48 *See, e.g.*, Art. 19 and the International Association of Privacy Professionals ("IAPP").

49 Bertin Martens, *European Union AI Act: Premature or Precocious Regulation?*, BRUEGEL (Mar. 7, 2024), https://perma.cc/7Z2P-K6XD; Mateo Aboy, Timo Minssen & Effy Vayena, *Navigating the EU AI Act: Implications for Regulated Digital Medical Products*, 7 NPJ DIG. MED. 237 (2024).

50 This includes the following US states: CO, CT, DE, FL, IN, KY, MD, MN, MT, NE, NH, NJ, OR, RI, TX, VA, *supra* note 35.

51 For a detailed overview of attorney-client privilege, *see* EDNA SELAN EPSTEIN, THE ATTORNEY-CLIENT PRIVILEGE AND THE WORK-PRODUCT DOCTRINE (4th ed. 2001).

52 For an in-depth analysis of digital legal services and issues around the lawyer–client relationship, *see* Paige A. Thomas, *Online Legal Advice: Ethics in the Digital Age*, 4 ST. MARY'S J. L. MALPRACTICE & ETHICS 440, 459 (2014).

in legal representation, the information exchanged between the client and the AI tool could be subject to privilege.[53] This raises further concerns about how the AI systems would effectively protect and segment privileged data while continuing to learn from the data they process.[54]

15.3.3 *Balancing Justice with Privacy*

This brings us to a seemingly impossible question: How can society preserve the privacy rights of individuals while creating effective and accessible methods for equality in justice? On the one hand, the potential benefits of generative AI and LLMs in the context of access to justice are exceptional. The ability of indigent persons to seek support from AI without concern for the costs of potential legal representation would undoubtedly remove many barriers that currently prevent adequate opportunities for equitable legal rights.[55] However, there appears to be a trade-off for the rights of those who have come before: individuals whose data is necessary for the appropriate training of LLMs are not likely to have had sufficient opportunity to review their data rights or provide informed consent for their data to be used in this context. Additionally, given the complex and advanced nature of many AI tools, it is unclear whether the human beings behind these systems have developed the understanding necessary to provide adequate notice to impacted individuals (if they can even be identified). The sheer volume of data on which most LLMs and generative AI systems are trained would likely prevent relevant disclosures from being made or clear risk advisories being prepared – precisely the challenge the EU AI Act aims to tackle.[56]

To a certain extent, technological safety measures have been developed in tandem with many of the AI tools currently in use that could balance the risks associated with using AI in the justice context. For example, de-identification mechanisms (including pseudonymization and anonymization tools)[57] have made it easier to comply with the GDPR's obligations for data processors to handle personally identifiable data only for as long as is reasonably necessary, based on the legitimate purpose for which it was collected.[58] Similarly, systems that limit data gathering or scraping to

[53] Jordan C. Tye, *Exploring the Intersections of Privacy and Generative AI: A Dive into Attorney–Client Privilege and ChatGPT*, 64 Jurimetrics: J.L., Sci. & Tech. 309 (2024).

[54] Davinia Cutajar, *Balancing Efficiency and Privacy: AI's Impact on Legal Confidentiality and Privilege*, Int'l Bar Ass'n (Nov. 29, 2024), https://perma.cc/M3YT-9J7N.

[55] *See* Marc Galanter, *Why the "Haves" Come out Ahead: Speculations on the Limits of Legal Change*, 9 L. & Soc'y Rev. 95, 144–46 (1974).

[56] *Proposal for a Regulation of the European Parliament and of the Council Laying Down Harmonised Rules on Artificial Intelligence (Artificial Intelligence Act) and Amending Certain Union Legislative Acts*, COM/2021/206 final (Apr. 21, 2021).

[57] GDPR, *supra* note 21, art. 4(5) and Recital 26.

[58] U.K. Information Commissioner's Office, Anonymisation: Managing Data Protection Risk Code of Practice (Nov. 20, 2012), https://perma.cc/8HB6-NG8L.

data that has already been made publicly available or is otherwise open-sourced could mitigate the potential inclusion of sensitive or confidential information in the metadata leveraged by these AI tools. Finally, with a greater degree of regulatory scrutiny and oversight, platforms have placed significant emphasis on digital safety and security practices when handling, processing, and storing data, including within cloud environments where many AI tools exist. A key component of maintaining this balance lies with the individuals and companies that operate AI tools and in holding them accountable for preserving the privacy rights of users. However, as the world has seen with GDPR compliance thus far, enforcement through financial penalties is only effective where the company cannot justify its revenue growth against the cost of the penalty.[59]

15.4 CONCLUSION

This chapter examined several considerations surrounding assurance for AI systems intended for use by unrepresented litigants, focusing specifically on reliability and privacy. Looking to the future, improved assurance for unrepresented litigant-oriented AI systems will require new directions of research aimed at developing improved methodologies for measuring and verifying assurance. Improved assurance will also require new forms of interdisciplinary collaboration, specifically between technologists and legal stakeholders, to identify and define the contours of what assurance means. As the legal community increasingly investigates the development of AI for use by unrepresented litigants, centering assurance is essential to ensure that deployed AI systems appropriately balance risks and benefits.

[59] *See, e.g., Binding Decision 3/2022 on the Dispute Submitted by the Irish SA on Meta Platforms Ireland Limited and Its Facebook Service (Art. 65 GDPR)*, European Data Protection Board (Dec. 5, 2022), https://perma.cc/DA6G-JY5T (leveraging GDPR penalties against Facebook); *Decision No. SAN-2021-023*, Commission Nationale de l'Informatique et des Libertés (CNIL) (Jan. 6, 2022), www.legifrance.gouv.fr/cnil/id/CNILTEXT000044840062 (leveraging GDPR penalties against Google); *Amende de 746 Millions d'Euros Contre Amazon Suite à Nos Plaintes Collectives*, La Quadrature du Net (July 30, 2021), https://perma.cc/J72Q-2QB9 (leveraging GDPR penalties against Amazon).

PART VI

Recommendations

16

Technical Methods for Evaluating AI Applications for Legal Tasks

*Shraeya Iyer, Daniel W. Linna Jr., and Jaromir Savelka**

16.1 INTRODUCTION

A lawyer's duty of competence under American Bar Association Model Rule of Professional Conduct 1.1 requires an understanding of both the benefits and the risks of applicable technology. As AI becomes ingrained in the delivery of legal services, this understanding cannot be limited to the general benefits and risks of technology but must extend to the specific benefits and risks of using particular technologies in different contexts. This highlights a critical need: What are the applicable standards for legal-services quality, and what are the accepted methods for evaluating technologies and understanding the risks and benefits of using them in the delivery of legal services?

We lack satisfactory answers to these questions. Without established standards, performance measures, and a culture of continuous improvement, the legal industry will continue to struggle to assess the efficacy and value of both existing services and the introduction of AI technologies. Academic and industry research is beginning to fill these gaps, and legal organizations and legal technology companies can learn from and draw on best practices for the development of software and AI systems in other industries.

To realize the potential of AI in enhancing access to justice, it is imperative to address fundamental issues in evaluating the delivery of legal services. First, high-quality input and outcome data are essential for AI and data analytics to function effectively. However, current legal industry data often suffers from serious shortcomings due to the absence of quality standards and metrics. Second, a clear understanding of how to measure outcomes, and of what is optimal, is necessary to guide AI development and assess its impact. Yet the legal industry is severely lacking in evidence-based practice, as quality is rarely, if ever, systematically defined. Instead, the legal industry relies on communities of practice and defers to the judgment of individual lawyers regarding the quality of any given piece of legal work.

* We thank Marc Lauritsen for his review of this chapter.

We do not argue that the quality of legal work is subpar or low, but the content of outputs varies, sometimes dramatically. When there is substantial variance in a work product, there is bound to be variance in quality. But it is often difficult to reach a consensus on what "good" means. Whatever setting a lawyer has practiced in, the lawyer will tell you that not everyone produces the same quality of work product and outcomes. If we cannot define and measure the quality of work product and outcomes, we will be severely limited in our ability to develop and deploy AI systems that can produce high-quality work.

Establishing objective, measurable characteristics of legal work is crucial for facilitating automation, quality control, and continuous improvement. For example, early experiments demonstrating that technology-assisted review in e-discovery could outperform manual review highlight the importance of evaluating current methods to establish benchmarks for comparison. By undertaking projects involving legal technology and AI, the legal industry can be compelled to confront the status quo, improve processes, and create metrics for evaluating the quality and value of the delivery of legal services.

16.2 TECHNICAL METHODS FOR EVALUATING AI SYSTEMS

The first step toward effectively evaluating AI-powered systems in the legal domain is matching the evaluation method to the type of output the system produces. While all outputs ultimately aim to support legal reasoning or decision-making, their variations in structure can be defined by categorical, numerical, and open-texture evaluations.

Categorical outputs classify items or entities into discrete, predefined categories based on specific criteria. They are commonly used to group data, decisions, or outcomes into distinct categories (e.g., "relevant/irrelevant," "liable/not liable," "arbitration provision/not arbitration provision"). Precision, recall, and F-measure (F1-score) are standard metrics for categorical evaluation.

Unlike categorical outputs, which classify data into discrete groups, regression outputs produce continuous values and therefore require numerical evaluation methods. For example, a regression model could be used to predict the amount of money a plaintiff is likely to recover if a legal claim is pursued in court. The amount could, in principle, range from zero to an arbitrarily large sum. Example metrics to evaluate regression outputs are mean squared error and root mean squared error.

Finally, open texture outputs are the most complex to evaluate. See Chapter 2 for a discussion of open texture in the context of the language gap. An open-texture output includes the output of a system when the input is a request to provide legal guidance on a specific legal question, such as the conditions under which one is entitled to the return of a security deposit under applicable law.

Each of these unique output types requires different metrics, benchmarks, and validation approaches to assess accuracy and understand real-world utility. The following sections examine each of these categories and illustrate their specific challenges through a series of case studies.

16.2.1 *Categorical Evaluation*

In the early 2000s, it was common in large litigation matters for teams of associates to review truckloads of boxes of printed documents. For each document, it was necessary to determine whether it was responsive to an adversary's requests for documents and relevant to a dispute, thus requiring that it be produced to the requesting party. By the late 2000s, technology-assisted review ("TAR") tools became available that could be trained to predict whether a document was relevant. Legal professionals, however, were slow to adopt these tools. Skeptics pointed out that lawyers who could bill for enormous amounts of time to manually review documents were reluctant to switch to using technology that, while cheaper than manual review, was not cheap. Lawyers were also genuinely concerned about whether the use of TAR could be squared with their ethical obligations, including their duty of competence. It was widely assumed that human review was highly accurate, and it was known that TAR had a measurable error rate. If the choice were between presumably perfect humans and flawed TAR, how could lawyers choose TAR? But subsequent research demonstrated that human review was not nearly perfect, and that TAR could be as effective, if not more so.[1]

Grossman and Cormack used categorical evaluation to show that TAR in e-discovery is more efficient and effective than exhaustive manual review, challenging the generally accepted view that manual review is more effective than TAR. In terms of evaluation, their paper examines recall, precision, and F1 scores as metrics for evaluating document review effectiveness by comparing TAR and exhaustive manual review using data from the Text REtrieval Conference ("TREC") 2009 Legal Track.[2] They found that TAR demonstrated higher precision and comparable recall while significantly reducing human effort in the review process.[3]

Recall is the true positive rate ("TPR"), which is the proportion of actual positives (e.g., relevant documents) that are classified correctly as positives by the model.[4] Recall is calculated as:

$$\text{Recall} = \frac{\text{correctly classified actual positives}}{\text{actual positives}}$$

1 Maura R. Grossman & Gordon V. Cormack, *Technology-Assisted Review in E-Discovery Can Be More Effective and More Efficient than Exhaustive Manual Review*, 17 Rich. J. L. & Tech. 11, 12 (2011).

2 Bruce Hedin et al., *Overview of the TREC 2009 Legal Track*, 18 Proc. Text Retrieval Conf. 1, 1 (2009).

3 Grossman & Cormack, *supra* note 1.

4 Machine Learning, *Classification: Accuracy, Recall, Precision, and Related Metrics*, Google for Dev., https://perma.cc/MV6H-LRYW.

Assume that a population of 1,000 documents has 100 relevant documents. If a review process of all 1,000 documents identifies 60 of the 100 documents that are known to be relevant, the recall is 60/100 = 0.60.

Precision is the proportion of all positive classifications (e.g., documents labeled as relevant) that are actually correct.[5] Precision can be calculated as:

$$\text{Precision} = \frac{\text{correctly classified actual positives}}{\text{everything classified as positives}}$$

Assume that our review process of 1,000 documents identifies 120 documents as relevant, 60 "true positives" and 60 "false positives." Of the 120 documents classified as relevant, 60 are correctly classified, for a precision of 60/120 = 0.50.

Precision and recall often have an inverse relationship: precision improves as the number of false positives decreases, and recall improves as the number of false negatives decreases.

The F1 score (also known as the F-Measure) is the harmonic mean (a type of average) of precision and recall, and is intended to balance the importance of precision and recall in measuring predictive performance.[6] Whereas a true average would produce a middling score if either precision or recall is high while the other is low, computing the harmonic mean causes a low score on either to drag down the overall score more than a true average.

The F1 score is calculated as:

$$\text{F1} = 2 \times \frac{\text{precision} \times \text{recall}}{\text{precision} + \text{recall}} = \frac{2\text{TP}}{2\text{TP} + \text{FP} + \text{FN}}$$

Studies cited by Grossman and Cormack show that independent human reviewers often disagree on relevance assessments, with overlap rates (i.e., inter-rater agreement) as low as 28.1% between individuals. These inconsistencies raise questions about the accuracy of manual review. The lack of a universally accepted gold standard in e-discovery leads to difficulties in assessing the accuracy of manual document review. Many assessments rely on adjudication by senior attorneys to resolve disagreements – a historic practice that is now proven to introduce subjectivity. The authors show that the introduction of TAR results in a fifty-fold reduction in effort in comparison to exhaustive manual review, and that TAR also achieves substantially higher precision, recall, and F1 score than manual review. These findings urge the legal industry not only to consider the implementation of TAR in e-discovery but also to adopt specific methodologies for evaluating the effectiveness of their reviews.[7]

5 *Id.*
6 *Id.*
7 Grossman & Cormack, *supra* note 1.

16.2.2 *Numerical Evaluation*

In cases where algorithms are used to predict continuous values (such as monetary compensation, duration, or probability), numerical evaluation provides a standardized measure of a model's performance. Metrics like mean squared error ("MSE"), root mean squared error ("RMSE"), and R-squared (R^2, coefficient of determination) are common tools in numerical evaluation that assess how close a model's predictions are to actual outcomes. These metrics are especially useful when comparing different regression algorithms or when experimenting with feature selection methods to reduce noise or overfitting.

For instance, in a study of fatal car-accident cases in Taiwan, researchers aimed to predict discretionary damages awarded for mental suffering. They applied three different types of regression models: K-nearest neighbors ("KNN"), classification and regression trees ("CART"), and random forests. They used numerical metrics like R^2 and RMSE to determine which model performed best and to assess the legal factors that may have influenced the outcomes. The random forests model outperformed the others and showed the highest R^2 value and the lowest error values. This type of evaluation helped identify the features that were most predictive (like claimed damages and victim age), revealing the model's potential to support legal professionals in gauging case outcomes.[8]

It is important to recognize, however, that while numerical evaluation offers a standardized way to measure model performance through metrics like R^2, MSE, and RMSE, this does not automatically translate into a model that is practically useful or contextually sound. In this study, the high R^2 score of the random forest model may suggest strong predictive power, but without grounding those predictions in real-life implications of judicial decision-making, the evaluation is at risk of becoming an abstract exercise. A model that performs well numerically but fails to consider the ethical, legal, or societal weight of its predictions (like how damages affect plaintiffs or reflect judicial reasoning) may be accurate but ultimately misaligned with the needs of its intended application.

16.2.3 *Open Texture*

Tasks such as summarization, explanation, or argument generation are characterized by textual outputs that can be expressed in many different ways. As a result, there is no single correct piece of text for comparison to the system output, which poses a serious challenge for evaluation. For example, one can measure how similar the output is to the gold standard answer (e.g., a piece of text that has been

[8] Decheng Hsieh, Lieuhen Chen & Taiping Sun, *Legal Judgment Prediction Based on Machine Learning: Predicting the Discretionary Damages of Mental Suffering in Fatal Car Accident Cases*, 11 Applied Sci. (10361) 1, 1–3 (2021).

verified as correct). However, high similarity does not guarantee correctness; a single negation, for instance, can completely alter the meaning. While it is possible for an expert to manually evaluate each output, this is expensive and also prone to inconsistencies and errors. Automatic evaluation of outputs by large language models ("LLMs") (e.g., "LLM as Judge") has recently attracted considerable attention as a possible option, but it has its own shortcomings and must be validated for each implementation. Zheng et al. offer one such example of automatic evaluation, examining the use of strong LLMs as judges to evaluate LLM performance.[9]

Ever since the release of OpenAI's early ChatGPT models, concern has increased regarding the implementation of AI tools in the legal domain due to the possibility that an LLM will "hallucinate." Farquhar et al. define hallucinations as "LLMs generating 'content that is nonsensical or unfaithful to the provided source content.'"[10] A common example is an LLM citing a nonexistent case for a proposition of law or incorrectly stating the facts or holding of an existing case. This concern arises among practitioners across the field: preserving trust between law firms and their clients, ensuring access to justice resources provide users with reliable answers, and ensuring that court orders and opinions are not polluted with nonexistent or erroneous law.

The term "hallucination," however, has caused confusion and is an unfortunate choice. First, the term anthropomorphizes AI tools. A technical term used by some is "confabulation," which better describes the technical error that results in inaccurate outputs. Second, there is no widely agreed-upon definition of hallucination, which leads to problems when study statistics are cited without consideration of how this type of error has been measured. Often, studies define "hallucinations" broadly to include a wide variety of errors and outcomes under varying testing conditions, including adversarial testing. We argue that a better approach is to define specific quality metrics and methods of evaluation narrowly to better understand the capabilities and limitations of AI systems.

Moreover, in machine learning ("ML"), models have always been evaluated based on the errors they make on specific benchmarks, and complex tasks inevitably result in a certain error rate. Hallucinations in LLMs are simply a type of error. The key issue is not the existence of these errors but understanding and managing them effectively. This involves developing strategies to mitigate errors and ensuring that users understand the limitations, thereby leveraging LLMs' strengths while minimizing their weaknesses.

Magesh et al. aimed to evaluate claims by legal research platforms that their use of retrieval-augmented generation ("RAG") reduced hallucinations in the outputs

9 Lianmin Zheng et al., *Judging LLM-as-a-Judge with MT-Bench and Chatbot Arena*, ARXIV 1, 7–9 (Dec. 24, 2023), https://perma.cc/FKP7-EQSG.

10 Sebastian Farquhar et al., *Detecting Hallucinations in Large Language Models Using Semantic Entropy*, 630 NATURE 625, 625 (2024) (citation omitted).

of their AI tools. This study illustrates the challenges of evaluating AI systems that are used for open texture legal tasks.

Magesh et al. conducted an empirical evaluation of generative AI legal research tools, particularly those using RAG techniques, to determine their susceptibility to hallucinations. The study assessed the performance of proprietary AI tools developed by LexisNexis (Lexis+ AI) and Thomson Reuters (Westlaw AI-Assisted Research and Ask Practical Law AI) and compared them to the performance of GPT-4. The authors defined hallucinations as information generated by LLMs that is either incorrect or correct but misgrounded (i.e., the cited source does not support the claim). Using their definitions, test questions, and methodology, they found that these generative AI legal research tools hallucinated from 17% to 33% of the time. Based on their testing, while RAG can improve reliability in comparison to general-purpose LLMs, hallucinations persisted.

For the study, the researchers created a dataset of more than 200 legal queries to assess the performance of AI-driven research tools. These queries included general legal research questions (39.6%), jurisdiction-specific and time-sensitive questions (e.g., circuit splits, recent case law, etc.) (34.7%), queries with false premises to test the AI's ability to correct misinformation (10.9%), and basic factual recall questions (14.9%). Each of the AI-generated responses was manually evaluated for correctness (whether the response contained factually accurate and relevant information), groundedness (whether key factual claims were supported by appropriate legal resources), and hallucination rate. To validate the accuracy of the human evaluation of the AI-generated outputs, the study confirmed that inter-rater reliability scores between individuals were within acceptable ranges.

Magesh et al. found that, in this particular study, Lexis+ AI answered 65% of the queries accurately, 18% incompletely, and hallucinated 17% of the time. Westlaw AI was accurate 42% of the time, incomplete 25% of the time, and hallucinated in one-third (33%) of responses. GPT-4, the baseline, hallucinated at a rate of 43%, while answering 49% of queries accurately and 8% incompletely.

The authors concluded that hallucination-related errors often stem from issues like naive retrieval (failing to retrieve the most relevant sources), inapplicable authority (citing incorrect or overruled cases), reasoning errors (misinterpreting retrieved documents), and sycophancy (agreeing with user misconceptions instead of correcting them). The hallucination rates were also relatively consistent across different query types, indicating that AI legal research tools do not perform significantly better on simpler versus more complex legal questions.

In examining the study and its potential limitations and avenues for future improvement, Magesh et al. asserted their primary reason for pursuing the study as a response to the limited transparency of proprietary AI models, making it difficult to assess how retrieval systems select legal sources. They recognized that their dataset focuses on text-based research queries, which do not generalize to other legal AI applications, like those that perform contract analysis or e-discovery. The researchers also emphasize that hallucination rates alone do not measure the usefulness of the tool; even tools with relatively high hallucination rates may still provide valuable insights when used appropriately.[11]

It is precisely this need for the proper use of AI tools that raises concern. While Magesh et al. stress that legal professionals should not view the presence of hallucinations as proof that AI cannot be used in the legal process, it is important to note the impact of such findings on the potential adoption of these tools. They emphasize that AI tools' outputs should be carefully reviewed and verified by lawyers who use them and should be understood as imperfect yet useful assistants.[12]

It is therefore vital to communicate the findings of studies like these carefully, both when findings are favorable to AI and when they are not. Caution should be taken in the discussion of AI tools and hallucination rates, as these figure can easily become misleading if taken out of context. Many legal professionals may disregard the researchers' conclusion that AI tools can still be useful and instead interpret the results as an outright disqualification of AI tools, without considering the nuances of how and why these hallucinations occur. Miscommunication of these findings could further hinder the adoption of AI in the legal industry, which already faces significant skepticism. While studies like this are vital and AI tools require proper oversight, outright dismissal based on overstated fears of hallucinations could prevent valuable advancements.

In response to the paper's findings, Thomson Reuters released a statement committing to investigate the claims set forth by Magesh et al. and stating that the company would work with the authors to minimize hallucinations. Thomson Reuters also noted that "one reason the study may have found higher rates of inaccuracy than we have [found] in our internal testing is because the research included question types we very rarely or never see in AI-assisted Research."[13]

Additionally, it is exceedingly rare that a single study should be accepted as definitive, especially when studying complex sociotechnical subjects. Good research explicitly states the known limitations of a study. As the Thomson Reuters statement notes, the questions used to evaluate hallucination in the study may not be representative of the questions that arise in actual use. Likewise, it is extremely difficult to evaluate AI tools for law when we lack the metrics to properly evaluate humans performing those same tasks.[14]

The Thomson Reuters response evokes a critical issue in natural language processing ("NLP"): addressing the discrepancies between a benchmark and the

[11] Varun Magesh et al., *Hallucination-Free? Assessing the Reliability of Leading AI Legal Research Tools*, ARXIV 1, 23–24 (May 30, 2024), https://perma.cc/48T2-HM7P.

[12] *Id.*

[13] Jeff McCoy, *Our Commitment to Our Customers*, THOMSON REUTERS (May 31, 2024), https://perma.cc/2JPT-K9W3.

[14] Daniel W. Linna Jr., *Evaluating Legal Services: The Need for a Quality Movement and Standard Measures of Quality and Value*, *in* RESEARCH HANDBOOK ON BIG DATA LAW 404 (Roland Vogl ed., 2021).

corresponding real task. In NLP, benchmarks are essential for advancing the field and driving progress, often using carefully curated datasets that aim to represent real-world tasks as closely as possible. Despite these efforts, discrepancies between a benchmark and the corresponding real task cannot be fully eliminated. Researchers understand that reported performance on specific benchmarks does not equate to performance on real-world tasks. When a study reports a model's performance on a task such as summarization or translation, it reflects how well the model performed on the specific benchmarks used, not the real-world task. Understanding the specifics of the benchmarks is crucial for estimating real-world performance. For example, a summarization dataset of English news articles might closely reflect a model's performance on real-world news articles but not on court opinions. However, discussions around model performance sometimes conflate benchmark success with real-world utility, leading to potential misunderstandings of a model's actual capabilities.

In light of these considerations, it is crucial to approach evaluations of AI legal research tools with both rigor and nuance. While Magesh et al. provide empirical insights into the performance of these systems, their findings should not be taken as a wholesale indictment of AI in legal practice. Instead, they underscore the importance of contextualizing AI errors, refining evaluation methodologies, and fostering transparency in AI development. As AI in the legal domain continues to evolve, both researchers and practitioners must work collaboratively to ensure that these tools are assessed against real-world use cases, not just benchmarks, and that their capabilities and limitations are clearly communicated without fueling unwarranted hype or skepticism. By striking the right balance between caution and innovation, the legal industry can harness AI's potential while mitigating its risks, ultimately advancing access to justice and improving the efficiency of legal research.

16.3 DIMENSIONS FOR EVALUATING AI IN THE LEGAL DOMAIN

Another essential aspect of evaluating AI systems used in the legal domain is testing the consistency of responses from a specific AI system, i.e., performing stability testing. Atil et al. investigated non-determinism in five LLMs that were configured to be deterministic (temperature set to zero) over eight common tasks across five identical runs, in both few-shot and zero-shot settings. A deterministic system would provide the same output in response to the same input each time. But LLMs are not designed to be deterministic. Atil et al. found accuracy variations of up to 15% and a gap between best and worst possible performance of up to 70%. Ultimately, they found that no LLM consistently delivered repeatable accuracy across all tasks.[15]

[15] Berk Atil et al., *Non-Determinism of "Deterministic" LLM Settings*, ARXIV 1, 1 (Apr. 2, 2025), https://perma.cc/EEA6-MGVM.

In this sense, numerous other dimensions of evaluation are relevant to the evaluation of AI systems used in the legal domain. Bedi et al. introduced the following dimensions of evaluation for LLM responses in the medical field: accuracy; calibration and uncertainty; robustness; factuality; comprehensiveness; fairness, bias, and toxicity; deployment considerations;[16] transparency;[17] understandability;[18] and stability.[19] These dimensions can be readily adapted to the legal industry.

16.4 RISKS, HARMS, AND IMPACTS

Before evaluating any AI system, especially in high-stakes domains such as law, it is essential to understand the risks it poses and how the impact of those risks can vary. For instance, in the case of an access to justice chatbot providing legal information based on user-submitted problems, the consequences of an error depend heavily on the severity of the legal issue involved.[20]

Errors are typically communicated in binary terms – whether the output was correct or incorrect. This binary approach is overly simplistic. Mike Dahn, head of Westlaw Project Management, suggests three ways to categorize errors found in LLM-generated responses in AI-assisted legal research tools: incorrect references in otherwise correct answers, incorrect statements in otherwise correct answers, and entirely incorrect answers.

Incorrect references in otherwise correct answers occur when an LLM produces a correct output but provides incorrect supporting information or unrelated citations. These errors are generally low risk, as they are easily detectable through a review of the cited material. According to Dahn, such answers still offer value, as they guide users toward the right conclusions, even if the sources require correction.

Incorrect statements in otherwise correct answers involve inconsistent or irrelevant content embedded within an otherwise coherent explanation. For instance, if the entire response discusses the application of a legal precedent to a situation, and one line discusses an entirely unrelated case, that would fit into this category of error. The risk of harm with these errors also appears to be relatively low, since the inconsistency is typically obvious and the researcher would be prompted to analyze the source material to confirm their suspicions. Dahn also finds that

16 Suhana Bedi et al., *A Systematic Review of Testing and Evaluation of Healthcare Applications of Large Language Models (LLMs)*, medRxiv 1, 2 (Aug. 16, 2024), https://perma.cc/LRD5-6YQW.

17 Łukasz Górski & Shashishekar Ramakrishna, *Challenges in Adapting LLMs for Transparency: Complying with Art. 14 EU AI Act*, 379 FRONTIERS IN A.I. & APPLICATIONS 275, 275–80 (2023).

18 Margaret Hagan, *Measuring What Matters: A Quality Rubric for Legal Q&A*, MEDIUM (Feb. 20, 2025), https://perma.cc/T57J-HSYE.

19 Atil et al., *supra* note 15.

20 NAT'L CTR. FOR STATE CTS., *Tech for All – Applications of AI to Increase Access to Justice* (Jan. 29, 2025), https://perma.cc/KES7-YVDG.

there is some benefit to these responses, since they still point the researcher to relevant source material, explain the issues, and give an overview from which the researcher can work.[21]

Entirely incorrect answers pose unique challenges in detection and potential harm. Hagan states that misleading answers are far more dangerous than those that are completely incorrect, as they can be extremely difficult to detect, and authoritative answers from AI outputs invoke trust from users.[22] Meanwhile, Dahn notes that entirely incorrect answers are rare in testing and difficult to address. In some cases, Dahn states that entirely incorrect answers can be detected by checking the primary sources cited. However, in cases where the incorrectness of the answer might not be immediately obvious and reviewing the primary sources might not be enough to resolve the issue, these errors pose a greater potential harm. Even in such cases, Dahn argues that these answers offer benefits similar to those of using secondary sources. Though dangerous when solely relied upon, secondary sources are valuable additions to primary research, just as these incorrect answers can still effectively reveal relevant primary law.[23]

Hagan also cautions against merely presenting accurate information, as there is a substantial risk of misapplication and misinterpretation of the law on the part of the AI tool or the user. The law is filled with technicalities; without an in-depth understanding of the implications of any legal action, this information can do more harm than good when not accompanied by warnings about practical risks. For example, giving a user "accurate" information regarding their legal right to withhold rent could cause them to take action that ultimately violates a technicality in the law that the user was not aware of and could lead them into serious legal trouble. Therefore, Hagan argues that AI tools must warn about practical risks whenever stating a user's rights, in order to avoid potential harm.[24]

16.5 PROTOTYPING AND EVALUATING AI APPLICATIONS FOR ACCESS TO JUSTICE

The evaluation of AI tools in the legal domain is essential, yet smaller organizations and access to justice initiatives often face significant challenges due to the high costs associated with rigorous testing and assessment. By leveraging specific prototyping and evaluation strategies, these organizations can develop effective and reliable AI-driven legal tools without the extensive resources available to larger enterprises. Drawing insights from case studies, this section examines

[21] Mike Dahn, *How Harmful Are Errors in AI Research Results?*, THOMSON REUTERS (Aug. 2, 2024), https://perma.cc/SUY6-CD5Q.

[22] Hagan, *supra* note 18.

[23] Dahn, *supra* note 21.

[24] Hagan, *supra* note 18.

approaches to prototyping AI tools for access to justice applications in terms of the design thinking process and the corresponding evaluation methodologies. This section explores how access to justice initiatives can leverage the design thinking framework, with an emphasis on the prototyping and testing phases, to develop reliable AI-driven legal tools, with examples from existing access to justice tools and development processes.

The steps in the design thinking process consist of empathize, define, ideate, prototype, and test.[25] The prototyping and testing phases are most relevant to the evaluation of AI systems for legal tasks.

Prototyping is an iterative process, executed in the early stages of project development, intended to test possibilities, start a conversation with potential users, offer a space for problem solving, and ultimately help build a tool to solve the problem previously identified. Often, the prototyping and testing phases are deeply intertwined, with movement between phases. The testing phase is intended to refine prototypes and tools, learn more about the user, and refine the framing of the problem.[26] The following sections outline cost-effective strategies to navigate these steps in access to justice resource-constrained environments.

16.5.1 *Prototyping*

A compelling example of AI-driven access to justice innovation is Beagle+, a legal chatbot developed by the People's Law School in British Columbia in partnership with Tangowork. Designed to improve access to justice by providing tailored legal information in response to everyday legal problems, Beagle+ offers users conversational, empathetic guidance while directing them to human-authored resources for deeper insights. Notably, user feedback has demonstrated a level of satisfaction comparable to interactions with human legal professionals.

The development of Beagle+ exemplifies an effective and scalable approach to prototyping legal AI applications. The chatbot's prompt engineering adheres to the CARE framework (i.e., Context, Ask, Rules, and Examples), ensuring precise and context-aware responses. A critical component of its architecture is RAG, which dynamically retrieves relevant legal content to maintain up-to-date responses. The system continuously updates its knowledge base by scraping the People's Law website content nightly, breaking updates into 400-word chunks, vectorizing them, and embedding them into a vector database. This automated process, which runs for approximately ten minutes each night, ensures that Beagle+ remains current without requiring manual intervention.

[25] Hasso Plattner Inst. of Design at Stan., *An Introduction to Design Thinking Process Guide*, https://perma.cc/73AD-984R.

[26] *Id.*

The development and deployment of Beagle+ create the following roadmap: provide memory to the LLM in the form of an automatically updating vector database, manually test with difficult questions to evaluate safety and helpfulness, and use AI to automatically evaluate risks in the outputs, like unauthorized legal advice, severity of the legal issue, and hallucination. Beagle+ demonstrates how smaller organizations can create accurate, low-cost legal AI tools with LLMs, automated RAG updates, and rigorous evaluations, offering a model for safe, effective legal AI development.[27]

Hagan outlines what quality looks like to users and guides developers on important aspects of design in legal AI systems. Her study finds that users want AI tools to provide clear step-by-step guidance on next steps, offer jurisdiction-specific advice, refer users to real-world resources (like legal aid offices or court forms), and provide answers without legal jargon that are easy to read and understand.[28] Lauritsen and Steenhuis offer similar advice to developers in their proposed general framework to ensure legal software quality. Their framework suggests, "[The system] should not ever behave in a way that a similarly situated human expert presented with the same fact pattern would regard as wrong."[29] They advise that the system should provide a "right" response alongside some supporting information. If this is not possible, the system should return a message indicating that a proper response cannot be given.[30]

16.5.2 *Evaluation*

Ensuring accuracy and reliability in legal AI tools requires rigorous evaluation. Beagle+ underwent extensive pre-production and post-launch testing to measure its effectiveness. Initially, the chatbot was tested with a set of forty-two complex legal queries, achieving a 70% accuracy rate using the GPT-3.5 model. Early tests revealed some concern related to terminology – specifically, the chatbot's use of the word "recommend," which in legal contexts could imply unauthorized legal advice (see Chapter 14 on the unauthorized practice of law). This is an example of the iteration between prototyping and evaluation processes. After returning to the prototyping stage to make improvements, the developers implemented a manual review process to mitigate such risks, in which legal professionals assessed chatbot responses. Out of 5,354 reviewed responses, 54 contained inaccuracies, all of which

27 Nat'l Ctr. for State Cts., *Tech for All – Applications of AI to Increase Access to Justice*, *supra* note 20; Nat'l Ctr. for State Cts., *Tech for All – A Technical Deep Dive into AI-Powered Justice Chatbots* (Feb. 19, 2025), https://perma.cc/6HZT-SJUN; *Beagle+ Explainer*, People's L. Sch., https://perma.cc/7KGN-WYW8.

28 Hagan, *supra* note 18.

29 Marc Lauritsen & Quinten Steenhuis, *Substantive Legal Software Quality: A Gathering Storm?*, *in* 17 Proc. Int'l Conf. A.I. & L. 52, 60 (2019).

30 *Id.*

were addressed through refinements in prompt engineering, relevance scoring, and website content.

The implementation of RAG with a private dataset improved accuracy to 80%, while transitioning to GPT-4 further increased accuracy to 99%. Post-launch evaluation included continuous monitoring of user interactions, facilitated by metadata-tagged chatbot logs that categorized conversations by topic and subtopic. To further automate quality assurance, the tool's developers integrated AI-driven assessment mechanisms that analyze chatbot responses along three key dimensions:

1. *Hallucination detection*: Identifying and minimizing false or misleading information.
2. *Legal impact analysis*: Evaluating the severity of potential misinformation.
3. *Legal "adviseness" assessment*: Ensuring the chatbot does not inadvertently provide unauthorized legal advice.

Even with these automated safeguards, every chatbot interaction undergoes manual review, ensuring sustained accuracy and compliance.[31] The evaluation process underscores a critical best practice of combining human oversight with automated quality control to maintain high standards of legal reliability.

As with any interaction in the legal domain, communication often contains highly sensitive personal information. Ensuring this information is securely contained is essential not only for user privacy but also for the reputation of the tool.

16.5.3 *Security*

Moutopoulos et al. offer guidance to developers on evaluating the security of their tool, Hear Me Out, an AI-powered digital platform developed by the National Justice Project and Portable Australia. The platform is designed to enhance access to justice by simplifying the pathway for users to file complaints. The authors outline three main areas: (1) anonymization and encryption, (2) access control and IP filtering, and (3) ethical data collection and use. In the first area, anonymization and encryption, all data is encrypted to safeguard against unauthorized access, and all personally identifiable information is anonymized. In the second area, access control and IP filtering, the platform permits only authorized personnel to access complaint data, and IP filtering is configured to protect sensitive data from potential breaches by only allowing access from designated networks and locations. The third area, ethical data collection and use, ensures that only essential data is collected from users. This data usage is fully disclosed in the privacy policy, and consent is obtained prior to collecting data on complaint interactions. Moutopoulos et al.

[31] Nat'l Ctr. for State. Cts., *Tech for All – Applications of AI to Increase Access to Justice*, *supra* note 20; Nat'l Ctr. for State. Cts., *Tech for All – A Technical Deep Dive into AI-Powered Justice Chatbots*, *supra* note 27.

emphasize that maintaining the trust of consumers requires providing clear user consent and disclaimers, as well as ensuring all policies surrounding privacy and data usage are made completely transparent to users.[32]

16.5.4 *Consumer Protections*

Another important aspect of evaluation, Hagan suggests, concerns consumer protections. Hagan asserts that "evaluating accuracy alone isn't enough." Apart from accuracy, AI legal answers should be actionable, empowering, and employ strategic caution. Actionable responses should offer concrete steps users can take. These responses should empower users, meaning they should "help users feel capable of handling their problem." In addition, Hagan outlines the key concern of *strategic caution*: the response should "avoid causing unnecessary fear or discourage action." Discouraging action can manifest in unexpected ways. For instance, Hagan specifies that AI tools should avoid excessively pushing users to talk to a lawyer or seek formal legal assistance, since this often deters users from pursuing the issue at all. However, Hagan also outlines a key regulatory concern: policies should be put in place to prevent AI tools from deterring users from seeking legal aid when needed. This reveals a delicate balance that must be struck: AI tools should not deter users from seeking legal aid, yet they also should not push them to do so.[33] The role of the AI tool is primarily informational. Its job should be to present legal information in a digestible and accurate manner without straying too far in either direction. The concept of "digital nudge" is discussed further in Section 9.4.

16.6 CONCLUSION

The integration of AI into legal services is well underway, necessitating the creation and implementation of robust evaluation frameworks that address both technical performance and real-world impact. Throughout this chapter, we have discussed several evaluation methods: categorical methods (e.g., precision, recall, F1), numerical metrics (e.g., MSE, R^2), and approaches for evaluating open texture outputs. The categorization of potential errors, from partially incorrect references to entirely incorrect responses, requires nuanced frameworks for identifying associated risks in legal contexts.

For access to justice developers, we have consolidated five key approaches that have proven effective through the implementation of similar tools:

[32] Dean Moutopoulos et al., *AI-Powered Platforms for Access to Justice: The Case of Hear Me Out, in* UNSW L. & Just. Rsch. Series No. 25-13 (Feb. 28, 2025), https://papers.ssrn.com/abstract=5213638.

[33] Hagan, *supra* note 18.

1. implementing dynamic knowledge maintenance through continuously updated databases;
2. conducting rigorous pre-deployment testing;
3. deploying AI-driven tools for hallucination detection and legal impact determination;
4. adopting structured prompting methodologies (e.g., the CARE framework); and
5. establishing thorough privacy protections through anonymization, encryption, and ethical data-management practices.

The belief that legal work done by humans is inherently superior to work done with AI assistance is proving incorrect for an increasing number of legal tasks. Establishing empirical quality standards for AI used in the legal industry would increase trust in outputs for both clients and law firms. Importantly, quality and evaluation metrics are needed to improve feedback systems for machines to learn and also to create higher quality training data. By creating a culture of continuous improvement and evidence-based practice, the legal industry can harness AI's potential to make legal information and services more accessible while also ensuring that the technology does not introduce additional barriers or risks to vulnerable populations.

17

Institutional Reforms for AI in Legal Services

*Izak C. Rosenfeld**

17.1 INTRODUCTION

Even with the best AI tools available, access to justice remains at risk of being stifled by the legal profession, regulatory authorities, and the justice system itself. Without fundamental shifts in the rules, awareness, education, funding, and safety mechanisms surrounding AI, it is hard to imagine these technologies fully empowering unrepresented litigants. However, there is still hope. With renewed emphasis on promoting AI, updating rules, creating and implementing guardrails, and standardizing laws and regulations to facilitate machine interpretation, the power of AI tools can be harnessed to expand unrepresented litigants' access to otherwise challenging or overwhelmingly complicated justice systems. This chapter identifies crucial recommendations for change across these thematic areas. As Martin Luther King Jr. once said, "Human progress never rolls in on wheels of inevitability."[1] The path toward meaningful AI-enabled access to justice requires deliberate action, collaborative effort, and an unwavering commitment to equitable legal systems for all.

17.2 INTEGRATE AND PROMOTE AI TECHNOLOGIES

Many legal regulatory authorities and professional membership organizations create and promote access to justice through a number of existing pathways, including legal aid, pro bono work, and self-help resources. These entities include bar associations, professional membership groups, and law societies (collectively, Legal Practice Bodies). They must widen the scope of access to justice to include AI by investing in and encouraging the use of AI tools. More specifically, Legal Practice Bodies should promote AI tools, develop educational initiatives for their responsible use, and support the deployment of AI to help bridge the justice gap and

* This chapter is published with the permission of the MITRE Corporation. I thank Marc Lauritsen for his review of multiple drafts of this chapter.

[1] Martin Luther King Jr., Letter from a Birmingham Jail (Apr. 16, 1963).

facilitate public access to such systems. Ensuring sufficient funding for AI programs should also be a priority for these organizations, just as many already fund pro bono initiatives and bar association foundations that facilitate greater inclusion and access to justice.

This section sets out specific ways in which Legal Practice Bodies can continue to advance access to justice by:

1. Promote AI tools;
2. Develop educational initiatives on the responsible use of AI tools;
3. Create sandbox environments for the development of AI tools; and
4. Dedicate resources to AI tools.

17.2.1 *Promote AI Tools*

Setting aside the uniquely challenging task of interpreting and applying laws and regulations to nuanced fact patterns and circumstances (addressed in Section 17.4), Legal Practice Bodies should strive to promote AI-based legal resources to the public and to members of the legal profession.

Many unrepresented litigants may already have benefited from the efforts of Legal Practice Bodies to promote awareness of pro bono and self-help resources. Additionally, some Legal Practice Bodies advocate for increasing the provision of pro bono services by lawyers. For example, the American Bar Association's ("ABA") Model Rules of Professional Conduct recommend that all lawyers engage in at least fifty hours of pro bono work each year.[2] Pro bono activity is also strongly encouraged and, in some US states, required to enter the legal profession (see, e.g., the NY State Bar's fifty-hour pro bono requirement to seek admission to practice law).[3] A similar approach to promoting the use of AI tools should also be adopted.

In the US, each state regulates the practice of law, from entry as a new lawyer to ongoing compliance with ethical rules and practice requirements. Similarly, in Canada the rules for legal practice are set by each province. However, in some countries there is a national system for regulating legal practice, which facilitates mobility within the country and ensures consistency in practice standards for lawyers nationwide (see, e.g., the UK's Solicitors Regulation Authority ("SRA") Code of Conduct).[4] Despite differences in geographical scope, many Legal Practice Bodies look for guidance from the more prominent authorities and their corresponding professional membership organizations (such as the ABA, which is frequently cited for its model rules, ethical guidelines, and recommendations for standards of professional practice).

2 Model Rules of Pro. Conduct r. 6.1 (Am. Bar Ass'n 2024).
3 N.Y. Comp. Codes R. & Regs. tit. 22, § 520.16 (2015).
4 SRA, *SRA Code of Conduct for Solicitors, RELs and RFLs* (Dec. 1, 2023), https://perma.cc/4NHP-2XEC.

In the context of AI in the legal profession, the New York State Bar Association ("NYSBA") (the legal regulatory authority for legal professionals in New York) was among the first bodies to identify best practices and recommendations for using AI in legal contexts. In April 2024, it published the *Report and Recommendations of the New York State Bar Association Task Force on Artificial Intelligence*, which set out the following key recommendations on the use of AI in the legal profession:

1. Adopt AI guidelines;
2. Focus on education;
3. Identify risks associated with new technology that is not currently regulated; and
4. Examine the function of the law in AI governance.[5]

Similarly, in Australia the Law Society of New South Wales, the Legal Practice Board of Western Australia, and the Victorian Legal Services Board and Commissioner produced a joint statement to help lawyers understand expectations around using AI tools in their legal work.[6] The statement emphasizes the importance of maintaining ethical obligations under Australia's legal practice rules (the Legal Profession Uniform Law)[7] around client confidentiality, professional independence, and the competent delivery of legal services. It does so by cautioning lawyers to implement risk-based AI policies, to limit the use of AI tools to "lower-risk" tasks, and to refrain from using them for tasks that should be "independently verified."[8]

Finally, in the UK, the Law Society has published guidance on generative AI that provides a broad overview of considerations for the legal profession when deciding whether to use AI technologies.[9] This report, akin to the recommendations outlined by Legal Practice Bodies in the US and Australia, emphasizes the implications of adopting AI tools for legal professionals rather than for litigants without lawyers. Recommendations range from ensuring ongoing compliance with legal ethics and professional obligations to considering the regulatory landscape in which such AI tools will be used.[10]

While there appears to be uniformity in the cautionary guidance from Legal Practice Bodies, these publications fail to capture the benefits or consequences of litigants without lawyers using AI tools. Despite their willingness to promote or

5 NYSBA, Report and Recommendations of the New York State Bar Association Task Force on Artificial Intelligence (Apr. 2024), https://perma.cc/9TUM-MU45.

6 *Statement on the Use of Artificial Intelligence in Australian Legal Practice*, Law Society of New South Wales, Legal Practice Board of Western Australia & Victorian Legal Services Board and Commissioner (Dec. 6, 2024), https://perma.cc/A2WV-YDF3.

7 Legal Profession Uniform Law 2014 (NSW) (Austl.).

8 *Id.*

9 *Generative AI: The Essentials*, The Law Society (Aug. 7, 2024), https://perma.cc/S9TG-XA47.

10 *Id.* at Part 3.

even require pro bono advocacy, Legal Practice Bodies appear too risk-averse to encourage unrepresented litigants to engage directly with AI tools when seeking legal services. Instead, these organizations appear myopic in their focus on warning members of the legal profession about the many risks and challenges that may arise from the use of AI in the context of legal practice. To that end, Legal Practice Bodies should prioritize the promotion of AI tools as mechanisms to improve access to justice for unrepresented litigants.

17.2.2 *Develop Educational Initiatives on Using AI Tools Responsibly*

Legal Practice Bodies should develop educational initiatives for both lawyers and unrepresented litigants on the responsible use of AI tools. As discussed above, Legal Practice Bodies around the world have published reports and guidelines on how legal professionals should (and should not) use AI tools in providing legal services. However, these Legal Practice Bodies have not yet provided guidance that seeks to educate or inform the *public* on how AI tools can be used responsibly in the legal context. This presents a stark contrast to the variety of efforts by regulatory authorities to implement and publicize guidance on the responsible use of AI (see, e.g., the NIST AI Framework and the EU AI Act, discussed in greater detail in Section 17.3.3).

Legal Practice Bodies are best equipped to advise and guide individuals on how AI tools can be used responsibly in legal contexts. This is due both to their integration within legal practice and to their insight around the day-to-day operations of legal systems, as they regulate legal professionals, oversee justice programs in conjunction with or alongside courts, and provide expertise on the administration of legal practice. Additionally, these organizations are already deeply engaged in assessing and understanding the potential impacts of AI on the legal profession, demonstrating their investment in the interplay between AI and the law (as explored in Section 17.2.1). It would not significantly burden Legal Practice Bodies to adapt their existing efforts, moving from a focus exclusively on practitioners to a broader mandate that balances their priorities with the needs of the public at large.

17.2.3 *Create Sandbox Environments for Developing AI Tools*

The legal profession is inherently risk-averse. Lawyers are held to strict standards in the practice of law and must continuously abide by ethical rules when carrying out their trade. As a result, much of the legal profession's history has demonstrated hesitation in embracing change, both in technology and in innovation. Furthermore, as discussed above in Section 17.2.1, Legal Practice Bodies have tended to be more willing to caution against innovation than to encourage it. To accommodate this risk-averse culture, Legal Practice Bodies should reduce barriers to engaging with

AI by investing in and creating sandbox environments. Doing so will help ensure accessibility for contributors, such as AI developers and content providers, and facilitate greater engagement by legal professionals. If members of the legal profession are given room to participate in testing or providing inputs to AI tools without fear of repercussions, there will be a greater chance that these mechanisms will improve and become more effective. One of the more significant aspects of this limitation arises in the context of the unauthorized practice of law ("UPL"), which is addressed in more depth in Chapter 14.

In 2023, the Organization for Economic Co-operation and Development ("OECD") published a policy paper discussing the use of regulatory sandboxes in AI. It highlighted a variety of benefits, including fostering innovation, ensuring regulatory compliance by developers, facilitating ethical experimentation with these tools, providing accountability and regulatory oversight, building public trust, and facilitating access to AI tools.[11] Using such sandboxes has already produced positive results in contexts outside the law and the justice system, which should dispel some of the resistance or hesitation that may come from Legal Practice Bodies, as there is already tangible proof of their feasibility. In the UK, the Financial Conduct Authority has implemented a regulatory sandbox that provides businesses in the financial services industry with the ability to engage in controlled testing of new AI and technology tools while vetting consumer protection safeguards and validating market demand for the tools themselves.[12] Since this sandbox program was implemented, participating organizations have seen an increase in business activity and improved access to services for more risk-averse consumers. Regulators have also gained fresh insights into new technologies and their associated risks.[13] This is just one example of the use of sandboxes to promote the responsible development of AI tools, but it reflects a consistent trend of benefits to consumers, businesses, developers, and regulatory authorities themselves.[14]

The case for sandbox environments as a vehicle to promote the responsible development of AI tools has already been made in contexts outside the legal profession. Where Legal Practice Bodies are engaged with the development of AI tools, they will benefit from a deeper understanding of how AI technology functions. This insight,

[11] OECD, *Regulatory Sandboxes in Artificial Intelligence*, OECD Digital Economy Paper No. 356 (July 2023).

[12] *Regulatory Sandbox*, Financial Conduct Auth. (May 9, 2024), https://perma.cc/9YJE-QNCA.

[13] Giulio Cornelli et al., *Regulatory Sandboxes and Fintech Funding: Evidence from the UK*, 28 Rev. Fin. 203, 204–05 (2024).

[14] *See, e.g.*, *Enhanced Regulatory Sandbox*, Australian Sec. & Inv. Comm'n (Austl. 2020), https://perma.cc/KHH6-MBUZ (introducing the Australian Securities & Investments Commission's "enhanced regulatory sandbox" regulations); Norwegian Data Prot. Auth., *Regulatory Privacy Sandbox*, https://perma.cc/BMB9-9AT8 (introducing the Norwegian Data Protection Authority's "regulatory privacy sandbox" regulations).

coupled with a dedication to expanding AI tools in the legal profession, should alleviate uncertainty and empower Legal Practice Bodies to regulate AI tools in a more considered way. Overall, AI sandboxes can help bridge the gap between technological advancements and regulatory frameworks, promoting the responsible development and deployment of AI tools for the benefit of the public at large. Regulatory sandboxes for legal AI tools are discussed in more detail in Chapter 14.

17.2.4 *Dedicate Resources to AI Tools*

Legal Practice Bodies have taken considerable strides toward the promotion and engagement of traditional pro bono and diversity initiatives, with a particular emphasis on access to justice. This has included anything from the establishment of pro bono centers within bar associations and legal regulatory authorities to the formation and funding of bar foundations and charitable branches.[15] As mechanisms for access to justice evolve – either due to technological advancements in tools like AI or as a result of emerging challenges in the pursuit of justice – Legal Practice Bodies must adjust and reassess the focus of their efforts.

To that end, it is crucial that these organizations shift their focus away from unscalable human solutions and instead prioritize the beneficial impacts of investing in advanced tools that empower unrepresented litigants. To be clear, community justice worker programs are a scalable human solution. What is not a scalable human solution is pairing a human attorney with each person who needs legal help. There are simply too few lawyers, and the need is simply too large.

However, it is essential to emphasize that AI should complement, not replace, existing legal aid resources. By integrating AI tools with current programs, Legal Practice Bodies can create a more robust and accessible legal support system. This synergy between AI and legal support programs could serve a broader population more efficiently without diverting funds from existing efforts to improve access to justice, thereby bringing greater balance to the activities of Legal Practice Bodies in advancing access to justice. In 1974, Marc Galanter astutely highlighted that differences in the quality and quantity of legal services greatly affected the fate of participants in the legal system.[16] The goal should be to leverage AI as an additional tool in the pursuit of justice, enhancing rather than supplanting the valuable work of legal professionals and existing legal aid structures.

Few stakeholders are better equipped or more attuned to the needs of individuals in pursuit of justice than legal institutions and lawyers. It is essential that Legal Practice Bodies are responsive to evolving challenges to access to justice by

[15] *See, e.g.*, in the US, the ABA's "American Bar Foundation" and, in Australia, the Victorian Bar's "Victorian Bar Foundation."

[16] Marc Galanter, *Why the "Haves" Come Out Ahead: Speculations on the Limits of Legal Change*, 9 L. & Soc'y Rev. 95, 144–46 (1974); *see supra* Sections 1.4.3–1.4.4.

advancing fairness in the public's engagement with legal systems – especially for unrepresented individuals navigating complex matters to protect their rights – and by mitigating the costs associated with modern justice systems.

17.3 UPDATE LEGAL PRACTICE RULES AND REGULATIONS FOR AI USE

Legal Practice Bodies have already dedicated extensive resources to providing guidance on the use of AI tools in legal practice (see Section 17.2.1). The natural progression is for such Legal Practice Bodies to modernize legal practice rules and regulations to align with the evolving technological landscape that intersects with the law. This would involve:

1. Changing rules that restrict or unnecessarily limit the use of AI (such as those around the UPL);
2. Adding AI and legal technology-centered professional development obligations and competency standards to the practice of law to ensure sufficient education for legal professionals as they engage with AI; and
3. Regulating the use of AI in legal systems to create guardrails that ensure quality control and suitability for legal needs, including through the implementation of sandboxes to promote testing and structural boundaries.

17.3.1 *Change Rules That Restrict or Unnecessarily Limit the Use of AI*

One of the current roadblocks to the effective use of AI tools by unrepresented litigants is the risk that submissions or other materials prepared by an AI tool on their behalf may be disallowed by the legal body receiving those materials. This challenge arises mainly in the context of regulatory restrictions on UPL (see Chapter 14). Andrew Perlman posits that existing regulatory regimes (such as the ABA's Model Rules of Professional Conduct)[17] already permit the use of AI tools by lawyers.[18] However, where existing rules prevent lawyers from providing AI-enhanced services or prohibit litigants from lawfully accessing such tools, Legal Practice Bodies must reform these regulations to ensure that professional conduct rules facilitate, rather than frustrate, access to justice.

17.3.2 *Add AI and Technology-Centered Competency Standards*

Legal Practice Bodies should view an understanding of AI tools and technology as a fundamental aspect of legal competence for lawyers. Whether serving clients or interacting with legal systems, it is already almost impossible to imagine navigating

[17] MODEL RULES OF PRO. CONDUCT (AM. BAR ASS'N 2024).
[18] Andrew Perlman, *The Legal Ethics of Generative AI*, 57 SUFFOLK U. L. REV. 345 (2024).

the justice system without technology. Continuing legal education and professional development obligations must include a specific emphasis on technology and AI.

It is a common gripe of legal professionals that they are required to comply not only with a comprehensive set of professional and ethical rules of practice but also with laborious continuing education and professional development obligations. For example, in New York, experienced lawyers are required to complete twenty-four hours of accredited continuing legal education every two years (which generally equates to twelve hours per year).[19] In Australia, lawyers must complete ten hours per year.[20] However, in some jurisdictions there is either no requirement for continuing education (e.g., in the UK) or merely a recommendation to participate in professional development (e.g., with the District of Columbia Bar in the US).[21] In both contexts, there is ample opportunity for legal professionals to avoid exposure to AI tools or legal technology, such that they do not develop sufficient awareness or understanding of these tools in legal practice.

While Perlman argues that rules of professional conduct are already aligned with the use of AI tools by lawyers,[22] a gap exists between whether lawyers *can use* AI tools and whether they *must understand* them. In 2023, New York State implemented a requirement for lawyers to complete one hour of continuing education in the category of cybersecurity, privacy, and data protection.[23] Although it reflects a positive approach to improving technical literacy for legal professionals, this requirement is an insufficient measure for ensuring expertise in AI and other technologies that directly impact the law.

17.3.3 *Create Guardrails to Regulate the Use of AI in Legal Systems*

An AI guardrail is a safety mechanism designed to ensure that AI systems operate within ethical, legal, and technical boundaries.[24] These guardrails serve as protective measures to prevent misuse, manage unintended outcomes, and maintain public trust in AI.[25] Many Legal Practice Bodies lack comprehensive guidelines on the use of AI. However, even experienced attorneys are known to fall prey to misuse of AI or to risks associated with its use, such as hallucinated legal authorities.[26] To ensure quality control and suitability for legal needs, Legal Practice Bodies should create and test frameworks and implement guardrails to govern the use of AI in legal systems. This could most easily be accomplished by modeling such guardrails on

19 N.Y. Comp. Codes R. & Regs. tit. 22, § 1500.22 (2022).
20 Legal Pro. Unif. Continuing Pro. Dev. (Solic.) Rules r. 6 (Austl. 2015).
21 D.C. Rules of Pro. Conduct r. 1.1 (D.C. 2023).
22 Perlman, *supra* note 18.
23 N.Y. Comp. Codes R. & Regs. tit. 22, § 1500.22(a) (2022).
24 Margaret Rouse, *AI Guardrail*, Techopedia (Dec. 24, 2023) (on file with Mia Bonardi).
25 *Id.*
26 *See, e.g.*, Mata v. Avianca, Inc., 678 F. Supp. 3d 443 (S.D.N.Y. 2023).

existing national and international guidelines, such as those used in the US, EU, and Singapore (each jurisdiction's guidelines are explored further later in the chapter).

In the US, there are two widely adopted frameworks that provide guardrails on the use of AI:

1. The National Institute of Standards and Technology ("NIST") AI Risk Management Framework (the "NIST AI Risk Framework");[27] and
2. the NYSBA Task Force on Artificial Intelligence's Report and Recommendations ("NYSBA Guidelines").[28]

The NIST AI Risk Framework structures its risk management approach around four interconnected functions: "Govern," "Map," "Measure," and "Manage."[29] The "Govern" function centers on establishing clear governance structures around the use of AI through internal policies and procedures. These structures should be developed with risk awareness in mind. The "Map" function encourages users to contextualize potential uses of AI systems to identify related risks. The "Measure" function is aimed at quantitatively analyzing and assessing AI risks according to their impact. Finally, the "Manage" function focuses on prioritizing and addressing identified risks through technical controls and procedural safeguards. This final function allows stakeholders to respond to, recover from, and communicate incidents or events. Overall, these functions are designed to be iterative, allowing organizations to continuously improve their risk management strategies as AI systems evolve.

The NIST AI Risk Framework also identifies three primary categories of harm that organizations must consider:

1. Harm to people;
2. Harm to organizations; and
3. Harm to ecosystems.

Finally, the NIST AI Risk Framework emphasizes seven essential characteristics that contribute to the trustworthiness of AI systems:

1. Validity;
2. Reliability;
3. Safety;
4. Security;
5. Resilience;
6. Fairness; and
7. Management of harmful biases.

[27] Nat'l Inst. of Standards & Tech. (NIST), *Artificial Intelligence Risk Management Framework: Generative Intelligence Profile*, Dep't of Commerce NIST Spec. Pub. 600-1 (July 2024), https://perma.cc/M587-D5B8.

[28] NYSBA, *supra* note 5.

[29] NIST, *supra* note 27.

To introduce effective guardrails that safeguard the use of AI tools in the legal context, regulators should aim to build on existing guidelines created by organizations like NIST.

The NYSBA is one of the few Legal Practice Bodies in the US to release a comprehensive framework for the use of AI in legal contexts. Although state bar associations in California, Florida, Michigan, and New Jersey have issued guidelines on the use of generative AI in legal practice, the emphasis has been on lawyers maintaining their competence and client confidentiality when doing so. The NYSBA Guidelines, though mostly centered on recommendations for legal professionals, provide tangible measures for ensuring guardrails are in place to facilitate the safe, effective, and ethical use of AI technologies. Key recommendations include implementing data protection measures, training on the effective use of AI, monitoring and updating guardrails, complying with legislative regulations, and, perhaps most crucially, ensuring that the use of AI aligns with ethical standards, particularly regarding the accuracy of AI-generated content.[30] On the whole, the NYSBA Guidelines aim to prevent overreliance on AI and to limit the potential legal risks AI can cause.

In the EU, the EU AI Act regulates AI use by outlining clear responsibilities for AI developers and users.[31] It creates four categories to monitor AI risk:

1. No risk,
2. Low risk,
3. High risk, and
4. Unacceptable risk.

The EU AI Act defines unacceptable risk as the potential to be a "clear threat to the safety, livelihoods and rights of people." Most legal AI applications automatically fall in the "high risk" category because this classification encompasses AI systems supporting judicial processes, including evidence evaluation, legal interpretation, and dispute resolution. However, there are opportunities for an AI provider to plead an exception to the "high risk" categorization if they can substantiate that it does not pose a significant risk to people's health, safety, or fundamental rights.[32] Within the EU, legal technology and AI developers must diligently test their products and communicate harmful incidents.[33] The EU AI Act also mandates that member states establish at least one regulatory sandbox at the national level or participate in an existing sandbox with other member states by August 2026.[34]

[30] NYSBA, *supra* note 5.
[31] Council Regulation 2024/1689, 2024 O.J. (L 212) 1.
[32] *Id.* at art. 6.
[33] *Id.* at art. 16.
[34] *Id.* at art. 57.

As discussed in Section 17.2.3, sandboxes offer a controlled environment, allowing for constant monitoring while testing AI models in limited real-world situations. AI models should be thoroughly tested and approved for specific uses. Creating sandboxes to mimic real-life scenarios, such as specific legal issues, can help identify appropriate situations where unrepresented litigants can most effectively and safely use AI. The safety of a sandbox environment would also encourage greater confidence in engaging with AI tools in a legal context, as it mitigates the risk of UPL allegations (see Chapter 14).

In Singapore, the Model AI Governance Framework is intended to guide organizations in maintaining good corporate governance over their use of AI.[35] This framework emphasizes the use of "Ethical AI" through eleven AI ethics principles:

1. Accountability;
2. Accuracy;
3. Auditability;
4. Explainability;
5. Fairness;
6. Human centricity and well-being;
7. Human rights alignment;
8. Inclusivity;
9. Progressiveness;
10. Responsibility, accountability, and transparency;
11. Robustness and security; and
12. Sustainability.

Additionally, the Cyber Security Agency of Singapore released the *Guidelines on Securing AI Systems* and a corresponding companion guide to advise system owners on how to protect AI systems against both classical and more novel cybersecurity risks throughout the lifecycle stages of the AI system.[36]

Combining AI risk analysis with ethics principles emphasizes the need to maintain security while focusing on the user (who, in the legal field, is an individual needing legal assistance). Novel AI frameworks built for use in legal situations should therefore comply with robust ethical standards. Large language models ("LLMs") and other AI tools can be useful in legal systems, but only if appropriate guardrails are in place to ensure that the AI does not cause harm to an unwitting unrepresented litigant. The best way to understand how to use AI effectively in a legal context is to establish a framework defining the circumstances in which AI use is appropriate and the conditions that could lead to unacceptable risk. To test

[35] InfoComm Media Dev. Auth. & Pers. Data Prot. Comm'n, Model Artificial Intelligence Governance Framework (2d ed. 2020), https://perma.cc/23VM-HZY2.

[36] Cyber Sec. Agency of Sing., Guidelines and Companion Guide on Securing AI Systems (Oct. 15, 2024), https://perma.cc/9LNV-6P6Z.

that framework, sandboxes should be used to emulate realistic experiences, where possible. Finally, Legal Practice Bodies could provide advanced monitoring and oversight mechanisms to identify risks arising out of the use of specific AI tools and to increase awareness of responsible AI practices.

17.4 STANDARDIZE LAWS AND REGULATIONS TO FACILITATE MACHINE INTERPRETATION

To promote the implementation and use of AI in legal matters, laws and regulations should be developed in a user-focused manner based on human–computer interface best practices, with a focus on:

1. Investing in conversion processes to ensure compatibility between the content of laws and their interpretation by AI tools; and
2. Modernizing current law-making and documentation practices to align with machine learning ("ML"), including the preparation of explanatory guides to facilitate computation.

Though it may be argued that the advancements within AI, ML, and LLMs have been such that these tools can process data in a wide variety of formats and from a broad spectrum of sources, the central challenge is how these AI tools can *interpret* and *rationalize* such data. This is especially significant when considering the complex nature of laws and regulations and the judicial decisions that apply them. Legal theorists have debated for centuries the appropriate methods for interpreting law, with multiple approaches still permeating the legal profession.[37] Even the most basic linguistic elements can dictate the intended meaning of a law; the placement of a comma or the use of list connectors (e.g., "including, but not limited to") has led to significant debates in courts around the world. This challenge is well recognized by experts in automated legal decision-making and the use of AI in the legal context; for example, L. Karl Branting stated, "a logical representation of a statutory rule is simply one interpretation among many possible interpretations."[38] Members of the legal profession take solace in the fact that AI tools do not currently appear to have the ability to engage in the deeper analytical thought

[37] *See, e.g.*, Aharon Barak, PURPOSIVE INTERPRETATION IN LAW (Sari Bashi trans., Princeton University Press) (2005); Paul Brest, *The Misconceived Quest for the Original Understanding*, 60 B.U. L. REV. 204 (1980); Ronald Dworkin, A MATTER OF PRINCIPLE (1985); Owen M. Fiss, *Objectivity and Interpretation*, 34 STAN. L. REV. 739 (1982); Mark Greenberg & Harry Litman, *The Meaning of Original Meaning*, 86 GEO. L.J. 569 (1998); Herbert Lionel A. Hart, THE CONCEPT OF LAW (2d ed. 1994); Richard A. Posner, *Statutory Interpretation – in the Classroom and in the Courtroom*, 50 U. CHI. L. REV. 800 (1983); Antonin Scalia, *Originalism: The Lesser Evil*, 57 U. CINN. L. REV. 849 (1989).

[38] L. Karl Branting, *Data-Centric and Logic-Based Models for Automated Legal Problem Solving*, 25 A.I. & L. 5, 8 (2017).

or contextual interpretation required to grasp effectively the effects of these laws.[39] However, this also presents an obstacle for individuals seeking access to justice: If laws require advanced legal reasoning and interpretation attainable only by those embedded in the legal profession, then unrepresented litigants do not have the necessary tools to advance their rights under the law.

One solution is to codify the intended meaning, impacts, and effects of statutes and regulations in a manner that is accessible to AI tools, such that the processing of legislative instruments is not without guidance. Additionally, because some judicial decisions alter the plain language meaning of what would otherwise be fairly straightforward laws, there should be a practice of identifying situations where judicial interpretations have varied. In many cases, the outcome can turn on a difference of opinion on how a legislative instrument governs the unique facts and circumstances present in that case.

For example, in the infamous US Supreme Court case of *Yates v. United States*, the Court overturned a criminal conviction based centrally on its interpretation of the words "tangible object" and its conclusion that this phrase was not intended to cover all kinds of physical objects, including, as was the subject of this case, seventy-two undersized fish.[40] The Sarbanes–Oxley Act of 2002 includes a provision under which it is a crime if a person "knowingly alters, destroys, … [or] covers up … any record, document, or tangible object" a federal investigation.[41] A fisherman, John Yates, was convicted under that provision not for destroying records or documents, but for disposing of seventy-two undersized red grouper.[42] In overturning John Yates' conviction, Justice Ruth Bader Ginsburg, writing for the majority, contrasted the ordinary meaning of the statute with the context of the legislation and Congress's intent.[43] Referring to the title of the section ("Destruction, alteration, or falsification of records in Federal investigations and bankruptcy") and the heading of the enacting piece of the legislation ("Criminal penalties for altering documents"), the Court concluded that Congress would have needed to be much clearer if it had intended for the statute to serve as an all-encompassing prohibition on the destruction of physical objects of every kind (and not just for obstructive acts in financial contexts).[44]

39 *See, e.g.*, Gizem Halis Kasap, *Can Artificial Intelligence ("AI") Replace Human Arbitrators? Technological Concerns and Legal Implications*, 2021 J. Disp. Resol. 209 (2021); M. M. Bues & E. Matthaei, *LegalTech on the Rise: Technology Changes Legal Work Behaviours, but Does Not Replace Its Profession*, *in* Liquid Legal 119 (K. Jacob, D. Schindler & R. Strathausen eds., 2017); Gary E. Marchant, *Artificial Intelligence and the Future of Legal Practice*, SciTech Lawyer (Nov. 1, 2017), https://perma.cc/PYX8-KL9V.

40 Yates v. United States, 574 U.S. 528 (2015).

41 Sarbanes-Oxley Act of 2002, 18 U.S.C. § 1519 (2002).

42 United States v. Yates, 733 F.3d 1059, 1061, 1064 (11th Cir. 2013).

43 *Yates*, 574 U.S. at 536.

44 *Id.*

Although we could identify countless examples of cases whose outcomes seem to be determined by minute or otherwise incidental circumstances, this is a fundamental element of the practice of law – the devil is in the details (and the details are often subject to interpretation). If seasoned legal professionals struggle to get things right, how could we expect AI to do better? There are two pathways: (1) limiting the scope of legal reasoning and interpretation carried out by the AI tools that are available to unrepresented litigants; or (2) more accurately capturing the logic and reasoning behind judicial decisions such that the general public can understand the rationale of precedent and its impacts on legislation. The former represents an unjustified repression of technology to fit within existing practice, while the latter calls for greater initial effort ultimately to improve the accessibility and equality of justice in the modern world.

17.5 CONCLUSION

The integration of AI into legal systems represents both an unprecedented opportunity and a significant challenge for improving access to justice. While the potential benefits of AI tools for unrepresented litigants are substantial, realizing these benefits requires systematic changes across multiple dimensions of the legal landscape. Legal Practice Bodies must take proactive steps to promote and facilitate the responsible use of AI tools, moving beyond their current risk-averse stance to embrace innovation while maintaining appropriate safeguards.

The recommendations outlined in this chapter form a comprehensive framework for action, from adapting access to justice programs to integrate AI technologies to updating legal practice rules and regulations. Key to this framework is the recognition that Legal Practice Bodies must shift from merely cautioning against AI's risks to actively fostering its responsible development and use through educational initiatives, sandbox environments, and dedicated resources.

Modernizing legal practice rules and regulations is particularly crucial, requiring a careful balance between enabling innovation and maintaining professional standards. This includes reconsidering restrictions on the unauthorized practice of law, implementing AI-focused professional development requirements, and establishing clear guardrails for AI use in legal contexts. These changes must be accompanied by efforts to standardize laws and regulations to facilitate machine interpretation while preserving the nuanced understanding necessary for proper legal analysis. Success in these endeavors will require sustained commitment from all stakeholders in the justice system. Legal Practice Bodies must lead by example, demonstrating that embracing AI technology need not compromise professional standards or ethical obligations. The development of comprehensive regulatory frameworks for AI use in legal contexts, drawing on existing models from various jurisdictions, will be essential for building public trust and ensuring consistent, responsible implementation.

As we move forward, the focus must remain on the ultimate goal: improving access to justice for all individuals, particularly those who cannot afford traditional legal representation. The recommendations presented here provide a roadmap for achieving this goal, but their implementation will require ongoing dedication, resources, and a willingness to adapt as technology evolves. The future of access to justice lies not in choosing between traditional legal services and AI-powered tools but in finding ways to integrate both approaches effectively while maintaining the highest standards of legal practice.

Conclusion

Mia Bonardi

Today, domestic abuse survivors in certain jurisdictions can access a court-provided online portal that guides them through filing a protection order in plain language, automatically prepares their documents, and helps them understand their rights, all at no cost. Yet a survivor facing similar circumstances in another jurisdiction may have no such assistance, not because the technology does not exist, but because their court system lacks the resources to implement it or has chosen not to adopt it. This disparity reveals the nature of our access-to-justice crisis: it is not a problem of technological capability, but of financial capacity and institutional will.

The initiatives profiled in Chapter 13 demonstrate that technology can have a significant impact. Pro Bono Net has helped millions of people through its legal assistance websites and other tools.[1] British Columbia's Civil Resolution Tribunal ("CRT") has handled over 52,000 claims through a fully online system.[2] Upsolve has helped eliminate over $783 million in debt for more than 13,000 people.[3] Rentervention has served more than 50,000 Chicago residents since 2019.[4] The Kansas Protection Order Portal ("KSPOP") conducted over 92,000 eligibility reviews and facilitated the filing of more than 30,000 protection orders in just three years.[5] These are not experimental prototypes; they are working systems serving real people today.

Yet while some jurisdictions embrace similar innovations, others maintain the status quo. KSPOP demonstrates capabilities that are court-funded and could be replicated elsewhere but still are not. AI-powered tools like Rentervention or

[1] Ray Brescia, Lawyer Nation: The Past, Present, and Future of the American Legal Profession 180 (2024).

[2] Video Interview by Mia Bonardi with Shelley Lopez, Chair, B.C. Civil Resolution Tribunal (Nov. 7, 2024).

[3] Upsolve, https://perma.cc/4V73-GHZC.

[4] Video Interview by Mia Bonardi with Conor Malloy, Former Dir., Rentervention (July 17, 2024).

[5] Video Interview by Kiernan Moran & Mia Bonardi with Ayyoub Ajmi, Prof., UMKC Sch. of L. & Founder, CiviLaw.Tech (Sep. 26, 2024).

JusticeBot are not available in every city. The same document automation tools that streamline court processes in some jurisdictions remain absent from others due to a lack of funding, institutional resistance, or both.

The technological capabilities exist to improve access to justice dramatically. Computational logic, explored in Chapter 6, can translate complex legal rules into clear, actionable steps. Machine learning ("ML"), examined in Chapter 7, can automate routine legal work and predict outcomes to inform decision-making. Document automation, detailed in Chapter 8, can empower unrepresented litigants with procedurally compliant forms and get them quite far in the process. Generative AI, as discussed in Chapters 4, 9, and 12, can bridge the language gap explored in Chapter 2, making legalese more accessible in plain language. Online dispute resolution ("ODR") platforms, examined in Chapter 11, help level the playing field against well-resourced opponents. The integration of these technologies, explored in Chapter 10, can create support systems that adapt to users' distinct needs.

Some of the legal AI assistants and technologies described in this book represent powerful interim tools – bridges that can span the justice gap while we work to eliminate the need for such bridges entirely. These technological innovations are both necessary and transformative, enabling millions to access justice today. Yet they also illuminate opportunities for deeper collaboration among technology developers, courts, legal aid organizations, and bar associations to create more accessible justice systems from the ground up.

The barriers to broader adoption are primarily financial, cultural, and institutional rather than technological. As discussed in Chapter 1, the access-to-justice crisis reflects choices about how to structure proceedings, regulate the practice of law, design procedures, and allocate resources – choices that courts, regulatory bodies, and legal institutions can and should reconsider. The remarkable tools presented in this book demonstrate their greatest potential when developed in partnership with institutions that have the capacity to deliver justice. Examples include the CRT, JusticeBot, the Nevada Self-Help Chatbot, and KSPOP. When institutional leadership, adequate resources, and technological innovation align, meaningful integration becomes possible, though rarely without significant effort and adaptation. As Professor David Colarusso, Co-Director of Suffolk University Law School's Legal Innovation and Technology ("LIT") Lab, observed, "the challenges the Assembly Line faced were never technical … [T]here were always problems with adoption."[6] CRT Chair Shelley Lopez offered simple advice to other jurisdictions considering similar institutional innovations: "Don't be afraid."[7]

When gaps exist in institutional capacity or will, technological bridges built by nonprofits and companies serve an essential role. However, these tools may remain

[6] Video Interview by Kiernan Moran with David Colarusso, Co-Dir., Suffolk Univ. L. Sch. Legal Innovation & Tech. Lab (Oct. 30, 2024).

[7] Video Interview with Shelley Lopez, *supra* note 2.

undiscoverable or inaccessible to the people who need them most. These technological innovations prove most effective and scalable when they complement, and are integrated into, institutions with the capacity to deliver justice. Embedding technological tools directly within courts and other institutions where unrepresented people naturally turn for help will ensure that technological assistance already available reaches those who would otherwise never find it.

Funding constraints have often proved as significant as resistance to adoption. As Mark O'Brien, Co-Founder of Pro Bono Net, explained, "It's easy to get money to build the first iteration, but very difficult to build version 2.0 and 3.0."[8] Many innovations emerged from crisis funding or volunteer efforts that cannot be sustained in the long term. Courts and legal aid organizations often lack the technical infrastructure to build and maintain AI tools, or the financial capacity to hire someone to do so, even when institutional willingness exists. Transitioning to sustainable models while maintaining accessibility requires creative approaches and institutional support from courts, legislatures, universities, foundations, and others.

We must be honest about the limitations of technological bridge-building as a strategy for improving access to justice. Technological bridges require constant maintenance, regular updates, and continuous adaptation to changing conditions. More fundamentally, technological bridges can serve only those who are aware of their existence and can access them. The very populations most in need of legal assistance may find even the most sophisticated technological tools beyond their reach due to digital literacy barriers, inadequate internet access, or basic discoverability challenges. Even when these tools are embedded within courts and other institutions with the capacity to deliver justice, they must function as alternatives that expand access, not as single options that create new forms of injustice.

Despite these limitations, encouraging signs of institutional engagement are emerging. Forward-thinking courts are beginning to host AI tools directly, as demonstrated by Nevada's Self-Help Chatbot, a project of the Supreme Court of Nevada. Similarly, as discussed in Chapter 14, unauthorized practice of law rules that unnecessarily restrict access to legal services are being reconsidered. Meanwhile, law schools are increasingly recognizing their role in training students to use technology to bridge the justice gap, as demonstrated by Suffolk University Law School's LIT Lab and other innovative programs.

The technological recommendations outlined in Chapter 16 demonstrate how to evaluate and improve AI applications for legal tasks. The institutional recommendations detailed in Chapter 17 highlight the need to simplify legal procedures, increase funding for legal services, and reduce restrictions on the unauthorized practice of law. These reforms, working in tandem with the AI technologies explored in this book and with institutional leadership driving change, represent significant steps toward addressing the access-to-justice crisis.

8 Video Interview by Kiernan Moran with Mark O'Brien, Co-Founder, Pro Bono Net (Oct. 25, 2024).

We hope that the bridges we are building today become unnecessary. Courts and other institutions with the capacity to deliver justice should be designed for the people they serve rather than solely for the professionals who operate them. The technology exists to transform how justice is accessed. The examples in this book prove that courts, bar associations, and legal education institutions can successfully lead this transformation when they have effective leadership and adequate resources.

True progress cannot be measured by technological bridge-building, which is stunted within an inequitable system. Rather, it must be measured by whether we have eliminated the barriers that force people to navigate complex legal systems without representation in the first place.

The choice before us is not between gradual reform and technological disruption but between a legal system that serves all people and one designed to serve only those who can afford representation. The innovations documented in this book show that we have the tools to choose equitable justice. What remains is the institutional will and financial commitment to implement them universally, not just in jurisdictions fortunate enough to have leaders who are, in the words of CRT Chair Shelley Lopez, unafraid to try.

Index

Page numbers in *italics* indicate tables, figures/charts.

For EU product safety concerns, contact us at Calle de José Abascal, 56–1°,
28003 Madrid, Spain or eugpsr@cambridge.org.

www.ingramcontent.com/pod-product-compliance
Ingram Content Group UK Ltd.
Pitfield, Milton Keynes, MK11 3LW, UK
UKHW020838290926
15470UKWH00004B/1423

* 9 7 8 1 0 0 9 7 7 9 4 3 2 *